To   Jim
Enjoy reading this.
(and then let me)
Love from   Mum & dad.
Christmas 1994

D1439178

Years of Hope

TONY BENN

Years of Hope

Diaries, Letters and Papers 1940–1962

edited by Ruth Winstone

HUTCHINSON
LONDON

1 3 5 7 9 8 6 4 2

This edition first published in 1994 by Hutchinson

Random House (UK) Ltd
20 Vauxhall Bridge Road, London SW1V 2SA

Random House Australia (Pty) Ltd
20 Alfred Street, Milsons Point, Sydney, NSW 2061, Australia

Random House New Zealand Ltd
18 Poland Road, Glenfield, Auckland 10, New Zealand

Random House South Africa (Pty) Ltd
PO Box 337, Bergvlei, 2012, South Africa

A CIP catalogue record for this book is available from the British Library

ISBN 0 09 178534 0

Set in Baskerville by SX Composing Ltd, Rayleigh, Essex
Printed and bound in Great Britain by
Mackays of Chatham plc, Chatham, Kent

With love and thanks to my
family and friends, past and present.

Contents

Illustrations

Editor's Note

This book, spanning as it does the important years from 1940–62, is chronologically the first in the series of Tony Benn's diaries. Unlike the previous volumes, *Years of Hope* is a mixture of youthful manuscript diaries, taken up, laid aside, resumed again over a period of years, and of yellowing cuttings, papers and letters filed away in the labyrinth of Benn archives. As editor, it was my job to unearth this mass of material, to put it into order and to extract from the total – amounting to some 1.5 million words – a personal and political record of Tony Benn's early life: from a fourteen-year-old school-boy to an ambitious young Labour MP. It is by no means a continuous record; there are some noticeable omissions when Tony failed to keep a diary at all for months or years at a time, but when he did, such as during the war and various crises of his parliamentary life, the record is vivid and detailed.

The selection of extracts has therefore been mine; Tony Benn has entrusted the raw material into my hands uncomplainingly, providing linking passages where appropriate. It is not a history and chapter notes have been provided only to enlarge upon a point in the text; thus the Suez crisis of 1956 is left to speak for itself, whereas the arrest of John Stonehouse in Africa did, I considered, merit a note. Such are the vagaries of political diaries.

For a number of reasons it has been the most enjoyable volume of *Diaries* to edit: full of unexpected insights into a younger Tony Benn, and into life in the 1940s; but also of shocking reminders of how seriously another war was being talked about so soon after the end of the last. It has also been a salutary lesson in how little domestic political life really changes over the decades: the modernising tendency of the Labour Party is nothing new, nor the internecine strife of the Conservatives.

The checking of names and places from the earlier years has been undertaken in the knowledge that it is impossible, at this remove, to get them all correct, errors for which I apologise in advance. I am grateful to David Butler for the use of the transcripts of interviews with Tony Benn 1960–62 and to David Benn for help with the early letters between members of the Benn family.

Thanks are due to Tony Whittome at Hutchinson who gently advised and guided, and his assistant Dawn Fozard who managed everything

with the least trouble or fuss; to Beth Humphries and Esther Jagger who
knocked an impossible typescript into shape in record time; and to the
incomparable Neil Bradford, production director at Hutchinson.

Ruth Winstone
July 1994

Foreword

Looking back at the political life of half a century ago, a perspective emerges which is not available to the contemporary observer of events.

In the years following the Second World War, for example, we were all told, time and time again, as I record in my diary, that the Soviet Union and its allies were threatening the military conquest of Western Europe and the world.

In retrospect, the Cold War and all the anti-communist propaganda that it released can be seen in a very different light. For it was an Orwellian creation of a deadly foreign enemy and anyone who criticised the status quo was easily presented as a secret agent of the devil; thus that status quo was buttressed in the west and Britain harnessed to a new war machine that we did not need and could not afford.

In this diary, I was critical of Nye Bevan's resignation speech in which he attacked the rearmament programme and the cuts in the Health Service which had to be made to pay for it. But Nye was right, and everything he forecast came true. For the Cold War hysteria was used politically against socialists in the west and the burden of weapons crippled our capacity to build an industrial base as a foundation for our future prosperity.

Yet for the decade that followed, it was Nye and his supporters who were accused of having damaged Labour's chance of electoral success where, in truth, the responsibility lay fairly and squarely with those who had imposed this arms programme on us at the diktat of the United States.

Just as we were dismantling British imperialism a new imperialism centred on Washington was growing and, despite the setback of the Vietnam War, it is now reappearing under the more glamorous title of a New World Order.

European pre-eminence lost in two bloody wars is now being patiently reconstructed in the European Union with NATO as the world's policeman designed to reimpose the control of the white nations of the north on the rest of the world under the effective control of international capital.

Meanwhile Britain itself, weakened by the arms burden and with a fundamentally undemocratic constitution, a tiny part of which the

Peerage campaign exposed, has slithered down to a near Third World status, concealing its decline by the rituals of a monarchical state, losing confidence in itself and handing over real power to Commissioners in Brussels who are intent on making us a province of a capitalist Europe.

One other advantage of a historical perspective is that you realise, as you get older, that nothing is inevitable and that change, when it comes, can come quite quickly and unexpectedly.

The signs of change are to be found at the bottom and never at the top.

As children we can only think in months or years, but as we get older it is easier to think in centuries and see the movement of power as it ebbs and flows when one system gives way to another.

Young people of my generation were full of hope and in 1945, after the fears and hardships of the war, we believed we really could change society – and we did, which is why this volume, which covers the years 1940–62, is called *Years of Hope*. It begins during the war-time Blitz on London, and the war-time diaries as an RAF pilot under training, though personal, contain a lot of early political observations and commitment.

My family radicalism and experience in Africa were to lead me later to become active in all the anti-colonial liberation campaigns.

The Movement for Colonial Freedom maintained close contact with all the main Nationalist leaders and it was in 1960 that I tabled the first motion in the House of Commons calling for a boycott of South African goods after attending the All-African People's Conference in Tunis held earlier that year.

As a one time BBC producer, I realised earlier than most in the Labour Party the great possibilities that radio and television held out for political campaigning and was an early advocate of the broadcasting of Parliament.

During the peerage campaign itself I was just too preoccupied to keep a proper diary, and the book ends with an account of that campaign as recorded by David Butler in interviews with me in 1962 for his Oral History project. In an Epilogue I describe the lessons the battle taught me for future political campaigning that are just as applicable now.

Change takes place when people have decided they will no longer tolerate injustice or unfairness.

At a time when we are supposed to be a rich and democratic country, young people have been paralysed by a sense of powerlessness which is totally false and very destructive of any serious campaigning for social improvement. But I am certain that, as in the post-war years, the tide is turning and people are rejecting the Eighties as they once rejected the Thirties, and demanding a fairer society.

Tony Benn
July 1994

Chronology

1940

School evacuated to Sussex, Devon and Hereford and back to London

Nov   Elder brother Michael joined RAF

1941

Dec   Father, William Wedgwood Benn MP, made a peer, with title of Lord Stansgate

1942

Oct   New College, Oxford

1943

24 July   Joined RAF

1944

11 Jan   SS *Cameronia* to Africa for training as pilot

23 June   Brother Michael killed in RAF

1945

10 Mar   Gained Pilot's Wings

May   Egypt and Palestine

VE Day celebrated in Palestine

Sailed home on HMS *Carthage*

5 July   General Election

July   Transferred to Fleet Air Arm

28 July   Father made Secretary of State for Air

4 Aug   Atomic bomb dropped on Hiroshima

1946

Jan   Return to New College, Oxford

July   Trip to Belgium with Peter Blaker

1947

May   President, Oxford Union

Oct   Sailed to USA on SS *Marine Tiger* for debating tour with
                      Edward Boyle and Kenneth Harris

1948
Jan   Return from USA
2 Aug   Met Caroline De Camp in Oxford
11 Aug   Engaged to Caroline

1949
20 Jan   To USA in SS *America* as salesman for Benn Brothers
Feb–May   Magazine salesman
17 June   Marriage in Cincinnati
Aug   Return to London
Nov   Producer with BBC North American Service

1950
23 Feb   General Election. Labour majority reduced to 6
26 June   Korean War began
30 Nov   Elected MP for Bristol South East

1951
8 Feb   Maiden speech
9 Mar   First BBC *Any Questions*
23 April   Bevan resigned as Minister of Labour
21 Aug   Stephen Benn born
25 Oct   General Election. Conservative Government elected
25 Oct   Re-elected for Bristol South East

1952
6 Feb   Death of King George VI
2 Sept   USA trip. Meeting with Adlai Stevenson, Ohio

1953
11 Feb   Ten-Minute Rule Bill (Paget Bill) on peerage case
                      defeated
21 Oct   Cheddi Jagan and Forbes Burnham to House of
                      Commons
26 Nov   Hilary Benn born

1954
11 April   Movement for Colonial Freedom founded
30 April   H bomb National Committee formed
31 Dec   H bomb National Petition presented to Number 10

1955

8 Feb	Bristol Corporation petitioned Parliament in support of peerage campaign
15 Feb	Instrument of Renunciation signed
5 April	Churchill resigned. Eden Prime Minister
14 April	Letter of support from Churchill re peerage
26 April	Lords Committee rejected Peerage Bill
26 May	General Election. Conservatives re-elected
7 Dec	Attlee retired
14 Dec	Gaitskell elected Leader of Labour Party

1956

14–27 April	Israel trip
27 June	Suez Canal nationalised by Nasser
16 Sept	Trafalgar Square demonstration over Suez crisis
30 Oct	Israel attacked Egypt. British intervention
30 Oct	Soviet troops entered Hungary
31 Oct	Anglo-French bombardment of Port Said
6 Dec	Appointed Shadow RAF Minister

1957

9 Jan	Eden resigned
17 Jan	Met Willy Brandt in Germany
8 Feb	Letter to *Pravda* re Hungary
20 Feb	Melissa Benn born
1 July	Met Kenneth Kaunda
7 July	Dinner with Kwame Nkrumah
29 July	Motion of censure on Speaker
3 Oct	Bevan opposed to unilateralism
4 Oct	First Sputnik launched
17 Dec	Life Peers Bill Amendment rejected

1958

3 Mar	Resigned as Air Force spokesman over nuclear weapons
9 May	Joshua Benn born
15 July	Paul Robeson to tea at House of Commons
1 Sept	Race riots in Notting Hill

1959

12 Mar	Select Committee on Procedure report published
27 May	Visited Tunisia
July–Sept	Trip to USA
13 Sept	Soviet rocket landed on moon
8 Oct	General Election. Conservatives re-elected

9 Nov	Appointed Shadow Transport Minister
28 Nov	Elected to NEC

1960
25 Jan	To All-African People's Congress, Tunisia
28 Feb	South African boycott, Trafalgar Square demonstration
16 Mar	Clause 4 retained by NEC
17 May	U-2 spy incident
6 July	Nye Bevan died
24 Aug	Visited Soviet Union
2 Oct	Resigned from NEC over nuclear weapons
17 Nov	Father died
22 Nov	Returned Letters Patent to Buckingham Palace
15 Dec	Appeared before Committee of Privileges

1961
27 Feb	Bristol Petition
21 Mar	Privilege Committee confirmed disqualification
13 April	Commons confirmed disqualification and issued writ for new by-election in Bristol South East
21 April	Readopted for Bristol South East as Labour candidate
26 April	Joint Select Committee on peerage law announced
2 May	Churchill's letter of support circulated in Bristol
4 May	Re-elected for Bristol South East
8 May	Excluded by Speaker from House of Commons
	Commons voted to confirm exclusion
	Petition to unseat presented to Election Court by St Clair (Conservative)
10–21 July	Election Court met
28 July	Election Court seated St Clair
1 Aug	Bristol Fund launched

1962
25 Mar	Joint Select Committee set up
2 Oct	Re-elected to NEC
17 Dec	Joint Select Committee recommended peerage renunciation

1
Growing Up in the War
1940–46

The diary begins in early 1940; I was fourteen and a pupil at Westminster School in London which, because of the Blitz on the capital, was evacuated to different sites in Sussex, Devon and Hereford, from where some of my earliest letters were written.

My father, then MP for Gorton, had been a pilot in the First World War, and a former Cabinet Minister in the 1929–31 Labour Government. At the age of sixty-four he had rejoined the Air Force and served at first in the Air Ministry, later in Italy, returning to England in 1944 to train surreptitiously as an air gunner.

My mother was keeping up his constituency work from our home in Millbank, London which was burned out during the Blitz. As a consequence, she and my younger brother David were moved, to my great delight, to a girls' school, Blunt House, in Oxted, where she taught theology, and to which I was a regular visitor. David was frail in health as a child and was educated at home for a time, during the war years.

In 1940, Michael, my elder brother, joined the RAF and was trained as a pilot, serving in North Africa and Italy, and becoming the heir to a peerage when Father was created a viscount in 1941.

I signed up for the RAF in 1942, and while awaiting my call-up went on to New College, Oxford, until I was eighteen and could start my training.

Throughout this book various family pet names are used in my diaries and letters to and from members of the family. To confuse the reader, I was known to my parents and close friends as James, Jimmy or Jiggs; my mother I referred to often as Yerma and Dearie, and my brother David as 'The Proff'. Later, once my own children were born, Mother and Father received their own pet names, 'Tappa' and 'G-ma'.

Busby's
Lancing College
Shoreham-by-Sea
Sussex

[February 1940]

Dearest Dearie
    Thank you so much for my three parcels, so beautifully packed and

arranged for me. The jams, marmite, sauce, cake and sweets have all been in use and you have no idea how they cheer me up in this awful place.

Take care of Dad and in an air raid do hurry to a shelter, don't yield to him and stay at home.

Let us hope that the war is over soon. There is nothing wonderful or glorious about manslaughter. Just so again is this shown by the terrible loss of the German submarines and the *Royal Oak* and *Courageous*.

Give love and kisses to Father. Oh Oh Oh how miserable I am in this dump.

    Love

      Jiggs

                                Buckenhill
                                Bromyard
                                Hereford

                          November 1940

Dear Dad,

    Thanks very much for the 5/-.

Dad I got your letter today and what a happy time we did have at Oban. I have been discussing things in general with a particular friend of mine and my idea now is as follows.

I shall take and most likely get School Certificate next summer. After that I have got about 20 months before I can join up.

At 18 I shall join up and by 19 (things will I hope have changed by then) I shall I hope be commissioned as a pilot or observer. I shall fight through the war and if I am still alive I shall go to Oxford. After Oxford I shall try to get a short service commission in the RAF for four years . . . saving carefully I shall try to get a job running or helping to run a Benn Brothers paper. I shall do that probably for 3–5 years.

Then at 30 or so I shall hope to get an unsafe constituency, and at 32 get into Parliament. At 82 I shall die.

Life here is rough but good. We at least 'dig for victory' instead of rowing or football.

Westminster School Report 1940
Wedgwood-Benn A Age: 15.8

Greek: Place 18   No. in set 22

Does not work hard enough in school or out. He prefers to think Greek is too difficult and therefore not worth attempting to master.

French: Place 24   No. in set 25

His learning French is really a quite unsatisfactory performance. He could do very much better but it would now cost him a great effort.

History: Place 14

Lively and intelligent, as always. He is keen to get on and works hard and I think he ought to do well in the Certificate. His knowledge is patchy, eg he will sometimes take a political allusion which no one else in the form sees, and at other times he is ignorant of commonplace matters. He still has a rhetorical style of writing which is unsuitable for history essays.

Saturday 11 January 1941
Start 'Twelfth Night', I am Viola. Sinclair scarlet fever.

Tuesday 21 January 1941
Contract German measles.

Thursday 23 January 1941
In bed, blotto and scarlet rash. Decision to join Air Training Corps made, in bed.

Wednesday 29 January 1941
Came downstairs for first time to 'staff' convalescing room.

Thursday 30 January 1941
Came down again, deadly bored. Doctor didn't come – can't mix with other boys.

Wednesday 19 February 1941
Read the lesson, Acts Chapter 17 verses 22–23. The RAF lowers age to seventeen and a quarter. I am sending up papers.

Sunday 23 February 1941
Neuralgia. Awful service. I am afraid that I *am* playing for Juniors (right half).

Tuesday 25 February 1941
Feel better. Inspection of gas masks.

Wednesday 26 February 1941
Lent begins. Give up sweets, etcetera.

Saturday 1 March 1941
Complained about taking part of Viola.

Sunday 23 March 1941
Worked very hard. Did essay. Guy is very annoyed with me. I wonder why?

Monday 24 March 1941
Bottom in Maths exam. Got shown up by Bill, Hamburger and McMahon.

> 52nd Westminster Scout Group
> Westminster School
> Dean's Yard
>
> 29 March 1941

Dear Benn

It is a pity you couldn't attend the Scout meeting today for two reasons.

1. I want to tell you the result of a talk this week with the Headmaster on the ATC
2. Your marks haven't been up to scratch and not appearing, although you were apparently in school, gives the impression that you didn't feel confident of getting a decent standard in today's tests.

With regard to the ATC, I came to the view that, if it must take place simultaneously with the Scout meetings, boys who feel bound to join would have to leave the Troop. So I'm afraid we must lose you. Obviously in a case like this the proper thing is for you to make up your own mind and stick to it.

Yours ever
        Scout Master
PS Your journey report omitted all bearings and distances.

Sunday 6 April 1941
Germany attacks Greece and Jugoslavia. Went to early service. Practised unarmed combat.

Westminster School Report May 1941
Wedgwood-Benn A Age: 16.1

Greek: Place 18   No. in set 20

I am still unconvinced that he really tries.

History: Place 6

He has worked very hard indeed and deserves success in the Certificate. From being rather casual he has now swung to the opposite extreme and takes himself very seriously. I like his enthusiasms and admire his drive but I hope he won't lose his sense of fun.

Housemaster's report:

He has been working well and apparently to a definite plan. He has high and rather grown up ideals but in carrying them out, especially if this entails hard and perhaps dull work, he often fails. This gives the impression – which I think is unjustified – that he is not really sincere. He is a strange mixture of a grown up and quite a young boy.

Buckenhill
Bromyard
Hereford

[Summer 1941]

Dear Mike
    I haven't written to you for a long time . . .
    We have done projections of maps, advanced aircraft recognition, the ATC Library has got the manuals of navigation, signalling, gas and flying training, which I have on loan.
    The Russo-German war may possibly postpone the invasion until next spring or autumn – in the former case, I would be in the Home Guard in the latter the Royal Air Force.
    Your affectionate and admiring brother

Buckenhill
Bromyard
Hereford

[Autumn 1941]

Dear Mike
    How are you? The ATC uniforms arrived the day I arrived back here. I was promoted that afternoon to one stripe. I hope to get my corporal's stripe before the end of term. Tonight I go on a Home Guard patrol. From 10 to 6am there are patrols of two in 2-hour shifts in the Church tower and the streets.
    Your affectionate brother
        L/Corporal Benn ATC

Tuesday 18 November 1941
Mikes leaves RAF Church Fenton. Offensive opens in Libya.

Tuesday 25 November 1941
Mike joins his operational squadron. Ayr.

Buckenhill
Bromyard
Hereford

26 January 1942

My dear Mike

There is little to report.

I am meeting tremendous opposition to Dad's peerage.

I am sending this letter via Dad as I am not at all sure where you are. On Tuesday another L/Corporal and I have got to run the parade so I expect it will be chaos.

Your affec and adm. bro

James

Buckenhill
Bromyard
Hereford

8 Feb 1942

My dear Mike

I had a letter from Nursey saying that she hadn't received a letter from you. Ferg has allowed the nearly 17s to join the Home Guard. I have got battle dress, gaiters, anklets, tin hat with camouflage net and Service gas mask.

Our job is that of a fighting patrol behind the lines of an enemy attack on road blocks.

Let me know the exact date of your leave and I will come up to London.

Buckenhill
Bromyard
Hereford

12 Mar 1942

My dear Mike

What a good weekend we did have. My first exploit on the motorbike was entirely your fault! When I join the RAF proper I shall probably see even less of you than I do now.

I am so glad that I found that you have the same view about females that I have. It is the only major omission that the parents have made in our upbringing. I suppose if we had a sister we should have met her friends. I don't know anything about them. I don't know what they are interested in, what they think about, and when I do meet them I feel most embarrassed.

We are having lessons in unarmed combat and I have bought an instructional book on the subject.

> Air Ministry
> King Charles Street
> Whitehall
> SW1
>
> 24 March 1942

My dear James (Tony)

I am afraid I have been a poor correspondent. I shall send you a letter whenever I get the chance but please don't consider that the letters call for any answer. I just wanted you to know that you are not forgotten.

I hope all goes well with the Home Guard and the ATC. I expect you are a sergeant by now.

What about the School Certificate and University Entrance Exams? The Proff [David Benn] is extremely well and very lively and now seems to be engaged in close correspondence with Willie Gallacher, the Communist MP. I hope Herbert Morrison will not decide that I must be interned on this account under 18B!

> Tons of love . . .
> Pa

> Buckenhill
> Bromyard
> Hereford
>
> 20 May 1942

My dear Mike

Re: the fair sex. Why don't you take out a correspondence course of the same kind I have adopted. I shall certainly see Anne next holidays. She is a very nice girl. I am thinking of subscribing to the *Girls' Own Paper* so as to make up my deficiency.

I have completely recovered from the depression, for I recognise just what it is.

> Your affec and admir. bro
> Sgt Benn

> New College
> Oxford
>
> 30 October 1942

My dear family

I arrived at New College about 3.30 and met a friend of mine who helped me carry my bags upstairs to my rooms. There I found a number of notes including an invitation to tea next Sunday with Mrs Fisher [H.A.L. Fisher's widow]. There was a note from my Moral tutor asking me to go and see him.

I decided to leave out economics from the intensive course and tackle only politics and philosophy since I cannot do PPE in the time available. I am enjoying myself immensely. Nobody takes the least interest in me or cares what I do – which is very pleasant.

Blunt House

17 November 1942

My dear James (No. 1850035 I should say)

Your very kind and welcome telegram came over the phone just as I was sitting down to write this letter.

Of course *the* news of the week for us all is about your entry into the ROYAL AIR FORCE. I am very, very proud of my three and if Father asks me what I would like to celebrate the inordinately long time I have been married to him I shall suggest that he should give me two more brooches so that I can really fly the proper formation on my frock. Tell us what the next step is and when you begin to go up.

     Yer Ma

New College
Oxford

Jan 14 1943

My dear old Mike,

It was grand seeing you last weekend. I am sending this to the Air Ministry to be redirected. I have phoned EW twice this week and I am having lunch with her tomorrow. I haven't actually kissed her yet.

This intensive course is getting a bit of a bore, we even have lectures after dinner. Last night the local security officer of the district came to talk about 'National Security'. In the course of the lecture he told this anecdote which is quite irrelevant and very funny.

Here it is:

'In the course of the French campaign we lost most of our equipment and the evacuated British Expeditionary Force was poorly armed. In the House of Commons Churchill was making his famous speech ('We shall fight on the beaches, we shall fight on the landing grounds, we shall fight in the streets.') There was a tremendous response and Churchill is reputed to have shuffled his papers and turning aside to have said 'And we will bash the buggers about their heads with bottles which is about all we've got.'

Well Mike, good luck in your affairs both of the sword and heart.

Your most affec and admir. Bro.
    James

                                     18 January 1943

My dear Ma
    I hope you are all right after the raid on London last night. I had no idea that it was serious until after dinner tonight when I glanced at the evening papers. It must have been quite a blitz for ten planes to be shot down.
    In any one week I have seventeen lectures, three essays, three tutorials and one and a half days doing Air Squadron work. I have got two more maps for my rooms and the walls are full up and very cheerful.
    Your affec
    James

Letter from Michael Benn, Tony Benn's eldest brother, who by 1943 was a pilot officer, just posted to North Africa.

                             103589 F/O M W Benn
                                 A. 9631 RAF

                              January 24th 1943

My dearest family
    I am going to settle down in real earnest and write to you all. Before I start to describe the various things I have done in the last week, I must ask Father if he ever sees the Night Combat reports from this area. Because if he does he will have noticed that on the night of Jan 20/21 one Junker 88 was shot down by one F/O Benn. My first victory! But more of that later.
    The trip out was marvellous. The weather superb and visibility incredible. You could see nearly 100 miles of coast.
    The bright blue sky was such a change too from the weather in England. We arrived at the place where I posted my first letter to you at three in the afternoon. I felt for the first time that I was really in the war at last. I noticed immediately the spirit as compared with an English station. Everyone was much more helpful and the 'Erks' more friendly and obliging. Strange as it seems, everyone at home [in the services] is either a Pole or a Czech or a Canadian or a Yank. Here they are nearly all English.
    We live in a requisitioned hotel about ten miles outside a large town. Nothing like England. How I hated the pettiness which was so common in stations in England. Back there people had plenty and were constantly

complaining, but here we have much less but are very happy; it's the activity of course which makes the difference.

I spent the first few days eating tangerines and chasing round getting some kit. We wear khaki battle dress here and so I spent an hour sewing on my wings and stripes on to this new jacket. It looks quite smart.

Now I come to the most exciting part of my letter. As you can imagine, I must be careful of the Censor.

I arrived at the Squadron and I was due to fly for the first time on the night of 20/21. It was the first time Lunan and I had flown together at night. I can't say too much about it, but it was quite simple and I regard it as a 'piece of cake'. I hit the Jerry's starboard engine with my first burst and set it on fire, it then dived away and I followed it round, fired again and hit the fuselage. The poor fellow went down in flames and hit the sea. We could see him burning on the water. I felt rather miserable really, it seemed such a bloody awful thing to do, but it's just part of the war. It was him or me. He fired back actually but he missed me. Let me say here – knowing the imagination of parents – that I was not injured, scratched, touched or affected in any way, neither was Lunan.

As you can imagine this has given me a pretty good start in the squadron and so a little modesty combined with some hard work should see me under full steam. The chaps – although some were a little disappointed at seeing an absolute newcomer step straight in and get one – are all very nice. It was just a question of luck you know, being in the right place at the right time.

> Take care of yourselves my precious family
> > Ever your affectionate and flourishing eldest
> > M.

> > > New College
> > > Oxford

> > > Jan 29th 1943

My dear Proff

Just a line to let you know how I'm getting on. I made my maiden speech at the Union a week ago about the Beveridge Report. The *Oxford Magazine* said that in a 'satirical' maiden speech I showed the wider implications of the motion 'which made even the Beveridge Report itself seem irrelevant'!

Last night we had another debate about helping the Jews in Europe. The motion was 'that this House urges that a more energetic and practical policy be pursued by the Government towards the rescue of Jews in Europe.' At the beginning of the debate there were an equal number of people for and against the proposal. But after Victor Gollancz had spoken, everyone supported the motion, including those who had *spoken against* it. The motion for helping the Jews was carried by 188 votes to 21.

     Much love
       James

            New College
            Oxford

            Jan 30th 1943

My dear Mike

    Not much happened today except an invasion exercise.

    At lunchtime all the shops closed and civilians were advised not to use the streets. All the civil defence services including fire-brigades were mobilised and besides the main town all the colleges held individual shows. Wellingtons and Whitleys flew over the city at roof top level. The gunners were swivelling their turrets and aiming their guns at the civil defenders. Fires were lit all over Oxford and the brigades pounced on them to have the fun of extinguishing them. In one of the main streets loudspeakers were broadcasting the noise of an air raid – machine guns, whistling bombs, flak, aircraft, explosions. There was so much crackling on the record however that even from thirty yards it sounded like a hosepipe.

    I returned to the College and was about to get down to some work when there was a knock at the door. In walked a Fellow of the College (a very distinguished historian incidentally). 'Excuse me,' he said, 'but I must ask you to vacate your room and become a casualty. I am about to light an incendiary bomb outside your door. You will have to go to the first aid post.'

    'Would you be so very kind as to give me some superficial wound, sir,' I said. 'I am very busy.' 'I think we can manage that,' he said as he fixed a label on me bearing the word 'slight burns'.

    The Fellow lit a bomb of tar and straw at the bottom of the stairs and I stood next to it with a friend of mine. After nearly quarter of an hour five or six gas-masked figures arrived and tripped over the stirrup pump. Luckily for them they just got the pump working before the fire went out!

    Tomorrow there are military operations and tanks, artillery and trucks rumbling around Oxford.

    All the best Mike
       Your affec and admiring bro
       James

            New College
            Oxford

5 Feb 1943

My dear Mike

This morning I wrote five or six letters and then went to a tutorial. After the tutorial I saw R. How fickle I am. You know, I can hardly bear the sight of her now.

This evening I went to a meeting of the Democratic Socialists which Kingsley Martin was addressing on the subject of 'The USA and the war'.

Martin has just returned from a tour of America. I agreed with most of what he said but as with all socialists there was one point on which I could not concur. He said that after the war there would be a Poland friendly to Russia or not a Poland at all. That displays – to my mind – a disregard for individuals and their wishes and throws me and other Christian reformers into the arms of the Liberals, whom I don't really think are progressive enough. There is a need for a new political party – a Christian progressive party which has a place for the individual. Masses of sensible people from all parties and 'classes' would acclaim such a party I am sure.

It is along these lines that I intend to work.

    Until tomorrow

        God bless you

        James

In 1942 a new political party, called the Common Wealth Party, was established by Sir Richard Acland and other socialists. Sir Richard had been elected Liberal Member of Parliament for Barnstaple in 1935 and represented it until 1945. In 1942, however, he and like-minded people decided to set up a Christian socialist party with a very radical programme, including the public ownership of land, to be instituted once the military victory was won. During the war it put up candidates in by-elections against what it termed 'reactionary' candidates, breaking the truce on contesting by-elections which had been agreed by the other parties. Its success was spectacular but short-lived. The Party won three seats – Eddisbury (J Loverseed), Skipton (H Lawson) and Chelmsford (E Millington.) between 1943 and 1945 and put up 23 candidates in 1945, but won only one seat. Acland himself unsuccessfully fought Putney in 1945 as the Common Wealth candidate. He then joined the Labour Party and in 1947 fought and won Gravesend in a by-election. In 1955 he resigned from the Labour Party over the Party's stand on the hydrogen bomb and lost in the General Election of that year as an Independent. The Aclands were an old-established Liberal family in Devon, and in the 1930s Sir Richard had handed the Acland estate there to the National Trust; after he left Parliament he became a lecturer, while his wife practised as an architect.

My brother Michael and I were attracted to this new party at its inception and in early 1943 I invited Richard Acland to address the Oxford Union on the motion 'That in the opinion of this House reconstruction in Europe and in Britain is impossible unless all the major productive resources entirely cease to be owned by individuals.'

4 March 1943
Visit of Sir Richard Acland, Bt, to the Oxford Union.

Mr President, Sir

My first task is a pleasant one, for it is to welcome Sir Richard Acland here tonight. I won't insult you – or for that matter him – with a long introduction for he is well known to you all as the founder and leader of that new political organisation, Common Wealth, which seems to me to be very much more idealistic in its conception and very much more realistic in its approach to political and economic reform than anything of that nature which has gone before.

You must all have heard by now of Sir Richard's gift to the National Trust of his family estates. With an acreage of 17,000 and a value of nearly a quarter of a million pounds it stands out as the largest gift that has ever been received by the National Trust. This act of generosity is even more noteworthy since the land has been in his family for three hundred years.

It surely serves to show Sir Richard's sincerity in living up to his political creed of the common ownership of large properties and economic resources.

On behalf of us all I would like to thank him very much for coming.

Extract from the Oxford Magazine

The speech of Sir Richard Acland, who was making his first visit to the Union since founding Common Wealth, enlivened the proceedings which culminated in an equal division of 82 votes for each side. The President gave his casting vote for the motion.

The Hon A. N. Wedgwood Benn proposed the motion, and began by maintaining that the prevailing popular distinction of domestic from international problems largely rested on false assumptions. The economic system at home was dependent upon the conditions of our foreign trade and both involved the fundamental issue of capital versus socialism. The natural outcome of industrialisation had been amalgamation and combination among capitalists, the essence of whose system was to restrict output and so increase prices ... which had helped to force Germany into Nazism. He concluded by referring to the Malvern Conference, which emphasised the ethical and religious arguments against capitalism ...

In reply, Sir Richard Acland Bt MP contrasted the political crisis at home, where the Government was being conducted by an eighteenth-century aristocrat in uneasy partnership with a sorrowful ruling class, and the outside world, where the war was being won by the forces of common ownership ... Our need was to

GENERAL ELECTION
1944 or 1945
●
COMMON WEALTH'S
Socialist Programme

1. We affirm our belief in complete democracy and our determination to preserve and improve British democratic institutions. Therefore, we pledge ourselves, if elected, to electoral reform which will abolish plural voting and the anomalies of the existing system of election, so as to secure that Parliament represents the wishes of the people, and as an immediate measure to introduce or support legislation either abolishing the House of Lords altogether, or depriving it of any power to veto or delay the enactment of any Bill passed by the House of Commons.

2. We believe that society must be based on the public ownership of the means of production, distribution and exchange, and that the immediate establishment of such a society is necessary and practicable. Therefore, we pledge ourselves, if elected, immediately to introduce legislation which will:—

    (a) Transfer to public ownership all banks, insurance companies and financial institutions, land, public utilities, mines, and all forms of transport;

    (b) Give the Government power to transfer to public ownership as soon as practicable any other industrial, financial, commercial or distributive undertakings;

    (c) Establish the principal that compensation to former owners is not to be worked out by reference to the alleged former capital value of their holdings and paid in interest-bearing transferable bonds, but is to take the form of pensions or grants related to the hardship-needs of the owners concerned.

3. The British people cannot themselves determine the solution to all international problems. They can determine the direction towards which British influence shall be exerted. We believe that Nationalism, Imperialism, and the forces inherent in competitive Monopoly-Capitalism have been the main causes of world war. Therefore:—

    (a) We will work to prevent the powers of finance-capital from reinstating the representatives of the old economic and political power cliques upon the liberated countries of Europe;

    (b) We mean business when we speak of economic and political independence for India forthwith and for the other Colonial Peoples at the earliest possible moment, and we accept "What we have we pool" in preference to "What we have we hold" as the watchwords of British Colonial Policy in the coming age;

    (c) We reject unrestricted national sovereignty, and therefore the relevant sections of the Atlantic Charter, as a basis of the coming international order. Against whatever difficulties it must be the firm determination of British policy to promote a peace which rests on the democratic liberation and unification of Europe and to establish effective democratic international government over all those aspects of human activity which affect equally the peoples of all countries.

Published by MARGARET WIMBUSH, *National Agent of* COMMON WEALTH, 4 *Gower Street, London, W.C.1 and printed by* GEO. STEWART & CO. LTD., 92 *George Street, Edinburgh,* 2.

General Election Series No. 7.

Extract from Common Wealth Party's draft war-time manifesto.

combine political with economic democracy, since the country that
first did this would lead the world . . .

Capitalism could not meet the crying needs of Europe for food
and fuel after the war. In England it would be nonsense to raise
again the objection that it 'doesn't pay' when we had men, machines
and materials enough to meet all our needs . . .

Mr C. A. R. Crosland (Trinity), ex-Treasurer, ably endeavoured
to refute the argument that work is less well done by the State's
employees than the capitalist's, though admitting that he found
himself in uneasy partnership with Sir Richard Acland.

7 March 1943
Letter from the Oxford University Labour Party Association to Transport House

We the Committee and members of the OULPA wish to place on record
our disapproval of the Government's handling of the Indian situation
and to express the hope that Indian self-government will be at once
promised and the scheme put into operation within a definite number of
years after the war or as soon as is compatible with the immediate needs
of the United Nations in prosecuting the war, with a view to securing
victory at the earliest possible moment. We also urge that the Labour
Party itself make clear its own attitude to the Indian problem and that in
accordance with the clauses of the Atlantic Charter, Indian freedom be
publicised more widely as one of the main war aims of the allied nations.

21 March 1943

My dear Ma

Thank you very much for the letter and telegrams. Yesterday was
rather a strain. I had a three-hour paper on moral philosophy in the
morning and another lasting for two hours on the same subject in the
afternoon. After that I went to the cinema and saw some real American
sentimental slush by way of contrast. Tomorrow I am moving my room.
Food has attracted a mouse which comes out in the afternoon. Although I
am not fond of him, I still leave the door shut to exclude the cat – which is
lucky for the mouse!

The final Air Squadron results are out and I have got through the
course successfully. That means I cut my training by about five months. I
shall go straight to flying school in June.

It isn't likely that I will be on operations until August next year –
which is a long time ahead and I sometimes wonder if the war will be
over by then.

Your loving son

J

New College
Oxford

17 March 1943

My dear old Mike

Your letter arrived this morning.

I was very interested indeed to hear you say that you were disillusioned about life, morals and beliefs. So am I. You have seen life in an Arab quarter and in a French colony, besides the ordinary RAF life and that has set you thinking about whether the English moral code is valid. I have been doing philosophy which has proved to my temporary satisfaction that everything men do they do because it makes them happy. I get rather upset at this disillusionment. I have given up Christianity completely because the more I think about it the more inexplicable it becomes. One wonders whether anyone would be a Christian if (a) it meant living a hard life and (b) no real satisfaction could be derived out of it and (c) there was no fear of damnation in after-life.

James

Blunt House
Oxted
Surrey

March 31st 1943

My dear old Mike

On Monday night I bought eight bottles of fizzy drinks, some chocolate, cigarettes, rock cakes and buns, costing 6/6, in all and got two half tins of salmon. I woke Lesley, Linnet, Barbara and Fiona at midnight and they all came into my room in their pyjamas. After eating we tried a game. I suggested that we should play a game where we gambled our clothes. I couldn't find any cards, so we decided a spelling game. Barbara is very bad at spelling . . . I think I can say that a good time was had by all.

Mike, what do you feel about Fiona?

Now to politics and the Beveridge Report. You wrote to the effect that you didn't think that the Beveridge Report solved anything. I don't agree with you there. Remember that Beveridge was asked to make a report on 'The social insurance and allied services', and an idea sprang up that it was a complete plan for post-war reconstruction. As a scheme for uniting in one state controlled body all the piecemeal inefficient and wasteful systems of social insurance which exist from the Elizabethan Poor Law to the Prudential Assurance Company it is very significant. Firstly because it would have a very important part to play in any state, planned and worked along socialist lines and secondly . . . it could work very well as a remedy for a capitalist state as it is today or in the transitory stage between capitalism and socialism. I absolutely agree with you that socialist planning is necessary. Capitalism is obsolete. It has ceased to perform the function for which it originated. It is not possible for a man to set up a business in competition with say HMV or Imperial Chemicals or the Nuffield combine. They can afford to push him out of business because of their superior capital.

The working man knows that he is working for the profit of his employer and his heart is not therefore in his job. He knows that if he 'goes slow' he is creating work for his friends – the unemployed. So he goes slow. We can't blame him, but nevertheless we can't have people going slow when we will need everyone working to capacity if we intend to make up the appalling destruction which we are wreaking today.

Out of 32,000,000 men and women who are employed in this country – 14,000,000 work in factories, docks, railways and other big privately owned concerns. They must be enlisted on our side and as is quite evident from their membership of the trade unions, they want national control. It ought to be quite evident by now that a changeover to nationalised industries and services is necessary. What part does the Beveridge Report play in this changeover? I am myself against a sudden breakaway from things as they are today. The new must evolve from the old and the evolution must be accomplished with as little fuss or disruption as is possible with the needs of the moment.

Well, Mike, I feel that this letter is some sort of compensation for a week's neglect.

Your most devoted and affectionate bro
James

Wednesday 19 May 1943

Extract from speech to the Oxford Union, Thursday 13th May 1943 on the motion 'That the state should design and build the Englishman's castle'.

A lot of light has been thrown recently on town dwelling conditions. Manufacturing areas generally have a higher infant and child mortality rate than country towns. The Registrar-General attributed this to the crowding together in towns, the crowding of too many people into houses, the aggravation of this condition by the ill-effects of poverty, the effects of a smoky sunless atmosphere. I will not put it to you that English men, women and children ought not to have to live in such conditions for I know full well that appeals on moral grounds have very little effect and are usually dubbed as emotional. Instead I will be realistic – very realistic. Think, my friends, of these people – potential workers in your factory or your office or your gasworks. Don't you agree that it is a pity to see such a lot of good raw material going down the drain – that is if they had so much of a drain to go down. In many ways, they haven't.

We are the customers of planning. On us and people like us will depend the tremendous but exhilarating task of making the paper plans into fact. This can only be achieved by putting the power into the hands of our democratically elected representatives, our government of the people. Blake was not being unrealistic when he wrote those immortal words.

'I will not cease from mental fight,
Nor shall my sword sleep in my hand
Till we have built Jerusalem,
In England's green and pleasant land.'

Saturday 22 May 1943

The *Oxford Magazine* last Thursday was critical of my speech to the Union. I 'must avoid treating the House as a class or a Salvation Army meeting,' it said.

The criticism of my speech was due to the fact that I was over-confident. In my earlier speeches I was absolutely terrified, but by this time I had conquered my fear and though it is a good thing to do that, fear serves a useful purpose in that it restrains conceit . . . I haven't got the fluency of speech in public that is required. However I intend to persist. Another urgency is to find out how to work in at least one really good joke.

Since I gave up Christianity I have felt that I have lost the purpose in life and though I suppose that I am gradually finding one – the fitting of myself for public service – it makes self-organisation much more difficult because I feel that any improvement is self-brought-about and I at once become a prey to my own vanity – which is perhaps the most crippling and deadly of all faults.

I am very jealous of the people with scholarships here. At Westminster I was most terribly jealous of the Busby monitors and I wanted desperately to be made one. In the ATC of course I got somewhere and I think that did me good. I don't work as hard as I could or should and therefore through my own fault I slip behind others, and my only remedy is jealousy. Jealousy and a sense of grievance are very closely linked and do a great deal of harm.

Wednesday 9 June 1943

I regard my death in the RAF as very possible. I am aware in vague bursts that entering the RAF is a great and dangerous venture. When I think of the technical knowledge necessary before I can fly and the number of things I will have to think of and do it fills me with foreboding, but I suppose that all can be done if I work hard at my training. That is only the learning side; it is the problem of judging the exact moment for

YOU
are going to be a
PILOT

flattening out and worse still the problem of whether I can keep my nerve in a spin or when the flak is at me. I am filled with depression and then I cheer up and say, 'Well, what if I do get killed? I shall be a hero and I won't have to plan my life which I realise will be an almost impossible task.' I think my new and most earnest wish is that Mike should survive the war unhurt.

Why am I fighting? In short it is because I think there is something worth fighting for. If I think that it is worth fighting for – it is presumably worth making any sacrifices possible?

I shall be terrified most of the time but the conquest of cowardice is a personal struggle and I can say that it will never be my policy to be a coward. I can't guarantee that in a panic I shan't give way – God preserve me from doing so – but I can't do anything now about it except prepare myself and train myself.

In July 1943 I joined the RAF at the Air Crew Receiving Centre in London, and was sent first to Stratford-upon-Avon, then on to RAF Elmdon, Birmingham for my first flying training on Tiger Moth aircraft. From there I was posted to Heaton Park in Manchester to await a troopship to Africa, where trainee pilots were sent to complete flying training.

At this time I began to keep a proper manuscript diary, and kept up a regular correspondence home to my family until my return to Britain on board HMS Carthage *in May 1945.*

Tuesday 27 July 1943
On Sunday I lay in the sun all day. Monday was the first real day and after being woken at 5.30 we had breakfast, moved out of our room, took our kit downstairs and marched to Lords Cricket Ground where we filled up endless forms. Then we were marched to the stores where we were kitted out. These manoeuvres were accomplished after endless reversals of plans and I was quite exhausted by the time we got back to Grove Court where we were rebilleted. I saw *The Life and Death of Colonel Blimp*.

RAF Elmdon
Birmingham

Sept 1943

My very dear brother
    In case you haven't had my last two air letters let me congratulate you on (1) your DFC and (2) your 22nd birthday. A junior brother and friend is very proud of you.
    At last I am at an aerodrome and I am happier than ever before in my life. We are only here for three weeks but in that time we are really taught to fly Tigers – and go solo – I simply can't believe it. We wear blue

battledress and with my pipe I really look quite operational. We are called 'pupil pilots'. On Sunday I shall have my first lesson. Details of the 'drome I can't give you by letter but I know you will understand how every little aspect of this sort of life appeals to me.

Sunday 12 September 1943

Towards the end of my time at Air Crew Receiving Centre I was on guard (security piquet) as a reserve with Air Gunner flight. One of the chaps I met there was a very good man and as I talked with him I heard of the shortness of his training and envied him. He hopes to be on operations by Christmas. This, combined with the fall of Mussolini a few days earlier and the subsequent cracking up of the Italian war machine, produced in me a queer feeling which I have now quite recovered from.

I had a sudden feeling that I ought to be an air gunner. This obligation was caused entirely by the feeling that I was becoming a pilot for the wrong reasons. Whatever else may have changed, my views on why I am in the war and why the war is worth fighting have not changed and so I realised that I should go into that branch of air crew which would put me in a position to do my own bit of fighting as soon as possible. I felt that my own desire to be a young pilot officer with wings was overshadowing this original sense of duty. I came to the somewhat hasty decision that it would be better to do six months' operations as an air gunner than graduate with wings and see service only as part of the army of occupation. A commission I want, but if it holds up my operations then I would sacrifice it willingly.

The family wholly misunderstood me when I tried to explain what I felt and they secretly felt that I had decided that I wasn't suited nervously or physically for pilot.

If I can't be a pilot I will remuster as air gunner.

We arrived at Stratford on August 14th and were billeted in The Firs hotel in Rother Street.

I shared a room with four chaps called Dick, Ken, Johnny and John.

We lived in a back room overlooking a garden full of coal and coke and with two extra beds in it. The Firs had practically no sanitary arrangements at all – all forty of us having two bathrooms with a WC basin and bath. The water was almost always stone cold. I learned again a lesson I had forgotten, it concerned my relations with the other people in the room. For some reason I was awarded a yellow lanyard and it was very interesting to note the effect authority had on me and the impressions I and authority had on the others in A Flight. I made a number of blunders with respect to my personal behaviour at the Initial Training Wing but it is luckily an advantage of the RAF especially under training that you are constantly being posted away from your companions and so you have every opportunity to start afresh every month or so.

Here are the main things I did wrong:
- I made myself cheap with terrible jokes.
- I lost the respect of my friends that way.
- I failed to psycho-analyse these people and so trod frequently on their soft spots, thus annoying them.
- I made fun of John Wilson and discussed others too freely and critically, laying myself open to the same form of attack.
- I talked too much, thus laying myself open to more attacks.
- I made myself cheap, thus generally encouraging others to score at my expense.

My future advice to myself is:
- don't cheapen yourself with feeble jokes.
- show to others the respect they deserve.
- be reserved and quiet: 'Better to keep your mouth shut', etc.

Tuesday 28 September 1943 – Elmdon
I was posted to Elmdon on September 10th and this brought a number of changes. In the first place the living conditions were very different – recreational facilities were very much better, we had a billiard table, darts board, chess, draughts and dominoes, a radiogram, ping-pong and a canteen. Nevertheless the Nissen hut we lived in was very cramped – sixteen of us in a small space.

The Welsh were very obstreperous and noisy which was all right, as long as they didn't choose your bed to fight on. I was the only Oxford University Air Squadron man at Elmdon. This breakaway provided me with an absolutely new start among people I hardly knew, and I didn't mess things up quite as much as at ITW. The yellow lanyard was resurrected and for a little over a fortnight I was second in command of B Flight.

Sunday 3 October 1943
At Elmdon I did my first flying training – twelve hours of dual instruction on DH82A Tiger Moth aircraft. The purpose of this school was to grade candidates according to their abilities as potential service pilots.

Ever since I can remember I have been struggling with the family notion that Mike was the mechanical member of the family, I the political member. My efforts to prove that I was able to manage things mechanical have met with considerable success of late. I worked the motor mower at Blunt House this spring and handled the engine fairly intelligently. I am perfectly able to have a look at clocks, typewriters and other mechanical devices.

But my flying training these last few weeks has proved me to be wrong. Not only in flying but in any physical exercise or test I have felt inferior and afraid. For at least two and a half years I dreaded the RAF inoculation and any form of sport.

I have become a different person these last eleven weeks. In July 1942 I was a Westminster Schoolboy, warped and undeveloped in mind, unfit and nervous in body. A year at Oxford changed my outlook and advanced me intellectually. The RAF has made me fit and braved me against my previous fears.

1850035 AC2C BENN ANW
Hut 41
F Flight
No 1 Squadron
RAF Station
Heaton Park, Manchester

[December 1943]

Dear Family,

Here is my address. I am almost certain that I have been selected for pilot training. This will be overseas though I cannot say where. On the nominal roll prepared by the RAF we are divided into two groups – potential officers and NCOs. I am in the first group. The prospects of leave are uncertain.

Conditions here are dreadful. Rains all the time. No baths, and no hot water. There are twenty of us in a Nissen hut which is unheated. But I mustn't go on. I came into Manchester today to have a bath and write some letters. The latter is almost impossible in a crowded canteen and there isn't a bath in the city.

Love James

AC2 A N W Benn 1850035
RAF Heaton Park
Manchester

12 December 1943

My dear old Mike

How glad I was to get your letter. It was grand to see you last Saturday week. I think we covered more ground in those three hours than we have ever done before.

At the moment circumstances prevent me from working properly along the lines we discussed.

I wouldn't miss my personal war experience for anything, particularly now that I am in the ranks, I have opportunities for meeting all sorts of people whom I should never come in contact with in the ordinary way of life. My hut at the moment contains an ex-policeman from Liverpool, a Scots engineer from the Merchant Navy, a railway worker from Barnstaple, a radio operator, a Welsh undergraduate, a fireman, a chemist's assistant. I have certainly learned one thing above all else and that is that the ordinary people have a deep distrust for the left or right wing politicians and their methods. This distrust has created a gap and an honest party on the lines we discussed could step in and cash in on these potential political forces, which are at the moment powerless through lack of organisation.

As it looks as though the European War will be over by next Autumn I can't reckon my operation service as being any other than against the Japs . . .

I can't say anything about my movements at all I am afraid. I will try and phone you one night at the end of next week as I might be able to give you some gen on the pukka possibilities of Christmas leave. My heart bleeds for you when you say you live in a Nissen hut! So do I – with eighteen others, a tin roof and a concrete floor.

> Yours in the same struggle
> James – an affec. bro

Letter written 'only to be read in the event of my death in the RAF'

December 1943

My precious family,

I can't think of anything which helped me keep going more than the feeling that behind me was a wall of love against which I could shelter. Apart from the terrific advantage that this gave me over the other people I met, who were not as lucky, it formed a foundation for many of my views and I came to see that it is not unrealistic to suppose that national and world happiness can only be built up on a basis of unselfish devotion to the cause of others. Not only must the structure of society itself be built on our family model, where all the tasks – pleasant and unpleasant – are shared . . . It was because I thought that if we lost this war something terribly evil would envelop the world that I wanted to help win it. I certainly was not fighting to preserve the world of 1939 but I could see that a German victory would have been worse and that unless we won we wouldn't even have the opportunity for making a lasting peace . . .

Thursday 30 December 1943

I did join the RAF to fight this war and I must lay personal considerations aside . . . I therefore intend to apply for an interview to get remustered (as air gunner) and use every trick I know to get it through.

Favourite tunes: 'Crown Imperial March' by Walton; 'When I look at you I hear lovely music'; 'Sunday Monday or always'; 'Mignonne', from *Colonel Blimp*; 'Ain't I ever going to get a girl in my arms'; 'I'm dreaming tonight'; 'Coming in on a wing and a prayer'; 'Silver wings in the moonlight'; 'The Trumpeter'; 'Cafe by Notre Dame'; Handel's 'Largo';

'Rose of Tralee'; 'She wheels a perambulator'; 'Perpetuum Mobile' by Strauss; 'We are the Royal Air Force'; 'Poor little Angeline'; 'Tonight'.

Tuesday 11 January 1944

In the morning we had a lecture from Air Commodore Howe in the Heaton Park cinema. His talk was on embarkation and he hinted broadly that we would be going to South Africa, and although I was convinced at the time, we all agreed later that it might be bluff. I finished marking my kit in the afternoon.

Wednesday 12 January 1944

We had a lecture on troopships this morning from F/Lt Peters and it was abominably dull and unpleasant as we stood to hear it in the mud and wet in front of the bandstand, while he almost read it from a booklet. In the evening I went to the ENSA show in the hangar.

Friday 14 January 1944

I woke up occasionally but it was not until about 6.15 that I began getting up. A quarter of an hour later we stopped at Glasgow.

We moved off again at about 1430 and about half an hour later came aboard the SS *Cameronia*. I went down to our mess and attempted to settle in. We were situated on D4 Mess Deck where in an area not more than eighty feet square and not higher than six foot five, 296 of us were accommodated. There we ate, sat and wrote. At night the space above the floor and tables was crowded with the hammocks slung from bars on the ceiling. Our kit was stored on wooden racks above these bars and the crush was incredible. Many had to sleep on mattresses on the tables. The first few hours were desperate – you could not be certain what was yours and where were your possessions. However, after the evening meal it was more tolerable and I went on deck. Four enormous cranes were at work loading the ship, two powerful lights shining on each crane, illuminating the decks like the streets of London before the war.

I slung my hammock at 8.30 and slept soundly.

Sunday 16 January 1944

Woke at about 6, got up and folded my hammock. Before there was time to wash, the mess orderlies had brought breakfast. This I ate with relish and then attempted to have a wash. It was quite impossible and I had to give it up in order to be in time for a fatigue parade under Flt. Sgt. Bishop.

As we were supposed to sail at one I made my way up to the deck and hung on to the rail. Sure enough we cast off and with the assistance of two tugs we slid away from the dock into the middle of the Clyde. I stood there in a sort of dream, leaning over the side, wondering when I would be back.

Monday 17 January 1944

In the course of the afternoon the sky was clear and the sea blue. I came below and wrote this journal and then just after 7 pm a message came across the Tannoy saying we were in submarine-infested waters and that we must carry our life-belts with us wherever we go, however short the distance.

Everyone is very calm and they can be seen reading, writing, sleeping, smoking and playing records in a quite unconcerned manner. Today I really felt better for I must admit that yesterday I was pretty seedy and giddy, even though I wasn't actually sick. Tonight we heard there was a shortage of water and we were rationed to a little over half a mugful each.

I didn't sleep very well.

Wednesday 19 January 1944

I watched the sunrise and it was a wonderful sight. The sun, like a red ball of fire, rose very quickly above the horizon, colouring all the ships in the convoy with a rosy tint and as it climbed higher the dark grey and deep blue of the twilight sky lost its dullness and gradually lightened through the most gorgeous shades of pink, orange and yellow. At about 3.15 we heard deep rumblings and bangings. When I got on deck I learned that some of the destroyers which comprise our escort had broken off and dropped about six depth charges on our starboard and about three on our port bows. As I stood I could see the destroyers altering formation and on the horizon two or three were visible searching for what must have been a U-boat or U-boats. The general opinion was that they would lie low until dark and then move in for an attack. However, as a matter of fact we had a quiet evening and I started a long letter.

Thursday 20 January 1944

I slept well and got up at 6.15 which enabled me to have the first really good wash since I came on board. I heard from a fairly reliable man on the next mess table that about eight depth charges were dropped early this morning. After the boat drill we had action stations and were bollocked for various errors in kit layout.

In the afternoon I wrote more of my letter to my darling Mary Anne and also managed one to the family. The mess deck became very hot, rising from 81 or 82 degrees in the day to 85 degrees at night. More depth charges in the afternoon – I suppose that the U-boats are still after us. There is an order today that water bottles are not to be filled till February 1st and that when we empty out old water we must use it for washing purposes. Water is very short.

Friday 21 January 1944

I didn't get out of bed till ten to seven. I felt weak with the stink of 300 bodies in so confined a space. We have nothing but artificial light twenty-four hours each day on our mess deck and the fresh air comes through air conditioning vents.

Tuesday 25 January 1944
I went along to a lecture on aircraft recognition which later turned into a discussion of the colour bar, and instructions on how to behave towards negroes and half-whites. We had a few phrases of kaffir language. I went downstairs and started an argument with Stan, Ken and Johnny on the colour bar.

Thursday 27 January 1944
I queued for biscuits and tea, got paid ten shillings, and went to the cinema. To my annoyance *Garrison Follies* was on again. However having nothing else to do I saw it through, then came out and read until tea; tried to write a poem on England almost entirely without success.

Sunday 30 January 1944
I got up this morning and heard straight away that we were lying off Port Said. After breakfast I went for a moment on deck and there was the convoy facing west in formation and moving off singly under the direction of a fussy little tug marked PILOTE. We cheered everybody – the little RAF air-sea rescue launch, the Greek ships, the men on the shore, the millions of Arab boats which were all over the harbour, and the advertisements for the various brands of 'English' whisky. The blue coated, red-fezzed police waved.

The landscape was as flat as a billiard table. I went on deck after dinner with Ken and there was a small rowing boat with Arabs in it, collecting pennies and sixpences in a basket.

Monday 31 January 1944
We sailed into the lake where a lot of ships were anchored including two Italian battleships which had surrendered to Admiral Cunningham last year. We dropped anchor.

I went up on deck in the evening and a remarkable sight met my eyes. There on the other side of the lake were six or seven groups of bright winking lights, illuminating the village or town. They were the first night lights I had seen for four and a half years. People were singing on deck and a mouth organ struck up the old favourites – 'Tipperary', 'Pack up your troubles', 'Bless 'em all' and so on.

Wednesday 2 February 1944
A tanker came alongside of us and while it was filling us up the mechanics on board the tanker sold us handbags, wallets and bracelets,

which they sent by rope to the ship on previous receipt of money sent down in a tin.

We are more cramped now. There are twenty-eight on a table designed for eighteen as two tables have been given over to the Army and there are a number of stories about women coming on board – WRNS, WACS, ATS and so on. I must say that I hope that they are true.

The Tannoy played music by Victor Sylvester and I lay watching the moon and stars and the lights of Suez.

Thursday 3 February 1944

We sailed from Suez early. I had a long talk with a Yugoslav RAF cadet of 22 born in Slovenia who was captured by the Germans and forced to join the Austrian army. He surrendered in May in North Africa to us although his brother is still a German soldier. He was very philosophical about it all. A typical victim of the war – not understanding it but carried along in the backwash. He laughed and smiled and we talked in English, French and German. I got my tropical kit ready tonight.

Sunday 6 February 1944

I lay in the sun after breakfast which was a great relief after the heat of the mess deck – 96 degrees F.

In the evening . . . an argument started with a chance remark by one of the men. 'I can't understand,' he said, 'why so many really great minds in history have been Roman Catholics.' From there we discussed Roman Catholicism, its appeal and history, logic and faith, cause and effect, utilitarianism, the validity of instinctive morality, the nature of the soul, men and animal compared. By a superhuman effort I got the conversation over to divorce – my pet subject after reading A. P. Herbert's *Holy Deadlock*. Once we had covered this the way was open to sexual perverts, local gossip and sexual murders.

Saturday 12 February 1944

We approached what appeared to be a wide estuary – a number of white villas with red roofs were scattered about the outskirts of – I suppose – Mombasa. It is rumoured that we are getting Italian prisoners of war on board in this place. First came some officers whom I didn't see clearly, but some of whom were of fairly high rank. The soldiers were rather ordinary, sad, tired and didn't seem to deserve the awful fate which the watching soldiers, airmen and South Africans were demanding for them.

I met a South African soldier, Oswald van Blerk, in the evening and we discussed education, co-education and homosexuality. His psychological explanation of the purpose of homosexuality to delay heterosexual intercourse was new to me. Tonight was the first night that there was a total lifting of the blackout. Portholes were left open, blackouts down, lights streamed into the harbour. I slept on deck and listened to the drunken seamen coming on board.

Monday 14 February 1944
I argued until tea with John Boss, Leslie Fewtrell and Johnny Harris as to whether the Christian Church could sanctify marriage based on love of a black woman by a white man.

Wednesday 16 February 1944
A ground staff RAF fellow died this morning in sick quarters of heat stroke. He was evidently working in the bakery where there is a constant temperature of 115 degrees. The flag is at half mast and he is being given a military burial tonight. We were also told that a sailor has gone blind from the sun.

After pay I got dinner and read, showered and talked. Then I attended the funeral of the airman. It was quite impressive though, despite the fact that it was the first funeral, I didn't feel at all spiritually or emotionally moved. It was rather cheap and everyday in a way. In the first place I think his life could have been saved and then the funeral arrangements weren't quite perfect and it went off rather like a parade not quite up to scratch, with all the shabbiness that that involved.

I slept on deck again.

Saturday 19 February 1944
The OC Troops interviewed me earlier in the week and asked me whether I was willing to give a talk on the war aims. I agreed and he asked me whether it would be political. I had to explain that it was bound to be expressed in terms of policy but if he meant 'Was I going to give a ranting party speech?' the answer was no.

By tea time we could see land and we docked at Durban in the course of the evening. The 'war aims' meeting came off at eight delivered to an audience of merchant navy men, soldiers and airmen of England, Scotland, South Africa and so on. I suppose that I spoke for twenty minutes, hardly referring to my notes. It definitely went down well and I was given tumultuous applause. Then Whitehead got up and rambled on for ages.

The question of the democratic value of the House of Lords was raised. I attacked it vigorously to the amusement of those in the know, and we finished up debating whether or not bloodshed would be a necessary prelude to the political and economic change that would undoubtedly come. I couldn't come to any conclusions on that matter.

I slept on deck feeling very excited and with mixed feelings of pleasure and sorrow at the voyage being over.

[No date]

My Dearest Dad,

Just a very short note to tell you that I have arrived at my port of disembarkation. I don't know where you are or how you are so I am sending this to your ME address.

I was addressing a meeting on Saturday on board ship. The subject was 'War Aims'. Had an interview with the Wing Commander last night in which he asked whether it was political, to which I replied that all war aims had to be expressed in terms of policies.

I couldn't prepare it as carefully as I would like for I had no reference books, and no privacy, which I miss so much. However, it is very different from the Union and my first experience of an ordinary public political speech with heckling and cat calls.

You've no idea how much I've thought of my Pa these last weeks on board and missed him.

Ever your loving son James

Sunday 20 February 1944

We got the South African currency, had dinner, paraded and disembarked. A native wallah was selling ice-cream and I ate three of them. Then a train took us to Clairwood Imperial Troops transhipment camp about five or six miles out of Durban. We settled into windowless, bedless, cowshed huts; the ablutions and showers are in the open. I went to bed about ten feeling a little nervous about snakes.

Wednesday 23 February 1944

After we had paraded we were marched off to the camp station and entrained for Bulawayo.

We moved off at about 10.30 and then we all slept until lunch which we had in the luxurious dining car. The food – what there was of it – was wizard. We passed through Durban, Pietermaritzburg and on over the Drakensberg mountains to Ladysmith climbing to 5000 feet in great sweeping curves through lovely open wooded fertile country. Then on through wider, more barren valleys to Newcastle.

Thursday 24 February 1944

Johannesburg 10.50 – great mines and piles of slag. We passed on today through more of the bush country. The gradient was sometimes as steep as 1:4 and the train went on so slowly that some people jumped off it and ran beside, stopping to pick wild peaches and jumping on again. At one station some kind ladies distributed tea and grapes etc. free. At Mafeking (where I relieved myself!) there were a lot of natives though no town to speak of. Periodically we would pass through native settlements or villages and very rough they were. Mud huts made of lumps of clay hewn in brick form, with hay rather than properly thatched roofs, and very often no windows but a wide space for a door. The natives were sitting around quite lazily outside watching, although I fancy there were railway workers, leaving only their old, infirm, children and womenfolk at home in the daytime. Tonight we passed into British Bechuanaland and stopped at Francistown, where we met a British Army sergeant who had been stationed there since 1940. He told us that two RAF cadets had been forced down and on arriving at a bushmen's camp had been eaten by them.

When we moved off, 'Goodbye' he said, 'and don't get eaten.' The true story, it later appeared, was that two RAF aircrew on being forced to land went to a bushmen's camp where they were feasted on some excellent food, including some especially good meat which they learned on enquiry to be giraffe meat. Now it happens to be an offence to kill giraffes out here and that night the bushmen, fearing they should report the matter and so get them (the bushmen) into trouble, went to the hut where the visitors were sleeping, shot one dead and wounded the other whom they finished off with an axe. Whether or not they then ate them I don't know.

Friday 25 February 1944
In the afternoon we passed from Bechuanaland to Southern Rhodesia and by 7 o'clock we were at Bulawayo where we disentrained and were marched to Hillside Camp. There we were issued with bedding, given huts and a meal, and left. The camp had been a dairy farm and the buildings were originally cattle sheds.

Sunday 27 February 1944
I went to Holy Communion at 8.15 and fainted and had to be taken out by Paddy Woodhead.

Saw the Padre and explained my interest in native and local political problems. He was very friendly, and suggested seeing Padre Roebuck.

Tuesday 29 February 1944
At the break I went to see Padre Roebuck and he was very friendly. 'What is your name, friend?' he said.

He asked me about my interests, political inclinations and education and assured me that he had no axe to grind. His consideration for the native was incredibly sympathetic and a trifle tragic. 'They are a simple people – lost – without a friend, and in South Africa iniquitously barred by law from practising a skilled trade.' I went away very impressed with the man.

Since this diary began I have completed my Oxford year and polished off many edges, while beginning a course of political philosophy which should be invaluable to me when it is fully evolved and operated – I refer to political speaking and organising. Although a small thing really, I derived considerable satisfaction from the success of my speech and the meeting on 'War Aims' that we had on the last night on SS *Cameronia*. I spoke with only the scantiest reference to notes and with considerable fluency, so I hope. Anyway it was an experiment and a practice in speaking to a working class audience which will prove quite invaluable. I have lived a simple, fairly hard-working life with people of all sorts, professions, classes (though I hate the word, it does have a meaning here I am afraid), ages, religions, upbringings.

I have been to a burial at sea and lived with 300 men in a mess like cattle with the temperature nearly 100 degrees at night. All this adds up to one thing – experience of life – and it is going to make me a very much stronger political opponent and more realistic organiser when the day comes.

Thursday 2 March 1944
I walked into town with John Boss and we went to the Services Club. We walked back to camp to hear Miss Gordon, the headmistress of the Eveline High School for Girls give a talk on 'The Rhodesian Girl' – a sub-tropical product compared with her English counterpart. She spoke extremely fluently and well, with of course a complete knowledge of her subject. It is impossible to describe fully what she said but a number of points rise in my mind as important and revealing. The first one is that the climate has two effects on girls.

Firstly it develops them physically at least one year before English ones, which means that they become physically adult at fourteen or fifteen. Secondly it has the effect of slowing down their mental development by a similar period if not longer. These two results are attributed to the heat and altitude and so on. Combined, the two factors resolve into a difference of four or five years between the physical and mental ages. This puts them, as she pointed out, at the mercy of unscrupulous men who may meet a girl of apparently eighteen, mentally developed to the age of thirteen or fourteen who may not understand her own reactions to stimulation. Among other points she discussed was the native question. When she was at school, her two prefects had to chase a native from the dormitory with hockey sticks. Girls were not allowed to go anywhere alone, which means an almost complete lack of privacy which tends to affect them, as quiet thought becomes difficult, which may also account for their academic backwardness. The superiority in their attitude can be attributed to their power over the coloured servants. This however has its own snags as the bringing up of the young cannot be entrusted to Bantu nannies and the parents are very unqualified to superintend and direct the emotional development of their daughters. It is interesting to hear that children have no colour prejudice and that it is induced artificially by the home or parental influence.

Anyway I got an insight into some problems which had never previously occurred to me.

Saturday 4 March 1944
It is very amusing to hear the natives in the compound in the morning. A native comes in about 0615 and shouts in Bantu, interspersed with the emphatic imperative 'WAKEY, WAKEY'. There is more shouting and laughing followed by silence when the 'waker' departs as sleep regains its prey. This continues until the man returns and reawakens us, which he may have to do two or three times.

Saturday 11 March 1944
After lunch we bullshitted up and went into town to enjoy ourselves for the afternoon. In the Services Club we met a very attractive girl of about twenty who served us. She was very sweet and we thought of asking her to come with us to the cabaret at the Grand Hotel. However when we came back from a tour of the town she was gone and we went out again feeling very depressed and there was sweet B-all to be done.

Tuesday 14 March 1944
I awoke this morning as depressed as ever and wishing to commit suicide as I always do first thing in the morning. Life really is as black as it possibly can be before the morning break and I often wonder how I last. I must be a very moody person although I doubt whether that is apparent to the outsider as when I am happy I bubble with natter and enthusiasm and when I am miserable I throw off a protective film of worthless jocularity and surplus verbosity.

18 March 1944

My dear dad,
    Many thanks for your airgraph.
    I am fit and well and the weather is heavenly. Nobody knows just how long we will be waiting but it will probably be another month or so, which delays our 'wings' until the end of the year and then I suppose about this time in a year we will be on our way to Burma or some other God-forsaken place. The aircraft we will start on are new American kites. They have scrapped the old Tiger Moth that Mike learnt on and we will use a 200 hp power trainer called the Cornell, with a cockpit cover, involving a pre-flight check on nearly fifty items. I am very keen to get cracking on it.
    Well I must close now Dad and if this doesn't get to you until May – a

happy birthday to you, old boy. It is grand having you on a war job at the
age you are.

    James

1850035 Cadet Benn

21 March 1944

My dear old Proff

    I have been neglecting you of late. We have some examinations coming
off in a week or so which call for a lot of preparation.

    I am glad you have made some progress with the Oxford business. You
were very wise to choose Balliol I think, as it is a college which doesn't
specialise in sports so much, as sets out to be learned. A reputation which
is not always true – but will be when you are there. Also, it is very left
wing in tendency, from Lindsay down. I expect that the fact that the
Daily Worker is read in the Senior Common Room convinced you of that!
Go all out for that scholarship – a scholar's status is better in the
University itself.

    Well, Proff, all my love and thank you for your share in the Christmas
parcel of books.

    Ever your old James

Tuesday 21 March 1944

I got my late pass this evening and found my way to the Women's
Institute where a certain Mr Sibson was to speak on 'Constructive
Democracy – Planning or Chaos'. It was typical middle-class socialist
circle I thought and smug as could be, lacking the realistic idealism of
Acland who is I suppose the very best of the Fabian middle-class
socialists . . . A Communist at the back of the hall started advocating
physical violence as the only means of establishing socialism. I took him
up on that and we argued away merrily. Anyway afterwards I began
talking to Mrs Friend, the Secretary, and she asked us to come along to
her flat with her husband, a prominent member of the railway workers'
union here. We sat and had coffee in this room of theirs where a picture of
Lenin stared down at us and where the walls would have done credit to a
socialist bookshop.

Thursday 30 March 1944

This evening the much-discussed Matabele warrior Ginyilitshe came to
address the discussion group.

    We were all seated in the quiet room where chairs had been placed
ready. The Commanding Officer (Wing Commander Walters), Wing
Commander Abel, the Padre, the Native Commissioner (Mr Huxtable)
and his two deputy commissioners were followed by the old warrior,

Ginyilitshe, and a native interpreter dressed in the khaki tunic and trousers of the Native Department.

Ginyilitshe was in the full war dress of his regiment, the Insukamini, and a very impressive sight he was: his headdress was a great black feather pom-pom which flopped over his eyes. Round his neck, upper arms and ankles were rings consisting of more of these black feathers. He wore a loinskin of jackal-hide. In his hand he held an oval shield, covered with the toughened skin of an animal, strengthened by a wooden stick.

He carried himself very erect and I was extremely impressed with his build and physique, for he is seventy-four. He did not sit down, but stood with the interpreter in front of us.

The meeting was opened with a few remarks by Huxtable. 'I've brought this old boy along to tell you the story of his life, and also to give you an account of how, together, we found King Lobengula's grave last September. I will try to answer any questions you put to me afterwards, but,' he said, 'I'm really not a Matabele man myself, you know – I am more of a Mashona man, you know.'

I felt rather disgusted at the general lack of respect towards the old man, considering his age and prowess.

Ginyilitshe began in a rather toneless way in short sentences, translated for us into remarkably good idiomatic English by the native interpreter. But later on, when he came to the various battles and skirmishes in which he was engaged, gone were the dull monotone and expressionless face and figure. He became alive and gesticulated wildly. You could see him relive every moment of the scenes and his description revealed a remarkable memory. He harped on details and not generalities.

'I was born when Lobengula became King of the Matabele after much strife in the tribe and my father joined Lobengula's army. I was later admitted to the Insukamini regiment, the third senior, numbering about 1,000 men.

'We were sent to the southern and eastern borders of Matabeleland, with our cattle.'

From what Ginyilitshe said it seemed that the King would enlist men into a new regiment all at the same time and normally they would remain together, all starting as junior soldiers. They were allowed to marry when they reached the age of forty, and their wives and cattle would stay with them in the ordinary course of events, remaining behind when they were away fighting. It was therefore possible to talk of a young regiment and an old one, of an unmarried regiment, and a married one.

In the late 1880s there were a few white men at the court of King Lobengula – three missionaries and a Colin Brandon, a prospector for diamonds who was also engaged in gun running. Lobengula liked the white men. In about 1890 there were stories that Europeans were coming north to attack the Matabele, so Ginyilitshe's uncle, Lorche, Lobengula's oldest and most trusted chief, was sent down to the Cape to see how powerful the white armies were.

Ginyilitshe continued: 'Lorche reported that the Europeans are very powerful and that they have rifles and guns on wheels which fire Boom-boom-boom-boom, Boom-boom-boom, from ammunition in a sort of string' – Maxim guns – 'and Lorche told Lobengula that it would be unwise to fight them.

'Now when Lorche returned and gave this message about the European strength, the younger chiefs were jealous, and told Lobengula that Lorche was a spy for the whites, and that when the whites arrived, he would depose the king and take that position himself.

'It happened that Lorche brought back with him from the south a candle, and the chiefs said to Lobengula, as proof of Lorche's treachery, "You, O king, have only the sun in the daytime; Lorche has a sun in his hut at night as well – indeed that is a sign that he wishes to be king."

'So Lobengula agreed that Lorche must die and he was killed in his hut one night by the knobkerries of his fellow chiefs.'

The Europeans became established at Fort Victoria and, at about the same time, cattle belonging to the Matabele tribe began to be stolen on the Mashona frontier. These reports came in frequently to Lobengula, at his kraal near Bulawayo, and it was a source of worry to him. He himself was inclined to believe that it was the Europeans who were responsible, but his chiefs persuaded him they were sure it was the Mashona men who were the thieves. 'I cannot believe that they would steal my cattle,' Lobengula would say. But the thefts continued and so he wrote a letter to the officer commanding Fort Victoria asking for an explanation and dispatched the Insukamini regiment, with strict orders that on no account were they to attack the Mashona on the way.

Ginyilitshe went on, 'However, the Insukamini's hot-blooded young chief, Chadoga, disregarded the instructions and engaged the Mashona forces. The latter, who were on fairly good terms with the whites, sent word to Fort Victoria.

'White troops arrived at the scene of the skirmish and captured Chadoga and the letter he carried. The officer demanded of Chadoga why he had disregarded the orders of the king. A peaceful pow wow was then arranged and the white officer said that, owing to the bloodshed, he could not trust the Matabele, and he gave them a message for Lobengula. On a pledge of good conduct, the men were allowed to leave the Fort and return to the royal kraal without interference.'

Ginyilitshe told us that despite this promise, European cavalry followed them and attacked with rifle fire. Chief Chadoga was killed and his body captured by the Mashona, who were supporting the whites. Chadoga's stomach was split right up and his gall bladder removed, which was a great indignity and had deep religious significance. One more action was fought by the Insukamini regiment before it was finally defeated.

They were encamped on one side of a river; on the other side they believed the white troops were encamped, but in fact the camp housed the Mashona, the Europeans being some distance off. The Insukamini could see great fires as the sun set, and decided to wait until these died down, believing that the Europeans would be asleep and that they could massacre them easily. However, when they reached the camp, the Mashona woke up, panicked and fled, to tell the white troops, who attacked the Insukamini with machine guns and rifles.

'The guns went boom-boom-boom-boom-boom,' Ginyilitshe said.

He went on with this noise for at least fifteen seconds, and each time he looked like stopping he would burst afresh, squashing the embarrassed and amused interpreter's attempts to translate his description. He gesticulated wildly up and down and was apparently demonstrating that everyone thought that the heavens would fall. It was funny, I admit, but also very pathetic. One could see these poor gallant warriors taken quite unawares by the new and terrible methods of war and thrown into frightful terror and confusion.

He ended his description of the battle with tragic and poignant words which were translated as 'We all died that night.'

They retreated and met a senior warrior who asked 'Where are the enemy?' 'There!' replied Ginyilitshe, pointing across our room, and repeated it as if he was reliving the moment. 'There!'

The Insukamini returned to Lobengula and Lobengula said, 'I do not want to fight the white men, for they are stronger.' But all his chiefs compelled him to go on. 'I agree,' he said, 'but under protest.'

He decided that it would be unwise to take on the enemy in open country, as their machine guns gave them an inestimable advantage. 'When the whites discover I have gone up country they will attempt to follow me, and we can lure them away and defeat them.' So he ordered the Insukamini regiment to follow him and told the senior warriors to remain in the less open country, surround the whites, and kill them.

When he had gone, sure enough the whites arrived in Bulawayo and started after him, and the senior chief, instead of doing as he was told, said, 'We are not young and inexperienced, we will take them in the open country and beat them.' Of course they were mown down by machine gun fire. The Europeans hastened after Lobengula. The king left his wagons one afternoon, riding on horseback with the Insukamini, and that evening an advance patrol under Major Allen Wilson caught up with the wagon, and finding the king gone gave chase.

They crossed the river at a place called Shangani, not knowing that the Insukamini were lying low on the banks, and when they crossed, the warriors rose up and surrounded them. It was here that Allen Wilson's patrol put up its famous last stand.

Ginyilitshe went on to describe the scene. He said that there were thirty or more of them and that the Matabele numbered hundreds. Wilson sent two men back for a machine gun but they couldn't bring it across as the river was in flood.

It was now just a question of time. The patrol had formed a square behind their horses from where they fired. When their ammunition was exhausted they used their small arms. At last a white flag was held up and, through an interpreter, a truce was requested, the whites promising that they would 'go away and not return at all'. But the Matabele chief told them they would go on fighting. 'Why have you followed us?' he asked. It was during the revolver fighting that Ginyilitshe was wounded – we saw the scar on his leg, where a bullet had passed through.

'You must forgive what we did,' Ginyilitshe said to us, 'but it was a time of war. We surrounded them and they started singing. It sounded like "Hee hee hee heway". One man' – Ginyilitshe seemed to think it was Wilson himself – 'stood out and fought alone when the others were dead. He was stabbed from all sides by the spears of the Matabele.'

Then news of this victory was taken to Lobengula and he said, 'It is good that we have beaten the white men, but I never wanted to fight them and I have betrayed my people,' whereupon he rode away and with another chief, Magnas, he committed suicide (although a story goes that he died of smallpox.) On the afternoon that he died he is reported to have said, 'O that I had Lorche with me today.'

He was buried with his treasure by a group of the Insukamini regiment, who swore never to reveal where his grave was and that if anyone else revealed it, he would be killed by the others.

This was the end of the first story and we questioned Ginyilitshe on several points. I asked him, through the interpreter, if he was carrying the weapons he used at the battle, but he replied 'No! They were thrown down before the white people' – I think he said before Rhodes himself – 'as a sign of disarmament at the end of the war.'

Ginyilitshe was not at the Indaba, or gathering, of the Matabele which Rhodes addressed but he had been there later. When someone asked how many Europeans old Ginyilitshe had killed himself, he didn't need it to be translated, but said 'Ah', and lowered his head to his knees and refused to answer.

When we all clapped the old warrior at the end, Ginyilitshe clapped as well, and the Native Commissioner explained that he did it as a sign of politeness.

There was one man present, a Rhodesian pilot, wearing his wings, who must have been at least sixty-five himself, and who must, I think, have known Allen Wilson personally, for he kept pressing Ginyilitshe about the last man who fought, with a view to establishing that it was definitely Wilson. He wouldn't clap at the end.

The second part of Ginyilitshe's story was most interesting. Lobengula's grave remained undiscovered until summer last year (1943), when a native woman approached Ginyilitshe and told him she was the Rain Goddess. All over the country, natives made her presents in return for rain, and she asked Ginyilitshe if he would help her count her cattle for the Native Commissioner.

Ginyilitshe agreed and they set off, but no cattle appeared and finally the old woman was too tired to go on, but Ginyilitshe continued alone. After crossing a river, Ginyilitshe came to a burial place and realised at once that this was King Lobengula's grave. He knew that it was roughly about there but kept the secret. Without intimating that he realised what it was, he returned to the Rain Goddess and said that he had come to a certain place and wished her to accompany him (to see how much she knew). She told him that 'spirits would lead her' and under her direction, they arrived there again. Ginyilitshe asked her what the place was and she replied that she thought it was the grave of King Solomon and his treasure. Ginyilitshe then said, 'I *know* it is the grave of Lobengula. Why did you lead me here?' The woman was frightened and told him she was a daughter of Lobengula which, according to Huxtable, the Native Commissioner, was quite untrue; the woman is an impostor.

Old Ginyilitshe returned to Bulawayo, told Huxtable about the grave, fearing that the woman might have shown it to white men, who might be rifling the treasure. Together they returned and the tomb was by this time open, but the treasure was intact. Huxtable asked Ginyilitshe's permission to enter. There was Lobengula's body, most of it removed by jackals but sufficient to be recognised. Lobengula was known to be an exceptionally large man and there was a tremendous shin bone; and the skull was peculiar, having not knitted together at the top, a peculiarity of the old king. There his tomb remains, up-country somewhere.

Finally the old warrior left the hut. When I am an old man of a hundred I will be able to tell my great-grandchildren that I actually talked to a man who fought at a battle 130 years before.

Blunt House

April 5, 1944

My dear old James

First of all birthday greetings.

The Proff and I are taking appropriate action regarding your bank.

We spent the afternoon of April 3 in the Study with the gramophone and it was as near a celebration (of your birthday) as could be.

I took out Fi, but she is very dull and I didn't enjoy myself. I shan't do it again. I am fairly busy when I get the time reading all the Common Wealth bumph. It seems to me the only party I could ever really agree with. The Labour Party (which I consider badly led) can't really see further than the end of its nose and will I fear do very badly out of the coalition. The Common Wealth MPs are not really behaving themselves very well at the moment. The CW will do itself a great deal of harm if even its three members cannot knit together.

Thanks for all your letters, look after yourself.

Affectionately Mike

Monday 10 April 1944
Today I was very depressed indeed. I think that the boil on my face, the sore on my behind, and the blister on my toe tended – if anything – to worsen things. This depression squashes life itself and any interest in it. Anyway this evening I saw Rita Hayworth in *Strawberry Blonde* and this cheered me quite a lot.

Wednesday 12 April 1944
I seem to have got over my depression now. The boil on my face has burst, which is very pleasant. I had a two-page airgraph from Mary-Anne. She was very affectionate and sweet and I really think that I am still very much in love with her. I felt wizzo tonight and not at all depressed.

Thursday 13 April 1944
I went to the discussion group in the evening and heard Major Bugler, Assistant Commissioner, talking about the history, traditions and organisation of the British South African Police. They were a second column of mounted infantry to the original pioneer column of 1893, who apparently fought in the Matabele war and were then partially demobilised, later being reformed as a body 500 strong to police the country (Southern Rhodesia) in a civil capacity, retaining the military ranks and organisation but assuming a less aggressive attitude and being transformed from the servants of the British South Africa Company to the servants of the Rhodesian government. They are now the sole police and still only consist of 500 Europeans with many more native police working under them.

Wednesday 19 April 1944
I went to the Services Club this evening for a meal especially to watch Gloria, who is a very attractive girl. Then Les, John and I went to see *Reap the Wild Wind*, a first-rate film.

April 21st 1944

My dear old Proff

Life here is settling down. I have joined the South African Institute of Race Relations which is concerned with studying the native problem in Africa – much as the Fabian Society deals with socialist and working class problems at home. Until I arrived in this part of the world I really had little or no conception of the intricacies or complications of South African or Rhodesian problems.

There is much that should be done and I don't see why I shouldn't do what I can when I get back to Oxford.

Ever your old James

Monday 24 April 1944

Today I wrote to Gloria under my assumed name. All I sent her was the poem dedicated to her with 'In all sincerity – Neil' at the end.

Salisbury

Southern Rhodesia

25 April 1944

My dear old Mike

At last I have managed to get hold of some extra air letters above the one per person per week ration.

Common Wealth is an organisation very well worth investigating. I know that Sir Richard Acland's own published books have been difficult to get. I am sure that you will be in full agreement with the CW political theory and its relation to Christian doctrine. Acland criticises the Labour Party for its rather strict Party discipline but as you point out he may weaken his own position by lack of it. I am a member of the LP more for what it could be than for what it is. If the LP wakes up after the war and makes a clean break with the Tories instead of trying to continue the coalition half-heartedly, I think that Common Wealth would find that it had very little the LP hadn't got. Possibly the finest combination after the war will be possible with a newly animated LP combining Common Wealth and Fabian enthusiasm with LP steadiness, organisation and capability for consistent work.

Wednesday 26 April 1944

We were woken this morning at 03.30 hrs but as I had gone to bed early I didn't feel too bad. We were issued spats, maps and compasses and we boarded the lorry just as the dawn was lifting. The lorry moved off and the flight began to sing as we drove through Bulawayo, the old sentimental soldier songs which in these surroundings were very pleasant. The sky in the east was yellow and orange and above a bank of

black cloud shone Venus, the morning star. We were dropped at a gate
with a course of 168 degrees and fifteen miles of rough bundu ahead. I
pushed on and gradually as the heat increased and the country grew
more difficult I stumbled more often, and began to swear under my
breath.

We had lunch at a hotel and the lorry came back at 2.30. I had a
deadly headache and I felt pretty ghastly but some Anadin soon put that
right and despite my sore feet, I went into town to see Gloria. She was
there and I noticed a definite difference. She was dressed very much more
attractively and when she came over to the table she was much sweeter
and her earlier chilliness had completely vanished. I went to bed tired
but happy with feet that hurt like the devil.

Thursday 4 May 1944
In the evening Noel Coward came to the camp to give his one-man show.
John, Les, Ken and I queued up between 6 and 6.30. The doors opened
at 7.30 and from then until 8 the 'Hillside Scamps' played. Then the
great moment arrived and Coward came on with his pianist Norman
Hackforth. He was very smartly dressed in a khaki shirt and tie, light
brown soled suede shoes. His programme which lasted a little over an
hour long was absolutely first rate. He sang

> 'Don't put your daughter on the stage Mrs Worthington'
> 'Let's fly away'
> 'London Pride'
> 'Don't let's be beastly to the Germans'
> 'I'm in love'
> 'Senorita Nina'
> 'Always be nice to the gentlemen'
> 'Let's do it – let's fall in love'
> 'Epilogue from *In Which We Serve*'

After the interval it carried on well, the best one of all being the last song,
'Grandpa ate a large apple and made a rude noise in the Methodist
Chapel'. I admire Noel Coward for being so low despite the ladies
present. He used the words 'bloody, bitch, Christ, bastard, short arm
inspection, sexy' and so on despite them.

Saturday 13 May 1944 – Trip to Victoria Falls
We had navigation first this morning and it wasn't too easy. The theory
part was all right but I was rather rushed for time in the plot and the
general uncertainty didn't help to give me confidence. Then I stowed my
kit bags and we had airmanship, which was easy. Then we were paid
(£5/10/-).

I packed up and had lunch in camp, after which we all walked to the station. After a certain amount of wrangling, we all got into one compartment and the train moved off through the bundu. We stopped at a number of small stations and passed a few native kraals where there was the usual profusion of natives to be seen, some with piccaninnies which ran about stark naked. We bought a whacking great water melon off a native.

We must have all slept till past nine when the train pulled in at Dett Junction where we were to eat. An open lorry then took us to the Dett Hotel, a ramshackle old place the verandah door of which was flanked by two dilapidated elephant skulls. We had to wait a bit before we got our rather shaky half-crown dinner.

We were picked up by the same dangerous lorry at breakneck speed and driven to the train.

Sunday 14 May 1944

We were woken by the guard who wanted our tickets and who told us that the Falls were twenty minutes away. The usual chaos which develops when six people try and get up at the same time ensued.

We were shown to our rooms in the Victoria Falls Hotel and after we had collected rain capes we all walked off in the direction of the Falls. As we came through the lounge of the hotel we could see ahead of us what at first appeared to be a layer of white cloud and the air was full of a thundering which was as deep and powerful as the beating of the sea on rocks. Before us we could see the boiling pot – the deep sheer gorge and the frail bridge which spans it. Round the hotel itself there were baboons playing.

The deep blue sky above, the sheer-sided gorge, the wide majestic river, the falling water and the turbulent stream in the chasm below – all these are partially obscured by the mist which fills the air.

The natives call it 'Mosi-oa-tunya' – the smoke that thunders. It is almost impossible to describe adequately the sensation of personal insignificance it produces.

Behind us as we stood there was a statue of David Livingstone, the first white man to see this sight.

We descended down the many steps to a position beside and half-below this part of the Falls, known appropriately enough as the Devil's Cataract. The spray was terrific and although I was wearing a cape I was soon drenched. We came to the danger point across the knife edge and then we saw a rainbow and next to it an inverted rainbow which curved elegantly across the water and seemed to disappear into the ground at our end.

The native troops guarding the bridge were very friendly and we crossed over on to the Northern Rhodesian side of the river. We walked through the native military camp which bore the inscription 'Though different in colour equal in loyalty' in Latin.

Tuesday 16 May 1944
Went to the curio shops and went to see some live crocodiles. Then we all had dinner and caught the 2005 train. A sing-song in the dining car wasn't much of a success owing to the Chief Steward's unpleasantness.

Saturday 20 May 1944
John Boss had collected the marks from the camp and I have an all-round percentage of 81 which is perfectly satisfactory and puts me in the first twenty or twenty-five. That means if anyone from here flies I am almost certain to be one of them.

Sunday 21 May 1944
In the evening I went to the Services Club and Gloria was there. She was very sweet and charming to begin with – in fact extremely so. All the signs were OK and Les Boughey came over to my table and said that she had been miserable until I came in and then she had cheered up like billyo. This optimistic statement I should have taken with a pinch of salt, but anyway she did appear to be favouring me so I determined to say something tonight. Unfortunately I found that my heart was throbbing so fast and I felt so hot I was blushing a deep red.

   Stubborn in my determination to get somewhere I asked her to 'come and sit at my table and make the last evening of my leave gay', but she turned scornfully away and said, with a sting in her voice, 'I think I'll get you a glass of water to recover.' That finished me. I got up and left at once, muttering to myself and fuming with rage and almost self-pity at this sudden humiliation which had fallen so swiftly after my seeming victory.

Friday 26 May 1944
Up at 0730 today as we were leaving at 9. I handed my bedding in, drew rations, stacked my kit and paraded ready to move off in the lorry. Our last view of Bulawayo at any rate for some time to come.

   At about five we passed close to Moffat and on to Gwelo itself where we de-trained. There waiting on the platform were the people who had been posted six weeks ago to Thornhill.

   Were taken to Guinea Fowl itself by lorry through the bundu and when we got down we were marshalled by the sergeant i/c cadets and allocated billets. I am with Basher Boardman.

Saturday 27 May 1944
We all had to fill in a form in duplicate which gave our particulars, including next of kin, father's occupation, hobbies, sports, flying experience etc, and 'politics'. Now this is in my opinion very wrong. In the first place it is a purely private matter which doesn't affect the RAF and secondly it carries with it the stigma and a black mark if you are, as I

am, a socialist. I could have left it blank and perhaps it would have been wiser to do so or I could have put conservative and played it safe but as it was a question which affected my own basic self I felt compelled to write down in all honesty what I am. For to me my political beliefs will achieve reality through victory and it is only because of them that war becomes a worthwhile job and the victory something to be desired. These stodgy RAF officers however will probably have some notion that socialism is subversive and that its supporters will be unsuitable for positions of responsibility.

Monday 29 May 1944
I was up early this morning or at 5.20 to be precise as I was down for early flying. I put on warm clothes, wandered over to dispersal, collected my 'chute and joined the rest of my flight who were wheeling the Cornells out of the hangar and on to the tarmac in front of our flight hut. We – that is the newcomers – went in to F/Lt Hill's office (he is the flight commander of D Flight) and we had the standard talk on discipline and local rules and regulations.

Then I did a little revision of my cockpit drill, but my instructor, Sergeant Crownshaw, neither called to see me nor made any attempt to take me up.

I ran for about an hour in the bright sunshine and got a very bad headache. I hadn't been feeling too grand and this started me off on a few hours of real physical misery. I seemed to get a fever – it must have been the sun – and I burned and shivered in turn and my face was as hot as the last time I spoke to Gloria.

The following three lectures weren't pleasant but luckily I had a free afternoon except for the swimming which didn't help . . . I strained a muscle in my thigh.

Wednesday 31 May 1944
This morning I felt wizzo and was up to fly at 6.15. My instructor is definitely good and I found the Cornell very steady and easy to fly. Turns are a piece of cake, spins easy to recover from and aerobatics comfortable to do. We flew round a bit and I think I did OK.

Thursday 1 June 1944
In the afternoon my flying didn't materialise because Crownshaw was playing football. I was very cheesed but later cheered up and spent the evening scrubbing my locker, tidying my box and generally clearing up for tomorrow's inspection.

Friday 2 June 1944
I got up at ten past five as I was early flying. It really is a deadly hour but I am quickly getting used to it.

Crownshaw took me up just as the sun was rising and it was wizzo. The ground lay below us clouded with purple-tinted mist and the fine blues, oranges, and yellows of a Rhodesian sunrise were giving way to the bright glare of the new sun. We flew to Senale and there practised take-offs, circuits and landings.

Saturday 3 June 1944
After breakfast we had kit inspection and F/Lt Goulton said, 'I want to ask you a personal question. Was your father, your uncle, or your grandfather an MP who used to cause great disturbances? I have a bet on it.'

'Well, sir,' I replied, 'both my father and grandfather were MPs but it is my father who was, I fancy, the most fiery!' After a short break in the canteen we had one period of armaments and then twenty minutes' drill.

Monday 5 June 1944
In the evening I went along to F/Lt Goulton's private music recital. He was very friendly and asked us what we would like to hear. I asked for *Iolanthe*, which we heard almost all through, but by the end of the record we were discussing education which, he being a schoolmaster, is his pet subject. He is a most determined and persistent talker but on the whole what he says is sense.

Then the Padre, who is aptly named Christian, came in and the conversation got on to other service matters including the length of the war (Goulton said 1950 and no second front this year).

Tuesday 6 June 1944 – Liberation Day for Europe and the World
I went up for over an hour and a half during which time I finished spins and started on my final and crucial task – finding out whether I will ever be able to land an aircraft. It was not until breakfast time that I heard the great news. The story was consistent and persistent, then during the airmanship period F/O Freeman told me the real 'gen'. He had heard General Eisenhower's broadcast announcement to the world of an Allied invasion of the French coast and containing the gist of issued orders to the underground movement. According to German News Agency reports Allied landings have taken place on the Cherbourg peninsula near Le Havre and on the mouth of the Seine, reports which I heard confirmed later in the day on the BBC. It appears that paratroopers have been dropped inland to capture aerodromes and that the beach landings were effected after an armada of 4,000 big ships and many thousand little ones, escorted by detachments of the RN, had crossed the Channel, and that the fire of enemy shore batteries had been mostly quelled.

This news and also a statement that besides the enormous numbers of aircraft involved we had a workable reserve of 11,000 allowing losses to that number was given out by Churchill. At first all this news made little impression on me, and had it not been for the service that the Padre arranged at once, which took us all from our work at a quarter to twelve and gave us a moment to meditate on it all, this great day, perhaps the greatest day in the world's history, might have slipped by without the notice it deserved in my own mind.

But when the work station gathered at midday, with clerks and fitters, the officers, the instructors and the pupils, and the air was quiet from lack of planes, and we sang 'Onward Christian Soldiers' and 'Fight the Good Fight', I thought at once of Mike and sobered up at the prospect of the dangerous work which had been assigned to him with the skill and courage which distinguished him from the ordinary run of pilots. Then I thought that perhaps the war with Germany would be over by August. That depressed me terribly for I couldn't go on training while there was peace in England. It is only the prospect of operations which lends a purpose to this very small contribution to the war effort.

Basher Boardman and I talked about remustering to Air Gunners in order to see action and I felt just the same sensations and conflicting sense of duty which characterised my earlier struggle.

I read part of the afternoon and Basher Boardman came in and, with a forced smile, he told me that he had been scrubbed. At first I couldn't believe it. He is very brave about it but it nearly breaks my heart to see him who is so keen and whose heart was so on the job, forced to give it up.

I was on staff parade at 10, so I heard the King's speech at nine and tumbled into bed very tired.

Wednesday 7 June 1944
Ma's birthday and I had her particularly in my mind. The strain of having old Mike in the front at a time like this must be very great, for the burden is probably more heavy on those near and dear to the fighting men who are left behind than on the men themselves. I am still depressed.

Thursday 8 June 1944
The WingCo's inspection was strict and searching. We were all in best blue and the sun came down blazingly on the ranks. One man half-way down our rank suddenly fell forward limp on to his face with a soft thud, he was carried off and Basher himself led another fellow off. At the end of our rank the WingCo turned to the adjutant and told him that he did not propose to continue the inspection owing to the heat. So we gave the royal salute and the flag was hauled up, after which the WingCo addressed us. It was a real peacetime imperial address.

He began by saying that he was sure that we all agreed that the occasion of the King's birthday was significant at this time and that our minds were probably not only turned to the King personally or to all that the Crown stood for but also to the men engaged in the second front. I for one certainly failed to see why the King's birthday mattered at such a time since everyone was solely preoccupied with the European onslaught.

Then swinging to the right after an order to remove headgear and give three cheers for the King which was certainly not rousing, the WingCo walked over to the native Rhodesian Air Askari Corps and addressed them through an interpreter in this manner. Everything here, the land, the hangars, the aircraft are all the King's and it is all your duty to guard them. Do your duty well. I felt sick at the failure to thank them or refer to Matabeleland as their country, used by us. It was a dictatorial speech that Goering might make to the conscripts of an occupied country about Hitler.

12 June 1944

My dear old Pa

Now that the great onslaught on Hitler's fortress has at last begun our thoughts are naturally turned to old Mike who is in the thick of it all and then to Yer Ma on whom all the burdens of this extra worry falls. The casualties are bound to be heavy.

I fly nearly every day and am managing to cope with it. Up to the time of writing I have only done seven and a quarter hours.

I have got a lot of literature on the native question and a great deal of help from an Englishman who lives in Bulawayo, a missionary for 22 years who is now becoming the political champion of the natives. It is a comfort to know that such men exist in a country where the German Herrenvolk theory of race – in this case white over black – is in full swing.

  Take care of yourself, Dad
    James

Wednesday 14 June 1944

At six this morning Crownshaw told me to get into 322 straight away, a PT-26A Cornell trainer. I apologised to him for boobing the check yesterday and he remarked that they were really only nominal things and that they didn't really matter. I thought that he was just being kind and I liked him for it but all the same I was pretty depressed as I got in and we took off. We decided to keep to RAF Guinea Fowl and not go to Senale but conditions weren't good. In the first place the 'T' was straight into the sun and that blinded everyone taking off and landing, and in the second place there were an enormous number of kites flying round this morning, and in the hour and thirty-five minutes we were up we were nearly killed twice by one of them (whose pilot forgot to close his throttle when he touched down on an engine-assisted approach, thus taking off and landing three or four times before banging it right open and going round again) and came very near to an accident while landing when two aircraft were converging on us from behind. The last landing I did was as near perfect as anything I've done yet and there wasn't even a judder.

We taxied on to the tarmac and I got out and walked back with Crownshaw. He said we'd just have a cigarette and then go up again. I was very surprised, but put it down to a desire on his part to finish me off ready for another check tomorrow. However we took off, did a circuit or maybe two, and then as we taxied up to the take-off point, he said to me: 'Well, how do you feel about your landings?' I replied: 'Well, that's really for you to say, sir.' He chuckled. 'I think you can manage one solo,' he said. 'I'm going to get out now and I'll wait here for you,' he went on.

So this was it, I thought. The moment I had been waiting for came all of a sudden just like that. 'OK, sir,' I replied. 'And don't forget that you've got a throttle,' he said. 'Don't be frightened to go round again – OK? And by the way,' he added – he finished locking the rear harness and closing the hood then came up to me, leant over and shouted, in my ear – 'you do know the new trimming for taking off?' 'Yes, sir,' I replied, and he jumped off the wing and walked over to the boundary with his 'chute.

I was not all that excited. I certainly wasn't frightened and I hope I wasn't over-confident but I just had to adjust my mirror so that I could really see that there was no one behind me. Sure enough it was empty and I was alone. I did my vital actions very deliberately and carefully, I looked round and paused, then opening the throttle slightly I swung into wind until my directional gyro read '0' for I had set it on the last circuit. Then I opened up to full throttle as smoothly and yet as quickly as I could. I pushed the stick forward and connecting the swing which developed with my rudder I loomed across the drome, swaying rather from side to side, but keeping her under control and well into wind.

The 'drome at Guinea Fowl is bad and we bounced about like a wheelbarrow but gradually I felt the pressure come off the stick and as the airspeed read 70 mph I applied a gentle pressure and we rose off the ground. I took my left hand off the throttle where I always keep it during the take-off and placed it on the trimming lever which I juggled with until I could climb 'hands off' at 75 mph. I tried to sing but I couldn't hear myself very well and I still couldn't believe that I was alone. I glanced behind me quickly to reassure myself and I felt as happy as a schoolboy.

Then I remembered my brother Mike's words: 'Whatever you do don't get over-confident; it is that that kills most people and I only survived the initial stages through being excessively cautious.' So I brought my mind back to the job, checked the instruments, looked all around and when we had reached 500 feet began a gentle climbing turn. It was very bumpy and the wind got under my starboard wing and tried to keel me over, but I checked it with my stick and straightened out when my gyro compass read 270 degrees. Then I climbed to 900, looked all round and turned again on to the down-wind leg. By the time I'd finished that turn we were at 1,000 feet, so I throttled back, re-trimmed, got dead on 180 and I felt pretty good about things.

There isn't much to do on the down-wind leg and I was tempted to put my elbow on the side of the cockpit and look professional, but once again Mike's words were in my ears and I thought that on a first solo a fellow has enough to do without wanting to look professional. I noticed that the circuit was almost empty of other kites – perhaps that one down there was going to take off, and there, I could see one turning out of wind after landing. By this time I was – if anything – a little too far, so I silently cursed myself for letting my mind wander off the job on hand.

I opened up on the turn which I started very gently in good time to about 1,400 revs and we came in just opposite the path I had selected. I always thought that I would feel a sense of panic when I saw the ground coming up at me on my first solo, but strangely enough I didn't feel anything but exhilaration at the approach which had turned out so well. No need to use so much engine, I reflected, so I made the final adjustment to the trimmer and then rested my hand on the throttle for the first moment. I thought I was a little high as I crossed the boundary so I eased back to 800 rpm, and as I passed over, I distinctly saw Crownshaw standing watching where I had left him. Now we were coming in beautifully and I eased the stick and throttle back. A quick glance at the ground below showed me to be a little high, so I left the stick as it was, gave a tiny burst of engine and as we floated down I brought both back fully. We settled, juddered and settled again for a fair three-pointer.

I was as happy as could be. Remembering not to use the brakes too heavily, I applied them as we came towards the opposite boundary for I had touched down a little late if anything, but that's a small fault compared with under-shooting. I turned out of wind, hauled my flaps up and trimmed fully tail heavy; then I swung round on to the perimeter and, defeating the devil of over-confidence for the last time, I taxied slowly round to where Crownshaw stood. With him was another instructor from our Flight whose pupil, judging by the intense look on his face, was the one coming at that moment over the boundary. I saw him strain eagerly forward, his hands twisting the handkerchief he held this way and that. His pupil made a good three-pointer, but I shan't forget that man's taut expression and his shoulders thrown forward in an effort to see how it went. He relaxed as the fellow slowed down and smiled weakly to Crownshaw.

I taxied up, stopped and braked. Try as I did, I couldn't restrain the broad grin which gripped me from ear to ear and Crownshaw, seeing it, leant over before he got in and said ironically with a smile, 'Happy now?'

I was more than happy, I was deliriously carefree, and as he taxied her back I thought about it all and I realised that the success of my first solo flight was entirely due to the fine instruction I had received; it was a tribute to that instruction that I never felt nervous once, and all the time had imagined what my instructor would be saying, so used had I got to doing everything with him behind me. We climbed out, and attempting to restrain my happiness I listened while he told me where and what to sign. Then I wandered back to my billet and one of the greatest experiences of my life was behind me. The lectures were pretty ordinary, and it being my free afternoon I had a bit of lemonade in the canteen and then wrote this which took me over an hour and a quarter.

Thursday 15 June 1944
I wrote a few letters in the afternoon and after beginning my preparations for tomorrow's bullshit inspection, cleaned myself up and went along to the Padre's church fellowship and discussion group. There were only a couple of others present, much to my surprise, but I did think it worth going to. I am going to have to face up to my own procrastination and laxity on moral matters.

The book the discussion group is reading is C. S. Lewis's *Christian Behaviour*.

Tuesday 20 June 1944
The whole afternoon Ken Brown, Phil James and Johnnie Walker were in my hut and the time was wasted absolutely in worthless nattering. I tried to keep my temper and in fact never showed any annoyance at all and pretended that I was in a listening competition or that this was practice for political work. The evening went in the same manner though the room became more crowded still.

Thursday 22 June 1944
I went into Gwelo in the afternoon with Otto Fialla. He is an Austrian Jew, son of a technical engineer who was a captain of the German army in the last war and he told me the story of his life. His father had a factory outside Vienna and when the Germans annexed Austria in 1938 his office and factory was taken over before he had time to remove his own papers and clear up his business. The SS men came in one day and told him to clear out straight away and they even refused to let Otto have his motorbike when he went for it that afternoon. Moreover Max Fialla had invented a number of engines and modifications and so on which were his life's work and even though he could not get hold of them he didn't want the Germans to get them.

That night therefore Otto, who was at the time only a boy of fifteen and a half, tried to get into the office to get hold of these papers. The SS heard

him and a chase ensued which finished up with Otto hiding in the boiler
which worked the central heating. He was not able to escape until four
the next morning when he walked out to a farm a few miles outside the
city and stayed there for three weeks as he knew that the SS would be
waiting for him to return home. His mother was frantic when she heard
that he was wanted by the police but a letter from Otto reassured her and
she and Max Fialla came out to see him. Three weeks later he was
smuggled across the Italian border and from there he made his way to
Trieste where he got employed aboard a ship sailing for Palestine. In this
way he worked a passage across the Adriatic and the Aegean, and at
three o'clock one morning he dived overboard as the ship was lying off
the 'promised land' and swam ashore.

When he reached land he had only the clothes he was wearing and they
were soaking wet; he had no papers, no passport but he found his way to
some relatives and there he started work on a farm. He drove a tractor
and later on he got a job as driver to a certain English colonel who later
was instrumental in getting him into the RAF as a driver in 1940 and he
served in that capacity – the last two years a corporal – for four years in
active support of the 8th Army in the Desert Air Force which earned for
him the Africa Star and Clasp. Then long investigations having proved
that he was not a fifth columnist he was allowed to remuster for pilot
training. His family escaped after him to South America, where they are
now earning some sort of a living in Bolivia.

I asked him if he intended returning to Austria and he said he didn't
know about permanently but 'I will go back. I have a score to settle.
They pinched my motorbike.'

Sunday 25 June 1944
In a 5,000-word letter to Mike I wrote out a full description of my flying
and the lessons I learnt. It gave me a chance to clear my mind. After tea I
went along to listen to the Padre on this text, taken from the Christ-
child's visit to the temple where he amazed the professors. After which,
according to the story, he 'waxed strong in body and in wisdom and
gained favour among men and with God.' He constructed his talk round
the belief that everyone should make their life like the life of Christ and
should develop in those four ways – bodily, mentally, be a tower of
strength among men, and be close to God. On physical fitness, which the
Padre started with, the three main reasons for developing and
maintaining it were: first because our bodies are the temple of God,
secondly because if we are really fit we are less likely to fall into
temptation, especially the temptations of drink and sex. And lastly
because we must keep as fit as possible so as to do our own work the
better for the glory of God. Very sound arguments, I thought. He bitterly
attacked those who despised an intelligent interest in religion. Gaining

favour with men did not mean that we should be so ordinary and popular
that we didn't strike a line of our own.

After the service I went along to the last of F/Lt Goulton's gramophone
recitals. He played Chopin's first pianoforte concerto which was
absolutely wizard and the *Dance of the Hours* which I must get when I'm
home again.

Tuesday 27 June 1944
We did PT this morning and the first lecture was meteorology.
Gannicliffe brought the mail in and there was a telegram for me. I don't
like telegrams as a rule so I didn't open it immediately, and when I did it
was quite unhurried.

R5 OXTED 41 24 1440
1850035 BENN

DARLING JAMES OUR PRECIOUS MICHAEL GAVE HIS LIFE JUNE
23RD AFTER OPERATIONAL ACCIDENT DAVE AND I REACHED HIM
DONT GRIEVE DEAREST HE SUFFERED NO PAIN IS SAVED
COMPLETE PARALYSIS FAMILY HOLDS TOGETHER FOR ALWAYS
DEAREST LOVE.

YERMA-STANSGATE.

When I saw the words at first, I was stunned and felt as if something
inside me had stopped.

For a few minutes I didn't think about it really, and I just went on
writing meteorology notes. The realisation of the desolation came to me
in waves. For the rest of the period I was either on the verge of tears or
quite calm.

When at last the lesson ended I went into the Post Office, picked up
some telegraph forms and walked to my hut. There I let go and sat
sobbing for ten or fifteen minutes. It was good to give vent to my feelings
– it eased things a lot. I was sick at heart. I never knew how much Mike's
example, his interest and advice, were responsible for maintaining my
desire to be a pilot.

The outburst over, I sent a telegram to mother:

MIKE'S GREAT SACRIFICE AN INSPIRATION TO US ALL. FAMILY
MORE UNITED THAN EVER. GOD BLESS YOU ALL. JAMES

Then I went back into the lessons and stayed until lunchtime. I wanted
to share my sorrow but it was difficult to speak about it. I was eating my
dinner with Jim Boulton, Ken Brown, Tony Evans, Budgett and Peter
Smith and Bob Morgan when a fresh wave of realisation caught me. I

was asked whether I had bad news. They were very kind and after just expressing their sorrow they went on as usual and I was glad for the diverted attention, as try as I did, my lower lip was quivering.

When I got back to my room I made my bed and lay on it once more in the grip of the instincts of affection and friendship which tie me double to old Mike who is a brother and my best friend.

I went and sat in the station chapel where before and beside God and with Mikie very near me I began the task of pulling together the shattered fabric of love and companionship which had protected me. I began to realise that the greatest blow fell not on me but on Mother and Father and little Dave. They gave him life and nourished him to healthy boyhood and courageous manhood.

I went across this afternoon to fly with Crownshaw. We did steep turns and forced landings, spinning and compass courses and all the time I thought of Mike. It wasn't until this evening, when I faced the problem squarely, that I reached a new peace and harmony. I did realise when I was flying that a new determination had entered me and that his courage was to become mine. I felt a special sense of mission and of duty that while a Benn still flies with the Air Force, my standard would be as high as his. I asked Crownshaw when I came down how I could get on twin-engined bombers.

After tea I dressed myself up in my battledress and great coat, I pushed my cap on my head, took my pipe and tobacco and went out to have a walk round the aerodrome. I thought of Mike as a pilot flying in North Africa or over France and Germany. I felt proud I was following in his footsteps. I thought of him as a companion through life and as a partner and a colleague in times of struggle for a better world which we can and will create out of this war. I thought of him as a friend with whom so many plans had been made.

When I had finished thinking of the past a great calmness came over me.

Wednesday 28 June 1944
I went up for an hour, climbed above 6,000 feet and decided to do a spin, my fear subdued by his courage. Then I pulled out and spun again. My voice is rather like his when it is muffled and so I picked up my speaking tube and said, 'Hello James, this is old Mikie speaking' – but it made me cry so I stopped. Then I had another hour's solo and came down for breakfast.

Friday 30 June 1944
Prepared for the weekend in Salisbury. Changed my clothes and packed the stuff in my blue pack.

Saturday 1 July 1944
Tony Evans wouldn't stay at the hotel with us. The lower classes, munts, people who speak with an accent, people who like Gilbert and Sullivan as well as or instead of Beethoven – all come into his disfavour. He did condescend to have breakfast with us but it was on sufferance, so I was glad to see him go to spend his time and money at Meikle's, the most expensive hotel in town.

Thursday 6 July 1944
Went along to the Padre's discussion group. We discussed sex and Christian moral teaching concerning it. Lewis, who is a bachelor, says sex is over-developed and hints that it should be on a par with the hunger instinct, also decrying those who say that free discussion will help.

Monday 10 July 1944
I had a letter from Mike today written on the day before he was killed – bless him. It was full of his activities – how sweet and natural it was. It finished 'Oh James, how I miss you – but we must see this through. Ever your old, M'

Tuesday 11 July 1944
Woody woke me with tea this morning.
   It was a fortnight today that Mother's first telegram arrived telling me of Mike's death and I had a third today containing news of the beautiful service in London which was attended by the Padre of Mike's station, the Wing Commander and officers, with family music. I suppose that Mike had full military honours. I hope so anyway.

Wednesday 12 July 1944
What upsets me is the knowledge that in time I shall get over my misery and forget – almost forget – all that he meant to me. Death now, for me, would mean reunion with him and for that reason I would welcome it, but I couldn't bear the family to suffer his sorrow again and I would weep over my own departure with them, not for myself, but for them.

Thursday 13 July 1944
I darned my socks and sewed on buttons after lunch and flew for an hour and a half in the afternoon, doing stalling, spinning, steep turns, loops and slow rolls, which I still can't do properly. A Hurricane, piloted by a group captain, came down today and when he had taken off he did slow rolls and aerobatics just above circuit height. I took a very dim view of that, for at rock bottom it was his own vanity and desire to show off his superior ability in a superior kite over us sprogs with the old Cornells.
   I went to the discussion group this evening and Christian marriage was

tackled. Taking the Christian view of what marriage is and should be, I supported A. P. Herbert absolutely on the issue of easier divorce laws. A strict division of civil and religious marriage would solve the problem for an enforced union prolonged without love or a fusing of character carries no moral value in the scale of things.

The question about the headship of the husband is nonsense. Lewis says that a point will be reached when either one or the other must give way or separate and no one seriously suggests that the woman should be the head. I agree with the last point but if the situation Lewis postulates arose – if separation or domination were the only two alternatives – something much more radical would be wrong than a mere bad arrangement as to obedience of wife or husband and something un-Christian and unloving would have entered into their life which unwilling obedience would never cure.

1850035 Cadet Benn

14.7.44

My dearest Dave

I have written you a long air-mail letter which I hope you will get soon. This is only a note in case it becomes delayed.

This is a very sad moment for us all, but I know that you are being as brave as he would wish you to be. We must be proud – and grateful too – that he did what he did and it is up to us to carry on with his work as best we can.

I had a letter from Mike three days ago written the day before he gave his all. It ended 'I miss you so much – but we must see this through' – and so we must each in our own way. I don't forget that you are at home in the front line now.

Don't you forget either that you have a loving older brother in your affectionate and devoted

James

Tuesday 18 July 1944

Crownshaw told me I could try alone so here I was doing my first night solo. Mikie was especially in my thoughts and I had the familiar snaps in my pocket over my heart, the Jerusalem cross I always wear round my neck, Mike's mittens and Ma's scarf on with Dad's watch on my wrist.

Wednesday 19 July 1944

I had many letters today about Mike. They were so sweet and sympathetic that I had a new outburst of emotion which I could not control. I wept bitterly when I read the inspiring words with which the RAF Padre concluded his sermon at Golders Green. The hymn was 'I vow to thee my country all earthly things above'. This made my sob as I haven't since I heard the news.

This afternoon I only did one circuit and afterwards when I was waiting across wind I saw an aircraft touching down not a hundred yards from me and right behind. It careered towards me but I didn't move lest he should become confused and hit me. He swung away but another kite lay in his path and when he was fifty yards nearer he swung back and I sat facing what I thought might be the end of me and very scared in a detached and fatalistic way. However, he passed to my left and I taxied back feeling weak at the knees after the experience.

Friday 21 July 1944
I had three air letters from Mother today, all with different aspects of the story of Mike's death – one, the bare facts about the circumstances which caused the crash, the second about how mother and Dave visited the hospital, and the last about the lovely service at Golders Green. Mother is quite magnificent.

I find great inspiration in a sentence from H. E. Bates's short story, 'You are the living'. It runs like this. 'He is dead now – you are the living. His was the sky – yours is the earth because of him.'

Wednesday 26 July 1944
When I returned to the flight F/Lt Hill called me into the instructor's room and said, 'Benn, the Chief Ground Instructor has given your name in to the Chief Flying Instructor as being below average in ground subjects. If your name appears on any other such list or if your flying is deemed below average by the CFI then you are automatically scrubbed, so I should pull your finger out if I were you.' This shook me badly as I have reached such a stage in my flying that I was actually under the impression that I could fly and therefore keener than ever to finish the course. If I am scrubbed then, for ground subjects, I should be utterly devastated.

The CGI has got his knife into the Junior Course and he is out to get rid of as many of us as he can. This of course is grossly unfair but there is nothing that can be done about it.

Thursday 27 July 1944
I went along to the Padre's discussion group where Stan Becker was opening up on pride and charity. A new man has turned up – a certain Sergeant Avery from Thornhill who had a strong Oxford accent – though I wonder whether mine is as bad. Anyway, we argued and argued about the sin of pride and the various aspects of it – spiritual, material, personal, objective, conceited, satisfied, absolute, relative, justifiable and so on. All the conclusion we came to was that the puffed up, personal

pride in oneself was a serious sin but that contentment in a job well done was justifiable up to a point.

The next problem of charity, or Christian love, was much clearer. C. S. Lewis states and I believe rightly, that 'Feelings do not matter, treat all men in the way you regard as productive of the most good for them. In this way even intense initial dislike will be turned to liking and love and any emotional hatred of them checked at once by self-discipline and remedied for the good of all men.'

The only difficulty here was one I brought up, and it is this. That although I agree with Lewis absolutely on this point it involves a change of the definition of sincerity for Christians. Feelings must be ignored and therefore whereas to the non-Christian a sincere man is one who acts according to his feelings consistently and is prepared to say so, a Christian is being sincere when he goes against his feelings, acts on what he believes to be right and treats all men equally, though for some he may have an intense dislike.

Friday 28 July 1944

Did an hour's solo aerobatics and I saw the sun rise twice. There is a story by H. E. Bates called 'The man who saw the sun rise twice' and I remember receiving a letter from Mike when he was in North Africa in which he told us how he had done the same thing whilst on an operational patrol.

As I opened up above the ground I looked over to the east and there was the faint yellow of approaching dawn. I climbed up once more and as I reached a greater height the whole splendid scene was recreated and I flew again in lightness while below me the first glimmer of the new day was showing on the tops of the mountains. I continued my climb intoxicated by the beauty of it all and when I had gained 5,000 feet I started work.

After tea I sturdily declined to go to the flicks.

When Wood came back from it he was full of even more than his usual hatred of the Yanks. I feel rather strongly about the subject, for these reasons.

We must win the war as quickly as possible for obvious reasons and the saving of life; we must see that there is never another war to prevent the recurrence of this bloodshed. Therefore, justified or unjustified criticisms of allies, especially of such a big and close one as America, must cease, or both reasons will suffer.

I don't necessarily defend the Yanks but I think a lot of stories get exaggerated and anyway our record isn't particularly a thing to be proud of.

Monday 31 July 1944

I am in the demonstration squad for the visit of His Excellency Sir Evelyn

Baring, the Governor of Southern Rhodesia – bullshine, bullshine, bullshine.

Tuesday 1 August 1944
After lunch I had to go along to the gym for the PT demonstration as I was chosen as one of 18. We were all stood to attention while Sir Evelyn Baring, Lady Baring, the Wing Commander with various RAF and civvy stooges stood round and nattered.

The PT went off OK except that in long vault I hit the box ends with my buttocks instead of clearing them and, so I am told, raised a laugh from everyone, though I did not notice it myself.

It is obvious to me that official occasions breathe the very essence of deceit from start to finish. In the first place the Commanding Officer of a station or unit that is to be inspected is determined to see that the visitor does not see things as they are but as perfect as last minute panic and faked bullshit can make them. Then in the second place the visitor only expects this and would not wish to see things as they are normally, willingly playing the part of the hoodwinked VIP and thus being able to unreservedly congratulate the CO afterwards. They must realise that it is all deceptive and unlike everyday life on a station. *If* in the distant future I am ever connected with an inspection or official visit either as CO or visitor or inspecting officer I should do well to re-read what I have written now – by one of those forgotten many.

Wednesday 2 August 1944
Crownshaw and I took off just after 1300 hours for low level cross-country. Tall trees reached above my wings and the numerous mounds of rocks were often above me. I had a wizard time mainly because we passed over so many native villages and I had an audience – truly a pilot's weakest point is his vanity. It was an extremely revealing experience too, for I saw life in the bundu as it is.

The rivers or smaller tributaries were almost dried up but the natives were all settled near one of the parts where water lay even in this season and I imagine that the carrying of that water to the huts is one of the biggest routine jobs that has to be done – and is probably done by the women. I didn't see many men about and I supposed that they were working though I am not quite clear what work they do – I am pretty certain they don't work in mines and I saw none about and anyway there were never more than a few huts – say fifteen at the most – in one locality.

Most of the flight was carried out over the native reserve. Of the natives I saw the majority were women. Stark naked, jolly little piccaninnies waved and jumped about. If we were passing fifty yards or more to the side of a village they would stand up and wave. But if we passed closer or over them, they ran in all directions, or crouched on the

ground. At the eastern side of Longwe in the foothills, I saw one poor
mother kneeling with her two children, attempting to shield them, as we
roared across. I felt quite ashamed and I was preparing to climb Longwe
when Crownshaw took her off me and began to beat up this village
mercilessly. I was really sorry to see him do that because I felt so warmed
in my heart at the spontaneous welcome they all gave when they first saw
us, that to frighten them, as our dives undoubtedly did, seemed
needlessly unkind.

As soon as we had gone over, out they all came to watch and the whole
process was repeated.

Previously to our shoot-up at Longwe we had been up and down the
Lundi river looking for crocodiles. We saw three hippos in the centre of
the river and as we flew over them they submerged like U-boats.

I went back to the billet to gloat over the tobacco and cigarettes that
my dearest Ma had sent me. I had reached the stage where my pipe was
laid aside because I couldn't find any smokable tobacco for it.

Saturday 5 August 1944
I got up late as we were given an entirely free day to celebrate the
station's fourth anniversary.

I really wasted the morning utterly, which I could ill afford to do as our
exams are in a week's time. The Rhodesian Air Askari Corps band were
playing before lunch and then we all went in to be waited on by officers
and senior NCOs, which was good fun.

I wasted the afternoon and then in the evening I got ready for the dance.
There were quite a few attractive girls there. Sergeant Stanton's popsy was
there, the girl who works the central cashier's machine at Meikle's in
Gwelo was there. Also a blonde job in a pinkish frock who looked as though
she had character, and an innocent-looking fairy in a white dress.

I went into the canteen first of all and there was assailed by Bill Fowler
and Joe Ley who tried to get me to have a drink. I was worried less they
were far enough gone to try and make me have it forcibly. Old Joe bought
me a bottle of beer and I blew the froth at him and made as if to drink it.
However I think they realise I am as adamant as ever and they gave up.

I saw and heard things which have strengthened my determination to
remain teetotal all my life. There was a cabaret show which I left after a
few minutes. There were only two sorts of turn, those that were dirty and
in thoroughly bad taste, and those that were clean and not funny at all.
The dance was rather a flop. You couldn't hear the band and most people
were tipsy. I paid a visit to the Corporals' Club and saw Crownshaw
obviously having had too much to drink but quite steady as a policeman
invariably is, the only visible sign being that he was enamoured of some
deadly popsy well in her thirties. I was caught in a conversation with a
drunk Rhodesian sergeant with whom I nattered for five or ten minutes

and was then shaken warmly by his hand and bidden good-night and lifelong good luck.

As I wandered by the dining-hall I saw in a corner two men fighting. One was lying on the ground and the other was standing over him, picking him up only to knock him down again. Then he hurried back into the dance and as he passed me I saw that it was Taffy Hinds – quite a pleasant fellow when he's sober. Jim Martin and I hurried over to where the other fellow lay, his face a mass of blood and his clothes crumpled and bloodstained. He was unconscious – in fact he looked half dead.

With the help of a couple of ground staff wallahs we started to carry him across to the sick quarters. However, he woke up half-way, started to mutter and swear and began to kick. I wasn't prepared to help someone who for two pins would have attacked us so we all dropped him and he ran, or rather staggered, to his billet and sat up in a stupor on the steps there.

It all arose because Hinds called De Sylva a bastard and De Sylva called Hinds a Welsh shithouse.

Monday 7 August 1944
I was sent solo for an hour and a quarter. I decided to do an inverted flight and I got 130 on the clock, rolled on my back and wobble-pumped. The engine cut so I decided as I had bags of height to half roll out of it. I pulled the stick back and blacked out completely in respect of my eyes though I remained quite conscious. When my sight came back I was diving towards the deck and my instruments showed me that in the panic of my engine cutting I had forgotten to close my throttle and I had over 3,000 revs on – ie I had over-revved my engine by 500–600 rpm.

I decided to force-land. I had bags of height so I opened my hood, locked my harness and looked for a suitable landing ground. There was a fairly flat stretch of almost unbroken grass with a few trees on down on my right so I began my S approach as per practice and pumped the throttle a while to see if I couldn't get the engine to pick up – but in vain. So I throttled back and concentrated on the approach. As I write this I am reliving those dreadful moments again. I was very frightened.

I actually contemplated baling out but I realised that I had a very good chance of getting away with it so I decided to stick by the kite.

As I glided down I had quite a bit of space available – so much so that the aircraft could have been flown off again, once repaired.

To my intense relief I heard that musical note – the engine picking up and I raised the nose and climbed towards the 'drome. Then the full implication of my stupidity came home. I thought of the inevitable interviews, the scorn, the end of the pilot's course for me, the court-martial.

Monday 21 August 1944
Sat in bed late and read *I, Claudius*, the pseudo-autobiography of that
Roman emperor which I found very interesting.

In the evening to see Rita Hayworth and Fred Astaire in *You Were Never
Lovelier* for the sixth time. Even the sixth time it is wizzo.

Saturday 26 August 1944
Nattered to Dave Williams and the crowd. Dave Williams was a Post
Office technician before the war and he told me some 'gen' on telephones.
Apparently, if you lift the receiver and tap it once, twice, thrice, and four
times (if your number were 1234) you get through without paying.

I must remember that for peacetime. I went to bed after a discussion
with Don Nicolson as to whether or not contraceptive apparatus was un-
Christian. We came to the conclusion that

(a) If sexual intercourse between a man and his wife is just a means of
    producing children then any device which enables them to have
    that pleasure without children is unnatural, wrong and very
    possibly a sin.

But on the other hand

(b) If sexual intercourse is more than that, as Dr Herbert Gray says,
    and is in fact symbolic and cementing as a spiritual and
    psychological union between them, then it is not wrong or
    unnatural. I rather tend to agree with Gray.

> 1850035 Cadet Benn A N W
> c/o HQ RATG Salisbury
>
> 27.8.44

My dearest family
I have had a telegram from you this week and a letter. I am very glad
to hear that the RAF have found a job for you, Dad, and it will be a great
thing to have been in uniform from the early days right to the end. All the
same I don't think you should stay in any longer than the European war
lasts.

In your letter, Ma, you tell me about Mike's letters which have been
left untouched. That's good, I hope you won't deal with them until I get
back. There are many private letters which we must, in fairness to him,
destroy.

He wrote one or two short stories which I was allowed to read – one
which particularly struck me which was about night flying while he was
operating as a night fighter pilot in England.

You ask me about my financial position, Dad – well I have £20 in my

Rhodesian Post Office Savings Bank, and £5 in my pocket which will probably go during the week's leave we are getting in a few days' time.

I have finished the elementary part of my training now.

Your loving son

Wednesday 30 August 1944

I had an hour and a half's solo this afternoon in which I had a real pukka dogfight with Costello and Roy Hinds.

There is something about dogfighting that I enjoy. Whether it is the cooperation with other aircraft or the manoeuvrability I do not know but the sensation of tearing about with a purpose, evading the other man, the feeling of power and the knowledge that the aircraft you fly must be cherished and understood if it is to be used, the quick thinking that is required, the battle of wits, all combine to turn the dummy attacks into a schoolboy's dream.

I went along with Shag Butler to Meikle's where we met some others. We had a few rounds of drinks and after the mental struggle which usually arises I ordered a lime juice in a loud voice. They laughed and I find that being quite determined and making a joke of it usually does the trick, without offending anyone.

Sunday 3 September 1944, Salisbury, Rhodesia

I went along to the Anglican cathedral for Communion this morning and it was packed. Naturally I was thinking especially of Mike and I had clearly in mind that day exactly five years ago when we were all at Stansgate and war broke out. I remember that all through the morning there were announcements especially concerning the Prime Minister's speech at 11 am, and in between programmes of martial music. At a quarter to 11 in the morning Nursey asked Gladys to fetch a few bottles of ginger beer so that we could celebrate the last quarter of an hour of peace, little knowing that the war would last until now.

To the Aulds.* There I met Mr and Mrs Auld, their married daughter Mary and her baby son John. Old Mr Auld is a civil servant administering the Industrial Conciliation Act, a kindly Scotsman. He is extremely verbose but very interesting. Mrs Auld is as hospitable as her husband and a more friendly Scot you couldn't wish to find. Mary is very charming and though she has young John to look after has returned to work as a nursing sister in the native hospital, from a sense of duty and because her husband is fighting in Italy. I like her very much; in her mannerisms she is like Nursey.

She has said that I may visit the native hospital some time.

* A Rhodesian family in Salisbury who befriended me during my time in Rhodesia.

Wednesday 6 September 1944

Mr Auld took me to the legislative chamber in Cecil Square, and introduced me to Mr Ferris, Clerk of the House in the Rhodesian Parliament.

The building has been adapted from a hotel. The debating chamber consists of a long hall, three-quarters the length of the King's Robing Room at Westminster, of which the end part is roped off for spectators. In front, the House itself is divided into two sides – on the left the Opposition, and on the right the Government. There are no benches but large padded armchairs with round backs and arms. The ordinary procedure of the Commons has been adopted.

The Speaker's chair is tall-backed upon which is carved the crest of the British South Africa Company and above and behind, on the wall, is the Imperial Crest. The acoustics are not very good and there are a number of microphones about, a sight which is rather strange for a British Parliament, I think.

Mr Ferris pointed out that smoking was not allowed in the chamber, though I noticed a dirty great ashtray on his – the Clerk's – table full of cigarette stubs. The Clerk has a number of sand glasses for keeping a check on speeches and three switches by him which operate different coloured lights.

I stood talking to Mr Ferris in the porch. At first he had been a trifle cold and haughty I thought, but now he was becoming more friendly and he talked of the Union and the very strong influences there. It is his opinion that, within a year of the death of Smuts,[1] the Union will eventually break all connection with our British Commonwealth of Nations and declare itself a separate republic.

I noticed the great suburbs which are springing up around Salisbury – fine little houses with tiled roofs, which indicate that Salisbury will develop fast after the war. I must say I don't feel the same horror of living here that I do about Bulawayo or Gwelo.

Mary had told me that tonight was the night when I could get over to the Native hospital. So Harry and I walked over there at 7.30.

The hospital itself was built in 1924 and consists of an H-shaped brick whitewashed building with wooden beams supporting a corrugated iron roof.

The operating theatre is a discarded building from the old European hospital and stretcher bearers carry the patients across there, rain or no rain.

Mary is a trained sister; she is on duty from 7.30 in the morning till 9 at night and she is the only white nurse in that native hospital. She has a hundred patients under her, sometimes many more, and at night two junior inexperienced probationers take over. Under her there are six male orderlies, and a few native female orderlies. These orderlies are not only untrustworthy as regards administering medicine, but are often insolent.

Mary is a quiet, efficient and determined girl but all the same when I was there I heard her having to 'shout like a fish-wife' (as she termed it) to get a couple of slack ones to do a job of work.

The supply of medical stores are very short. Mary gets as much as she can from rags and so on. I went into one ward and there was a tiny tot lying in bed – it can't have been more than three or four – with both legs broken, bandaged and I daresay plastered, with its feet suspended by string from a bar above.

In another was a man who kept sitting up and throwing his blanket off. He was shackled by the legs to the bed to keep him on it and the orderlies tried to keep him covered.

Mary pointed out three that would die. There was no moaning and Mary tells me that natives are very good patients, never complaining and always making the best of everything.

The nurses like Mary carry on under these conditions. It is magnificent really.

Well I have seen something tonight that I shall never forget and it makes me realise what a lot there is to do in the world.

I realised what a sweet girl Mary is. Her husband is a lucky man. Perhaps long segregation from women makes me fond of all I see, or perhaps I see in Mary a girl of real value. She is a very fine specimen. I must keep clear of my Barbara Ann and Gloria tendencies and stick to those who are like Mary.

Thursday 7 September 1944
Mr Auld took me to see Victor Robinson, chief adviser to the Attorney-General. He is quite disillusioned with bureaucracy and finds all sorts of little annoyances in the native problem.

The example he gave was of the museum, which is crowded out with natives on Saturdays and Sundays thus preventing the Europeans from taking their children and yet, as no colour bar is legally allowed, they cannot prevent the natives from going, so it looks as though the only solution is closing the place on those days altogether.

Difficulties like this are real and the idealist must bear them in mind when he considers the possible solutions of the problem.

Monday 11 September 1944
I am absolutely bored stiff with flying the old Cornell, so completely disregarding Crownshaw's instructions, I climbed over a large bush fire which was burning and carried by its thermal I reached a height of 9,000 feet above the drome.

Friday 15 September 1944
We arrived in Bulawayo about six and after a cup of tea at the canteen we

walked to the Services Club for breakfast. Our luggage had all been left in error on Gwelo station.

We embussed and arrived at RAF Heany in due course where I was billeted in the old church – an extremely grim building with no box, locker or wardrobe.

Monday 18 September 1944

Met my new instructor Flying Officer Porter who seems a very sound type. He is a North Country police constable in civvy street.

After flying I was very trembly and shaky. I have come to the conclusion that it is a delayed nervous reaction. It isn't at all pleasant while it lasts but it wears off after a while. It takes the form of apprehension such as I used to experience at school or before any public speech I make – except that it is more acute and accompanied by actual physical shaking. Thank God it is delayed, for I don't know what I would do if it actually attacked me while I was flying. I am quite calm and collected while in the air.

Sunday 24 September 1944

I really wonder whether with all my experience in the RAF I shall ever settle into Oxford again. I wonder if I shall find the Union toffee-nosed or think the college and its members intolerably smug. In a way I hope so, because seeing university types from the outside, as it were, I really can't say that I want to be one again. Mike noticed it and commented on it and now I see just what he meant – bless him.

Wednesday 4 October 1944

My Polish WAASIE was at the flicks tonight and I noticed her looking at me as I was gazing in her direction.

Monday 9 October 1944

After a five-minute dip in the baths, I had tea, then went to bed early, having restrained myself from going to the flicks although I would give anything to see my Polish WAASIE friend. However just as I had written this and was going to bed Eddy came in and asked me if I was going to the prayer circle.

I didn't like the jocularity much, nor the jibes at the Roman Catholics who were holding confession next door.

Eddy gave a 15-minute address on 'Watch and Pray' with frequent references to Satan and his craftiness. This doesn't appeal to me I must say. I feel sure that we are bound as brothers under Christ, and therefore these criticisms tonight are simply skin deep and do not touch the real springs of religious belief. I can't make up my mind whether to go next week.

Sunday 15 October 1944
I went down to the Baths and there was that fellow who is going to introduce me to the Polish WAASIE. He was damned abrupt I thought, and I hadn't a clue what to say to her. She [Jozia] is quite a nice creature really and I daresay that in time everything will be organised. I found out something of her history. She lived in Livow or Lemburg and her father and brother are still there. In 1939 she was sent by the Russians to what I presume was a concentration camp on the White Sea. She was in Russia for two years. She said 'Russia is a bad country – bad people.' I suppose for many of these girls the Russians are almost as big a bogey as are the Germans – a thought to bear in mind when the post-war statesman attempts to build up a new world. What she suffered I can't say but she left Russia after two years and went to Iran where she stayed for a year before coming to Africa. She joined the WAASIEs in February 1943 and has been in Pietermaritzburg, Jo'burg, Lusaka and now Heaney.

Tuesday 17 October 1944
There were three letters for me in the sergeants' mess. One from Dad was on the subject of standing for Parliament. Apparently he had opened a letter for me, from John Parker, in error, in which Parker requested me to consider contesting a seat at the next General Election as a Labour Party candidate. My first sensation was amazement, then of intense pleasure, in the first place at having been remembered by my Party friends and in the second at having been considered as a suitable candidate by Parker, the MP for Dagenham, whom I hardly know. Pa wrote a few words of sound advice. I know that it is his heartfelt wish that I should finish at Oxford. Bless him for promising to use his influence with the Party to get me a good seat if I decided so, and also for his generous offer of the necessary financial support.

Wednesday 18 October 1944
I am afraid that Porter wasn't very pleased with my taxiing, my single-engined landing or my precautionary one this morning and I felt pretty cheesed.

After tea I went along to *Band Waggon*. It starred Arthur Askey and Richard Murdoch but somehow it didn't quite hit it off. The sense of humour we have must have altered since the war, for the film was made in 1938 or 1939 I suppose. Anna was sitting in the row in front and Jozia was sitting farther along the same row as me. This made things very tricky and I couldn't smile at Anna without Jozia seeing. When I smiled at each of them in turn both looked glum so I've put two blacks up and boobed badly.

I worked at my Christmas cards until 10. I have never seen such continued and heavy rain as we had tonight. The thunder was louder than falling bombs, the lightning as bright as day, and the water pouring down as if a bucket was being emptied on each square foot every minute.

Friday 20 October 1944
After lunch I finished my Christmas cards and took them to the Post Office, believing that they all went free. However to my amazement I discovered they required stamps and I was obliged to withdraw 30 shillings from the PO and pay 11/- for stamps. It raised the cost of my Christmas cards to £1.9.0 but it was worthwhile expenditure.

Saturday 21 October 1944
The sergeants' mess social seemed to be promising and I changed into blue and went along. It really wasn't all that much of a success. Sgt Lamb is disgusting and aggressive when he's drunk. Otto Fialla is obscene and very rude. I saw the girl from the barrack stores there – a more toffee-nosed type you could not wish to see, but I think despite this, immensely attractive.

Monday 23 October 1944
In signals we did a Radio Telephone exercise and my voice came out so like the BBC that everyone laughed heartily. It was all meant in good humour so I took it as such and laughed at what I now always refer to as my atrocious accent. It's good for me to be teased about it as long as they don't take exception to me on account of it. I am quite happy to let it go on. The time when it is really a hindrance is when I meet people for the first time and they judge me as a supercilious, toffee-nosed type.

Wednesday 25 October 1944
The flick was not very good except for Veronica Lake, who is lusho. Anna was pretty unresponsive tonight and I almost had a crick in the neck. I wonder why she is like this, because she is always very eager when speaking to me.

Saturday 28 October 1944
I wrote a couple of letters this afternoon and in the evening went with Tommy to try to find Anna. We couldn't so we took up a position on the verandah at the entrance to the sergeants' mess. Bob Willshire and George Brown joined us.

Bob bought the first round of drinks and got me a small sherry, which I tipped unobtrusively down a crevice in the concrete of the verandah. To avoid further trouble, I bought the next round of drinks and got myself a dry ginger ale which I like with a pipe. We decided that Anna must have gone to the dance, so we went there.

She was very attractively dressed in a blue frock – which unfortunately got torn. I can't dance at all but we staggered round and it made me even more determined to do something about my dancing.

F/Lt Long came over and started talking; I think he was slightly pissed as he told an enormous number of stories. He was very friendly and as good as told me that he had recommended me for a commission.

I do hope Anna enjoyed the dance. She looked lovely and I am glad that they took a photo of the group as it will probably be the only one I have of her. We walked back to the WAASERIE together. I couldn't kiss her good-night outside the lighted WAASERIE so I arranged to meet her at the flicks tomorrow. Then I came back to my room and had a natter with Thorpe, who is getting his 'wings' on Tuesday – lucky man.

Sunday 29 October 1944
Everyone warns me that these Polish girls expect you to marry them if you get in the least bit intimate. I do not intend to go as far as that and I certainly won't marry Anna even if I want to. In the first place I may be killed in Burma and even if I survived it is an altogether different life in England. It is too absurd even to consider. However I don't want to upset her as she is very sweet. Therefore I must not raise her hopes.

Monday 30 October 1944
We had the first fatal accident on the station since I have been here this morning. An instructor and a pupil hit the high-tension cables while on low-level cross country. The kite caught fire and they were burnt. As a matter of fact, of course, they were killed by the kite striking the deck probably at 140 mph, so they were already dead. It is just another example of what unauthorised low flying does for you. I feel strangely calm about it, and everybody jokes about it. I can't make up my mind if this is wrong or not. If I thought of it too seriously and pondered each implication it might worry me to the extent of affecting my morale and my flying.

Frankenstein's Monster meets the Wolfman was on tonight and I took Anna. The question of popsies arose and she asked me if I had one in England. I made a joke of it and said 'I have six – one in England, two at Heany, two at Bulawayo and one at Salisbury.' This solved the problem.

Wednesday 8 November 1944
This afternoon I found myself telling Sewell and Stout about Mike, and it all seemed remote, and with a shock I realised that it didn't mean what it used to.

In the evening I went into Bulawayo and met Anna. She is a very dim girl really. After the pictures were over I took her to the City Hall gardens and we sat and talked. I said, 'Anna, do you expect me to marry you?' She said she didn't but to make it quite clear I talked about it. I said that

I would be going to fight the Japanese, and I might be killed, and that then I go back to England, and she goes back to Poland. She agreed.

I asked her as we sat if she minded if I kissed her and she said that she didn't understand. I leaned across and kissed her but she was queerly unresponsive. Then she asked me why I had kissed her if I didn't intend marrying her and it showed that she has a thoroughly Victorian attitude, at once moral and prudish, and strange now. She said she had only known me for three weeks and she was shy. In fact she even cited a friend of hers who had known an RAF fellow for ten or eleven months before she let him kiss her. She told me that I had stolen her first kiss.

I walked back to the YWCA with her and kissed her goodnight – she was more responsive at that moment than before. Then I came back in the transport with Jerry Lacey and Bill Thorpe who had spent the evening with their own Annas.

Thursday 9 November 1944
Met my new instructor today, F/O Bostock, a short man with fair hair, thinning on top and a neat darkish moustache. What I liked about him especially was the way he offered me a cigarette while explaining the gen on formation flying, which I am beginning tomorrow.

Monday 13 November 1944
Bostock took me up today and showed himself to be a very fine instructor.

I coped far better than ever before and learned his method of doing a controlled rate of descent, which is excellent. He sent me off solo and then after breakfast we did armaments.

Wednesday 15 November 1944
Two more people were killed this morning, when two Oxfords collided in mid-air. In the one kite were two pupils. They collided with Paddy Woodhead from our course.

By a miracle Cotton was thrown clear. What I hate is the tremendous outburst of gossiping which accompanies it, though I am sometimes a participant.

Paddy Woodhead was on the mess table next to us in SS *Cameronia*, and I learned to appreciate his real qualities and amiable nature.

It seems a wasted life and there is none of the excitement or romance which people imagine makes a death in the service any better than a death in a motoring accident.

Sunday 19 November 1944
I went to the flicks in the evening and there was Anna sitting with another girl about five rows ahead. I signalled to her to come and sit with me and she brought her friend – another Anna. I could see by her

expression that trouble was brewing. She asked me somewhat tartly where I had been for the last two weeks.

Clearly they thought that I had a popsy in Bulawayo and I said quite clearly that I had not. After a long muttered conversation in Polish Anna came out with this ultimatum: 'If you like a Rhodesian girl – all very well. If you like speak to me say so.' I replied that I had no other popsy and that 'I like speak to Anna.'

A moment later she stated that I must not go into Bulawayo on Sunday. I declared that I would not be bullied by her, nor any of her friends, that I didn't have a popsy in Bulawayo but that I intended to go into the town when and how I decided.

I chuckled merrily but she was near to tears so I left it at that. Her parting shot was that there were plenty of boys at Heany and one with two buttons on his armband had wanted to be her boyfriend but that she had refused.

I walked back to the WAASERIE with her but I don't propose going to the flicks tomorrow night.

Tuesday 21 November 1944
Turned up at the flights, but we weren't going to fly. Long came in and said he would rope in someone to give us a talk. No one volunteered and as I expected he chose me.

'Come on Benn,' he said, 'talk about something.'

'Certainly, sir, but I fear I shall bore you, for what interests me usually bores everyone else.'

'What's that?'

'Politics!'

'Come on all the same and let's hear you.'

I started straight to the point and said that I proposed to base my talk on General Smuts' speech on native policy which he called 'The Basis of Trusteeship'. I outlined two schools of thought which Smuts declared 'outworn' and described the theory of trusteeship. Having established that development was necessary or at any rate inevitable, I touched lightly on the question of parallel development within the existing framework. I wasn't idealistic as I knew that would not appeal. However I tried to show that change was inevitable and that we had better be prepared for it. Porter took me up and suggested that this change would take hundreds of years to come. Finsbury stated that mission schools would be responsible for trouble if it came and we shouldn't educate the Bantu.

I tried to hold my own but Porter went off muttering that he didn't care about the wogs and 'Roll on the Boat'. I defended the missions and shut up Finsbury, Bostock defended imperialism and I was led on to say a word or two about international finance, which annoyed him as too progressive.

Then interest lagged, the audience diminished and I called rather a lame halt.

Wednesday 22 November 1944

My formation flying this morning was very bad and for the first time, Bostock practically lost his temper in the air. I apologised for my cluelessness afterwards and he was quite friendly.

Saturday 25 November 1944

At a quarter to ten Bob, Ken and I were summoned to the Chief Instructor's office. We had to wait an hour and three-quarters while he interviewed five scrubs.

He saw us individually and the conversation went something like this:

CI: 'Benn, you have been recommended to me as an under-officer. Do you want to do this and live in the officers' mess?'

'Yes, sir.'

CI: 'You are young and may find it difficult at first – a lot of men older than yourself will be under you and you will have to use tact. Don't be put off by the 'old chum' racket. If an old chum disregards an order he will expect you to report him and you must do so.'

Then we went across to the Chief Ground Instructor's office. He gave us a long talk referring especially to home troubles. When he had given Willshire two buttons and Ken and me one each as cadet leaders he told me that I was to be moved to the other group so that Willshire could keep an eye on me and give me a hand with discipline. Then he dismissed us and told us to meet him at the officers' mess for lunch.

We went into lunch and it was the best scoff I have seen in Rhodesia. I suppose I shall get used to it but at the moment it is strange. I find that I have forgotten some of my table manners. It is an ideal place for spare time and I enjoy the easy chairs and the music from the radiogram. I was going to go to the flicks tonight but I can only sit with the officers and that cuts out Tommy Stout and Anna, so what's the use?

Monday 27 November 1944

I found Johnny Harris to pay him the 15/- I owe and there were some of the boys, so I stayed and nattered. When I looked back, I felt a despair and was unhappy about it while it went on, though the company was friendly enough. I wasted two or more hours; I sunk into the lowest and cheapest form of humour, partly because I hadn't sufficient determination and strength to clear off and partly I suppose because I wanted them to know that even though I have a blue band on my sleeve I am still one of the lads. As it was I stayed and talked and laughed over the lowest filth and lost complete control of myself. I writhed when I thought of it afterwards and lay awake for half an hour conscious of self-disgust.

Tuesday 28 November 1944

I learned quite a lot tonight in the officers' mess. I learned that as men, officers are no different from ordinary ranks, or for that matter any middle class community, like Oxford or air crew generally. They get disgracefully drunk, their conversation is the same, sexy, uninformed petty level, and seen close to, they command no special respect. It debunks the picture the Air Force hopes to build up of its officers. I am not toffee-nosed at heart at all and all I want to be able to do without giving offence to anyone is find my place and settle down in it.

Thursday 30 November 1944

After tea I spoke to cadet officer Bay'lani of Belgrade. I asked him about the political situation in Yugoslavia and though he wasn't really interested in politics he told me one or two interesting facts about Marshal Tito and General Mihailovich.[2] Bay'lani was a law student at Belgrade University for a year before the war and then he was in the capital for six months or a year after the German occupation and he escaped to Switzerland and through unoccupied France to Spain and Portugal, where he came to the Middle East and then on here. His social background (his father was a Belgrade banker) makes him conservative in outlook and clearly royalist in sympathy. He was broadminded enough to recognise Tito as a great war leader. At first, so he said, the partisans fought under Mihailovich but because of Serb–Croat rivalry, made worse by local disputes, they gradually broke away and formed what is now Tito's army. Later they had clashes with Mihailovich's Chetniks and this probably developed into first-class warfare. Mihailovich too, so he fancied, had made local agreements with the Germans, and his opposition to them was at times half-hearted.

This combined with the fact that Tito was receiving Russian support and recognition, might account for that force being communist in backing and anyway it was pretty clear that the Balkans would be in the Russian sphere of influence after the war. As far as King Peter himself was concerned he believed him to be completely or almost completely under the influence of his corrupt and unreliable ministers. However the possibility of a rapprochement between Tito and Peter did exist and we should soon see.

Saturday 2 December 1944

After lunch I went to the Quiet Room and read the AMWIS [Air Ministry Weekly Intelligence Summary]. In AMWIS was a copy of a pamphlet issued to Japanese intelligence officers who are engaged in interrogating British and American POWs. It was interesting and rather terrifying – particularly this paragraph:

'Torture by beating, kicking, starving, or murdering is a clumsy method and *should only be resorted to when all other methods fail.*'

It is not at all impossible that I shall be taken prisoner and I shall have to adjust myself mentally to that possibility and also prepare a plan.

I should be very frightened of torture or the threat of it and I might prefer an easy way out – suicide before or after capture.

I have to remember that I am not the only one involved. Physical weakness under torture could cost other people's lives and that changes the nature of the problem. I would not be justified in *not* committing suicide if by refraining from doing so I gave in under torture and my weakness resulted in greater loss of life. In this sense suicide would be in a sense the ordinary self-sacrifice which war service renders possible in the ordinary course of air operations and that I must be prepared to do, if it seems necessary.

Cadet Pilot Benn

Bulawayo, Southern Rhodesia

Dec 8th '44

My dear old Proff,

I have been must lax (ha ha) of late in writing to you.

Anyway Proff old boy, a Very Happy Christmas. When in the not too distant future I am among you again Proff, I shall have all sorts of anecdotes to add to the old impersonations.

Our Native boy in the Officers mess is called Jeremiah, and a very good boy he is. However I still can't get used to asking an Old Testament prophet for 'another dollop of spuds'. The natives have very funny names. My friends in Bulawayo once had one called 'Motor Car'. He came from a very remote village miles out in the bundu, with hardly more than a track out to it. My friend, out of curiosity, asked him whether there were any motor cars where he lived. 'No, Sir' replied the boy, 'I'm the only one.' That is a perfectly true story.

Loving good wishes, James

Tuesday 12 December 1944

Long is friendly but damned rude sometimes to the most docile and pleasant people. Very often just for the sake of showing off – the Italian head waiter, the native boys in the mess, pupils, ground staff.

Friday 15 December 1944

I am well and properly in the shit with Long these days. He is rude to me and he means it, he is unpleasant and when a man like Long gets his knife into you, he keeps it there. It all came of my letting him become too familiar and becoming so myself. Now he will take delight in upsetting me and I shall have to watch out carefully – thank heavens I have only got another week to go and then it will be farewell to 2 Group.

Saturday 16 December 1944
I am very depressed this morning for many reasons. I have put up a black with Long. I have been extremely childish in the mess and have antagonised a lot of people. I have also dropped off with my flying. All these contribute to a general feeling of depression which is really upsetting me and I feel lethargic and miserable.

Sunday 17 December 1944
I didn't get to sleep until about midnight. It was very hot and three-quarters of an hour later I was woken by Bert Banks and Buck, who had been in town on the booze. Buck asked me if I wanted to buy a submarine and Bert if I wanted to buy a battleship. Drowsily I declined both offers. Then Buck came across and said he saw an ant on me. When they went I had a job getting to sleep again.

Friday 19 January 1945
I had a heated argument with Tom Stout about Churchill, Greek policy and wartime criticism in general. It has always seemed to me to be despicable that ambitious, ill-informed, ultra-critical civilians (like Shinwell) have any right to launch general attacks on a war government, though naturally political differences and points must be exploited and attacked – that is vital. It is not a very productive subject for discussion this but I do feel the greatest sympathy for a man who is really doing his best to win the war and who in his trouble becomes a target for all these attacks.

Afterwards I went to the canteen for a bottle of pop and staggered to bed.

Sunday 21 January 1945

My dearest family
This is I hope positively the last time that I shall be forced to make a skimpy letter like this serve as my total correspondence to you all.

By this time next week the Wings exam will be over and done with and if I have passed it then my spare time will be my own . . .

Thanks for your letter, Pa. I agree with you about 'no politics' now but don't extend that to the Jap war. The political side of things is getting nearly as important as the military now and when it becomes more so I want to see you change back into parliamentary uniform and open a 'second front' in the Lords, straight away.

Bless you Proff for your news.

Tuesday 30 January 1945
I got the 2 o'clock transport into town and restarted my search for uniform. I saw Marcus and he measured me for tunic and slacks which will cost me £15.15.0. Then I ordered a Simpson greatcoat for £13.13.0. I

made enquiries about khaki and bought a couple of pairs of shorts and a couple of pipes. Today's efforts pretty well finished my uniform hunt.

We heard today that apart from Peters who failed airmanship, everyone else is through the Wings. Somehow the thrill isn't as great as I thought, but I expect the edge is taken off it by the long months of waiting.

Thursday 1 February 1945
I had hardly got ready for bed when Cotton came in as pissed as a fart and told me that he had been ordered to bed by Sqn. Ldr. Alexander, the CFI, after planting a meat roll on his head. I listened to him for a while, took him across for a pee, waited in his room while he spewed out of the window, undressed him and put him to bed. The disgusting spectacle confirmed for me, though I needed it not, that teetotalism is a wise policy.

Saturday 10 February 1945
Got up for breakfast at 8.30. Saw Horace Long and bade him goodbye. All he said was, 'Well cheerio Benn. I am glad I met you.' Very simple but I felt he meant it and I was pleased.

There is a panic at the moment about postings and of course the question of instructors has come up again.

I have handed in an application to be posted to the Far East. My reasons are that the Sayles and their children were in Shanghai when the Japs entered and haven't been heard of since. I *must not* be made an instructor.

After dinner I went to see *Road to Morocco* for the 3rd or 4th time. Bing Crosby, Bob Hope and Dorothy Lamour are a grand team. Mike was very fond of them.

Tuesday 13 February 1945
It seems fairly certain that between ten and fifteen people will be wanted as instructors. This worried me so much that I decided to act at once.

Barney (the CGI's clerk, a Communist and a very good fellow) advised me to be blunt to the CGI. When I went in he said: 'Yes Benn, what do you want?'

Me: 'Sir I have come to see you about an application I made to be posted to the Far East. I have strong reasons for wishing to go. My uncle, his wife and three children are in Shanghai and nothing has been heard of them for three years; my brother was killed a short while ago and my father is in the Air Force himself again, at the absurd age of 69.'

CGI (smiling): 'So you want to have a crack at the Japs yourself?'

The CGI explained how postings are worked and suggested I see the CFI, Sqn. Ldr. Chinnery.

So I went through same thing with Chinnery.

Chinnery: 'Well, Benn, you will not go to Norton [as an instructor] but we do not post direct from this command to the Far East – they do that from the Middle East. So you are almost certain to go there.'

I felt as happy as a pig in shit, to use an old RAF expression.

Cadet Pilot Benn
Bulawayo, Southern Rhodesia

14.2.45

Me dearest Proff

I am delighted to hear that you are a candidate for the executive of the Oxted and District Society for Anglo-Soviet Friendship. General discussions will give you practice in addressing an adult audience which will stand you in good stead at Oxford, and later on in national politics – unless you decide to take up comparative philology.

I have asked Ma not to post any more letters to me after Feb 28th, until I cable a new address. I shall know tomorrow definitely whether I am going to get a commission or not.

You are a wonderful correspondent and always in the thoughts of your affectionate brother.

Thursday 15 February 1945

This morning we were told that CI wanted to see sixteen of us at 10.30. I went in first and the CI and CGI were sitting at the desk. The CI asked me what I intended to do after the war. 'Life as an officer in peacetime is a great one and the training is better,' he said.

'Yes sir – I wish to remain in the Reserve for some years if that is possible.'

CI: 'Yes. You have a flair for politics?'

'Well sir it has always been my interest at school and at Oxford and now I am trying to learn something about the political situation here . . . '

CI: 'What impressions have you formed of this country?'

'Well I am trying to avoid impressions so as to devote as much time as possible to studying. But I do think the native position is unsatisfactory.' (Here I was skating on very thin ice for WingCos, who have hordes of munts to clean their boots, buttons, clothes, don't view proposals for the liberation of such munts with a very kindly eye.)

The CI then asked me what I thought should be done and I replied that I considered that there should be a goal towards which the native policy, however slow the improvement might be, should be working. I came out rather worried in case any reference to politics should upset my chances.

Later in the day we all had to report to the Group Captain's office. I went in to see him first, and he was sitting looking through my documents. He asked me about my permanent commission and I replied as before that I did not intend to remain in the RAF. I should probably be in the Air Force for a long time as it was, but that my real interest was politics.

The Groupie smiled. 'Well Benn, when you get into Parliament you can tell them how underpaid we are!' He was quick to add, 'or rather were so before the war'.

It seems more than likely that I shall get on to Liberators, Baltimores or possibly Wellingtons. It isn't impossible that I shall end up on fighters – Spitfires, Typhoons or even Tempests.

Friday 23 February 1945
I just had time to wash and have breakfast before I was due back for the eye test, which I failed again. The Medical Officer said, 'Benn, I'm afraid I shall have to send you to Salisbury for a medical board. I have to cover myself. You will probably be flown there and back in one day.'

I was disconsolate.

Friday 2 March 1945
I sewed my wings and PO's rings on to my battledress, and spent the evening doing nothing.

Monday 5 March 1945
I had a delightful – if slightly premature – telegram of congratulations from the family today on my Wings. It was wizard and I showed it to a few friends. It ran like this:

> The happy three
> Ma, Dave and me
> Rejoice with our joy
> About our boy
> Our spirit sings
> He's got his wings.

The reply I sent was

> Your message in rhyme
> Arrived dead on time
> To greet me just when
> I became P/O Benn.

Thursday 8 March 1945
After lunch I had a bath and went on Wings parade. It was a queer sensation marching on to the parade ground and I was nervous. I was afraid that I should shout 'Sir 035' when my name was called. Nobby Ashurst in front of me actually did this but I was OK. Dixon (Wing Commander AFC) was giving the Wings. It was a great moment for which I have long waited.

I thought of Mike watching it all and my heart was very full as we marched past to the music of the Royal Air Force march.

I had a photograph of Mike in my pocket and I felt very much that he was being recommissioned in me to carry on. As the third PO Benn of this war (Father May 1940; Mike August 1941; me March 1945) I have a great tradition to keep up.

I went along (to the passing-out party in my blue at about 7pm) feeling very self-conscious. A lot of people tried to smear my 'Wings' with beer, which I took a poor view of. However everyone was very friendly.

Bob Willshire came round and told me that the CI, Dixon, was going to speak at 7.15. So at 7.12 I quickly went up to him and said 'Are you ready, Sir?' 'Yes, Benn.'

I plucked up courage and walked to the middle of the room. 'Quiet a moment please. The Chief Instructor would now like to say a few words.' At this Wing Commander Dixon leaned across and whispered huskily, 'No, Benn, no, I want another beer.'

The whole room was hushed and waiting on my next words, so, with . . . commendable presence of mind I raised my voice again and said 'I apologise, it was a mistake. The Chief Instructor wants another beer.' (Loud laughter.)

He was most genial and told me that it was quite all right but he couldn't speak until he had had another drink.

Tuesday 13 March 1945
I collected a package from the Post Office and closed my savings account. The package contained Mike's Wings – the actual pair that he wore on his battledress. They were taken off that tunic and sent me, so I at once removed the Wings that I had put on my own battledress and sewed on his pair. I prayed that I should be found worthy of the Wings I wore.

Eddy and I caught the transport into town and turned up at Mimosa House. Ibbotson* was most welcoming.

After lunch we set off in the car and entered the location reserved for married people – those joined by Christian or established native rites. In cases of doubt the native commissioner (Mr Huxtable, or one of his

* Revd Percy Ibbotson, a Christian minister to whom I had been introduced and who was kind to me during my time in Rhodesia.

subordinates) decides. The purpose of this is to check the habit of temporary wives and common prostitution, which is rampant and very liable to spread VD.

We went into one house after asking the native if we might and inspected it. It consisted of two small rooms. The front room was his bedroom, living room and where I presume he ate his meal. The back one was his kitchen and pantry, where a fire burned on the floor and led straight up to the chimney. There were a few shelves for his cooking utensils. The house was pretty disorderly, but that was almost entirely attributable to the size of it. This fellow was trying to turn his 10ft by 6ft ground into a garden and he has put a whitewashed wooden fence round it, which is rather a good example of the native's desire to improve his own property. For this house he pays 13/- a month plus 1/- for light.

We then went into a model house (of a type built since Ibbotson's report). This house is of a type which encourages self-respect and it was very tidily kept. The owner was very proud of it. The back door is very popular. It seems that natives are very fond of a back door.

We left the location and drove off – past the coloured (*definition*: man or woman with a strain of aboriginal blood) area. Here the coloureds rent plots. They are allowed to buy property and they can live where they like.

We went on to the Luveve shopping centre, built on three sides of a square, and a covered verandah runs round the inside. The intention is to see that in the location and also at Luveve the native needs should be met by native tradesmen, so as to ensure that they are not cheated by Indians, coloureds or white people. There is a haberdashery shop, a general stores (where we bought 10 Tom Tom cigarettes for 1d – rather strong and definitely not an indoor cigarette), a cobbler, cycle repairer, a tin worker. One man was making fine kitchen utensils out of old sheets of tin from petrol cans and so on. Apparently a beer hall will soon be erected to complete the picture.

(no address as yet)

24.3.45

My dearest old Proffy

I am glad to hear of all your work for the exam which will by now be over and done with.

I am fit and well for my next stage in training, for training it will still be for a month or so. The German war will be over in a few weeks thanks to that great Russian General Marshal Zhukov and his Irish colleague, old 'Tim O'Shenko'. The Allied armies in France are making magnificent progress. I don't see how Hitler can hold out for much longer. Then things at home will gradually return to normal and I shall at least feel that our positions are equalised – for the last fifteen months I have been living peacefully and safely in a country which hardly notices the war.

Well that's all for now, take care of yourself and the parents
　Your devoted bro.

Monday 26 March 1945
Today was a hectic rush of clearance, packing and getting kit ready.

Tuesday 27 March 1945
I have been made Officer i/c Draft to the Middle East. This is very
gratifying as I have worked hard on it and I must try to hold the job
down without upsetting anyone.

Wednesday 28 March 1945
I finished my packing and after saying cheerio to one or two people we
left Heany for the last time at 0945. The train journey wasn't particularly
exciting but I stood on the end of the railway carriage and saw the sun set
for the last time on Rhodesia. It was most impressive and I felt the magic
of Africa.

Thursday 29 March 1945
At 1015 we landed at Kasama in Northern Rhodesia, for a cup of tea.
This place is in the Tsetse fly area. It is a well planned airfield in the
middle of the jungle. We had tea inside the shade of a native hut. We
passed over to Tanganyika, then quite suddenly there was a complete
break, giving way to a bare canyon made up of ridge upon ridge of sharp
volcanic lava, like ripples on a wet sandy beach. To our right, clearly
visible, was Kilimanjaro, the highest mountain in Africa – its peak
disappearing into cloud.
　Just before we landed at Nairobi we saw Mt Kenya a hundred miles to
the north, majestically marking, as it does, the Equator. Below us lay
Nairobi, rather neat and inviting after a day's flying over such desolate
country.
　The natives here in the hotels wear long white coats from their neck to
the floor, brought in by a broad green sash round the waist – which
makes them altogether more dignified than Southern Rhodesian natives.
　We sat and smoked our pipes with a cup of coffee on the verandah of
the Officers' Mess. It seemed incredible that we were a thousand miles
from where we had spent last night – tucked away in the centre of Africa.

Friday 30 March 1945
Glad to get airborne again! The pilot did some low flying over a swampy
island, in the middle of the Nile. On this island there must have been
thirty or forty elephants and we flew over them, and the whole herd
started galloping madly away.

Saturday 31 March 1945

As we descended to land at Cairo I could discern the royal palace and the sea. However I couldn't see the Pyramids as I had hoped. We went to Heliopolis where we disembarked and, as Officer i/c Draft, I got the forms organised before we split up. Eddy Wilmot and I are billeted together in D9 – a tent. I was exhilarated by the whole atmosphere of the place, a real encampment under canvas, in which were an assortment of RAF officers and other ranks who had just arrived from the Far East and Italy, South Africa and Blighty and were going to other equally far distant places.

I laced up the tent and made up the beds, feeling that here at last was the beginning not of hardship but of some sort of life under active service conditions, which might serve as an expiation of the luxuries of the last year.

Then Eddy came in and started moaning – 'conditions are disgraceful, the ablutions are shocking, the lavatories are beyond comment, these tents should have been replaced by huts . . .' All this only served to upset me and I began to feel depressed. I told him if he had any moans I didn't want to hear them.

This incident was a sideline to Eddy's character (which is otherwise very fine) and I was rather sorry.

We decided to go and have a jolly in Cairo. So John, Eddy and I got spurred up and boarded the famous Heliopolis–Cairo tram – the fastest in the world. They belted along at a goodly lick. A well-dressed man was sitting opposite us and gave us all sorts of information and was most helpful.

Cairo is a strange city, much more like London than Bulawayo or Salisbury. The streets are crowded with people right up to eleven at night, there are hundreds of cars and taxi-cabs. The streets are full of wondering gyppos selling 'feelthy pictures, mister', 'dirty magazines, sir', or just plain 'wallets and handbags'. The worst pests are the ones who want to clean your shoes. It is fatal to attempt to argue with their price.

Sunday 1 April 1945

Eddy, John and I had put our names down for the Padre's tour of the Pyramids. Before we left the Padre himself told us something about the place. The Pyramid we are visiting today was built by King Cheops, and it took 100,000 slaves 30 years to bring the stone slabs (weighing between 19 and 60 tons each) across the Nile from the quarry 16 miles away.

As there was a tremendous crowd there, we went straight to the Sphinx. It has a body of a lion for strength, the head of a man for wisdom, the features of a woman for beauty. It is actually the Sun God himself, and at sunrise a priest sat in the hollow of his head with the people gathered round and they prayed to the sun as it rose.

Its nose was struck off by a cannon ball from one of Napoleon's cannons in 1814.

Across from the Sphinx are the temples. We went down into the catacombs and the guide lit some magnesium wire so that we should be able to see the sparkling granite, which was an incredible sight – the old Egyptian drawings and scratchings were still discernible. They looked, surprisingly, not dissimilar from the ones on the cushion covers of the green couch by the door of my room at 40 Millbank.

Down into the tomb we went and there was the coffin of blocks of granite eighteen inches to two feet thick. We could just see over the edge and with the aid of a torch I saw parts of the skull, fragments of the spine and well preserved leg bones, of this ancient high priest who lay as he had done for 4,600 years.

I was surprised when I saw the Pyramids to find that they were not smooth. This of course was pure ignorance on my part.

When they were completed they were covered with alabaster, however in about the fifth century AD (or have I got it wrong?) Egypt was ravaged by barbarians (which ones I wonder? what ignorance!) who, realising the value of the alabaster, stripped it all off. The tip of the Pyramid is lower by some 40 feet.

The second Pyramid (erected for what King, I wonder – what wasted schooldays!) has actually still got its alabaster top.

We entered the Gizeh Pyramid and climbed up a ramp into the King's burial chamber, right dead in the centre of the Pyramid. There was nothing in the coffin of course.

The tramp of many feet and the cries of the guides added to the rich atmosphere. I almost felt as though I was present at the actual burial in another age, of the King himself, as part of the procession.

Hot and tired we reached the open air and went to the police cafe for tea where, not so many months ago, Churchill and Roosevelt sat and refreshed themselves at the foot of the Pyramid.[3]

We boarded the bus and went back to Cairo where we were dropped at a little bazaar behind the Palace hotel. The Padre has made an arrangement in the bazaar that in return for cheap prices, everyone who goes on his tour will be taken there. (They couldn't understand why the Padre didn't want a rake-off!) All I bought was a filigree silver bracelet, brooch and locket for Ma, made by children because adults haven't got the patience to do the job properly.

Tuesday 3 April 1945 (my twentieth birthday)
We had an early call at 0345 this morning and we had to complete our packing, hand in our bedding, have breakfast and catch the 0530 transport. I was unpardonably rude to Eddy, for which I felt ashamed of myself.

At the window of the canteen we got a 'mug o' char' and after serving us they immediately served half a dozen East African Negroes. I rejoiced to see such striking proof of the fact that we have left the colour bar behind us, below the equator. It made me unhappy in my heart to witness it and be a party to manifestations of racialism.

The Egyptians live in slums. That is the only word for it, for the houses are tumbledown and filthy, as opposed to the kraals of the Rhodesian Africans.

Thursday 5 April 1945

We reached Alexandria and there was a lot to be seen and smelt. The place very much resembled the East End of London, with the tannery and soap factory smells. After we had passed the docks and station, we reached Muhammed Ali Square. The bay is rather magnificent, curving gently round to enclose a basin full of Mediterranean blue. There is a fine promenade round it – like Bexhill I thought, and big buildings of yellow brick on the far side of the road. I should think that to a sailor on a ship anchored offshore Alex must look a wizard place, sunlit and clean with fine houses. But as we drove along the promenade we got a really close view of the place and it had none of these virtues. The streets were dirty and unkempt, the houses shabby and badly needing painting and general repairs.

We were dropped off at a club in the Barclay's Bank building just off Muhammed Ali Square. Here we had a fine lunch for about four bob and there was a band there, whose efforts were very pleasing.

Monday 9 April 1945

I have often thought about life in an Officers' Mess as a young pilot and it quite comes up to my expectations. The curtains are drawn and the electric light turned on, the mess fills up with groups of officers, some in khaki, some in blue, wearing battledress and service-dress.

The dinner gong rings and we all move into the dining-room which consists of a T-shaped table with little smaller ones beside, all lit by electric lamps, which give a cosy intimate atmosphere.

One F/Lt is shooting a line to a few others. He turns and I can see his DFC and 39–45 Star. Perhaps he has reason to show it.

There is rather a subdued buzz of people enjoying themselves to a background of music from a gramophone.

Friday 13 April 1945

We heard on the news today that President Roosevelt was dead. We were all gathered round the sergeants' mess when the eight o'clock news was read and the first, long item concerned his sudden collapse and death. Everyone was absolutely hushed for some minutes, a more marked silence than is ever accorded to great items of war news.

Without a doubt, everyone was as shocked and as sad as if Churchill himself had died.

Service life – particularly in air crew – gets you accustomed to death of friends and colleagues. It was rather strange and impressive to be there.

Saturday 14 April 1945
I reminisced with Mike aloud and compared notes of my growing fear of operations. The implications of fighting in the air – responsibility for the crew – the possibility of ditching, crashing, being taken prisoner, torture by Japs, these things are working on my imagination and frightening me.

Tuesday 17 April 1945
Today a Warwick, doing fighter exercises with a Corsair at 2,000 on the 'drome, was violently thrown about, it spun in and hit the ground just across the canal, about 300 yards from where I was in the cinema. The petrol tanks blew up and all the crew of eight (six officers and two sergeants) were either killed by the impact or burned to death – a grim business. We heard the thud, rushed out, and a great column of smoke was rising in the air.

As I watched I saw two or three bits of plywood and fabric floating down. They landed very gently a few yards away.

The fire burnt for some time. Two dead and half-burnt men were brought out.

Thursday 19 April 1945
Nick Vice (pronounced Vitzay) is a Yugoslav who shares our tent and his story runs like this.

He was a lieutenant in the Royal Yugoslav Air Force before the war. Germany invaded his country and she capitulated. The reconstituted Croat state sent most of its Air Force to Germany and he went with it. They were sent there ostensibly to train on German aircraft.

Nick was commissioned as a Lieutenant in the Luftwaffe. No doubt they called him a 'free Yugoslav'. Then he and his squadron were sent to the Russian front for propaganda purposes – all 'volunteers'. The squadron were flying Messerschmitt 109s and 110s. It was engaged in the offensive on the Crimea and in the autumn of 1942 Nick was in action. I asked him if he had any Russian planes to his credit – 'Yes.' 'How many?' 'That must remain a secret until after the war . . . '

Stalingrad came and Nick was ferrying aircraft to the front. Then one day he flew back to base and saw his chance. Stealing a sports-plane used by the squadron for communications purposes, he took off and set course for Turkey. 'I flew bloody low,' he said 'for the Germans were after me. I force-landed on a beach and the Turks interned me and I was later released under an agreement made with the Allies.' In Egypt, Nick was treated as a friendly POW. He gave the RAF plenty of information about the Luftwaffe and they asked him thousands of questions. Subsequently he was commissioned in July 1944 as a pilot officer in the RAF. ('I never seem to get any promotions' he said.) He was given three hours on Harvards and sent to Italy. Now he is back here waiting for an Operational Training Unit on Twins.

When I heard that he was fighting the Russians and had actually some 'victories' to his credit I was disgusted for here was a man so recently an enemy by alliance. But this mood passed and I am just a listener. He knew many people in the British embassy before the war (he is a cultured man) and these, coupled with his value to the British Intelligence, made him a valuable man and gained his commission for him.

I saw *Mrs Miniver* tonight – a fine film, true to life but lacking, because of its Hollywood origins, some of the finer details which might make it even better. I enjoyed it and find Greer Garson and Walter Pidgeon almost as perfect as a pair as one could wish to see.

Thursday 26 April 1945
After lunch we went across to the orderly room and learnt that we had got our leave, plus a railway warrant to Jerusalem. This is joyous news.

I washed and walked across for a drink and dinner with John Downham. I started talking with him about the native question. He has a very much greater grasp of the principles of African native policy than I have, which made me very ashamed and annoyed to think that I was so ignorant and *damned lazy*. He is a very intelligent fellow indeed who says little and when he opens his mouth speaks sound sense, based on some knowledge. The more I see of the industrious and intelligent university type the more I realise how I have wasted my opportunities.

Sometimes I get quite worried about my inability to get on with people. I really cannot get on with Eddy and I feel that it is not his fault. I get nagging, short-tempered and rude. He is patient most of the time and I wonder if I shall ever be able to get on with my crew later, and later on with my wife, if I am so intolerable to live with.

Friday 27 April 1945
Our leave to Jerusalem is all fixed up. Five of us are going – two pilots and three observers. We leave here the day after tomorrow and spend the night in Alex. On Monday we catch the train and should be in Jerusalem by 11.25 on Tuesday. I am also hoping to get to Capernaum, Jericho, Tel Aviv and generally round the place. I look on it almost as a pilgrimage. I am reading H. V. Morton's *In the Steps of the Master* and also one by Dr Lowdermilk of the US Soil Conservation Commission on *Palestine – a Land of Promise*, a consideration of the new Zionist settlement. I wrote a letter to Ma of our plans.

Saturday 28 April 1945
Tomorrow we go on leave.

The American–Russian link-up is broadening and Germany is rife with rumours and trouble. The Himmler offer[4] provides the headline of course, but whether or not this actual incident is true, it is indicative of the state of turmoil inside Germany. The end cannot be far off now.

I wonder if we shall be in Jerusalem to celebrate it – what an appropriate place it would be. In the evening we saw *The Lamp Still Burns* with Rosamund John and Stewart Grainger, produced by Leslie Howard. It was a fine tribute to nursing, and also pointed out some necessary reforms in a fine profession.

Monday 30 April 1945
I got up early this morning and cleaned everyone's shoes, partly because I consider that self-discipline is necessary as I hate cleaning shoes, partly because if this leave is going to be a success it must call for unselfishness from everyone and partly because I like being thanked for performing little services.

We travelled through the night to Ismailiya. Beside the line were many lights, of 'dromes and houses.

We had a drink in the dining car and came into El Kantara, where the train stopped. Here we had a proper meal at the NAAFI officers' restaurant and came back to the train. We settled down to sleep or attempt to sleep.

Tuesday 1 May 1945
I woke up early – it was cold. The train was steaming through the Sinai desert and by the light of the full moon I could discern an expanse of silver sand.

We got up and washed before the train pulled into Gaza. Here we had breakfast at the NAAFI and afterwards we wandered up and down the platform and were attracted by the quantity of lavatories. There was one for British officers, one for nursing sisters, one for women officers and one for Indian officers, and separate ones again for women other ranks, British other ranks and South African other ranks – class distinction *par excellence*. Beyond Gaza were green fields well cultivated – I was quite reminded of Blighty – the hedges were well tended, the farm houses fine stone buildings, that pink granite that in England we associate with churches and buildings like the New Bodleian. None of the tumbledown plaster and mud house-huts that mark the Egyptian agricultural land. I saw straight away that this was the land of promise.

At Lydda we changed and there were crowds of peasants waiting for the Jerusalem train, whom we took to be pilgrims to the city for the Eastern Holy Week. The journey from Lydda to Jerusalem was full of surprises. The train twisted and turned through the valleys and climbed painfully between the rough bare mountains. Finally, on the dominating summit we reached the Holy City.

After seeing the service police we started hunting for accommodation and we went to the Church Army hostel. This was very cheap and very comfortable.

After a bath, John and I walked round and visited the Zionist bureau in Ben Yehuda St. We found it closed but a middle-aged, grey-haired little Jew wearing a cap and rather resembling Trotsky opened the door. Inside we found a young lean-faced rather intellectual looking Jew. The first thing he asked us was 'Who sent you?' After explaining that we were on leave and wished to learn as much as we could about Zionism in Palestine, he became very helpful and suggested drawing up a programme for us. He told us the places we must visit including the Hebrew University.

Wednesday 2 May 1945
At 9 we went along to the Zionist office for a tour of the Hebrew University. We caught a bus and passed through New Jerusalem, past the British last-war cemetery, and were met by a student of the University.

He took us out to the open-air theatre, which commands such a fine view of the upper slopes of the Jerusalem hills, with the Dead Sea and the mountains of Moab in the far distance – a magnificent backcloth.

Here we sat and our friend spoke to us. His English was good and he told us of the founding of the University by Dr Chaim Weizmann[5] in 1917. It was dedicated by Arthur Balfour, whose Declaration is the kingpin in the Zionist argument.

He outlined the difficulties of the University – they had to integrate the various cultures represented by immigrants and refugees. They had to teach Hebrew so as to overcome language difficulties. He pointed out that whereas in a pioneering country the culture is usually the last thing to develop, in Palestine the University was one of the first institutions – built and maintained by voluntary contributions.

He ended by saying that the Hebrew University was creating an individual culture of its own and hoped to be able to give something to the world. He then showed us the Botanical Research Museum which consisted of a collection of flowers mentioned in the Bible – with their old and technical names.

There was a fine specialised scientific library consisting of thousands of books mainly in German, French and English, as Hebrew translations are not readily available, but there are some there already. We walked through the fine woods to some new excavations on the site of a cemetery of 100 AD. There was nothing much to see except the steps leading to the old vaults.

22 May 1945

My dearest family

To take your letters first, Pa. The grandest thing is to hear that you have applied for your release. As I said before, the emphasis is shifting – or rather has shifted – to the political field and clearly that is now your line once again. Your war record is magnificent. That is more than I can say for myself who have only been in for two years and never been near a German, nor heard a shot fired in anger.

The Blackpool Conference seems to be the beginning of a new chance for the Labour Party . . .

27 May 1945

My dearest family

We arrived at the Services Club in Tel Aviv on the sea front. We had elevenses there and the hostess came across and invited us to tea with her later – the Jewish hospitality in Tel Aviv is renowned. We accepted and went for a pre-prandial walk. We came to the fish fleet anchored in the harbour, with the fishermen mending their nets. It was very romantic. We saw the house of Simon the Tanner (whoever he may have been). Walking back – through the out of bounds area – we came back to the Club for lunch. Afterwards we walked round the streets of new Tel Aviv and I was very impressed with the architecture and planning of the town – a very fine example of what might be done at home.

On Saturday morning we had dragged ourselves out of bed at 5.15 am to climb the Mount of Olives. It was in the first grey of dawn that we walked through the streets which were awakening to the activity of a new day. We marched along the road that dropped into the Vale of Kedron, the redness of the dawn silhouetting the Mount of Olives above us.

We passed into the Garden of Gethsemane and started a long climb. The sun rose, alas, before we reached the top but looking back I saw a sight I shall never forget – the walls of the Holy City suffused with a bright golden hue and the roofs coloured the same tint.

27 May 1945

My dearest family

I left you in my last letter on the top of the Mount of Olives at dawn.

At lunch we revisited the old city of Jerusalem and found our way to the church of the Holy Sepulchre. I had been expecting to be disappointed. And it was frightful – orange peel and paper on the floor, shouting guides, jabbering masses, police and beggars. I lost the whole atmosphere of Christianity in the building which of all others in the world is – or should be – the focal point of Christian devotions. In the sepulchre itself, of all places, they collected money for the candles. I came away full of rage at this desecration and disappointment.

To the old city to watch the Abyssinian ceremony of 'searching for the body of Christ'. The Abyssinian monks (who are incredibly poor) live in hovels on the roof of the Holy Sepulchre and their church is a 'lean-to' tent. They broke away from the early Church in about the 5th century and have remained almost unchanged liturgically and doctrinally since then. For a while we could neither see nor hear what was going on. Then the crowd parted and from the church came one black brother, the Abyssinian patriarch, richly clad and followed by other Abyssinian dignitaries and monks. The music was provided by tom-toms, of all instruments, and the procession began.

On the morning of Monday May 7th we got up at about seven and went in for breakfast, which consisted of laban, bread and tea. Laban is a large dish of thick sour milk and lumps of cream cheese which I found hard to stomach but gallantly ate. After breakfast we set off through the fields, joined a dusty and rough road and walked across into Syria. We joined the road to Tiberias and got a lift in.

We hired a rowing boat and rowed out into the Sea of Galilee, trying to pick out Capernaum on the side of the lake further up. Coming in, we entered a little Arab restaurant for refreshment and as we walked towards the place, a Jew hurried up with a smile and said 'The war – finished!'

We didn't know whether to believe it or not so we smiled back. It seemed to be confirmed by a special edition of the paper. So we solemnly celebrated with an orange squash and ice cream each – hardly believing it could be true, hardly thinking of it, it seemed so remote. Returning later to Shaar Hagolan, via another settlement, we found them preparing for a festival to celebrate peace.

It was nearly ten o'clock and we understood that the King was to speak so we asked to listen to the wireless. As you know, he didn't, but in consequence we missed the gathering on the lawn when the leader of the settlement gave an address of welcome in Hebrew to 'the three English officers'. Think of the wonderful opportunity for replying with a speech – what we missed! I was disappointed.

Outside on the grass an effigy of the swastika was burned and the settlement crowded into the eating hall, where a little wine and lots of biscuits and nuts were laid along tables.

I asked for an orange squash and was given one, however one old boy emptied half a cupful of wine into it, and I drank it up – it was practically communion wine – rather an appropriate beverage to celebrate peace.

Then the national dances began – Germans, Czechs, Poles, Turks, Yugoslavs, all did their national dances. Then there was a pause and an announcement in Hebrew. Everyone looked at us and it was explained that the RAF officers would do an English national dance. Hurriedly deciding to do the boomps-a-daisy, two of us took the floor – it was an instantaneous success and everybody joined in.

That is how I celebrated the peace.
   Your devoted
      James (Tony)

At the end of my leave in Palestine I returned to Egypt and from there was posted home, returning in the troopship Carthage, *which was also carrying many servicemen who had fought with General Slim in Burma.*

The 1945 General Election campaign had already begun in Britain and it was decided to organise hustings on board ship, at which I spoke on 'Why I will vote Labour' (although at twenty I was too young to vote in the forthcoming Election!). The atmosphere on board ship was electric and it was at that moment that I realised that Labour might possibly win.

I was stationed at Harrogate on my return and came down to London to take part in the Election campaign, working in the Abbey Division of Westminster constituency. The Labour candidate was Jeremy Hutchinson, a young lawyer, and my job was to drive a loudspeaker van carrying his wife, Peggy Ashcroft, around the constituency.

She spoke to the Peabody housing estates about the need for a National Theatre and we drove to Downing Street, where Jeremy Hutchinson declared that he wished to canvass the occupant of No. 10, which was of course still Winston Churchill.

With no public opinion polls to guide us we never seriously thought we could win and there was a long gap between polling day, 5 July, and the declaration of the result, on 26 July, to allow the votes from troops serving overseas to be collected and counted.

On the day the Election results were announced I went to Transport House where they were flashed up on a screen using an epidiascope as they came in. As we sat in that darkened room and saw the Tory Ministers falling like ninepins, we knew there was a landslide Labour victory.

At one point the door opened and, blinking as he came out of the sunshine into the darkness, we saw the familiar figure of Clem Attlee, who had driven from Northolt Airport, after flying from Potsdam, where he had attended the Potsdam Conference with Truman, Stalin and Churchill.

The police car in which he travelled did not have a radio and it was only at that moment, as he came into the room, that he heard what had happened.

A BBC man came up to me with a microphone and said 'Will you shout, "Three cheers for the Prime Minister", but I was too shy to do so. That evening in Central Hall, Westminster, packed to the doors with Labour supporters, Clem Attlee walked on to the platform and amid tumultuous cheers announced that the King had asked him to form a Government.

Among his very first ministerial appointments before his return to Potsdam, this time as Prime Minister, was a new Secretary of State for Air: my father, then an air commodore in the RAF, complete with his Wings from the First World War, was sent to the Air Ministry.

At about that time, when the European War was over, and RAF pilots were being

VOTING PAPER

LABOUR
Total war on bad housing,
unemployment, poverty,
ignorance and ill health

X

TORY

Big business and landlords
blocking all progress

CHOOSE!

Published by the LABOUR PARTY, Transport House, Smith Square, London, S.W.1, and printed by ST. CLEMENTS PRESS, LTD., Portugal Street, Kingsway, W.C.2.

Election literature produced by

LABOUR ☒

- ● REAL PEACE—————————— *Cross*
- ● A GOOD HOME—————————— *Here*
- ● A GOOD JOB—————————— *for a*
- ● GOOD WAGES—————————— *Better*

Britain

- ● A CHANCE FOR THE CHILDREN————

WE have started to cross over from War to Peace. It won't be an easy crossing, but the main thing is to arrive at the right place. What you have always wanted is : Real Peace; a Good Home; a Good Job; Good Wages; and a Good Chance for the Children. A Labour Government would work to give you these things.

You didn't get them between 1918 and 1939 when the Tory Party had a majority in the House of Commons for 18 years.

Remember that, when the Tories try to wriggle out of their responsibility for the mass unemployment, the derelict areas, the poverty and social misery of those years.

Remember that, when the Tories tell you that your prosperity depends on private profit-making enterprise.

Remember that, when the Tories ask you to vote against Public Enterprise and Public Controls which will put the keys of economic power and prosperity into the hands of the people.

And Remember also, that political power for the Tories means economic power for Big Business.

p.t.o.

the Labour Party in 1945.

made redundant, I applied to transfer to the Fleet Air Arm in order to be posted to the Far East and was sent to the Royal Naval College for a 'knife and fork' course, so-called because the Navy did not believe that the RAF were gentlemen, and had to be trained as such if they were to be acceptable in the Senior Service.

From there I was posted to HMS Macaw, *a 'stone frigate' in Bootle, Cumberland and was then transferred briefly to Portsmouth to serve on HMS* Pretoria Castle, *a merchant ship converted with flight deck to become a mini aircraft carrier.*

I was serving in HMS Macaw when the atomic bomb was dropped on Hiroshima and heard the news in the ward room on the radio. That clearly meant that I would never be needed in the Far East. The Navy was only too glad to get rid of me and I was given a class B release to return to University which I did, that autumn. Post-war Oxford was quite unlike the University in pre-war years, for there was a telescoping of generations, servicemen who had served, and some of whom were wounded in the war rubbing shoulders with youngsters straight from school.

Thursday 7 June 1945
'Why I will vote Labour': Speech made from the 'hustings' on board the Carthage *en route for Britain*

'Until the Japs are defeated, they naturally remain problem Number 1. The Labour policy in this respect is the same as the Tory one. I do not for one moment believe that a coalition Government is necessary to handle this problem. It is in fact a Tory trick to persuade you that the Labour Party is putting Party before country.

'At home, we have the problem of release and resettlement. Beginning now, and reaching the climax at the end of the Japanese War, we have to demobilise our forces in a fair manner and resettle them in civil employment. The problems the resettlement will raise are manifold. Many have not got jobs to go back to. Many more, with jobs or without, will be returning to conditions which quite rightly they will not tolerate. This problem is very complex and closely bound up with industrial and economic problems generally. The comparatively simple task of getting you out of uniform will be achieved. The provision of full employment will depend on the proper operation of certain heavy industries and the right direction of the investment. There can be no proper resettlement of our soldiers into the post-war world without a radical change in our economic system.

'As regards this economic planning, I think we all agree that not many people hold our economic system, as it stood before the war, to have been a satisfactory one. A return to those bad old days is not only impossible but most undesirable. War – as you know – is an artificial boom, because production and employment are maintained by the never-ending call for more ships, tanks, aircraft and guns. Men and women are all provided with as much employment as they need in the armed forces and industry.

'After the war the needs of reconstruction, too, will call for tremendous efforts. But if the problems of economic planning are not faced, a great slump will follow that boom and we shall all over again witness all the misery that it involves.

'The Labour Party's policy is simple – take over coal, power, transport and steel, which employ such a large number of our people: by directing investment all along the peaks and depths of the vicious trade cycle it can gradually be ironed out. By maintaining employment at a steady relative level the ensuing prosperity will gradually raise the absolute level. The incentive of work under these conditions would be far greater than under the old system – when the role of an employee was to enrich his employer in booms and live on the dole in slumps.

'Opportunities for bettering yourself would be just as great, with the added advantage of an assured job and the knowledge that your efforts were directed towards the raising of the general standard – our old friend, the spirit of service.

'In 1944, 3.75 million days were lost by strikes, nearly twice as many as in 1943. Yet 1944 was the vital year, the climax of our attacks on Nazi Germany and I am not prepared to believe that the workers were sufficiently lacking in patriotism to disregard that fact – something is definitely wrong. It is impossible to identify the interests of the miners with that of the mine owners. The workers' production committees and the trade unions generally are very capable of assuming greater industrial responsibility.

'In this way, the farmers of this country have done a tremendous job. They have enabled shipping space – that would otherwise have been allocated to bringing our food – to bring over arms and men from the New World, with which we have defeated the enemy. We cannot expect, then, the farmers to fall back again into conditions they suffered for years before the war, when agriculture was neglected.

'The Labour Party has taken a hand in promising that prices will be guaranteed. Many whole-time or part-time agricultural workers in this war may want to settle on the land. The Labour Party gives full encouragement to these people.

'One of the most pressing problems of all is housing. Before the war, slums were a running sore – disease and squalor were rampant in many areas. The submerged tenth were a forgotten minority. The position is even more serious now than it was then. Inability to effect ordinary repairs and the damage caused by enemy action is incalculable. Are we going to let Jerry Builder do his worst and breed a new series of slums for the next generation or are we going to plan decent homes for the future?

'There will be no more Jerry Builder with the new regulations. Not only will his physical efforts be checked so that you will be protected against having to live in rotten houses but on the financial side his irresponsible investments will be checked for the public good.

'The control of land to prevent racketeering will also be necessary. The Labour Party does not intend to nationalise all land, yet – but control is very necessary.

'Europe lies devastated and the worst legacy of all is the hatred of one nation for another.

'We must not let the situation deteriorate. This is the second war to end war. Let it be the last.

'Just as we as a nation cannot let our economy slide, we as citizens cannot permit our own interests to be jeopardised by irresponsible international cut-throat economics. For make no mistake; the throat that is cut is your own.

A touch of socialist realism from Transport House, 1945.

'The Labour Party stands for international co-operation and will make a stand against the great combines which menace the consumer.

'The Labour Party stands for a policy of collective security, based on a world organisation with the will and power to prevent aggression.

'The eyes of the world are on the Commonwealth and Empire. In Africa, we see the first stirrings of native political consciousness – a natural and healthy response to our occupation. In India things have gone farther. I do not propose, before all of you who have served in India, with your wider knowledge of Indian problems, to go into any details now. But I do say – the policy of Colonel Blimp is long outmoded. You will remember what Colonel Blimp said: "I stand for no interference with the right of the Indians to do as they are damn well told." The Labour Party has drawn up plans for developing Africa economically and with this great untapped demand before us we have a promise of great prosperity for ourselves, for themselves and for the world. The same applies to India. The Labour Party wishes to see the unification of India and her emergence as a full Dominion.'

Friday 22 June 1945
Westminster Labour Party meeting with Mrs Hutchinson for afternoon, radio van.

March 1946 – Oxford
Last night I heard that Group Captain Cheshire was going to give a talk on the atomic bomb and I decided to go along.

I stepped into the University Air Squadron building and there were the pictures of past members of the Air Squadron around the walls and amongst them a picture of me. There were hardly more than one in six still alive.

The CO came in and asked us not to drop our cigarette ends on the floor, then he introduced Cheshire.

Cheshire is a young man of perhaps 26. He came up as an undergraduate in 1937 and joined the Air Force. He was described as the greatest air bomber pilot ever and he is probably the most highly decorated officer of the war. He started off his talk by describing more or less factually the events leading up to 'Operation Manhattan'.

In 1944 the Superfort bomber made a direct raid on Japan possible and the Pacific strategy was organised to procure bases for this. Guam was selected a year later as the base for the atomic raids. The utmost secrecy was required and no one, however senior, outside the project, was informed. They got the mechanism for the bomb transported out there, but the problem was moving the atomic cores. One went by cruiser, the other by C54 US Air Transport – carried by a Colonel and a Sergeant – in a little yellow box.

Cheshire did not go on the Hiroshima raid. He described the Nagasaki one. The aircraft (two for observations, one for the bomb) rendezvoused over South Japan at 9 o'clock and went in to the target at 10. They were flying at 34,000 feet. The kite was pressurised, heat and soundproofed so they were wearing khaki slacks and shirts, with no oxygen or intercom. They put dark glasses on, so dark that the sun was just a blur in the centre and when the bomb went off it lit up the whole scene as if a light had been turned on in a darkened room. The heat generated is 10 million degrees C, very nearly as hot as the internal heat of the sun. After three minutes they were able to take off their glasses.

At the moment the bomb dropped there was a flash of fire and a column of smoke rose at about 20,000 feet a minute, to 60,000 feet, where it flattened out into a mushroom shape. They dropped radio sets with instruments attached to record pressure waves, etc.

Cheshire said quite plainly he did not want to discuss the ethics of the thing but he sobered everyone up by putting to us quite plainly the facts. If we have another war it will mean the end of our physical civilisation, for man might survive but buildings can't. He spoke quietly and slowly. 'Realise this, that if these bombs are ever going to be used there is not much point in anything that you are doing now.'

He was quite remote and above us and no doubt the whole world seemed as unreal to him as he to it.

Notes

Chapter One

1.   (p.64) Jan Smuts was Prime Minister of the Union of South Africa, 1919-24 and 1938-48. An Afrikaner by birth he fought against the British in the Boer War, but during the First World War he commanded the Imperial troops in East Africa against the Germans. He died in 1950. He favoured a more conciliatory attitude towards Africans without conceding equality of races.

2.   (p.73) Draza Mihailovich was leader of the royal Yugoslav underground during World War II, forming the Chetniks who were initially supported by the British Government. When he was suspected of collaborating with the Germans, Churchill transferred his support to Tito and his Communist Partisans. Mihailovich was executed in 1946 for treason.

3.   (p.83) On 20 February 1945 Winston Churchill and President Roosevelt met in Cairo to discuss the war against Japan.

4.   (p.87) In April 1945 Heinrich Himmler, the Nazi Minister of the Interior under Hitler, tried to open peace negotiations with the Allies, via the mediation of Sweden. Hitler, hearing of this, ordered his arrest and Himmler fled from Germany, but was arrested by the Allies, and committed suicide while in Prison in May 1945.

5.   (p.88) Chaim Weizmann, a research chemist born in Poland, was a prominent Zionist, who advised the British Cabinet in World War One and was largely responsible for winning from the British Government the Balfour Declaration 'viewing with favour the establishment in Palestine of a national home for the Jewish people.' He founded the Weizmann Institute and became the first President of Israel, 1948.

2
Marking Time
1946–1949

In the summer of 1946 Peter Blaker, a fellow student and friend, asked me if I would like to travel with him by car to Belgium, in the liberation of which he had participated, because he wished to look up some friends.

We went in our car by ferry, toured around Belgium, and visited the friends he had known during the war.

While we were there it was arranged that we should go down a coal mine, the first one I had ever seen.

July 1946

Peter Blaker and I planned this trip to Belgium during the course of the summer term at Oxford. We made enquiries everywhere and got passports, visas and tickets, and in the day or so left before our departure we collected camp equipment, compass, car, maps and dictionary.

We set off on 1 July for Folkestone; the packet was the Belgian ship *Prinses Josephine Charlotte*. We docked at Ostend and disembarked in blazing sunshine. It was a Mediterranean day. An AA man was there ready to advise us on regulation and rationing concerning the car. By ten past six we were on our way through Ostend to Bruges.

The first thing that struck me was that every bridge had been blown up and we crossed over the many canals and rivers by Bailey bridge or other makeshift bridges.

We settled on the Hôtel du Grand Sablon in Bruges, changed for dinner and came down to a fine meal in uniform.

We sallied forth in the car in search of a ration card. The '*sens unique*' signs puzzled us for a while but the patient policemen were very tolerant of the two mad Englishmen (GB on the car stands for *grande bête* they told us afterwards) and we got along famously.

We were directed to the HQ of the police and we were ushered into the office of the Chief of Police, a genial grey-haired man with an enormous brow. He asked us if we liked Belgium, what we had done '*pendant la guerre*', and how we felt about the international situation. Did we think the Russians meant war? Everyone in Belgium thought we should have to fight the Russians – the hated Russians – 'it is inevitable'. We assured him that in England it was different. We must have peace. It is possible, it is necessary. There is the atomic bomb. 'The atomic bomb – it is no good,' came the response. 'The latest test – it is a failure.'

Bonjour et bon voyage, messieurs. We went off, all the constables smiling and laughing.

We found the food rations office and bought stamps in an old building by the canal. Wandering back to the middle of the town, I bought a beautiful pipe and a phrase-book of Flemish. Peter cashed a travellers' cheque and we packed up and paid at the hotel. Then set off in search of a restaurant for lunch. We found a place with a fat French proprietress and her skinny giggly 35–40-ish maid.

We had an omelette each with chips swimming in fat, and got out our maps. The maid came and said she liked English boys. She knew a soldier from Liverpool – he was so nice.

We didn't quite know how to ask for the bill at this stage. It was a long struggle. We tried *le menu, le compte, le cheque, le note.*

We took the road towards Zoute where cheerful seaside villas caught our attention. They are wonderfully painted and quaintly designed, no two are the same in design or colouring. On many villas we saw the skull and crossbones and DANGER – MINEN written on them, reminding us that the whole coastal area had been heavily fortified and defended.

Thursday 4 July 1946
We woke about 9 and drove to the beach, where we tried to get clean by having a bathe and then I sat on the bonnet with two canvas buckets full of sea water for a shower and a wash.

We filled the car up with petrol and set off for Antwerp; it was a hot day and we joined the main Bruges–Ghent highway where we came to the Canadian military cemetery at Adegem and there Peter located the grave of his friend who had been killed in Belgium. The cemetery was beautifully kept and on some of the graves there were some flowers and messages from people who had known the person during the liberation. Perhaps the most impressive graves of all were those simply marked 'unknown airman', or just 'unknown', with the date. There were photographs of some of the men hung on the cross. We were greatly moved and drove in silence for a while.

Saturday 6 July 1946
We stopped a while at the little village of Godinne and gazed across the Meuse at the rough rock which rose behind the line of houses and the railway. A tug with barges passed.

We drove off into Dinant and climbed up hundreds of steps to the great stone-built citadel which commands the town. The Belgians take enormous trouble to make their sights interesting. They had a tableau of skirmishes with Germans in 1914, with half a dozen soldiers in each of their respective uniforms, complete with rifles and bayonets and a suitable number of dead and bleeding men lying about. There was also a more recently constructed one of a Nazi torture chamber in Holland which was horribly realistic, with some poor wretches being branded, suspended and beaten by a few thugs in German uniforms. The citadel has been besieged seven times (or is it seventeen) starting with Charles the Bold centuries ago and ending with the Americans in 1945.

Descending to the river level, we had lunch and took a snap of the blown-up bridge across the Meuse, and the main hotel which the Germans had used as Gestapo HQ during the war and had burnt before leaving lest any of the documents should fall into Allied hands. The occupation seemed so remote, we could hardly believe it only came to an end two years ago.

At Ciergnon we came across our first sign of battle. A German Tiger tank lay by the roadside knocked out by a shell which had split and jammed the turret. We stopped and climbed over it, examining the damage inside. Nothing movable was left there, so our hopes of finding a vehicle intact or a Jerry tin hat were dashed.

We had a cup of coffee and a large slice of wild strawberry tart and set off for La Roche-en-Ardennes. La Roche was hidden away in the bed of a river. We could see as we swung round the last part of the road that it was heavily damaged but it was not until we were actually in the place that we could see that it was virtually destroyed. Whole areas of streets were flat. The centre of the town existed no more, and the bridges were gone. I felt quite ashamed at turning up here on holiday, when the townsfolk were living in shacks amidst the ruins of their homes. Here, as at Rochefort, we heard of street fighting and artillery duels, the burning of buildings by friend and foe in retreat. Apparently La Roche was recaptured by the Germans during Rundstedt's Christmas offensive in 1944 and held for only six days. Most of the damage, tragically, had been done by the American guns in the assault.

We set off for an evening expedition to Bastogne. On the way we saw more signs of battle. Across the river there was a knocked-out German tank. On our side were two burnt-out American armoured cars. I imagine that the skirmish had taken place during the last German retreat to the Ardennes, when an advanced patrol of Yanks had caught up with some Huns on the run; but it might of course have been the other way round.

Treading carefully in fear of mines, we examined some farm buildings. Inside there were lots of empty tins, the straw lay about and it might all have happened a week before.

We looked at the German tank and by it we found a pile of rusty live ammunition. A belt of machine-gun bullets, a few shells and a couple of egg grenades were in a heap. I took one bullet from the belt and kept it.

We went on towards Bastogne and just as we entered it we noticed a field on the right littered with tanks, guns and armoured cars. We jumped out and had a good look round. I was extremely lucky and found three Yanks tin hats. We chose the two best and left the third.

Monday 8 July 1946 – Visit to Belgian coal-mine
Monsieur Volders, an engineer, tall and broad, a jovial trade union leader type in his late thirties, leaned towards us and said '*Enchanté*' as we shook hands. We knew then that the phrase definitely was not – as we had previously thought – sentimental and effeminate. Volders had visited England and spoke good English.

We dispersed after this and Bastin led us to the engineers' changing room, where a complete miners' get-up was given us. From the changing rooms we went to the pit head.

We were told that the mine used 4,500 free workmen, including heads of departments, engineers and general employees, 1,800 German POWs, 600 *Belges inciviques* – collaborators sentenced to this form of punishment. Some of them have got 20 years to do. I questioned this and Volders said with a smile, 'Don't you think it is long enough?'

We descended in a matter of a few seconds to the main gallery 800 metres down. Here we found ourselves in a sodium-lighted tube station – that was how it appeared, with four to six railway lines side by side. They are very proud of their method of supporting the roof with concrete blocks and it is apparently streets ahead of English mines. The pressure was so great there was no alternative to concrete.

We clambered into an empty truck and we passed from the larger gallery into a smaller one and disentrained. As we were going to walk for a while Bastin ordered us to strip some of our clothing.

We found a gang of collaborators working. Their job was to dynamite the rock out, clear it away and as each section was emptied, install the guiders and fit the concrete blocks. Bastin got into a long argument with them over wages and conditions. He explained the arrangements as we walked away. They are paid full wages by the firm – but the Government gets the money. Part is granted to them for cigarettes, and sundry expenses from the canteen, part is sent to their families and part is kept by the Government as a gratuity when they get released.

They were not miners by profession – one of them was a student, another a tailor and so on. I enquired of Bastin for what offences they had merited so heavy a punishment. He told us that some had helped the Germans in one way or another, others had joined the anti-Bolshevik brigade, and so on. The poor men had done the latter to earn a little money. Gradually the injustice of it all came home to me. One could understand them punishing or even executing those who had given away to the Germans RAF escapees. But the members of the anti-Russian brigade, or the people who had carried on with their work and had thus come in contact with the occupiers in a business capacity – they surely couldn't be blamed for seeking to live ordinary lives, since the ultimate liberation seemed so far ahead.

But the *inciviques* were smiling and looking quite fit and happy.

From here we went on to a seam of coal that was being dug. The workers at this point were German prisoners of war who looked fit and well and even cheerful. I didn't feel so sorry for them, partly because they have in a sense deserved some sort of expiation for their crimes, partly because they would only have a comparatively short time to do as they would be sent home when peace was signed, and partly because by this stage I was beginning to feel quite sorry for myself as it was sweaty and sticky and tiring.

We clambered up a slope, we crouched and crawled and stumbled each with a lamp in hand. It reminded me of the ascent up to the Pyramid of Gizeh. Beside us ran a moving conveyor belt which carried the coal down. We finally reached the gang of miners working on the face itself. This lot were free Belgians, and their attitude was friendly and cheerful. The job is so hard, so dirty, so long, so noisy, under such bloody conditions, that the spirit which prevailed was of comradeship and good feelings of brothers in adversity.

Bastin showed us the caterpillar coal saw which undercut the seam so as to enable the drillers to work out the stuff above. The air was thick with dust, of course, but fresh air was brought by pipe to them as they moved forward and fresh sections were joined every day.

I shall never forget that trip and I hope the details of it remain fresh in my mind. Even in this, one of the most modern and efficient mines in Western Europe, conditions are appalling and the poor fellows who are compelled by economic pressure to work there deserve the best that we can give them. The firmness of my belief in socialism was strengthened beyond the power of an economist or padre to strengthen it.

We bathed and dressed in the engineers' changing room and went back to lunch at the Bastins' house.

The bitterness in Belgium and in most of Europe today between the various grades of resistance is very regrettable though I suppose that I, who have never lived in an occupied country, cannot understand or appreciate the heights of feeling on this matter, of those who have been through it all.

Normally all Belgium is Catholic (it was one of the major contributing factors to the outbreak of the liberation war against the Dutch in 1830), except for the socialist and Communist elements. Now the right-wing policy of the Vatican is estranging the resistance groupings even more, among whom, of course, are a great number of Catholic liberals.

The Russian prisoners of war had been made to work in the mines by the Germans who, being short of troops, had used Belgians to guard them. Many escaped of course. The Belgians helped them whenever they could and lots got away. On one occasion a recaptured Russian gave away his helper and this caused great bitterness.

At the end of the day we slept in great comfort at the Bastins', after a full and interesting experience.

Saturday 13 July 1946
We got to Ostend just in time, got aboard and found a seat.

The arrival at Folkestone was dismal indeed, the formalities of immigration and customs being badly handled and irritatingly executed. We cursed this country – its traffic regulations, its drabness, its officials and above all its women.

We finally crawled into London with the car, like us almost a wreck, sans hooter, sans reverse.

Sunday 25 August 1946
Last Saturday I went out with B. I didn't realise till I came to pay the bill (£3/10/-) what a waste of time and money it had been. The truth of the matter is that she is a shallow, selfish, dull and expensive little girl. She is very physically attractive, but she has no sort of personality, sparkle or life and absolutely no character. She has got nothing original to say about anything. I found conversation extremely difficult. It petered out almost entirely after a time. What is more she was utterly frigid and didn't respond at all to the pressure of my arm while we were dancing.

In July 1945, Father had been appointed Secretary of State for Air in the Labour Government. Shortly afterwards, he was sent by the Prime Minister, Clem Attlee, to Egypt to negotiate a revision of the 1936 Anglo-Egyptian treaty, with special reference to the future of the Sudan, then under an Anglo-Egyptian condominium, and to discuss the future of our Tel-El-Kabir base, the presence of which had caused a great deal of resentment in Egypt. Egypt was in effect a British protectorate, over which King Farouk was the titular head. Father, who had been in Egypt as a student at the turn of the century and served there in the First World War, was a firm opponent of imperialism.

While Father was away, Attlee decided to reorganise the Services and appoint a Minister of Defence in the Cabinet in place of the three Service Ministers, including Father, who had traditionally sat in Cabinet. Attlee also wanted younger ministers and Father was by then sixty-nine. Father returned from Egypt to be given this news in a rather peremptory way. In his very last days of office, Father went to Paris where the Peace Conference was in progress and took me as an unofficial ADC.

3 October 1946

An hour and three-quarters ago I met Father at Northolt on his return from Egypt. He has been out there since April, negotiating the treaty and this recall coincided with a crisis out there. The talk and gossip in the papers about Father's departure from the Cabinet has been incessant since last year and recently has reached higher ferocity. I knew that something was in the air and was wondering just how much of it was true. We lunched at the airfield with Sir Ronald Campbell, the Ambassador to Egypt, officials and the members of Father's staff. Then we got into the Rolls with the flag flying. Father spoke up straight away. 'This is the end of the Air Ministry job I should think.'

It appears that in April, a couple of nights before Father left for Egypt, Clem called him over to see him and said, quite bluntly, 'Bevin wonders if you would like to take over the chairmanship of the British Council . . . Younger men, you know.'

'I refused that post during the war,' Father responded. 'I was happier as a pilot officer.'

And that was that – not a word about Egypt or the treaty, no mention of good luck, or a kind wish.

He returned in June and left again for Egypt in July. Clem sent for him again; this time on the very eve of his departure. When Father went into the PM's study, he said 'Well Clem, I'm off to Egypt again tomorrow.'

'Are you?' said Clem. 'I thought Bevin was sending someone else!'

So all these months he has been alone in the Middle East, with this appalling threat hanging over him and no word of good will from his colleagues.

11.20 pm

Father returned from seeing the PM at 4.30. Clem had said to him, 'I am reorganising the Service Ministries and I don't want you.' Father accepted it of course without question, simply adding that he was in full agreement with the policy of putting youth at the prow. But what would be the reaction in Cairo of the dismissal of the man with whom they had been negotiating for the last six months? Clem hadn't thought of that and muttered that he thought that all that business would be settled by the Egyptian leaders coming here and dealing with Bevin personally.

That was that. Nothing further was offered or contemplated.

Later, a crawling phone call from the Foreign Secretary's Private Secretary who intimated that Bevin was most anxious to see Father in Paris tomorrow. Father accepted this and said he would be taking two assistants (Wood and me).

4 October 1946

Up early this morning and I went to Moss Bros to hire a hat. Wood,

Father and I left the Air Ministry in the Rolls with Flt. Sgt. Jacob – flying the Secretary of State's ensign for the last time.

We took off at 11.43 from Croydon and landed in France at 12.48. In less than half an hour we were at the King George V Hotel, lunched in Father's suite, and Father went off to see Bevin quite early.

He told me what took place.

Bevin said to him, 'Well, Wedgie, this must be a disappointment to you, coming back after six months' hard work to get the sack. You've done a good job.' These were kind words and Father deeply appreciated them. Bevin said he had hoped that the reshuffle could have been postponed until after the negotiations but that had not been possible. He wished however for Father to carry on in an advisory capacity.

Father said that this was no good.

The next development was at about five, when the PM's Private Secretary rang up to ask Father to alter his letter of resignation and add the words 'of which I entirely approve' after the phrase 'reorganisation of the Defence Ministries'.

Father said that he had not even seen the new scheme and he would not alter his letter of resignation. 'No. No. No, I will NOT.'

The next thing was that Clem himself rang up and said, 'Look here Wedgie, your letter looks as if you didn't approve of my changes – but surely you can't object.'

Father replied, 'My dear PM, I knew nothing about the new defence scheme, I was not consulted or advised and I have told you that I am all for close defence planning but I don't think that having Bert [A. V. Alexander] – a well-known enemy of the Air Force – in charge, will work. I think it is disastrous and I will not alter my letter.'

Father told me that the truth is the PM doesn't think Father can help him or be of any use and wants to get rid of him.

We dined with Mr and Mrs Bevin, Sir Ronald Campbell, Sir Walter and Lady Smart, Mr and Mrs Pierson Dixon, Sir Claude and Lady Russell, Frank Wood, Henniker-Major and Mrs Alexander.[1]

The conversation was dull, very dull, but Mrs Bevin and Mrs Alexander were most pleasant. Mrs Alexander (aged seventy-five) has been in Paris for seven weeks and she is loving it. The cost of her upkeep obviously never occurs to her and she is invited everywhere and goes out to night clubs – and on her own admission has come in at 3.30 am with gifts of roses on a silver tray.

She tried to persuade me to find myself a pretty young driver and go out for the evening with her. Mr Dixon was privately shocked but pretended to think it a great joke! The wives of Labour Cabinet ministers must be gravely embarrassing to the smooth public school Guards types who have to accompany them.

Ernie Bevin is a graceless man, with Ladies Smart and Russell on either side, but he kept up his end well on the subjects of rationing and controls, and the £75 limit. I heard him say, 'If you relaxed these measures a certain useless and extravagant class would spend English money here on goods, take them back to England and re-sell them.' Society women cut no ice with the Bristol docker, and good luck to him.

Extract from Isis, *an Oxford University magazine, 29 January 1947*

There is still, apparently, a Conservative majority in the Union. At least, on Thursday a strongly worded anti-Government motion was passed by 205 votes to 178 after a debate which was on the whole lacking in vigour.

The Hon G. E. Noel (Librarian) moved 'That His Majesty's Government is displaying dangerous incompetence and foolish indifference in the handling of Imperial and Commonwealth affairs'.

The Librarian declared that in presiding over the decline and fall of the British Empire, the Government were presiding over the decline of a great influence for world peace. It was easy enough to throw away the old Imperial responsibilities, but it was the Government's task to live up to them.

While he did not seek to defend Kiplingesque imperialism the Librarian claimed that the idea of a British Commonwealth was still worth working for. He was best on the subject of India, making out a strong case against premature withdrawal. The Librarian might have done better to retain his well-established practice of introducing an occasional word of wisdom amid the spontaneous flow of his wit.

Some people make idealism sound corny. Mr A. N. Wedgwood Benn (Treasurer) made it sound commonsense. He kept more closely to the motion than the Librarian, pointing out the economic implications of Imperialism and the attempt the Government was making to raise the standard of living of the Colonies. Many of the measures criticised by the proposition had been planned in the days of the Coalition government. On balance, said the Treasurer, our policy had been sane and high-principled. A little more fluency and the Treasurer would have become a really first-class speaker.

Oxford Union

16-2-47

My dearest old Proff

It is a month since I got your letter. I am sorry to hear that you had a bad cough. The family assure me it is nothing to worry about. I feel very cut off here.

I daresay that Father has told you that the Soviet MPs will be in Oxford on Feb 27th, the date of the Presidential debate at the Union and the President is inviting them to dinner. Afterwards they will come to the debate on the Government's home policy at which I shall be speaking first, and Sir Hartley Shawcross last. It will be very good fun, though I don't expect that they will understand why there is more than *one* candidate standing for election. They will be bringing their own interpreters and a sort of Nuremburg system of microphones and head sets with them. If I get the chance I will try and ask them if there is any chance of them fixing up opportunities for undergraduates to visit the Soviet Union in the summer.

I wish that you could come to that debate Proff.

Ever your old friend, James

18 July 1947

Today I witnessed an historic occasion – the formal ending of British imperial dominion in India. This took place a little after 12.30 o'clock in the King's Robing Room under the Victoria Tower, which has, since the bombing of the House, acted as the Lord's Chamber.

Headed by the mace-bearer carrying the mace, and followed by the Speaker walking beside Black Rod, came the Commons. At the entrance of the makeshift Chamber, the mace was taken to one side and the Speaker in his robes and wig entered the bar of the House. I was standing at the foot of stairs leading to the Gallery and the Prime Minister, the Chancellor of the Exchequer, the Minister of Food amongst others passed within a foot of me. At this point I went aloft to my place in the Gallery and watched the remains of the proceedings from there, between Peter Kirk, son of the Bishop of Oxford, and my brother, David. The Lord Chancellor spoke again.

'My Lords, spiritual and temporal, burgesses and members of the Commons, you are assembled here to hear the Royal Assent given to sundry Acts passed by both Houses of Parliament.' The reading Clerk then rose and read the Royal Commission.

'I George VI, Defender of the Faith, by the Grace of God King of the United Kingdom of Great Britain and Northern Ireland and the British Dominions beyond the seas . . . etc. etc.' (no mention of the Emperor of India).

The appointment of the Royal Commissioners was then read and as each was mentioned, the Clerk bowed to the peer in question, who removed his hat and inclined his head in recognition.

For example, 'And my right well-beloved cousin William Wedgwood, Viscount Stansgate', etc.

The Commission ended with the words 'signed by the King under his seal manual'. The Lord Chancellor then ordered the reading Clerk to enumerate the Acts that had been passed.

The reading Clerk then rose, bowed and read out the Acts one by one, including 'The Indian Independence Act', and bowed. The Clerk of the Parliaments then turned and faced the Commons at the bar and without bowing he spoke clearly the words of royal assent in Norman French 'Le Roy le Veult.' When all the Acts had been read the Speaker turned and left the Chamber, followed by the Commons.

Incidentally, among the bills enacted was the Trafalgar Estates Bill which concluded the generous arrangements made for the Nelson family after Nelson's death 142 years ago. The House of Peers remained seated, the Royal Commissioners left and the Lord Chancellor resumed the Woolsack until a noble Lord moved the adjournment.

Churchill was not there, nor were Simon, Salisbury, Halifax, Wavell, Templewood, nor any others. This was a sad way to treat a fine and statesmanlike piece of liberating legislation. What worried them no doubt was a short sentence from sub-section 2 of Clause 7 – 'the assent of the Parliament of the United Kingdom is hereby given to the omission from the Royal style and titles of the words *Indiae imperator* and the words *Emperor of India* and to the issue by His Majesty for that purpose of this royal proclamation under the great seal of the realm.'

In June 1947 I wrote a self-mocking piece for the 'Isis Idol' page of the Isis *magazine*

The facts about Anthony Benn's early life are simple and unexciting. Born in London just over twenty-two years ago he was educated at Westminster, a period unmarked by any distinction in the fields of school activity in which he participated. He left utterly convinced of the desirability of co-education.

. . . Along with most of the war-time generations, he spent his three terms [at New College] in a leisurely way before joining the RAF in Summer 1943. He spent a year in Southern Rhodesia, learning to fly which he thought was great fun, though his feelings were not shared by his new instructors.

His extremely youthful appearance had at least one amusing repercussion. After his first round of the cook-house, as a very new Pilot Officer, the sergeant-cook offered him an orange to take away. Benn accepted this gratefully and fled, blushing furiously. From there he went to the Middle East. His stay in the Middle East was brief and pleasant. It included a leave in Palestine, where he and two others stayed over VE Day as guests in a Jewish communal settlement. At the victory festivities there, the Jews of all nations did their traditional folk dances and the three English officers were asked to do an English national dance. Boompsa-daisy is said to be still popular in the Sea of Galilee area.

Posted home in time for the General Election he drove a

loudspeaker van round his local constituency in Westminster and soon afterward, full of boyish enthusiasm, transferred to the Fleet Air Arm for service in the Far East. However, armed with the atom bomb, the UN Supreme Command decided that Benn's services could be dispensed with and he was sent on indefinite leave . . .

What can be said of him as a person? He dresses scruffily, talks too much and is rather boisterous. His interests are mainly political (being a rather idealistic socialist) but he also enjoys discussing a great many other subjects of which he is even more ignorant. He collects pipes, believes in complete social and political equality as between the sexes, gets rather too easily embarrassed for comfort and laughs at his own jokes. Being by nature somewhat unmethodical he attempts to organise his life with three mechanical devices. A petty cash account (to keep him economical), a job list (as a substitute for imperfect memory) and a time chart (to give him an incentive to work).

Of the future he does not like to think overmuch. He is on the list of Labour Party parliamentary candidates (potential) and hopes to make something of this when he has had time to supplement his rather inadequate PPE education, by gaining a little first-hand knowledge and experience of some aspect of political activity.

Over the autumn and winter of 1947–48 I led a debating tour of sixty American universities, organised by the Institute of International Education in New York, and the debating team sailed in a liberty ship, USS Marine Tiger *which had been used as a troopship in the war. The conditions were immensely crowded as we slept in bunks grouped in five one above the other, and eight in a mess deck.*

On board was Maynard Krueger, who had stood as the Vice-presidential candidate in 1944, when Norman Thomas was the socialist candidate for the presidency, and we had many political discussions on our way out.

My companions in the Oxford debating team were Edward Boyle and Kenneth Harris. Kenneth subsequently wrote a book about the trip called Travelling Tongues.

Among the debates in which we took part was one on the desirability or otherwise of an Anglo-American alliance (which subsequently appeared in the form of NATO), on the question of the nationalisation of basic industries, and on the merits of a practical versus liberal education. This tour took us right across the USA and allowed me to visit and stay with Professor Reinhold Niebuhr, an internationally respected theologian of the Union Theological Seminary in New York who, with his wife Ursula, then teaching at Radcliffe College, was a very old family friend. I also took the opportunity while in the States to visit my cousin Betty Shinkman and her husband Paul.

My manuscript diary for this trip was necessarily brief and factual as we had an exhausting travel schedule almost every day, by train, plane and bus, and I had the additional responsibility of keeping records of our finances for the trip.

Saturday 27 September 1947

The first day of our American trip. We got aboard at Southampton at 12.15 GMT. The accommodation on board is bunks and the washing facilities are good with hot and cold fresh water and old lavs without doors.

On receiving our first copy of *Tiger Rag* we decided to volunteer for the editorial staff.

On deck it was too good to be true. There was almost a clear sky. The moon was full and lay right off our port beam. The sea was calm though rippled.

Just by us was a small group of students (French or Czech, I couldn't decide), who were singing some of their own songs. The deck was softly lit and crowded with multitudes of people – Mexican Boy Scouts wandering up and down playing softly on mouth organs, Negroes and Negresses, Americans from North, South, East and West, Canadians, a small group of nuns, Frenchmen in berets, Catholic padres and English émigrés.

The majority of American students are natural, unsophisticated and carefree. They dress in blue jeans, rolled up to below the knee, and sweaters. The girls display just that freedom from stiffness and awkwardness which mars the social behaviour of so many English girls.

Kenneth Harris and Edward Boyle are turning out to be splendid companions. Kenneth's sense of humour is good and we are finding each other's company very enjoyable.

Sunday 28 September 1947

Didn't sleep very well and hadn't heard that the clocks were being put back. Kenneth appeared at breakfast with that rather colourless face; it was clear that the transatlantic swell had been too much for him. He came up on deck with us but was sick and went back to bed. Most of the day he spent on his bunk with nothing but a Coca-Cola and a bar of chocolate.

Monday 29 September 1947

In the evening the film show was cancelled owing to a broken projector.

We got talking to Maynard Krueger who was on board and who explained the strength and position of the Socialist Party (on whose National Executive he sits and on whose vice-presidential ticket he ran in 1944), and the Communist Party. The CP has been a nuisance in the East, whereas leftish groups in the middle and far West, not having worked much with the CP, are working-class-unity minded.

The Americans for Democratic Action, with no sort of organisation at all, is preparing its supporters for a fight for Truman in 1948. The ADA realises that to stand as a third party would be impossible and being committed to the Truman and Marshall plans they will have to back the Democrats. The Socialist Party attacks ADA from the left as it is compatible with a general policy of keeping progressives together. As regards the Socialist Party itself, Krueger admitted that it could not be regarded as a potential third party and said that he regarded its greater value as a political educative force, much as the Fabian Society works at home.

As regards the election of the Republican candidate for '48, Krueger explained that Dewey was far and away the favourite. Stassen would get the Minnesota vote in the opening stages of the national convention, as most states back the local boy first time. In the later stages the real people, Dewey, Vandenberg and Taft, would come up against one another.Then, and only then, if a deadlock was reached, might someone like Eisenhower be offered the job. MacArthur was definitely out, but Eisenhower might well be pulled in.

The latter part of the evening I spent talking to the nurse from Bart's who is spending a year at the Johns Hopkins hospital.

Saturday 11 October 1947
Docked in New York. Edward and I go sightseeing. Liverpudlian overhears us talk and stops to shake hands.

Empire State Building. Edward 'tries to jump off'. I feel the same.

Wednesday 15 October 1947
Padre Alexander Marshall Laverty (Marsh) collected us. He was a charming man, had been an army chaplain, now first chaplain to Queen's University. Member of the United Church of Canada.

The United Church contains all Congregationalists, Methodists, Baptists and Presbyterians; it has women ministers – 17 of them. However, the Anglicans don't recognise the United Church orders and this difficulty reaches a head over ordination of women. If reunion does come off, the small Anglo-Catholic grouping will break off and may even go to Rome.

Laverty himself was not keen on women clergy – not on theoretical but on practical grounds. ('Men need holy orders if they are to give of their best, women don't'.)

Hot and crowded train [to Toronto]. No ice on board and no windows open.

Met a gentleman farmer and a semi-senile lower middle-class man. They were worried at the high prices and against price control. 'We need a slump. That will discipline the workers.' They were not anti-working man but distrusted all liberal, socialist and CP leaders. They should, broadly speaking, all be deported.

Arrive Toronto. Pleasant drive from Toronto to Niagara in a 1947 Buick, radio player, lovely tints in trees around road.

Saturday 18 October 1947
Met up with Elizabeth Rausch whom I had met on the boat. Dinner in ladies' dining room. Attractive girl. Things went not too badly tonight. Elizabeth is a strange girl. She is plump. I confess that in blue jeans I hadn't noticed it. Conversation didn't flourish but plodded on during dinner. I find her very attractive. She has a slow smile, slow reactions and a slow turn of speech. As Winston put it about the women of Cyprus – they have slow, sloe eyes.

Monday 20 October 1947
Up early for breakfast.
    Went to wrong bus station for West Point. Got a cab to right station. Taxi driver: 'West Point Debating is good. Rough time in Britain now. You can take it. Why the Hell dontcha clear out of Palestine?'

Friday 31 October 1947
We had breakfast downstairs in the Lafayette Union – typical union breakfast. Cafeteria system. Push tray past glasses of orange juice, grapefruit and tomato juice, cereals, bacon and eggs, toast and preserves. A good combination costs 60 cents. Packed in our room, taken to station at Lafayette by car and caught the train to Chicago.
    It was a luxury train with adjustable cushioned seats, reproduction art treasures at each end of the coach, dining car with white steward and Negro waiters, an observation car where we could get drinks, and *Life* and *Time* and *Fortune* in leather covers. There were large numbers of very attractive girls on the train going to attend a conference of women editors of company magazines.
    Chicago station was dull and dirty and we got a redcap to get us a cab. This drove us through the streets between drab towering buildings. The route to the University avoided the coloured quarter – a slum that the Chicagoans wished the visitor not to see.

Monday 3 November 1947
Arrived by Greyhound in Champaign-Urbana after lunch in Indianapolis. Met by Professor Richard Murphy – charming eccentric with illuminated bow-tie.
    Accommodation in Illinois Union. Then straight to give a talk on English debating to the debate squad. I talk about 'keeping one's pecker up' and learn later to my embarrassment what it means in America.

Wednesday 5 November 1947
Plane to Chicago – our first flight in the USA. Bad weather caused us to be late and we arrived just as the Madison plane left.
    We had a hot dog and coffee from a coffee-stand.

Thursday 6 November 1947 – Minneapolis
We had a good view of the twin cities as our train pulled slowly across the river. The mills and skyscrapers looked rather miserable in the drab morning light.

We had a quick breakfast and then went to see the General Mills. They gave us white cloth caps and aprons and we saw the whole grinding process in the grain elevator. These great machines on four or five floors worked away with scarcely more than a foreman standing by. The man-carrying belt fascinated me. On the first floor the flour was being packed into bags and cartons. Most of this was mechanical but certain processes were done by hand. The sight of a human being linked to a machine as part of a continuous process was very depressing: 99 per cent mechanisation is soul destroying for the 1 per cent human element.

Friday 7 November 1947
Arrived at Des Moines too late for our connection. At the station we had lots of coffee. One kindly woman at the bookstall, seeing me looking at the *Chicago Tribune*, said, 'It must be funny for you coming to a country where the press can say what it likes.' A chasm of ignorance opened up before me and I could only deny it weakly. We caught the train to Iowa City and arrived in the late afternoon. Accommodated at the Hotel Jefferson.

To a Fraternity House where there was a buffet supper. We sat and talked, and with so many charming women listening it was delightful (and made us conceited).

Sunday 9 November 1947
Drove to the station at West Liberty and found that no sleepers had been reserved – which was really my fault. There was time for a quick doughnut and Coke before we boarded. We couldn't get a sleeper so we settled in the coach. At about midnight the train stopped for a break at Burlington and we bundled out, silent with exhaustion, into the coffee shop where we had cheeseburgers, cherry pie and coffee.

Monday 10 November 1947
It was so horrible sitting up all night that we were hardly conscious as we dragged our luggage at the station. We were met and taken by car to the Forest Park Hotel.

There was a blood row with Kenneth over the laundry.

After the debate we refused all invitations so as to be able to go off with a party to a little night club in East St Louis. It was a dismal place, with dirty tables and chairs and waited on by two or three scruffy youths. There was a negro woman crooning into a small useless microphone by the piano. We sat round and talked and drank. After midnight we celebrated Kenneth's birthday and drove back to Forest Park.

Wednesday 12 November 1947
Caught the 9.30 'City of St Louis' for Denver. The station was exciting, with boards advertising trains to San Francisco and New York, Florida and Seattle, Texas and Montreal, Coca-Cola and Rita Hayworth.

Thursday 13 November 1947
I peeped through my upper berth window and saw the vast flat prairie flying past and realised that we were in Colorado. It was very exciting. We had passed through Kansas overnight. Here was the beginning of the Far West with red Indians on Denver station and cowboy types slouching and swaggering by. The air was like champagne and it was cool and invigorating.

Denver is a great cattle-ranching and mining centre. Our road northwards took us parallel to the Rockies.

Met the British Consul, who is very dry and amusing. On class distinctions in Denver: the upper set (Grandfather struck it rich); the middle class (Father struck it rich); the *nouveau riche* (you struck it rich).

Edward and I had to share a bed. Neon light flashing in window. Dance band playing below.

Friday 14 November 1947
Wonderful flight up to Cheyenne, over lakes and forested land. Wyoming is indescribable. The townships below look like architects' models put on a relief map. Not part of the terrain on which they lie.

Up to Billings. This is even more a Far West scene – there still are horsemen about and the Indians look more at home and the white men are rough and ready. We felt conspicuous as we looked.

We boarded a bus but it had to go slow as the roads were ice covered. We stopped once and saw revolvers on sale in the coffee shop bookstall. We trundled on between high ridges and tree-covered slopes to Bozeman.

There was a reception for us and we sat and talked with these 'uncouth' north-westerners. We were, we thought, the first Englishmen they had ever seen. 'Do you put it on?' asked one girl of our accents. I spoke about the tour, Ken about education and Edward about the royal wedding (very popular). We argued about food prices and went to bed in separate rooms. It is snowing hard.

Sunday 16 November 1947
Driven to the 8.58 Northern Pacific train for Missoula. We sat in great comfort – leg-rests in front of adjustable seats. The train took us slowly up through the vast reaches of the upper Rockies, climbing often at walking pace, and we saw the engine swinging round on the tracks until it nearly joined with the end of the train.

Peaks stood clearly on each side and rocky surfaces had sometimes had to be blasted through so the deep cuttings were frequently tight into each side of the train. There was snow lying everywhere and the clear blue sky contained a shining sun which gave the whole scene a panoramic beauty and an unearthly appearance of Elysian perfection.

The observation car at the end of the train gave an excellent view (until we were turned out of it as non-Pullman passengers). We lunched aboard and strolled round when we stopped. An Air Force officer on his way to the new air base in Alaska was the only reminder of a troubled world.

We were wonderfully received at Missoula and were driven to the Florence Hotel.

Monday 17 November 1947
We went off to see the campus, set below a steep wall of rock with U of C carved on it. Then coffee at the union and I spoke for 45 minutes to the convocation on the general topic, 'Anglo-American relations'. It was well attended and excellently received although not well-prepared.

Lunch at the hotel with the Lions. They are a lot of self-conscious grown-up schoolboys.

The debate was held in the Union building. We were asked how we would like to be addressed, and we said 'Edward, Kenneth and Anthony', but were given our full styles and titles [the Hon Anthony Benn, the Hon Edward Boyle and Mr Kenneth Harris] 'but they just prefer to be known as Ed, Ken and Tony so I won't give you their full pedigrees'. This was so embarrassing that I felt obliged in my reply to say, 'You must be wondering what is so odd about our pedigrees. I assure you that we all had fathers and mothers and were born at an early age.'

Bed almost immediately after the debate.

Wednesday 19 November 1947
After lunch we boarded the bus to Walla Walla. We had more than an hour's wait and wrote some postcards from an ice-cream soda bar. The driver always stops at railroad tracks, opens his door with its long handle, looks both ways and starts off again.

The little metal tag attached to it, which is hung in front of the bus, reads: 'Your Greyhound operator is A. N. Jones. Safe, efficient and courteous'.

To the Washington State Penitentiary. This grim, walled and turreted building stood within an outer wall, also guarded. Inside the gates a terrible oppression seized me. There was a little room full of novelties made by the prisoners – beautiful filigree work and leather goods all exquisitely crafted with great skill.

The chief warden hailed us – a great tough ex-boxing champion who looked rather a bully. We saw round the prison yard and glanced up at the guards in their glass and concrete pillboxes, armed with rifles, searchlights and machine guns.

The old cells were rather grim – great cages with double bunks. The new cells were well equipped with running water and porcelain lavatories. Many prisoners were listening to their radios and writing and we saw the shower baths (homosexuality is of course a real problem). We saw a little wooden hut where two Negroes live, rotting away with syphilis and segregated because treatment was no use. We heard about a boy of seventeen who was under a death sentence for raping and murdering his girlfriend. We saw the bare death chamber with its gallows and rope above the trapdoor through which the murderer's body would hang a few feet from the floor.

Wednesday 26 November 1947 – Hollywood
We were driven out to the MGM place at Culver City. Here we waited for Arthur Hornblower – a charming, cultured, tweedy man (very English and dry in his humour).

We went to Fred Astaire's set where the closing shots of a musical number were being taken. The Technicolor lighting was amazingly garish and yellow. Very good tempers all round and lots of cooperation. The great cameras swung forward and backward on huge rubber wheels on a platform. Fred Astaire's facial expressions were magnificent. He seems a pleasant chap. Then we saw a French fishing village and harbour with a tug on it. It was incredibly realistic. Storms were created by fans and hosepipes.

Ten men had been dismissed today (including Young, Chief Executive of Warners).

Young told us that the British Screen Writers' Guild had said it would find employment for all Hollywood people deprived of their means of livelihood on account of their liberal views – a strange and symbolic transplantation of the Statue of Liberty to the Thames Estuary. We met Charles Boyer and Cedric Hardwicke, and Mike Romanoff wouldn't speak to the real Prince Romanov because he spelt his name with a V.

We walked round to see the Don Juan shooting (Errol Flynn, Viveca Lindfors and Robert Douglas). The publicity woman on the set introduced us to the latter two. Vivien is a Swedish star with the loveliest eyes I have ever seen. She had her hair dyed black for this part (Queen of Spain) and was sad that her child hadn't noticed!

Just before we left Young asked us if there was anything he could do for us. 'Yes,' mumbled Kenneth, 'Tony would like to meet Rita Hayworth.' 'Who wouldn't?' came the retort.

Thursday 27 November 1947
We had a Thanksgiving dinner in the London Grill, a pleasant little restaurant attached to our hotel. After that Ken and I went to see *The Secret Life of Walter Mitty* – a cracking good film with Danny Kaye whose impersonation of an RAF officer was first rate.

Sunday 30 November 1947

The Grand Canyon. Up an hour before sunrise and we walked round to the left-hand promontory. The sky was greyish duck-egg blue and the far side of the Canyon was like a huge backcloth in dim and barely distinguishable shades. The colours brightened into pastel shades of brown and purple and brick red and yellow.

From that moment, until we left the airfield in the afternoon, the scene changed visibly all the time. The shadows shortened and altered, the bluish mists which curled in and out of the winding crevices at the bottom of the Canyon thinned out and disappeared. The colours changed like the lights on a cinema organ.

Tuesday 2 December 1947

We took off and flew north-east. We saw Santa Fe down below us, landed at Pueblo and by then the weather was getting appallingly bad. A great thunderstorm had blown up. As we were shaken by bumps and the plane ploughed on through the inky blackness it was a strange feeling to know that the cabin was only a few thousand feet above the bare mountains and one felt very isolated and nervous. We landed at Colorado Springs and ran for the coffee shop. They doused the plane with alcohol as she had got iced up and we completed our journey.

Thursday 4 December 1947

Caught the train to Winfield and we felt that we really were in the South at last. Discrimination in lavatories.

We had a few moments to ourselves in Winfield before the debate in the little hall (where the posters for European relief revealed a lot of good works). After the debate we smoked a cigar and went to bed on the train while it pursued its southern course for the great big world of Texas.

Friday 5 December 1947

When we awoke the train was still on the move. This was surprising as we had been due in Fort Worth at 6.50, but we learned that there had been a freight wreck and we were going round another line which would make us six hours late. In fact we were still in Oklahoma. Breakfast of sandwiches, milk and chocolates and row over distribution caused by my bloodymindedness and Edward's altered decision about fasting. Quite a nasty little scene. Texas countryside – rolling hills and green expanses. Might be parts of Hertfordshire on a bigger scale.

Arrived at Forth Worth and phoned for and got a booking on the afternoon flight to Austin. Arrived Austin about 4.30. Edgar Shelton and Jones met us and took us off to the Hotel Austin. At our hotel Edgar produced a bottle of scotch and a bottle of rye. I was rather bored by the prospect of a booze. Edgar with his blond hair and very Anglo-Saxon face and his splendid southern accent was a colourful and representative figure – the southern gentleman, a devil-may-care young blood. All this is romanticising – but one's first day in the real South presents a temptation to look round for a type.

To the debate in the Baptist chapel. The debate was fun – a lively audience and a friendly atmosphere. They just roared at the Texas jokes – provided they were kind; and at Englishmen jokes – provided they were unkind.

Saturday 6 December 1947
Roused from bed early by the porter and discharged dirty and sleepy on to the platform. Shaved, washed and breakfasted at the station coffee shop. We sat and wrote letters in the public waiting hall. We booked air passages to New Orleans over the phone and got in a cab to the airport. On the way we passed through the whole of the city – big, industrial, dirty city. The industrialisation of the south has caught it napping rather and the expansion is untidy and disorganised in the way of town planning.

We carried on to the airport through some Negro housing areas – tumbledown, unpainted, unbelievably drab, wooden weatherboarded shacks were crowded on to the streets. The sordid aspect appalled me.

We reached the airfield in time for a coffee and then boarded the giant four-engined Skymaster, which carried sixty people six abreast in a long compartment bigger than a train carriage. It was far less cosy and intimate than a Dakota.

At New Orleans we got a limousine (one of those fantastic car-buses with a long body) into New Orleans itself, along the pleasant highway lined with trees and new houses. The limousine driver suggested that we try the Chalmotte Hotel and we were dropped there. Our room was a tall dark room with a dirty green distempered door. The slatted door had some slats broken. The lock was defective. The dirty windows looked on to a wall. There was one low-powered bulb.

We washed and changed and walked out for dinner. The lines of lights, the bright signs, the Christmas trees, the streetcars, all contributed to a feeling of life. Across the way was the French quarter, narrow streets, old houses with iron tracery verandahs, little shops of antiques. It might have been a part of Bordeaux as the weather was warm and the night air refreshing. We dawdled through the streets looking into the bars and cafes from which music was issuing forth. Finally we went for a meal to the Court of Two Sisters. A little orchestra played in the darkest corner. Each table was lit only by a candle within a glass oil lamp shade.

We had a first-rate dinner and talked most amicably. It was a high point in tripartite relationships.

Tuesday 9 December 1947
We drove across a river and through cotton fields where coloured men
and women were working. Had a discussion as to whether we should
keep on to Birmingham or get off at 8.30 in Tuscaloosa. Decide to get off
early and catch 9 o'clock train. Kenneth not over-enthusiastic.

Wednesday 10 December 1947
Fell out of train at Tuscaloosa. Edward forgot one suitcase and I, half
asleep, unfed and bloodyminded am rather provocatively censorious.
The cab driver asks if we are part of the cast of *Madame Butterfly* who are
in town.

Dropped at hotel and sit in lobby until breakfast. Kenneth thinks he
has lost his hat. I fetch someone else's, plus his paper, and am pursued by
the flabby owner. Am so taken aback that I say, 'I assure you sir that I
had no intention of keeping it', as if I had just borrowed it to show Ken.
The man is nice and goes off obviously thinking 'the mad British'.

Sunday 14 December 1947
The schedule has been so intense here that I am glad to get away, though
our visit has been well worth doing. Woke up in the middle of the night
on the train to find we were in Montgomery, Alabama: green tropical
vegetation sliding by not unreminiscent of the view as the *Cameronia*
slowly moved down the Suez Canal north of the Bitter Lakes.

The train was a terribly slow one and very uncomfortable. I read one of
those Sunday papers and watched an old GI sergeant showing off. (They
are the same the world over).

Then to my surprise the train stopped in the middle of the main street
of Gainsville and the station buildings were just by the road – as were the
shops, houses and hotels. As it pulled out again I noticed that the train
had obeyed the traffic lights.

We parted and I got a cab to the Hotel Thomas and settled down in
my little room there. Had a quiet dinner, smoked a cigar and read horror
stories, relaxed and dozed off. The little courtyard in front of my window
with the tropical vegetation was very pleasant.

Tuesday 16 December 1947
I rang Professor Eubank this morning and he said he would come and
collect me. I packed and sure enough this lanky, handsome, sharp-
featured, sunburnt man arrived, took me to lunch at the Paradise Club.
He always shakes hands at every opportunity, is a practical joker and
always talks of out-Britishing the British.

With no notice at all, I gave two hours of talks on the BBC to his class.
They were really quite a success when one considers that I know nothing
about the BBC apart from what Ken has told me.

Later picked up a tired and travel-stained Ken and Edward. At the bus station there were jukeboxes showing films (the only ones I ever saw).

We had a quick bite of dinner and then went and did a 15-minute broadcast.

Wednesday 17 December 1947

We gave a long series of lectures from 8.40 to 2.40 ('The Social Picture', British Economic Policy, Palestine, and the Labour Party) and by the end I had hardly any voice left and I was exhausted. The most depressing thing was discovering that, after an hour's talk, the people who had been busy note-taking were just interested in our performance for its skill of presentation, posture, gesticulation, and direction of emphasis, caring not a button for content.

We felt rather sick about it.

After a short reception in the Union, I slipped away with Rush Foland for an ice-cream soda at one of those car pull-up bars, where you order and your stuff is hooked on to the door of the car on a special tray. Rush is one of those quiet, shy, puzzled but thoughtful American boys. He is mad on drama, has bags of money and doesn't know what to do.

I got back to the Union and did all the work on the accounts which we finished between midnight and 1.30, settling our finances for the fortnight's break.

Thursday 18 December 1947

We walk round discussing whether to buy a pin-up-girl tie and decide to do so – until we discover it costs 12–20 dollars. Edward goes off to St Augustine by bus, Ken and I go to see *Down to Earth* with Rita Hayworth.

Saturday 20 December 1947

Crowd of college kids pushing about and drinking and necking on the station. Rather a bore.

Sunday 21 December 1947

Breakfast in Washington on the train. Then the familiar journey through Baltimore, Philadelphia to New York (Penn Station). I rang Ursula Niebuhr and she said come straight along. I got in a cab and as we drove along the Riverside Drive, the watery winter sun shining over the East River and the clear cold buildings and a chilly wind biting in through the cracks of the cab, I felt I had lived in New York all my life. The tour had begun from there nearly three months before.

The Niebuhrs were most kind and I settled in. Christopher I had never met before and he is a tall boy of 12 or 13. Elizabeth doesn't give a damn for anyone and is really a very attractive little personality already.

Monday 22 December 1947
Walk up Fifth Avenue to see the great Christmas tree in front of the Rockefeller Center. People skating on the pool. All New York is ready for Christmas. The charity Father Christmases who are on the street are stamping their feet and ringing their bells and shaking their boxes. The steam from the manholes rises like the smoke from a small campfire.

Wednesday 24 December 1947
Rang Reinhold up, pretended I was 'Alistair McAlistair of the Presbyterian Church', and asked him to preach on Sunday. He said he couldn't (which wasn't true) and would be busy till June. Tells me he is going to Scotland and rings off. Reinhold tells us at dinner and we giggle and confess.

Thursday 25 December 1947
Went to Columbia Chapel with Ursula for communion.

We undid the stockings and distributed presents. Then Christopher, Reinhold and I went to morning service at the new cathedral on 112th Street.

The Niebuhrs spent the rest of the afternoon reading and hanging about.

After dinner Reinhold does a recitation, Elizabeth plays a piece and I do 'There was an old lady who swallowed a fly'. Then there is a tremendous Christopher–Elizabeth fight and after many tears this is straightened out. Reinhold clearly doesn't enjoy his duties when they include punishment.

A family scene of this kind (I can so easily remember from the child's point of view) is absolute hell for the parents and unbelievably silly to watch. The row was patched up, however, and Christmas ended happily and I set the time back five hours and visualised the gathering in England.

Friday 26 December 1947
The snow is so deep that cars just appear as great protuberances through the six-foot drifts. Traffic is stuck for miles in Broadway.

Saturday 27 December 1947
At about 12.30 I took my leave of the Niebuhrs and went downtown with a small bag to meet Elizabeth Rausch at the Astor. The feel of New York was entirely different and as I left the subway I heard the place as it probably never has been this century – absolutely quiet.

Wednesday 31 December 1947
Hear Big Ben on the wireless sounding midnight at 7 o'clock and the

1948 celebrations in London and Edinburgh – it makes my heart miss a beat – the announcer's dear English accent is wonderful.

Cocktail party at house nearby where son aged nineteen has married a nurse of thirty and is to introduce her.

Elizabeth and I walk and walk and sit down on a snow bank. While the kids rush by skating on the roads I kiss her. She is terribly shy and nervous. I am rather ashamed of myself. Back for the New Year's Eve party.

Friday 2 January 1948
Up latish, haircut.

Mrs Rausch knits in her study across the hall while Lib and I neck in the sitting room. It is too obvious for words and I feel an awful fool. But that is the way the Americans look at these things and 'When in Rome . . .'.

Thursday 8 January 1948
Woken at Penn Station by a prodding on the thigh by the Negro porter who had slipped his hand through the curtain. I poke my head out of the window. Kenneth's head pops out and so does Edward's. We all three are staring at the porter. 'You must be out of hyer ba seven.' Edward protests and the Negro goes away and returns with a white Pullman conductor who tells us we shall be towed away to the yard if we don't get off.

We are the last people on the train and pile out with our baggage.

Trip to Princeton. We are taken straight to the Colonial Club for lunch. Before lunch a Lucky Strike salesman is showing a film about Luckies and distributing free packets.

There are no fraternities at Princeton, but these eating clubs (which are non-residential) take their place. The row of eating houses is the most mixed I have seen. A Tudor cottage stands by a colonial facade, a Gothic building rubs shoulders with a Jacobean manor house. An oil painting of George II stared down at us as we ate lunch. After lunch we were free and Edward and I walked round the campus. We set off across the fields for the graduate college which is situated by itself – a couple of quadrangles and buildings of the real Oxford sort – ivy covered and presided over by an almost perfect replica of Magdalen Tower. Here was a dining hall reminiscent of Christ Church – and the whole thing is not more than 15-20 years old.

Walked back to the Colonial Club and got ready for dinner. There were about 25 Princeton people here and ten of our friends including the Rausches. The debate was hard to do. The subject matter demanded a forceful delivery but the size of the audience made it seem rather absurd.

I hardly had an opportunity for a word to Lib and I am afraid that she was rather upset.

Friday 9 January 1948
A horrible bumpy night in the train and hard to sleep. Disentrained at Washington bleary eyed and tired. We resolved not to accept a full programme and to demand some rest. We are grumpy. Truman can't see us – doing State of the Union message.

To a dance and reception in our honour. Chatted to embassy people and danced a couple of times. I was dropped off at the Shinkmans' and have a long 'family' chat with Betty and Paul. They have no help at all – except for a coloured woman once a week.

Monday 12 January 1948
British embassy for lunch. Talk to Mervyn Pritchard (Education attaché). Lady Inverchapel very attractive in Red Cross uniform. Inverchapel very friendly. Pleasant lunch.

We drive to House offices to see Congressional friends. Quick look round the Capitol (burned by us in 1814) with pictures glorifying British defeats.

Then on to the Chamber of Commerce auditorium: 1,100 people present and 600 turned away. Our opponents thought they were safe and we coshed them. Every Senator and Congressman had been invited and between 50 and 75 were there. One sensed that the first few rows were very chilly. However, after it was all over we were congratulated by the Burmese Ambassador.

We went back to the embassy with Inverchapel for a drink. We talked about Bob Boothby and Inverchapel said he had always tried to persuade him to join the Labour Party. He was pretty progressive himself, which encouraged me, but Edward dismissed it rather contemptuously as a diplomat working for a Labour Government, playing with the idea of being a socialist.

Inverchapel was very complimentary about our performance and lent us his Rolls-Royce to take us home. (It had been built for Queen Mary.) We went via the hot dog stall where Edward had left his wallet. He got it back with sterling but minus $200!

Tuesday 13 January 1948
Caught a cab to the Barclay at Rittenhouse Square, where I found Ed and Ken in the bar drinking with some young men, who came to have lunch with us. I started the Communist question and relations were rather strained. The basic assumption of so many Americans is that the CP is a subversive organisation and cannot be accorded the democratic privileges. When it goes hand in hand with the idea that a belief in God, the American constitution and free enterprise constitutes a rigid formula for the good life, the American way and democratic government generally, then I lose my temper.

There is a rough and ready egalitarianism in the USA. Reinhold's definition about the class system is a sound one. 'There is a class system in a country when the so-called lower orders recognise their position as such, and accept it.' Compare an English hot dog stall man with some of his American counterparts. The Americans all look forward with uncontrollable optimism to a rise in the world and they have the drive to work towards it. We accept life.

1948 – Thoughts on Socialism

I am a socialist. Advocating a change imposes a responsibility for proving capitalism a failure. The failure of *laissez-faire* capitalism is easily shown. It produced and allowed grave inequalities of income and capital that were quite unjustifiable on grounds of necessity or justice. For example in Britain in 1937, 3 per cent of the population owned 60 per cent of the property. One can legitimately indict such a situation for failing to give to each man a fair share of his national heritage of wealth earned by preceding generations. This indictment is even more telling if it can be shown, as it can, that as a direct result came poverty and squalor and undernourishment. Before the war in this country a medical survey revealed that only one in four had an adequate diet.

This state of affairs makes a mockery of the price mechanism as a means of translating needs into economic demand. How can it be said that the second yacht bought by Henry Ford is more necessary than the food and clothing purchased by the worker?

It is often said that businesses can be judged a success or failure according to their profitability. Yet no account of the social costs is shown in a corporation's balance sheet: the cost in health of factory smoke, the cost in wasted talent of education facilities that are withheld for financial reasons (low wages) and so on.

The old system was persistently unable to provide full employment. The cyclical trade depressions, which have occurred since the industrial revolution, reached their climax in the 1930s, when there were more than 15 million unemployed in the USA. The right to work and support oneself is one of the most basic rights of man. Yet in the present century there have been only two occasions when there has been full employment – in the two world wars, when production was organised for purposes of destruction.

Socialists assert that because of this failure – the results of which are so serious that for some people the machinery of political democracy is interpreted as a hollow sham – some new approach is required. So far we have been purely destructive. It is now that our task becomes more difficult as we are required to suggest an alternative.

So as to deal with one anti-socialist charge straight away, let us look at the requirements of the individual. First of all we must recognise that we are all made with different qualifications. Ultimately everyone will find his own level. But he must be given a chance to do that. So requirement number one is: *real equality of opportunity*.

Opportunity to get the basic education without which no one should have to enter life's struggle and beyond that any additional education that his peculiar talents deserve, to be attained competitively. Free enterprise, because it permits the inequalities of one generation to be inherited and increased by the next, does not provide this.

A certain basic minimum must be available to all, regardless of ability. Of course ability is largely inherited via wealth. Perhaps one day we shall be able to make reality of 'from each according to his ability, to each according to his needs'. That day is a long way off. Economic efficiency demands a degree of inequality because of the need for incentives. We can only hope to reduce inequalities to the lowest point compatible with these demands. And a certain standard of health, nourishment and housing must be maintained for all. No one else can do it but the state and in Britain a new paternalism is state paternalism: looking after those who cannot look after themselves. This involves interference, but if this interference is democratically controlled we need not fear that an unwieldy bureaucracy will clasp us in its grip. The socialist blueprint for achieving these two simple ends involves the use of a number of equally simple mechanisms.

Production must be carried on according to certain specific social priorities, not only in difficult times (as in Britain now or any country in times of war) but always. Economics is said to be the science of scarcity. We cannot, at least in this century, meet everyone's needs, so we must plan what we have to bring in the greatest benefits to the greatest number.

Full employment is a national and even international responsibility. If we can have it in wartime, why not in peacetime? While there are human needs to be met, the Government must see (if no one else will) that production is not halved as it was in the USA in 1931 because of the so-called lack of profit in business. Planned investment is the technical economic term for what is required. It simply means the planning of new capital expansion to give work to the people who are involuntarily unemployed because of an inherent instability in the system. It isn't of course as crude as that but the effect can be produced smoothly.

Last of all, public planning of industry through public ownership can resolve the dilemma to which I have referred: wasteful competition or efficient monopoly with the risk of consumer exploitation. If industries which face these two difficulties are rationalised it is possible to get all the efficiency that unified control provides and protect the public by democratic supervision through Parliament or Congress.

These then roughly and simply are the tools of socialist planning. It is sometimes said that they involve interfering with the liberty of action that is sacred. But liberty alone means nothing. Liberty for whom? To do what? We must answer those questions.

Socialism does affect some freedom, but a special sort. It prevents businesses from taking irresponsible economic decisions (to which they are answerable to shareholders alone) which affect thousands of people. The economy must be controlled by the people who work in it. It has for too long been our master and not our servant. By placing the responsibility for supervising its running on the shoulders of the people we elect we are organising an extension of democratic freedom into the economic field, whereas before it has only been in the political field.

One thing more – about democracy. Communists always say that democratic socialists are betraying true socialism, because they allow free speech to the capitalist and do not wage the class war ruthlessly. What they forget is that, put at its lowest valuation, political democracy as we understand it is the safest way of running your government. I believe that it is a great deal more important than that. We in the English-speaking world have created a wonderful machinery for peaceful change in parliamentary democracy. It has taken 1,000 years and we should not and cannot expect it to grow in Russia, Eastern Europe or primitive countries which have not our history of peace, plenty and stability. But we must treasure it ourselves and use it to achieve our own ends. Socialism is important, I feel certain, but socialism achieved by force is no good. The democratic machinery is at hand for us to use. We are more fortunate in that respect than were the Russians.

I may as well add that my credo, this faith, springs forth from a personal interpretation of a Christian faith. Put boldly, 'Love thy neighbour as thyself' is surely an ethical claim for a proper national health service and so on. The individual didn't always get a square deal under the old system and this is an attempt to put that right. Quite how the claim that everyone should work for his own interests is compatible with the New Testament teaching I could never understand.

Thursday 1 April 1948
All is not well with the Abbey Division of Westminster Labour Party. The growth of the organisation has produced cliques and endless bickering. Wilf Messer is a wonderfully reliable and steady chap. Jack Jones, the chairman, is the best type of trade unionist. But there is an ambitious, bitter and intriguing group. The measure of the tragedy is that it has reached the point where Mrs Hammond, a splendid woman, is resigning and if we can't keep a woman like her in the Party, what hope is there of increasing our membership? Abbey is, I hope, an exception.

Saturday 3 April 1948
My twenty-third birthday. Today the world is heading straight for war. I wonder whether these words will ever be read by anyone who survives.

I know that everyone tends to believe that every war is bound to be the last but this time with atom bombs and bacteria I can't see how life can go on in a form worth living, when it is over.

On this 23rd birthday of mine I am faced with the problem of what to do with my life. In a year's time I shall have left Oxford behind and shall be working for a living.

Is politics really my place? Should I earn my living in business? (Benn Brothers for example). Or should I go down a mine for a year? Just where do I stand politically? *Am* I a socialist? Am I prepared for the personal sacrifices that must necessarily involve?

I must sort out my own position and see if I can't resolve the present confusions and make out of all this a coherent whole on which to base everything.

While I am on my own weaknesses and faults, another shortcoming is that I want the limelight too much. This arises from a personal insecurity, for Mike was so clearly a better man than me, and Dave so courageous and talented, that I constantly felt the need for making my own presence felt. I am also very conceited. I like wearing clothes that draw attention to myself. Another thing that has always worried me is my self-consciousness. I have always worried terribly what people thought of me and made all sorts of efforts to please. This has probably done me more harm than good.

If I am really hated by someone even now it still worries me a lot, but generally speaking I am much more at ease with people and with women. A reputation for insincerity is rather a damaging thing, let alone the fundamental badness of insincerity itself. Am I insincere?

After the 1947–48 US debating tour, an American friend whom I had made wrote to tell me that a young American student whom he knew, Caroline De Camp, from Cincinnati, Ohio would be studying in Oxford, and he thought I might like to meet her.

Thus it was that I went to Worcester College to have tea with her and some friends on the afternoon of 2 August 1948. Nine days later, in the early hours of 11 August, I proposed to her on a park bench in Oxford.

That bench, which I subsequently bought from Oxford City Council for £10, now rests in the front garden of our home.

After coming to meet my family, Caroline returned home and during the next six months we conducted an immensely long correspondence describing in detail our lives, opinions, and hopes for the future.

I completed my finals in the autumn of 1948, and she studied for a postgraduate degree at the University of Cincinnati.

In January 1949 I set sail for America again to work as a magazine salesman for Benn Brothers, staying for a few days in Cincinnati at the end of January to meet her family. Then I set off on the lonely task of contacting possible customers for the painfully thin trade journals which were affected by the paper shortage.

Among other places I visited Indianapolis, Chicago and Philadelphia, where I addressed the annual meeting of Friends, ending up in New York working for McGraw-Hill publishing house to learn something of their marketing techniques.

This lonely mission, staying in tiny bedsits at night seeking out customers in the Yellow Pages and walking round these cities with my wares in a briefcase, came to an end when I returned to Cincinnati in May to see Caroline get her degree. We were married at the Church of the Advent on 17 June.

We went on honeymoon to Leland in Michigan, cutting it short to attend a political conference at the Summer Institute for Social Progress at Wellesley College, where I debated 'The Future of Europe' with a Polish diplomat.

We returned to Britain by ship in July and later that year Caroline began a second postgraduate degree at University College, London while I joined the BBC as a producer with the North American Service.

During this busy period for both of us, before and early in our marriage, my regular diary lapsed.

Trinity College
Oxford

11 March 1949

My dear Jimmy

How are you? All I've ever heard from you was a note saying 1. Carol was perfect, 2. the prospect of marriage was perfect 3. life in general is perfect and 4. you were perfect.

From all of which I deduced that you were happy and things were going well. I imagine you are now engaged in ceaseless entrepreneurial activity on behalf of this rather shady publishing firm. I hope the job hasn't turned out to be as disagreeable as you expected.

Nothing much happens or changes in Oxford. Of the Labour Club I now see little, being very much persona non grata as a result of certain goings-on at the Club dinner where I provided, during the speeches, a background of shrewd comment which was not highly appreciated by the more humourless members present (the majority).

The main things that have happened to me are that I nearly got South Hammersmith and that I have turned down Oxford. The South Hammersmith thing was disappointing. I was rung up by Gordon Walker to know if I would let my name go forward. I said yes: there was then a fight at the NEC level between me and Douglas Houghton (for the candidature). Houghton won and went down to the selection conference with full Transport House backing and was then quite unexpectedly beaten by Tom Williams, who was a Co-op nominee. Then Oxford fell vacant since they finally got tough and pushed Stewart Cook out. I was nominated by four wards, and had a terrible time making up my mind. But I finally said No, I think wisely. Lady Pakenham in the end was the only candidate and she has now been accepted.

The only person who is still optimistic about my chances is dear old Hugh [Dalton] whose reputation you will be glad to hear I have now entirely rehabilitated by a sensational article in *Tribune* saying he was the greatest Chancellor since Gladstone.

My love to Carol, God help her. And drop me a line with your news.
    Yrs
        Tony [Crosland]

                        Trinity College
                                 Oxford
                          4 June 1949

My dear Jimmy

I gather, both from your letter, and your elegantly-printed invitation which is (if I may say so) quite dominated by your lengthy nomenclature, that you propose to carry this thing through to the bitter end. So be it. You do so with my prayers and good wishes, and I shall think of you on 17 June 1949 at 6 o'clock.

It is a great relief to me that you are being married in evening dress, though I should hope that you will have a more elegant one than that which you used to wear here. Try not to make a fool of yourself at the wedding: I suggest that you keep off the ginger-beer: you know how it goes to your head.

I won't give you all my news now as I shall see you in a few weeks.

So my very best wishes for the 17th and afterwards: and give Carol an avuncular kiss on the forehead from me and tell her how much I look forward to seeing her.
    Yrs
        Tony

Notes

Chapter Two

1.   (p.106) The dinner guests in Paris, on that occasion were: Sir Ronald Campbell, British Ambassador in Cairo; Sir Walter Smart, Minister at the British Embassy, Cairo, Pierson Dixon, Principal Private Secretary to Ernie Bevin, (Dixon later became British Ambassador at the UN in New York and Paris); Sir Claud Russell, long-time diplomat and retired Ambassador; Frank Wood, then Principal Private Secretary to Father (the Secretary of State for Air), later Permanent Secretary at the Ministry of Posts and Telecommunications; John Henniker-Major, then assistant Private Secretary to the Foreign Secretary, who succeeded to the title of Lord Henniker, served as British Ambassador to Jordan and Denmark and became Director-General of the British Council; Mrs Alexander, wife of A V Alexander, the First Lord of the Admiralty and later Minister of Defence in the Labour Government.

3
'Baby' of the House
1950–55

In October 1950 Sir Stafford Cripps, the Chancellor of the Exchequer, was stricken with cancer, and resigned his office and his seat in Parliament as MP for Bristol South-East. Having been approached and shortlisted as a candidate to succeed him, I was selected on 1 November and resigned from the BBC the following day.

The by-election took place on 30 November. My Labour majority, though comfortable at 7,000, was 10,000 less than the majority Cripps had enjoyed a few months earlier. I took my seat on 4 December 1950 as the 'Baby' of the House, at the age of twenty-five.

By the time of my election for Bristol South-East the post-war Labour Government had really run out of steam and was shortly to lose the next General Election in 1951.

The great achievements of building the Welfare State and the National Health Service and the planned reconstruction of our industry had been completed but there were still acute shortages which necessitated the retention of rationing.

The pressure brought about by an American loan to Britain, and our inability after the cost of the war to pay for imports, led to a round of 'austerity' cuts in 1947 which included a reduction in rations, an end to 'pleasure' motoring and the banning of foreign holidays.

Coming so soon after the war, people were tired of hardship and wanted to enjoy the material benefits of peace. The Conservative opposition, still under Churchill, exploited the crisis and in the February 1950 General Election Labour had lost its huge majority and was left with a majority of only six seats over all other parties.

The Cold War had also begun to take its toll and the high hopes of 1945 for a new period of peace and cooperation had been threatened by a growing fear that another war might be on the way, fear accentuated by the 1948 Berlin 'airlift' mounted by the West to get in supplies to the western zone of Berlin which was being blockaded by the Soviet Union.

The Korean crisis beginning in 1950 stepped up the Cold War climate, as American forces were sent to South Korea to fight the Communist North Korean army which had crossed the border into South Korea. The Americans used the Security Council to pass a resolution justifying its action, in the absence of the Soviet Union from the Security Council.

The war became so serious that President Truman hinted, on 30 November 1950, the day of the Bristol South East by-election which took me to Parliament, at the use of the atomic bomb against North Korea.

At that time the prospect of a Third World War was seriously considered, and the Labour Government, with Ernest Bevin as Foreign Secretary, went along completely and uncritically with the American strategy, which was to build up NATO in the west, to resist a supposed Soviet attack, and to support Chiang Kai Shek in China against Mao Tse Tung.

President Truman had adopted the 'Truman doctrine' to use American power to contain the Soviet Union and to prop up any anti-Communist governments against threats from radical forces inside their own countries.

It is hard to believe, in retrospect, that the threat of world war should have reappeared so soon after the defeat of fascism in 1945. But with the benefit of hindsight it is clear that what we were witnessing was a return to the anti-socialist strategies of the Twenties and Thirties, strategies which had been temporarily suspended while the USSR was a wartime ally in the defeat of Nazi Germany. By 1950, in America the anti-Communist Witch-hunt was underway.

The internal and domestic crises affecting Britain put a strain on the Labour Government, which by 1951 had lost its radicalism. Herbert Morrison was urging caution and consolidation, which, however, proved unsuccessful in holding back the tide of conservatism – even though in 1951 Labour had the largest vote ever recorded in a British Election and had won more popular votes than the Conservative Party which replaced it.

The end of 1950 was therefore not an easy time to enter Parliament, when a weakened Labour Government was about to be driven by American pressure to policies which included a massive, unnecessary, and costly rearmament programme, while parallel pressures to 'contain' the threat of Communism ensured that Germany, within five years of its defeat, should actually be re-armed itself to strengthen western defences.

On the positive side Attlee's Government had ended British rule in India, though at the price of partition, and the process of decolonisation elsewhere had begun – thus sparing Britain the costly wars which embroiled France in Vietnam and Algeria, and Portugal in its colonies.

The anti-colonial movement was growing in strength in Africa and Asia and these campaigns, a continuing theme of the years that were to follow, greatly interested me after my experiences in Africa during my wartime service.

Southborne Hotel
South Parade
Bath

19 November 1950

Dearest Ma and Pa

I really don't know where to send this letter – to Millbank or Stansgate. Bless you for writing to us.

All goes well here. We are tired of course but we have both more or less recovered from our colds. The weather is appalling . . . it rains cats and dogs.

This morning we went to Mervyn Stockwood's church. There was a sung Eucharist, *five* officiating clergy, a short sermon on the meaning of the *mass* and tea and cakes in the vicarage. Next Sunday the three candidates are addressing a church meeting on 'Why Christians should vote Socialist/Tory/Liberal'. We shall probably leave here on December 1st (polling is on November 30th).

We might drive direct to Stansgate if that is all right with you.

> All love
> > In haste
> > James

January 1951
I am going to try out a political diary. What I want to do is to highlight the most significant events of which I am a witness and set down contemporary opinions and accounts which my memory would probably distort to suit current purposes were I to try and recall them later on. This is surely the politician's greatest weakness, if published memoirs are anything to go by.

I am a very new Member of Parliament and it is still exciting to bump into Winston Churchill in the members' lavatory, as I did the other day. It is still pleasant to be called by my christian name by Aneurin Bevan and to call him Nye.

Monday 29 January 1951
Returned to the Commons, still feeling like a very new boy. After Questions the Prime Minister made a long-awaited statement on the new Defence plans, involving rearmament costing £4,700,000,000 over the next three years and the call-up of 235,000 reservists this summer. It was received in glum silence on our side of the House. Some Labour MPs asked hostile questions and this was used by the Tories as fresh evidence of a Labour split. I went away wanting to discuss it with my colleagues, but I don't really know them well enough and this frustrated me.

At 4.30 the external affairs group of the PLP met to hear Milovan Djilas from Jugoslavia. He spoke for a while and then answered questions. Here is a summary of his remarks.

Causes of Jugoslavia/Soviet split

Economic exploitation by the USSR
Attacks on Jugoslav national independence that accompanied the above
Attempts to dictate Jugoslavian foreign policy

Soviet policy (backed by Russian people) unlikely to change

Nature of present Soviet pressure

Propaganda
Blockade
Armed threats by satellites

Relations with Peking

Jugoslavia has recognised Peking.
There is an element of Chinese expansionism similar to Soviet expansionism.
There is hope of a Chinese-Soviet split.
Peking takes the Soviet line on Jugoslavia.

Freedom in Jugoslavia

There is no press censorship.
The political parties freely publish newspapers.
There is no likelihood of a capitalist press 'like the *Daily Express*'.
Criticism of Government policy is allowed.

Likelihood of war

Jugos believe that an attack by the USSR would precipitate a world war.

Balkan affairs

Tito wants better relations with Greece. There is little Soviet strength in Jugo. 2,000 are in jail. Hungary shows sympathy with Tito but the feeling is ill-organised.

Trieste will ultimately be partitioned. Big federal grants are going to Macedonia.

The whole question of an independent judiciary is under discussion and attempts to achieve it are being made. Religious freedom is allowed to orthodox church but not to Catholics. (I may have misheard this.)

On broadcast propaganda, Jugoslav propaganda to the Balkans is effective. BBC propaganda to Jugoslavia is weak because they underestimate the importance and widespread support for socialism.

Wednesday 31 January 1951

This morning the Parliamentary Labour Party met to discuss foreign policy and the defence plans. It was an interesting meeting which I was glad to attend.

The Prime Minister opened the discussion. On the Far East he said our aim is to prevent not to foment war. That was the Commonwealth task at recent meetings. Korea must be seen in its Far East context and that is why the Government has advocated recognition of Peking. We must be careful not to get bogged down in the Far East. The PM worked for that with Truman, the Commonwealth and through UNO. But foreign affairs is bound to be a compromise and at the moment feeling in the USA and China has risen very high.

Dangers: Militarily the Western powers are weak relative to the USSR. The Soviet armed forces are controlled by a small group, though I do not believe that group wants war. The Berlin airlift and the rape of Czechoslovakia have been danger spots. Korea was the first actual military operation and it shows the irresponsibility of the satellites.

Britain has many world responsibilities and we are working for collective security because we cannot reach agreement with the USSR and we must be armed to deter military adventures.

What we can do: There is a difference between preparing for war and preparing to prevent war.

The dangers of rearmament are:

– that we might cause an incident;
– that someone might decide to leap in first;
– that we might start an arms race that would make war inevitable;
– the USSR doesn't want a peaceful world, preferring to see the disruption of the Western bloc. We must be careful therefore not to disrupt our economy.

The position in Western Europe is now dangerous because of her post-war weakness. But we can't commit too many forces to Europe and must keep some at home. The reserve recall is a preparatory scheme to get trained people ready and 15 days' training is just enough.

The production job is immense as obsolescence and wear and tear have used up our supplies from World War II. This will be expensive. But our aim is deterrence not threat.

German rearmament: We have to decide how to meet it. It must either be by the occupying powers or by the Germans themselves. We can't let them enjoy a privileged position and bear all the burden ourselves. What line is to be held? Germany cannot be a no man's land. All we have accepted so far is the principle of a German contribution within a unified command. The details are still under discussion. We still hope for an East–West conference.

America: there is a lot of anti-American feeling. They do talk too much – but they are essential for European defence.

After the PM had spoken, Glenvil Hall, chairman of the PLP, called for discussion.

Eric Fletcher [MP for Islington East] said the plan to rearm Germany is wrong in principle, premature and dangerous in that it will provoke the USSR.

A. J. Irvine [MP for Liverpool Edge Hill] supported the defence plans if a negotiated settlement is pursued by lively diplomacy. He feared that British restraint on the USA is ineffective. Peking is not an aggressor. Labour MPs feel impotent and the power of the Cabinet is too great. We need guidance.

Victor Yates [MP for Birmingham Ladywood] – This present rearmament and German rearmament are provocative. Delay over USSR offer of a conference is regrettable. He will vote against the Government defence plans.

Frank McLeavy [MP for Bradford East] – The people support the Government, at least the working class do. These damned intellectuals in the Party (the critics) don't count at all.

John Hynd [MP for Sheffield, Attercliffe] – German forces will be integrated and interdependent. The Nazis won't be rearmed. The alternative to a German contribution is a higher British military contribution, which is unthinkable. It is better to let the Germans in now than later on, when they might misuse arms.

Sydney Silverman [MP for Nelson and Colne] – The PM had mentioned public opinion in the USA and China. He should not neglect British feeling. If there were a General Election today the Labour Party would only win 100 seats. This is because the people voted Labour to achieve freedom from destitution, poverty and war. But our foreign policy is a Tory one. The Government have yielded to US pressure over (1) German rearmament; (2) the resolution branding China as an aggressor; (3) the present defence programme.

The immediate danger is in the Far East; there we have backed the US who are working against any negotiations.

He said he will vote against the Defence plans.

Dick Crossman – The divisional labour parties are discouraged and divided. He wished the PM had spoken as frankly as he did today (and as moderately) to the public.

Two main dangers today are the Russian threat and American war-mongering (MacArthur). We have succumbed to American pressure. Crossman would support the defence plans if it were not accompanied by weakness to America.

Woodrow Wyatt – We must have strong forces if we are to influence Washington.

Herbert Morrison – There are real dangers to the PLP in this split. If the PLP gets demoralised it will spread all over the movement. We daren't force an Election at this inopportune moment. We can't always rely on the Tories to save the Labour Government.

Jimmy Hudson [MP for Ealing North] (a pacifist) – Pacifists won't create trouble for the Government, because we know that bad as it is the alternative is Churchill. He deplored the dirty methods the US were using, quoting the hold-up in Congress of a grant of wheat to stem the Indian famine.

John McGovern [MP for Glasgow Shettleston, former ILP Member] – The Government have worked for peace but war is inevitable. But we must work for peace still and prove that we are doing so to the workers. The intellectual left is a danger but the workers are solid. Home issues are uppermost in their minds.

The Prime Minister replied to the points. The Labour Party has always been keen on collective security and we must accept the consequences of it now. I wish we could have halted at the 38th parallel but British influence with the US has to be related to our power.

Victor Yates had said we were slow in arranging talks – but why blame us alone?

We can't boast publicly about the pressure *we* bring to bear on the Americans, and so we are always accused of 'being dragged along'. Take the UN resolution branding China as an aggressor (passed yesterday by the Political Committee of the UN). Britain has delayed action and modified the American proposals. But we must support the UN and try to work with them. Americans are an inexperienced people and Truman and Acheson have had a tough time. We have worked hard to prevent a rift between Asia and the West.

On German rearmament, we can't let them escape entirely from the responsibility of defending themselves. It would give them a privileged position at our expense. The USSR are being very difficult and nothing would please the USSR more than a split in the Party now.

I have been very frank with Truman, Attlee said, and told him that I disagree with him about the recognition of Peking and the future of Formosa.

The meeting then broke up.

Clem's statements were moderate and I think he made a strong case for what he has done. But of course a call for party unity means that everyone must make concessions to different viewpoints. I am unhappy and undecided about German rearmament. And 100 per cent against Japanese rearmament. The defence programme I would be inclined to support as I do think that there is a threat of aggression in Europe, though I am not satisfied that enough has been done to negotiate with Russia about Germany or that we have made every possible effort to allay Polish and Czech fears. I think we might do well to guarantee the Oder–Neisse line and perhaps try direct negotiations with the Eastern European countries.

In Korea I am very fearful of MacArthur, but quite what we could have done about the American resolution at the UN I don't know. They would have carried it (without the modification we achieved) in any case as the Latin American countries are satellites of the USA. It is the same problem we Labour MPs have to face: whether we stay in as loyal members accepting what is done and try to shape policy or whether to rebel and become lone voices in the wilderness. What terrific pressure there is on us. A spell in Opposition would do us a world of good, if not for the grim prospect of Tory rule and the sad depletion of ranks that a General Election would cause.

Wednesday 7 February 1951
I made my maiden speech today on the advice of various people that it should be 'about the middle of February'.

Roy Jenkins suggested steel nationalisation. I know nothing about steel except what anyone can mug up and it was almost impossible to speak non-controversially about it.

Father had said, 'A maiden speech is like a canter at a horse show. You are just expected to show your paces in a graceful way.' As everything that could possibly have been said on the subject had been said – several times – the only way to tackle it was to set out the case simply and, if possible, amusingly.

I remembered Father's advice for all Commons speeches – 'simplicity, sincerity, modesty, clarity'.

I had stayed up half the previous two nights and had written a script, with notes for actual use. The debate was opened by Churchill, and George Strauss (the Minister of Supply) spoke second.

A message came from the Whips' office asking me to move to the benches above the gangway and shortly afterwards my name was called.

I would certainly have abandoned the whole attempt after the opening speeches had not the family all been present – Mother and Caroline, Father and Dave.

The benches falling away from below me made me feel very tall and rather conspicuous.

I stumbled a bit over 'right honourable friend' and 'right honourable and gallant gentleman'. At one point, speaking of the bad psychological effect of a profitable steel industry while rearmament threatened our living standards, I sensed a change of feeling – and a wave of hostility. But towards the end of my speech I was aware of growing friendliness and laughter. I could see our Front Bench – Strauss, Bevan, Dalton and Strachey – all looking up at me.

I sat down after about 15 minutes. Sir Ralph Glyn, Conservative Member for Abingdon, followed and paid a very warm tribute which Father enjoyed as much as I did. It had been a success. Conceit compels me to record that I had letters of congratulation from the PM, Strauss, Bevan, Steven Hardie (chairman of the new Iron and Steel Corporation), and others. I do feel much more at home in the place.

Thursday 8 February 1951

Hugh Dalton joined me at dinner tonight with Geoffrey de Freitas [Labour MP for Lincoln], Fred Mulley [Labour MP for Sheffield Park] and Fred Bellenger [Labour MP for Nottingham, Bassetlaw]. Allowing for the fact that Dalton hates the Germans with all his stomach, and likes to be thought left-wing leader in the Cabinet and wants the support and admiration of young men – allowing for that, what he said was very interesting on the question of German rearmament.

When the Foreign Secretary Ernie Bevin went to New York last September for a meeting with the American and French Foreign Secretaries, he was directed by the Cabinet against any form of German rearmament. What Bevin's views on the subject were, I am not sure. The French of course were dead against it. At this meeting the Americans came out in favour of German rearmament and laid it down as a condition of their economic and military participation in Western defence. No German participation, no American participation, they insisted. Bevin cabled the Cabinet for fresh instructions. According to Dalton it took three Cabinet meetings to get agreement on the position. Finally agreement to the principle was accepted, but since then the Government have worked (said Dalton) to see that the four-power conference secured a guarantee of disarmament in East and West. 'As time goes on,' he concluded, 'and there is no actual German rearmament people will realise how far practice can diverge from the principle forced on us by the Americans.'

I wonder how accurate this account is?

Later Crosland and I went in to the Smoking Room to join Nye, Hugh Dalton and Dick Crossman. Crossman was under attack by Dalton for the defeatist *New Statesman* policy. Nye's personality was electric. His vigour and grasp and good humour and power of argument paralysed me with excitement. Seeing him beside Dalton one could not but notice the difference. Dalton – saturnine, wicked, amusing, intellectual, roguish; Bevan open, honest, good-humoured, and devastating.

Sunday 11 February 1951

To Bristol for my first visit since the by-election. We got up to find Bristol in the middle of a full-scale atomic bomb exercise. What a sign of the times. The centre of the city, laid flat by the air raids in the last war, was full of military and police searching for 'radio-activity'. However, the traditional British imperturbability was well demonstrated by the fact that all the high-ups lunched in comfort at the Grand Hotel where we were staying.

After preaching at St Mary Redcliffe, I came back to a private meeting of Bristol Party members. One, Ken Howarth, drew me aside and said, 'We're all gunning for you tonight. So you'd better be on our side. The

Party's split from top to bottom. Alderman Harry Hennessy opened the meeting and then mentioned the fact that I had spoken at the Oxford Union in a debate on the Government's policy, which called for an explanation. I felt I was on trial and I was rather nervous. Howarth and Herbert Rogers asked very hostile questions, others were pacifistically inclined and were worried about the domestic implications of rearmament.

I answered as well as I could and Rogers created the greatest trouble by saying that there were only two possible foreign policies – a capitalist or a socialist one. The US was intent on depressing workers' standards of living all over the world, compared to the USSR, which was putting socialism into practice.

Others dissented from him but the rebels always speak in greater proportion to their strength and I was concerned at the situation getting out of hand, so I delivered a little pep talk on 'unity, loyalty and trust'. I got a vote of confidence at the end of the meeting *nem con*.

It gave me experience of a hostile audience. I had an opportunity to stand up for myself under attack – to establish myself as a person and a leader. To that extent I think I gained respect.

In February 1951 an unofficial strike of dockers took place, starting in Birkenhead and Liverpool and spreading to Manchester and London. The strike began over wages but, because the TGWU was led by the virulently anti-Communist General Secretary Arthur Deakin, it was complicated by allegations by Deakin of Communist 'agents provocateurs' creating 'unrest against capitalism'. He claimed that 'the clear intention is to strike at countries which do not accept the Communist outlook at the point at which they are most vulnerable'. The situation was embarrassing for the Government, and Minister of Labour Nye Bevan in particular, after three dockers from Liverpool and four from London were arrested and charged with conspiring to incite dock workers to take part in strikes. The strike was exacerbated and became a demand for the discharge of the arrested dockers.

Wednesday 14 February 1951
Another Parliamentary Labour Party meeting today on the economic repercussions of the Defence plan. But before it began, Glenvil Hall, the chairman, said that one matter was to be raised.

Then Bob Mellish got up to protest against the arrest of seven dockers. He said that until the arrest, the London dockers were showing that they were not being taken in by the Communist Party agitators, and had, in the main, resisted the appeals to come out on unofficial strike. He (Mellish) was appalled that police action had taken place and wondered why on earth the dockers' MPs hadn't even been consulted beforehand. This, he said, was just the way to break the Labour movement.

Bessie Braddock supported him for Liverpool Exchange. She added a personal attack on the PM for being completely out of touch. Then David Logan, another Liverpool MP, said he had been to an unofficial port workers' committee 'in Bessie Braddock's HQ', where the agitators were given their orders to go and get things started in London and were paid their fares. This had also included a sentence of death on a deviationist docker. I was a bit taken aback by this but no one asked for elucidation. The gist of his argument was that it was high time the Government clamped down on the CP.

At this stage, Herbert Morrison got up – the great big white chief, the statesman and placator. He warned us that the arrested dockers had not been tried and the matter was *sub judice*. No comment was permissible. The Attorney-General could not possibly reply. He was prohibited from taking political orders and the decision (on the dockers) was his and his alone. However, he (Morrison) was able to say that the Attorney-General had consulted the other ministers, including the Minister for Labour (Nye), before taking his decision and they had concurred.

Before we could absorb this news for ourselves, its significance was emphasised by Nye Bevan, who banged his papers on the table and half rose, saying, 'I cannot allow that to pass by.' Morrison sat down, so did Bevan, with explosive wrath and Glenvil Hall rose. But the cat was out of the bag. A back-bencher got up. 'Mr Chairman – as there is apparently a divergence between the Minister of Labour and the Lord President, the matter must be discussed.'

But it was not. Perhaps it was all for the best. I for one was very shocked by the Cabinet cleavage thus revealed.

Nye, summing up, said he had heard many appeals for Party loyalty and he felt that it should come from everyone, however exalted (looking at Morrison) – even those who had not had the advantage of experience in the trade union movement.

Subsequently two versions came out. Edward Shackleton (Morrison's PPS) suggested that Nye had begged the Attorney-General to arrest the leaders and that the Cabinet sub-committee which considered the appropriate action had accepted this. What seems more likely is the version Roy Jenkins and Woodrow Wyatt gave me on that evening, that Nye was against the arrests and had said so.

I came away wondering how the Government could last with such dissensions in it.

Thursday 15 February 1951
Defence debate was into its second day today. The opposition motion of censure was moved by Churchill.

Gaitskell has the intellectual qualities of the job of Chancellor and also, as last week's performance on meat and on India's sterling balances showed, fighting capabilities.

The Tory pressure to get us out is now at full pressure.

We were on the defensive until the end. Nye Bevan's final speech was a brilliant performance. It was quiet and contained no abuse. It cut Churchill particularly into little pieces by scorn and laughter.

Even Churchill really enjoyed it. For us it was a shot in the arm. It gave Nye his big chance to enunciate policy on the grandest scale and free him from the earlier limitations of health and housing and latterly Labour. It immeasurably strengthened his claim to the leadership of the Parliamentary Party and to the next premiership.

A majority of 21 for the Government, unexpectedly high, was the final triumph.

Thursday 22 February 1951
I went to Number 10 for tea today. The Prime Minister and Mrs Attlee make a point of entertaining Labour MPs in one way or another. Welsh MPs Llywelyn Williams and Dorothy Rees, and Coventry MP Elaine Burton were the other guests. We went over at 4.30 by car and up to the flat. Mrs Attlee received us and Clem came in later and stayed for half an hour. There had been a row at Questions, over the appointment of an American admiral over NATO sea forces and Clem had come out of it rather badly. We had been warned by Clem's PPS not to talk shop and so we were slightly taken aback when Vi went for Clem and asked him why he had knuckled under to the Americans yet again. Clem said nothing, but I got the impression that he really hadn't cared a bit one way or another and hadn't even known about the decision before Churchill put down his questions.

Tea was not exciting and Clem's conversation never rose above the ordinary except in his digs at Churchill. I think he has an inferiority complex.

Vi was very la-di-da in her latest creation, with long red fingernails. She might have been a leader of society and her comments were very 'upper class', especially her reference to the proposal to open Chequers to Festival of Britain visitors, which was 'How awful'!

Saturday 17 March 1951
I haven't written my diary for nearly three weeks and there are some interesting things to record.

The Prime Minister and George Thomas
George Thomas, the MP for Cardiff West, told me this story. In 1947 (he had been elected in 1945) he was asked by the National Union of Students to go to Greece as their representative at the trial of some Greek students, charged with helping the Republican rebels under General Markos. Having got there he 'decided' to go to northern Greece and try to cross the rebel lines to see Markos. With the help of his interpreter,

who he is convinced now was a spy, he walked through the mountains to a village where he was 'captured' and taken by donkey to Markos' HQ. He stayed with Markos and they had many talks. He was given letters to take back to the UN and had taken film and kept diaries.

After many tears and adventures he reached the Government lines and returned to Athens. He reached England to find himself a headline story. He spoke all over the place and was in the forefront of the attack on Bevin's policy of intervention in Greece. In fact, as he put it, he made himself a bloody nuisance to the Government. He even stopped the PM in the corridor and said, 'Mr Attlee, if I were a Greek, I should be fighting with Markos – terrible things are being done in Greece.' To this Attlee replied rather testily, 'Both sides are just as bad and we have to support the Greek Government.'

George was feeling the strain of this one-man campaign and his health suffered as a result. Then one day, Arthur Moyle, Attlee's PPS, said to him, 'George, the PM wants to see you.'

He went along, and Clem lit his pipe and began, 'George, you don't look at all well.'

'Well, Mr Attlee, I must admit I haven't been feeling too grand.'

'You must go to Switzerland for a holiday.'

'I can't possibly.'

'I shall send you to see my doctor. Here's the address. Go along and he will examine you.'

George was staggered and deeply touched. He went along and was given a thorough examination, and the doctor refused to tell George what his conclusions were: he had been ordered to send them direct to Number 10.

A week later the PM sent for him again. 'I have had the report,' he said. 'You must take a good rest. If you won't go to Switzerland then you must go away for three months' rest. The Chief Whip will make all the necessary arrangements.'

Since then he has had a very great affection for the PM, whose human feelings, so rarely shown, were very real.

A note on Hugh Dalton

Hugh Dalton, the Minister of Local Government and Planning, is a notably indiscreet man. He had to resign from being Chancellor of the Exchequer because he released the outline of the budget to a press man just before he opened the debate in October 1947.

Two or three days ago I met him just outside the Smoking Room. The Attorney-General (Sir Hartley Shawcross) was standing a few feet away reading the ticker tape. Dalton and I fell into conversation and began discussing the Divorce Bill which passed second reading last Friday. I said how angry I was that we were told it was going to be a free vote and then found that we were asked to oppose it.

'O well,' said Dalton at the top of his booming voice, 'that bloody Attorney-General hasn't got an ounce of political sense in his fingertips.' I thought he had seen Shawcross and was saying it in fun, but when he went on, 'He ought to leave politics and go back to the bar ...' I whispered, 'He's behind you.' Dalton glanced round quickly and his smile froze and his face went whiter even than normal. Without a word he turned and walked with me towards the Library. 'I can't help it,' he said, 'if the Attorney-General eavesdrops.'

Monday 19 March 1951
The present parliamentary situation is very uncertain. On a number of occasions the Government has been defeated but none have warranted a dissolution. The Prime Minister made it quite clear in fact that he would not consider resignation except on a major issue or on a vote of censure. With skilled leadership the Party has survived in power, despite various attempts on the King's speech and other occasions to dislodge it.

Then, about two months ago, the British Institute of Public Opinion (the British Gallup poll) published the latest figures on the state of the parties. The Conservatives had 51 per cent, Labour about 38 per cent. This was the lowest ebb for us since 1947. No doubt we shall pick up again. But meanwhile it was discouraging news.

Churchill phoned David Butler, whom he had consulted before the last election (on the strength of David's articles in the *Economist*). David rang him back and told him that while the figures had to be considered in the light of many factors, they meant (if they were accurate) a situation similar to that in 1935, with 480 Tory MPs to about 135 Labour. David subsequently sent a fuller analysis to Churchill and received a telegram of thanks.

Undoubtedly this report strengthened the determination of Churchill to call for an election.

On Thursday, 15 March a slip of paper was being circulated round the House (signed, I think, by Jim Callaghan):

GALA SMOKING CONCERT

IN THE SMOKING ROOM

THE HOUSE OF COMMONS MALE VOICE CHOIR

under its conductor

JIM

NO PAIRS   NO PACK DRILL

At about 10 o'clock the Smoking Room began filling up. There must have been 80 Labour MPs in there including 10-12 Cabinet Ministers.

Whenever a Tory came in they all sang: 'Why were you born so beautiful, why were you born at all.' When any Labour MPs went to the bar they sang: 'My drink is water bright, water bright fresh from the crystal stream.'

Then, they started singing a parody of 'John Brown's Body': 'We'll make Winston Churchill smoke a Woodbine every day, We'll make Winston Churchill smoke a Woodbine every day, We'll make Winston Churchill smoke a Woodbine every day, When the red revolution comes.' Solidarity for ever . . . ', etc.

It was great fun and we had certainly captured the Smoking Room from the Tories even if nothing more. They got back at us however by a brilliant tactical move. They challenged us to a division in the House and while we poured in to divide they called it off and by the time we had got back, the Smoking Room was theirs again.

Wednesday 11 April 1951

I must describe the events which have led up to the present crisis in the fortunes of the Party.

When Gaitskell came to consider his budget he was faced with the need for a considerable increase in revenue to meet the rearmament programme and the inflationary dangers that accompanied the rise in world prices.

He also had to demand, even more firmly than is usual for a Chancellor, that Government expenditure be held down tightly. The Cabinet Committee which considered the various ways in which these objectives could be achieved reached the provisional conclusion two weeks ago that no charge should be made for dentures and glasses on the health service. At about that time Nye Bevan made a speech in public at Bermondsey in which he said that no Government of which he was a member would introduce such a charge.

This was taken to be a statement of fact. It now appears it was nothing of the kind – rather an ultimatum to Gaitskell designed to intimidate him.

Perhaps I should say at this point that Nye's Celtic pride has been deeply hurt during the last six months. When Cripps resigned as Chancellor he was bitterly disappointed that he, Nye, did not replace him. Harold Wilson felt a similar resentment – of which more later. Then a few weeks ago, when Ernie Bevin resigned the Foreign Office, Nye felt that he should have had first refusal. Instead Herbert Morrison got it. These rebuffs and the emergence of Hugh Gaitskell, which shifted the old balance of forces in the Cabinet, produced all sorts of results. Nye, who had accepted the defence programme reluctantly, believed a socialist budget could make the sacrifices more palatable. When he learned, as late as Monday last, that Gaitskell intended to impose the health service charges, he decided to act.

The Cabinet met at 10.30 last Monday morning. The charge was disclosed as a definite feature and Nye announced his decision to resign if it were not withdrawn. Gaitskell, backed by the whole Cabinet (except Harold Wilson), stood firm. The Prime Minister, of course, was in hospital with a duodenal ulcer and he was kept in touch. By lunchtime no decision had been reached and so the Cabinet met again on Monday evening at 6.30 and sat for three hours. Nye and Harold Wilson decided that they would resign the following day and letters between them and the PM were actually exchanged with the understanding that they would be published the following evening at 7pm.

After the Cabinet had adjourned, Hugh Dalton (according to his own account) stayed late, with Nye, to dissuade him. Nobody seemed to care very much whether Harold Wilson resigned or not and from this one could learn that indispensability should not be assumed, nor tested too often.

On Tuesday morning, 10 April, Budget Day, Ian Mikardo, a 'Keep Lefter' and intimate of Nye's, had breakfast with Nye. That meal is shrouded in mystery. At any event when Nye reached the House the story had circulated and a number of junior ministers, including Jim Callaghan and John Freeman, signed a letter imploring him to reconsider. Callaghan himself presented the letter and Nye's comment was: 'You put me in a very difficult position.' A nice mixture of reversed thinking and understatement.

At about 3.40 on Tuesday, after Questions, Hugh Gaitskell, looking pale and nervous and complete with buttonhole, came along the Front Bench to open his budget.

I looked along the Treasury Bench. Dalton and Chuter Ede, Herbert Morrison and Douglas Jay – they were all there, even the dying Ernie Bevin. But Nye was not.

The Chancellor began. His speech lasted for more than two hours, a brilliant exposition: there is no doubt that speech made his reputation secure. When he came on to the detailed proposals we heard definitely of the decision to charge for glasses and false teeth under the health service. I looked at once to the group standing beside the Speaker's chair. Nye and Jennie Lee and Michael Foot had just entered and they stood there to hear the announcement. As soon as it had been made Nye peered anxiously at the Labour benches, eyes going back and forth up and down. The announcement was greeted without a sound. We all took it absolutely quietly. Nye looked crestfallen and disappeared through the glass doors.

The Tea Room and Smoking Room received the budget well. We had all expected far worse things and the most noticeable reaction was sheer relief.

By now the story of Nye's resignation was getting around. I dined with

Tony Crosland, Woodrow Wyatt and Roy Jenkins. Hugh Dalton joined us.

Most of what is set out above was culled from these four. The first indication had come on the Monday night from Tom Williams (S. Hammersmith). Gossip had it that Nye, feeling he could not carry the Party with him, had decided to postpone his final decision.

At 10.30 today the PLP had its meeting; it had been called to discuss Gaitskell's budget. We met in good heart. Early that morning, Truman had dismissed General MacArthur from all his commands and we felt that this would have an immediate effect on the prospects of peace in Asia.

Glenvil Hall opened the meeting. He said we should hear Gaitskell first. The Chancellor spoke briefly. When he sat down Chuter Ede rose and explained that there was a disagreement on the budget and the question had arisen as to how far collective Cabinet could be waived at a Party meeting. It had been decided (and the PM had reached the decision) that while Cabinet ministers could not argue with each other in public, it would be permissible for a statement to be made of the opposite point of view. Nye then got up. He was pale and angry. These were his remarks as far as I can remember them:

'Comrades. It is known to you that some of us find certain aspects of the budget very repugnant. We feel this so strongly that it is a question of principle that we contemplated taking a certain step. However, in the interests of the Party unity we have decided not to take that step. I will say no more than this: that the responsibility for maintaining Party unity should not fall on us alone. It is not too late for modifications to be made.'

The meeting proceeded. Various people spoke. Bessie Braddock said she would not defend the new charges on a public platform. After some discussion – which revealed more opposition to the budget than I had realised – Herbert Morrison spoke. He explained the difficulties with which a Chancellor has to contend, stressing the various pressures upon him, and the necessity for firmness.

At this point Nye got up to interrupt. He said, 'I must protest. It has been agreed that Cabinet ministers should not argue in public. I have contented myself with making a statement but if I am provoked in this way the situation will become intolerable.'

Immediately after Herbert I was called – my first speech at a PLP meeting.

I welcomed the budget and, since Gaitskell asked for honest criticism, I had some.

On this question of 'principle' of a free health service, it is nonsense. There are many national scandals it would be costly to correct. This is not a question of principle, but to the contrary, it is a practical matter. There is only one test we can apply and it is an overall one: 'with what we have and can get by way of revenue, how can we lay it to the best advantage of those who need help most?'

I believed that more should be done for the old age pensioner, hit hardest by the rising cost of living. He had to wait six months before the budget relief and within a year this would be swept away by the rising tide of prices.

To finance this increased benefit I would be willing to see the standard rate of income tax raised.

I added a word about MacArthur. I said we were all incredibly relieved and attributed it, in part, to British pressure. However, I hoped that no one would make any indiscreet statement of exultation. Truman faced tremendous internal difficulties and we should avoid anything that might add to his burden. We didn't want to see 'President' MacArthur elected next year.

I sat down, rather having regretted my intervention, which had contributed nothing in particular and had estranged me from the Nye group.

Miss Jones, who works in the PLP office, told me that when I was speaking, Ernie Bevin, flabby and pale and motionless, and half-asleep, woke up, looked up and asked, 'Who is that boy?' She told him and he replied, 'Nice boy, nice boy.' Three days later he died.

After the meeting Gaitskell and Douglas Jay came and joined me for lunch. Gaitskell is a strange man – donnish, slightly self-conscious, a little remote, as Crosland is when you talk to him. His success in presenting the budget and his personal victory over Nye in Cabinet hold out a danger that he may overplay his hand. Certainly he is a political personality to be reckoned with.

As to his own views, he tends to be right-wing. Four years ago Crosland told me that Gaitskell had been talking of the necessity of rearming the Germans. I was horrified at the time. I do not doubt that he is a first-class administrator, with every attribute that Winchester and New College can provide.

The row with Nye has been very unpleasant for him and I gather that the extent of Nye's personal attacks on him pass belief.

When he gets to hate a man his hatred knows no bounds.

Monday 23 April 1951

The resignation of Nye was announced this morning. Harold Wilson's position was uncertain though it was announced later today that he too intended to go. I arrived at the Commons at two and went up into the Members' Gallery. With the sunlight pouring through the windows opposite, the Chamber was suffused in a warm glow of light. Jennie Lee came in at about ten past three and sat, flushed and nervous, on the very back bench, below the gangway. At twenty past three Nye walked in briskly and jauntily and went straight to his seat three rows back. He looked pale and kept shifting his position and rubbing his hands. The Front Benches on both sides were very full – Churchill, Eden and the Tories sat quietly.

Morrison, Chuter Ede, Noel-Baker, Dalton, Gaitskell and the others sat unhappily together. Then the Speaker called Nye Bevan to make his resignation statement.

His rising was greeted by a few 'hear hears'. Not many. The Government Front Bench looked sicker and sicker as the speech went on and the violence of the attack intensified. Jennie Lee behind him sat forward and became more and more flushed. Every now and again he pushed back the lock of his iron-grey hair. He swung on his feet, facing this way and that and his outstretched arm sawed the air. He abused the Government, he threw in a few anti-American remarks for good measure. He attacked the Treasury, economists, and the unhappy combination of an economist at the Treasury. Gaitskell showed clearly the contempt he felt. Dalton looked like death once warmed up and now cooled down.

The fact is that though there was substance in what he said Nye overplayed his hand. His jokes were in bad taste. I felt slightly sick.

He sat down, the hum of conversation started and the exodus began. Nye stayed put for a few moments. He rose to go, and Emrys Hughes shook his hand as he passed the Front Bench.

It has to be said that he has written the Tory Party's best pamphlet yet. I predict it will be on the streets in a week.

Tuesday 24 April 1951

Nearly twenty-four hours have elapsed since I wrote the account of the dramatic scene in the House. Nye's attack was bitter and personal. His style was that of a ranting demagogue. But there was substance in what he said and his speech reads better than it sounded. Nye will never be in another Government until and if he forms his own. The rest of yesterday was hectic. I had thought Nye's statement would include some reference to his own intentions. It seemed inconceivable that he could overthrow the Government and yet while I listened it seemed impossible that the Government could last.

Rumours flew round all afternoon. Harold Wilson's resignation was confirmed and John Freeman's was thought very likely. I stood and gossiped a bit in the corridors and felt rather ashamed at doing so. Winston Churchill walked past with the Tory Chief Whip and said *en passant*, 'In all the streets the Party leaders stand, their own solution and a policy to hand.'

Last night I rang Pa and he came along to the House for a talk in the Smoking Room.

The comparison with Lloyd George and Asquith arose at once. He said he would have followed Lloyd George to the ends of the earth if he could have been sure of two things: that he would speak the truth and that he would stick to what he said. Therefore though emotionally for Lloyd George, he (Pa) stuck with Asquith. He warned me not to get mixed up with 'Nye' or 'anti-Nye'.

'You are yourself, the candidate for Bristol South-East. It is there you must fight to maintain yourself. When the groans of the members here, for whom Nye's resignation means political death, have subsided, you will settle in again.'

Today I picked up Pa and brought him to the Grand Committee Room where the Parliamentary Party had a special meeting. Many of the Party old-stagers, Christopher Addison, Pethick-Lawrence, Arthur Greenwood, and others were there. Glenvil Hall was in the chair and the Cabinet, barring the PM, were beside and behind him. The meeting was packed.

Nye and Jennie sat three-quarters of the way back on our side.

Glenvil Hall began by reminding us of the meeting that had been held there in 1931, 'when the Chancellor of the Exchequer was Mr Snowden'. The main figures on the platform then had passed into history (at this Pa shouted dissent!). Glenvil Hall read a message from the PM – written in his own hand – saying that the Party was bigger than each of us and we must have unity. This was greeted with cheers, though the reference to 1931 had done a great deal of damage. The next to speak was Harold Wilson. He gave a very quiet, dignified and impressive account of the reasons which had led to his resignation.

Wilson went on to agree with Nye that the defence programme had been wrecked by the continuing shortage of raw materials, caused by the dangerous expansion of US production designed to complete their own colossal rearmament programme and raise the level of domestic consumption at the same time.

Wilson argued that the charge on teeth and specs was only symbolic of his disagreement with the Cabinet. He said that, financial considerations aside, he detected a desire on their part to impose changes in any case. Finally, after making these points, he said that he intended to support the Government both inside and outside the House and to make this statement as uncontroversial as possible.

Next John Freeman spoke. He announced his resignation and stated that his disagreement with the Government went back far beyond the budget. He intended no disloyalty but felt that he was obliged to resign. 'In laying down the responsibilities of office I am also giving up the fruits of office.'

No one was more conscious of the need for unity than he and he intended to support the Government. This quiet, dignified but slightly pompous statement was well received.

Hugh Gaitskell was called. He began by congratulating John Freeman on his honesty and with a charming and disarming smile said, 'I quite agree with John on what he has said about the ethics of resignation.'

Turning to his budget and the issues it raised he affirmed that the defence programme was not as big as it might or could have been, if for example the Cabinet had believed that the Russians intended to attack this year or next. It was absurd to argue that no limits had been placed on it. On the contrary it was accepted only because it was compatible with our national economic independence and our present (or a slightly reduced) standard of living.

He had made it clear on radio, and in speeches, that it would mean sacrifices and that it was calculated with many reservations. Moreover, to his knowledge, Nye had never opposed the level of defence expenditure laid down for the current year.

At this Nye leapt up, highly excited. He shouted that this violated Cabinet secrecy and said, 'I won't allow it, I won't allow it.'

Gaitskell went on that he agreed with Nye that the US attitude to stockpiling was very dangerous indeed. Without divulging any Cabinet secrets, he felt it safe to remind Nye that he had frequently said this in Cabinet. The problem was one of allocation. Both we and the US were attempting to finance rearmament by increasing production and we could not grumble at that. Turning to the budget, he denied that it was unfair. To pick out a few items alone gave a wholly wrong impression. Profits tax, the purchase tax and increased income tax fell largely on the well-to-do and he believed it was a fair balance.

He also resented the suggestion that the cost of living was to be 'allowed' to go up. Mainly it was outside our control.

He bitterly resented Nye's charge that he had advocated payment for specs and teeth out of spite. There had to be a ceiling somewhere and that was for Cabinet to decide. It was grossly unfair to accuse him of cutting the social services when in fact they were to cost £50 million more this year.

In conclusion, the Chancellor said that we should do well to differentiate between the effects of world rearmament on us and the effect of our defence programme on ourselves. The two presented different but complicated problems.

He believed that this budget was a fair and honest one and that it should have been and could still be a popular one. Let us fight the Finance Bill through and win the next Election.

It was a stirring speech, clear and fair, put over with force and conviction. These twin qualities of intellectual ability and political forcefulness make up Hugh Gaitskell's greatness. It is rather ironical that Nye should have been largely responsible for making Gaitskell into the major political figure that he now is.

Glenvil Hall next called Arthur Greenwood. His gestures were weak and aimless and his remarks were punctuated by loud clicks from his false teeth.

He spoke of 1931, as one who had 'passed into history', and denied that there was any similarity. He upbraided the PLP for its gloom when we were making such headway in the country with membership going up and unity secure. He said gloom and disunity from the top would be the gravest act of treachery to the working class. I think his speech did some good.

After him Tom Proctor [MP for Eccles] was called. He began a long story about how he was on his way home from South Wales when the train, instead of going through the tunnel at Newport, went via Chepstow. Being a railwayman, this irrelevance by him was wildly cheered! The gist of his speech was that on the train he had met Archie Lush, Nye's agent at Ebbw Vale, who told him that the general council of the Ebbw Vale Party had met after the budget and decided to demand that Nye resign from the Cabinet. He, Archie, was on his way to London to present this ultimatum to Nye and tell him that if he did not resign he would not be readopted as candidate. Tom wanted to know if this was true.

When Nye rose he shook with rage and screamed, shaking and pointing and pivoting his body back and forth on his heels. His hair came down, his eyes blazed and I thought at times that he would either hit someone or collapse with a fit. The spectacle absorbed us completely. He accused Gaitskell of reckless frivolity of argument. He screamed, 'I have been martyred by the platform', a tragic insight into his persecution-ridden mind that shocked us all.

When he had said his piece Herbert Morrison shook his head with dissent. 'Don't shake your head, Herbert, it's no good you shaking your head,' he screamed. Tom Proctor intervened, and with contempt Nye turned on him: 'Shut up, shut up, you're a bonehead.' (Earlier, during Hugh Gaitskell's speech, Jennie Lee shouted something and Charlie Pannell told her to be quiet. Nye turned on him and said, 'I'll take you outside and knock you down.')

At one point even Nye said, 'I think I'd better sit down', but he didn't, demanding that we should face the facts, asserting that all the production departments had reported that the arms programme was impossible of realisation. 'We must influence the USA to release raw materials for our use and we must maintain the social services. The health service won us the last Election, you all boasted about it on your platforms and now you cut it. We cannot save ourselves as the man on the sleigh tried to do by throwing our children to the wolves.'

The megalomania and neurosis and hatred and jealousy and instability he displayed astounded us all.

Yet political memories are so short, and parliamentary parties so prone to change their composition, that though at this moment I could never trust or follow Nye, events might change my mind.

As the memorial service for Ernie Bevin was scheduled for 12.15 in Westminster Abbey there were no more speeches and Chuter Ede was called to wind up.

He said we had witnessed the most scurrilous attack on the Government he could recall (an allusion to *Tribune* of 17 April). At this Jennie Lee half rose and shouted, 'Right of reply, right of reply!' Chuter Ede paused and looked straight at Nye: 'In so far as this situation reminds me of 1931, it reminds me of a speech made by Oswald Mosley at one Party meeting.' This produced an instant uproar by Nye and Jennie who both shouted, 'Now you'll get it', 'You've asked for it,' and other unintelligible threats.

Chuter went on unhesitantly, to say that the maintenance of this Government was vital for the peace of mankind. The situation was difficult, the budget was hard, and all ministers had had to make sacrifices. He stressed that unity and unanimity were incompatible with any progressive Party – but loyalty was vital. Hugh Gaitskell had prepared the budget but the whole Cabinet – the *whole* Cabinet – accepted the responsibility for it.

Moreover, when the first proposal for making a charge on teeth and specs had come up there was no hint of rearmament at all. Nye shouted: 'Publish the papers, publish the papers!' This interruption began to develop into a new speech and Chuter sat down while Nye went on. 'I intend to ask the Prime Minister to ask the King to publish the papers.'

Chuter Ede got up: 'There are *some* people who hope this party will go into opposition so that a new Leader can emerge . . .' The rest of what he said was drowned in a chorus of disapproval from people who were anything but pro-Nye. Desmond Donnelly [MP for Pembroke] moved the adjournment of the meeting and Chuter Ede said that he had finished all he had to say and hoped that the unity of the party would remain secure. Glenvil Hall accepted Donnelly's motion and at 11.23 we adjourned.

At dinner Michael Foot came and joined us. He was quite friendly but there is no doubt this split has had and will continue to have the effect of creating barriers between friends – not of course that I am a friend of Michael's – but it is true of those like Tom Driberg and John Freeman whom I know slightly.

The day ended with the unopposed second reading of the National Health Service Bill.

May 17th '51

Dearest Proff

Just a line to tell you that I am on *Any Questions* again tomorrow night –

Friday.

I was asked at rather short notice to replace Woodrow Wyatt, who, as you know, has been made Under-Secretary of State for War and is not allowed to broadcast. The programme is 8.15–9.00 on the Light Programme I think. I'm not suggesting you listen, but I thought you'd like to know.

  Love, James

Between June and September, 1951 I failed to keep a diary despite all intentions to the contrary.

To our great delight, on 21 August 1951, our first child, Stephen Michael, was born, Caroline having just received her post-graduate degree from London University. We spent the summer at Stansgate.

My first year in the Commons had been dominated by the Bevan row, which had ended in his resignation as the Minister of Labour.

In May 1951 I spoke in the debate on compensation for Far Eastern Prisoners of War, who had been seriously ill-treated by the Japanese, arguing that the dropping of the Atom bombs at Hiroshima and Nagasaki was an equal atrocity and that throughout four hundred years of British colonialism similar atrocities must have been committed by our own troops.

This speech was heavily interrupted and it was my first experience of addressing a hostile chamber, and was followed by a few critical letters from those who had read press reports of the debate: I am still glad that I drew the comparison.

I spoke in two further debates in the Commons – the first on the future of the BBC and the second on immigration policy.

In the former I complained at the refusal of the BBC to recognise my own union, the National Union of Journalists, and argued for far greater decentralization of the BBC instead of the system under which all power was vested in the Director-General.

In the second debate I came out strongly against the tight restrictions on immigrants, pointing out that far more people left the country than entered it, drawing a comparison with the more liberal US policy and pointing out that, at that time, unemployment in Britain stood at less than one per cent while there were half-a-million unfilled vacancies.

In the autumn of 1951 Clem Atlee, the Prime Minister, dissolved Parliament to hold an Election one year before its term was out, although Labour still had a small majority in the Commons. In less than a year after being first elected at a by-election, I thus had to fight my seat again.

It was during that campaign that I was asked to help Hugh Gaitskell with the first ever TV election broadcast, beginning an interest in party political broadcasting that continued until Labour won the election in 1964.

Monday 8 October 1951

We wondered all summer whether there would be an Election and on about 12 September, when I was in London, the House of Commons was buzzing with the latest rumours. A week later, on 19 September, the Prime Minister broadcast his decision and I didn't go to the Scarborough Conference, nor in fact did I visit my constituency until today.

Caroline, Stephen and I drove down from London to Bath and got settled in Pratt's Hotel. At 7.15 we got to Unity House, the Party HQ, and went straight to a meeting of the General Council. The business was simple.

Then a resolution reselecting me was put and carried and I spoke for a few moments, stressing how we should concentrate on peace, planning and social justice.

Tuesday 9 October 1951
The big headlines were on the new Egyptian announcement that they intended to abrogate the 1936 treaty regarding British occupation of the Canal Zone and the Condominium in Sudan.

The Tories are going to play this up along with the Persian oil crisis and the evacuation of Abadan. I rang Pa straight away to get a background guide, as he knows more about this than anyone, having been there in 1946 for six months seeking to get the treaty amended.

At 4.30 I stopped for tea and Eric Rowe (my agent) and I dropped in to see John and Queenie Rees. John is making a most professional illuminated 'Vote Benn' sign for the car. The loudspeaker is broken.

Wednesday 10 October 1951
Tom Martin of the Tailor and Garment Workers' Union is lending us some loudspeaker equipment. There was just time to do 8 five-minute meetings before I picked up the Dayglo posters 'Back Benn Again'. They are red on black. Ideally one ought to be able to get elected independently of the Party ticket although in these modern times that is virtually impossible.

The large Gallup poll majority against us (still 7 per cent) seems too big to beat in two weeks.

People are apathetic and there aren't the young ones at meetings that there ought to be. The housewives are our weakest spot, and I am sure that with men alone voting we would win easily. Perhaps women are destined to be the floating voters, stirred against any Government in these days of the welfare state.

I do not trust the Tories to keep the peace or achieve success with production. But my only consolation would be the hope that they would keep their promise to reform the House of Lords and allow me to retain a seat in the Commons.

Monday 15 October 1951
Harry Hennessy took me to my first dinner-hour meeting, outside the

Co-op furnishing factory. Not a single soul came out of the factory to listen and I began to wonder what was wrong. We had a lot of kids from the school which made some sort of an audience, but either through a mistake in timing, or through hostility, we got no one out.

I disappeared after lunch to help Tony Crosland in Gloucestershire South. He did very well in his personal canvassing but I didn't think much of his speech.

Tuesday 16 October 1951

At 7 Caroline and I went over to the Central Hall, Bristol for the great rally which the Prime Minister was to address. There were nearly 3,000 people there. Harry Hennessy was a wonderful master of ceremonies. His introductory speech was blunt and honest.

Every Labour candidate in Bristol spoke and as I stood up to speak I felt sick with emotion. Mastery of an audience of that size is a strong task, but what an intoxicating experience it is.

We all did a second speech in an overflow meeting upstairs and Harry started a collection off. We collected £138.

Then Clem and Vi could be seen on the way to the platform. Everyone stood up and cheered lustily, shouting themselves hoarse. 'Hello Tony,' he said as if we were old friends! I shook Vi's hand as she passed. Harry took control again and we all sang 'For he's a jolly good fellow'. Then Harry introduced 'Comrade Clem Attlee', and pushed him forward. But the bouquet had been forgotten and Alderman Mrs Keel gave Vi the flowers with a moving little speech.

Clem quietly and sensibly reviewed the work of the Government abroad and at home, linking each to the work of two famous West Countrymen, Ernest Bevin and Stafford Cripps. 'They have both left us now,' he said, 'but other younger ones have come to take their place. Christopher Mayhew, one of the most brilliant young men, to replace Ernie Bevin, and Tony Wedgwood Benn, another brilliant man, to replace Stafford Cripps.'

When he sat down Tony Crosland moved his vote of thanks, and paid his tribute somewhat back-handedly by saying there has never been an anti-Attlee faction in the Party (which was both patently untrue and damning with faint praise).

We ended with the first verse of 'The Red Flag'.

Wednesday 17 October 1951

The way the Egyptian crisis is developing makes it far harder to draw a distinction between the two parties. Herbert Morrison's 'tough' policy and the delight with which the *Daily Herald* is unexpectedly playing it up have taken the ground from under our feet. I cannot understand why the public relations on this have been so badly handled.

Thursday 18 October 1951
Far too many council houses have Tory bills in the windows.

Sunday 21 October
To St Matthew's parish hall for a public meeting with David Goldblatt, the Liberal candidate for Bristol West.

My theme was to woo the Liberals to vote Labour. I proposed doing it by pointing out how we shared the same ideas but that in putting them into practice we differed. It was an appalling speech, muddled and badly delivered, airy fairy, and without form.

Goldblatt was brilliant. He out-debated me from the start and I was very ashamed of my performance.

Thursday 25 October 1951
The first thing to notice on polling day is the weather and today dawned clear and blue, with a good winter nip in the air. Everyone was cheerful and there was a crowd of small boys helping by running as messengers and checking numbers at the polling stations.

At about 7.15 all the helpers gathered and we set off on a grand tour. The flashing VOTE BENN sign with spotlight on the yellow flag and loudspeaker blaring was the centrepiece. I stood on the running-board for a while but it was too tiring and I walked behind and waved.

Leaving a group of tea-drinkers in the Committee Rooms, at 8.45 I drove back to Bath to pick up Caroline and have supper. As we sat, the first results began to come in over the wireless. We heard first of a recount at Watford, which in itself was significant as the Bevanite John Freeman was thought to be marginal.

His victory by a small majority was cheerful news even though one cannot rejoice over the personal aspect.

Then the results began coming in more quickly. The first indications were of a moderate swing – Labour majorities reduced by about 1,500 and Tory votes similarly up. It looked as if this would give a working majority to the Tories but only two Conservative gains were reported in the first hours.

We reached Wick Road School at about 11.45 pm after having left Stephen at Winifred Bishop's house. My agent, Eric Rowe, standing behind the returning officer, had a huge smile on his face. The growing piles of votes in 250s showed us to have about a two to one lead. We almost doubled the by-election majority, although it was down 2,000 compared with Cripps.

I spoke briefly in the count, about the efficiency of the official staff, the clean way the campaign had been fought, and the miracle of British democratic decision making. I was carried on the shoulders of supporters to Ruskin Hall where I thanked them more personally.

A very tired MP and his wife got back to their hotel at 3am. We listened to the results as they came in until about 3.45.

After the inflation caused by the Korean War, the arguments within the Party, and the drive towards rearmament in Britain and Europe, the defeat of the post-war Labour Government was perhaps inevitable. But the Labour vote remained high and was actually greater than the popular vote that carried Winston Churchill back to power.

Although Clem Attlee carried on as Leader of the Labour Party until after the General Election of 1955, it was obvious that the Party was moving to the right, with the rise of new leaders, of whom Hugh Gaitskell was the most significant; while the left under Aneurin Bevan's leadership was on the defensive. After the Election I resolved to keep my diary more regularly but succeeded only in an intermittent record of those years in opposition, as a humble backbencher.

Wednesday 31 October 1951
Parliament reassembled today and this morning there was a joint meeting of the Parliamentary Party and the National Executive.

Father came along and we sat side by side.

Glenvil Hall (whose victory over Lady Violet Bonham Carter in Colne Valley gave us so much pleasure)[1] welcomed new Members by name and told us he was writing to those who had been defeated. Next business was election of a Leader, and Clem was elected by acclamation. He took the chair, beaming and grinning like a cat with two tails. He bubbled with schoolboy jokes.

His next task was the election of a Deputy Leader. After Herbert Morrison had been proposed by the ever faithful Frank McLeavy there was a move to postpone a decision so that a private ballot could be organised. However, the suggestion was defeated by a show of hands. Frank rose again in support of Herbert. Then a voice could be heard (I think it was Emrys Hughes') proposing Nye Bevan and this was seconded. Aneurin rose and declined the officer, amidst a dignified mutter all round. Herbert was therefore unanimously elected.

I must record one most unpleasant incident that occurred at this time. Jennie Lee who was sitting in front of me turned to Father and said, 'You know Wedgie, despite your radical background this son of yours shows more and more sign of becoming a proper little Tory.' Father replied, 'Well I must enlist your help in trying to control him', to which Jennie replied, 'No, the best way is not to control him. Leave them alone and we find that everyone writes his own signature in his own way in time.' It was said with such bitterness and so meanly that it completely wrecked my day.

This evening David Butler came to dinner and his latest meeting with Churchill on the Saturday before polling day deserves a mention. He had been summoned before the 1950 Election to Chartwell and had spent the evening with the man discussing electoral possibilities, and he remained overnight as a guest.

This latest summons came and David presented himself at Hyde Park Gate at about 10.30 in the morning, where he found Winston in bed drinking a whisky and soda. The first thing that struck him was how he had aged in the last eight months.

He asked several questions about his chances of success in the Election. David was cautious and indicated that an overall majority of forty or so was likely. Putting it into betting odds, he got a more lively response and they had a little backchat.

Churchill remembered almost exactly David's remarks about 18 months before.

Before he left, Churchill asked him quietly and soberly, 'Mr Butler, do you think I am a handicap to the Conservative Party?' It was said without dramatic intent – indeed with a rather pathetic desire for reassurance. David did not answer for a while. 'Come Mr Butler, you need not be afraid to tell me.'

'Well,' replied David, 'I do not think that you are the asset to them that you once were ... the public memory is short, you know.'

'But the people love me, Mr Butler. Everywhere I go they wave and workmen take off their cloth caps to cheer me ...'

A Note on Hugh Gaitskell

Just before the Election was announced I wrote (as radio adviser to the Party) to Hugh Gaitskell asking him whether I could give him any help with the Party political broadcast he had been asked to give on 29 September. He sent a message asking me to come to his room at the Treasury and I asked Michael Young, Secretary of the Party's Research Department, to come with me.

Gaitskell walked across from his desk to greet us, and as we were ushered in his smile was welcoming. We sat round his desk and he outlined to us the script that he proposed to deliver.

He was immaculately dressed in a brown suit, with the very slightest aura of aftershave lotion and talcum powder about him. His curly hair and receding chin gave him a boyish but also slightly ineffective appearance. His smiles are slightly distant and complacent – his mind appeared to be working on its own and only part of it was devoted to the people who were with him.

After he had finished I asked him to what audience he would be directing his remarks – floating, middle class, trade unionist, unhappy Bevanite? He looked a little pained and bored when I pressed the point and countered by a reminder that honest politics meant speaking the truth, and what fine service Cripps had done to establish this tradition.

Under the mildest form of criticism, he always reverted to this slightly detached and hurt off-handedness so reminiscent of Tony Crosland. The similarity between the two was too noticeable to be missed and no wonder that Crosland thinks so highly of him.

I could see very clearly how the character of Gaitskell and his mannerisms would have driven Nye Bevan to fury. I won't say he is slippery because he is too straightforward to be that, but he could easily by a gesture or smile or frown or word-choice make it clear he wished to avert a head-on collision in argument with those who disagreed with him.

In a way it was his attractive, public school character that made him both pleasant and detestable.

I thoroughly enjoyed it even though it made me more sympathetic to Nye Bevan than I had been at the start.

Tuesday 6 November 1951
The King's Speech today was a dismal failure – nothing in it at all. Churchill looked a very sick man.

Wednesday 7 November 1951
Butler's début as Chancellor was the occasion for some Labour glee. The policy of austerity he announced was a complete vindication of Labour's policy and sounded the death knell of most Tory pledges. There were many glum faces behind him as he spoke.

Tuesday 20 November 1951
Reached the house at 5.15. and met Tom Williams (my own MP – South Hammersmith) and we stood and talked in the corridor.

He told me privately and before I was 'officially' approached that it had been decided to ask me to join the Bevan group. Apparently half a dozen people in the group had suggested it and Fenner [Brockway] was the man detailed to make the request. Tom – bless him – said he thought I might like to know before then, so that I could have some time to think about it. I said that I was undecided and very greatly appreciated his kindness.

Should I join the Bevanites?

I am not in sympathy with the methods used by the Bevanites since the resignations in April. *Tribune* has been scurrilous and the personal bitterness engendered has been far greater than was necessary. Particularly obnoxious do I find the complacent assumptions by the Bevanites that the ark of the socialist covenant resides with them.

From a personal point of view I am anxious to settle down independently. This last year has been very frustrating and I am only just starting to venture forth on my own.

22.11.51

Dear Fenner

Just a note to let you know that I would prefer to postpone any decision on the question you asked me on Tuesday.

Though I share many of the views held by the group, as a new member enjoying a little independence for the first time I don't want to bind myself in any way at present.

Yours ever
Tony Wedgwood Benn

Thursday 28 February 1952
PLP Foreign Affairs Group
Today there was another Foreign Affairs Group meeting to discuss German rearmament. It was interesting because for the first time decisions were taken. The characteristic of Party discussions all this time has been talk and no vote. The Foreign Affairs Group was the first to do anything but of course its decisions were not binding on the Party.

The following motions were moved:

Eric Fletcher: 'That this group is opposed to any proposals for a German contribution to Western Defence which would violate all four conditions laid down by the present Leader of the Opposition on 12 February 1951; and is of the opinion that the whole question of German rearmament should be postponed for the time being; and protests against Her Majesty's Government's support for the creation of what the Prime Minister has openly described as a German Army.' [Carried by 30 votes to 24.]

John Strachey: 'That this Party shall reaffirm the view that we shall not agree to German rearmament until the conditions laid down by Mr Attlee have been fulfilled. These conditions include in particular the condition that the building up of the forces in the democratic states must precede the creation of German forces and that the agreement of the Germans themselves must be obtained. That this party shall urge that the British Government shall indicate its willingness to become a member of the European Defence Community if a treaty containing suitable safeguards can be negotiated.' [Defeated]

Denis Healey: 'That this Party believing that the defence of Western Europe can best be achieved within a closely integrated European Defence Community, but that a European Defence Community limited to the nations of continental Europe is inadequate for this purpose, maintains that the British Government should approach the Administration of the USA to propose that both countries offer to place a proportion of their armed forces inside the European Defence Community.' [Defeated]

Emrys Hughes: 'That this Party declares its opposition to any form of German rearmament, welcomes the opposition to German rearmament recently expressed by the socialist parties of Germany and France and calls for joint consultation with our continental comrades with a view to halting armament in Europe, formulating a policy for disarmament and the reconstruction of Europe as a planned socialist economy.' [Defeated]

Freda Corbet [MP for Peckham]: 'That this group accepts the necessity for a German contribution to Western defences with safeguards against a resurgence of German militarism as laid down by Mr Attlee in his four points on 12 February 1951.' [Defeated]

Feb/March 1952 (Dictated June 1952)

The first two months of 1952 marked a general improvement in relations within the party. The Bevanite problem seemed to be on the way to solution. Tory policy was uniting us all and there was plenty of good feeling. Then in March the Government published the Defence White Paper. At once things got more intense. Crossman drafted an amendment to it and circulated it for signature. I was approached but refused to sign it. There was a Party meeting to discuss the matter. The official Party amendment was to add to the Government motion the words 'but has no confidence in the capacity of HMG's present advisers to carry it out'. Attlee sent out a special three-line whip to all Members to support this. The Bevanites refused.

I learned later that the Shadow Cabinet had framed this motion as a bridge towards the Bevanites. However, there is no doubt that the Bevanites took it as a direct slap in the face. On the day of the debate I was in two minds as to which way to vote. I went in to hear Crossman's brilliant speech and then I heard Attlee's winding up. Finally, having left it too late to go away and abstain, I found myself going to vote with the Party. The first question put was the amendment and to this the Bevanites and others abstained. The second was the main question which the Bevanites opposed, while the bulk of the Party abstained.

I was away from the House most of Thursday 6 March and all of Friday. It wasn't until Saturday morning that I heard from the *News Chronicle* that a great row was brewing with talk of expulsions of the Bevanites from the PLP.

I decided to do what I could and at first contemplated finding a group willing to resign from the Party if Nye were expelled. I wrote out a list of people who I thought might be sympathetic. The first person I rang was Kenneth Robinson.

I spent the rest of the day and all day Sunday phoning around.

I rang Hugh Dalton on Sunday night and asked him what the Parliamentary Committee would do when they were defeated at the Party meeting.

He refused to believe they would be. He was convinced the wind was blowing the other way and had set his sails accordingly.

On Monday the 11th I had lunch with Kenneth Robinson. We discussed the situation and agreed to get together later with those of our way of thinking to organise a bloc of moderates.

After lunch I went to the Tea Room where there was an 'expulsionist' group in action. I argued very fiercely with them and was rather rude, I fear, but so were they. It scared me stiff. I thought the Party had had it.

The 'Keep Calm' group came to meet me at 5. At 5.24 the meeting adjourned so that two MPs could see Clem before the 6 o'clock Parliamentary Committee meeting to present our views.

At this meeting a revised resolution was agreed on, which was presented at the Party meeting the following day. However it is now clear that the bulk of the Committee wanted to frame a motion that would lead to the expulsion of Bevan and his associates.

At 8 pm the non-Bevanite rump met under John Freeman's chairmanship (the real figurehead of humbug respectable rebelliousness) and they decided to await the outcome of the Party meeting.

On Tuesday 11 March the Party meeting was in the Grand Committee Room.

At 10 am Clem had not arrived and at 10.20 Herbert Morrison got up and said he had better begin the meeting with formal business.

At 10.23 Clem turned up. He had been delayed by fog on the line and he looked very nervous. He was shaking visibly when he got up to speak.

He said: 'This is the most serious situation I can remember during the seventeen years I have been Leader. It might put the Tories in power for many years. The Party meeting had reached a decision and the revolt was against the Party meeting, not against its leadership. Since standing orders were suspended (in 1945) democracy must be the basis of our decisions, allowing for the conscience clause.

'With regard to the debate last week; members of this Party advised others to defy a Party decision. The ostentatious abstention of some members was a deliberate act. I sent out a special whip to avoid confusion.

'The Party is free to choose its own leaders, but once chosen they must stick by them. We cannot overlook this situation and we must come to a decision. The Parliamentary Committee proposes the following resolution:

'That this meeting of the PLP severely condemns those 57 members who voted against the decision of the Party last week, calls on all members to give an undertaking in writing that they will abide by the decisions of the Party in future allowing for the conscience clause, and welcomes the reintroduction of standing orders.

'Everyone must sign.'

Bob Mellish was then called (no doubt because Clem expected him to be tough). He set the tone of the meeting. He said that the reporters were waiting to hear the news that the Party was breaking up. 'But it is bigger than all of us – including the Platform. I felt hatred last week but now I feel less. Surely we needn't sign . . .'

Archie Manuel [MP for Central Ayrshire] (one of the 57): 'I hope the chairman won't make iron-fist rulings. Our only crime is that we voted against a Tory Party motion – then abstained on conscience. Dick Stokes [Ipswich] has been absent from the House for weeks – isn't he just as guilty?'

Irvine: 'This is a serious Party meeting and I hope that tolerance and dispassionate feeling will prevail. The official amendment was drafted so that the three Bevanite ministers *couldn't* accept it. In the last analysis it is unrealistic to ask people to bind themselves not to oppose Party decisions.' He then quoted from Burke.

Clem: 'Please be brief.'

Irvine: 'Very well, I'll omit the second quote from Burke' (Laughter). 'This is not a split on principle – but we cannot mock or ignore the feelings of the dissidents. Only the dissidents can save the unity of the Party. The Parliamentary Committee *approve* of Tory defence policy and *only* disapprove of the personnel carrying it out.'

Fred Lee: 'No one should be asked to sign. Most of our difficulties arise out of the difference between being in power and being in opposition and we shall have to work out a better system for Party meetings. Majority rule must prevail, provided there is adequate discussion. Let's forget "Cabinet rules" and start afresh.'

Nye Bevan: 'I am very sorry that the subject of defence, as an issue, has been ruled out of order. In that case the NEC and the Annual Conference must consider it. Should the 57 be condemned? Who split the Party? Certainly not Scarborough – that united it. I have never attacked the leadership. I didn't stand for the Executive because I didn't want to speak with two voices from the Front Bench.'

Clem: 'Don't be personal.'

Nye: 'There are many groups in the Party – there is the XYZ Club – a group of ex-Ministers – and many others. You always have groups.

'A letter was sent to the Parliamentary Committee before the defence debate. It was very reasonable and could have united the Party. Instead the Committee conspired against me.' By now Nye was thoroughly heated and in full tide of wrath, finger quivering and pointing. 'Woodrow Wyatt was given a copy of this letter and the Defence Committee considered it.'

Callaghan on a point of explanation: 'A member of the Defence Committee had seen the letter as he was canvassed to support it.'

Nye: 'How could I agree to the official amendment? I had resigned on the

£4.7 million programme and I challenge Clem to come with me to the Palace to get permission to publish the papers of the decision.'

Clem: 'No – you resigned on the cuts.'

Nye: 'We resigned on arms.'

Jean Mann [MP for Coatbridge and Airdrie]: '*You* supported the £4.7m programme.'

Nye: 'Contain your bile, Jeannie. The Party could have been united. We could have fought it on the Election manifesto. The real splitters are the leakers. I know the names.'

Several members: 'Who? Who?'

Nye: 'The leak is in the background now.'

Freda Corbet interrupted Nye, who said, 'Shut up Freda, you're not in County Hall now. I will accept standing orders but the leaks must stop.'

Clem: 'There were no official leaks.'

Nye: '*No*, I didn't say that. Party meetings are inadequate, as was proved by the Foreign Affairs debate. Who are the wreckers?' (Nye screams this and Clem smiles smugly). 'Having a secret Party meeting caucus will wreck the Party and if a vote of censure is passed it will split the Party.'

Percy Daines [MP for East Ham North]: 'That was an eloquent plea for anarchy. This is a simple issue of majority rule. Of course there are groups, otherwise who were the "we" Dick Crossman referred to over the weekend?'

George Strauss moved his amendment calling for the reintroduction of standing orders. John Strachey seconded.

Tom O'Brien [MP for Nottingham North West] (in a very tough and effective speech) made five points:

1. He supports Strauss.
2. If Clem's motion is accepted the Party commits suicide within a few hours of Butler's budget.
3. Majority rule is necessary but minority rights must be respected.
4. We must have wisdom.
5. The official defence amendment should never have been tabled.

John Freeman (pompous and smug and urbane as ever): 'Grateful to Strauss – we want unity. We all accept standing orders – but Defence is of course a matter of conscience.'

Clem: 'Conscience can go too far and majority rule is the only way of running a Party. We think that the action of the 57 ought to be condemned and we shall press our resolution to the vote.'

The Strauss amendment was put and carried 162 to 73. The official resolution therefore fell. The meeting broke up, after the third example in a few weeks of the incapacity of the Executive.

At the next meeting standing orders were reintroduced and at the following meeting various amendments were considered and voted on. Gradually the hatred that had been stirred up by the debate and vote died down. The expulsionists had been beaten, the Bevanites had been rebuked, the moderates had won. The wounds healed and the Tory budget plus the results of the County Council elections (with sweeping Labour gains) united and heartened us so that we moved into the Easter recess with good spirits and good feelings, which are rare, it seems, in the Labour Party.

In the summer of 1952 Caroline and I, and our year-old son Stephen, visited Caroline's home in Cincinnati just as the American presidential campaign was moving into its final stages.

I took the opportunity of writing to Governor Adlai Stevenson, the Democratic candidate, who was Governor of Illinois, to ask if I might visit him for a talk.

When he agreed to see me David Butler, who happened to be in America at the same time, and I drove to the Governor's mansion. What follows is an account of that talk written shortly after our meeting. The following year, 1953, I let my diary cease completely until September while I became more and more absorbed with the anti-colonial struggle in Parliament and tried to retain a more independent role in the inner Party conflicts that were building up.

I joined a small group of active Labour backbenchers led by Geoffrey Bing and including Reggie Paget, Ian Mikardo, Leslie Hale and Fenner Brockway and we tried to use every parliamentary opportunity open to us to make political points that were not being made by the Front Bench.

Our daily meetings to plan our tactics gave me an understanding of parliamentary procedure and how it could be used to advance a political case that might otherwise go by default.

In February 1953 Reggie Paget, the MP for Northampton, introduced a 'ten-minute rule' bill designed to enable help me to retain my seat in the Commons at the moment that my father's death (then seven years away) would disqualify me from sitting, by virtue of his peerage. It was, needless to say, overwhelmingly defeated.

Tuesday 2 September 1952
I had written to Governor Stevenson to ask if I might see him. Mr William Blair, his assistant, cabled the invitation to come, and showed me in. The Governor was sitting at his desk at the end of a long conference table. He rose to welcome me and said that he had met Father during the war, in Italy.

Stevenson: I met him when I went over in 1944 to his headquarters in Naples. 'Wedgie' we called him, a famous name in British politics. Well, what are you doing over here?
Benn: I am over here for two months studying the campaign. So far I have been mainly in Cincinnati, where of course the Republicans are very displeased with the choice of the Republican candidate, Dwight

Eisenhower, and the treatment of Senator Robert Taft. As a result they are very pessimistic about the outcome of the Election. And of course the Democrats are very optimistic. What I wanted to do, if I may, is to ask you some direct questions about your policy, mainly in the form that they are asked me in Britain. Obviously our different views on China are the most striking and important. We have recognised their Government and I am often asked under what circumstances the American Government would recognise them.

Stevenson: Well, that's a difficult question. No one could recognise China now in America and keep his shirt. And if the Chinese attacked Indo-China the present public feeling would be much intensified. It's very difficult to see one's way clear on this. Certainly not while the Korean War continues. With regard to Korea – and this is off the record – I was very much opposed to crossing the parallel at the time, except in so far as it was necessary to establish a defensive position. That would have met the intention of the first resolution on Korea passed by the UN at the beginning. The second one, calling for the unification of Korea, for which I'm afraid we were largely responsible, seemed to me to have been a mistake. The trouble was that we left it all to the military. And also we ignored the one piece of good advice that we got – from the Indians – who warned us that the Chinese would come in if we went up to the Yalu River. It's a very difficult problem and I admit I don't see my way out of it clearly.

Benn: Do you feel that the present Chinese Government is there to stay, or do you think that it can be shaken by Chiang Kai Shek?

Stevenson: Oh, no, there can be no future for Chiang Kai Shek. He has long since ruled himself out, and in the United States the Administration's record on China has been badly distorted over the years. They say, 'The Democrats have lost us China'. I guess that no responsible official in the State Department or informed politician in either Party now believes that there is any future for Chiang. As to training Chinese Nationalist troops for use in Korea, it is a very difficult question.

Benn: Well now, related to this, and a thing that causes a great deal of worry in Britain from time to time, is the body of opinion which seems to be strong and which has important spokesmen, which despairs of peace and seeks, in the case of Korea, either to get out at once or to win by extending the war. In some cases they even urge a whole-scale preventive war.

Stevenson: Who are you thinking of?

Benn: In the Far East, General MacArthur, and with regard to the more general point covering Europe, Foster Dulles with his condemnation of containment and his advocacy of a more direct policy.

Stevenson: Ah, you must read a speech that I made in Michigan, yesterday. (He sent for a copy and gave it to me.) Dulles' policy is designed purely for internal political consumption. He realises that there are a lot of Czechs and Poles and Rumanians and Eastern Europeans in the United States worried about their captive brothers; and this is a cynical attempt to win their support. I cannot believe that the Republicans really mean this. It has created great disquiet among Eisenhower's internationalist supporters.

Benn: Well, I never realised that. I thought that it might be a wild statement designed to attack the Administration, but evidently I'm not cynical enough.

Stevenson: Oh, yes, that is the sole and simple reason for it. The Polish American Group has, as a direct result, come out for Eisenhower. It represents a sizeable part of the New York City vote.

Benn: Can I turn this from a negative to a positive question? How can one create the climate of opinion in the United States in which the hope of co-existence can be made to flourish over a long period of time?

Stevenson: It will be very difficult. So much emotion enters into it. And co-existence will soon be damned, like containment, as appeasement. The problem of democratic education in foreign policy will be one of the biggest problems of the next Administration.

Benn: I was delighted to read your speech to the American Legion, and to see you deal such a deadly blow to McCarthyism, and more than that, to give some meaning to that quote of Dr Johnson's ('Patriotism is the last refuge of a scoundrel'). It has never meant very much before – except as a cynical joke.

Stevenson: Oh, I am glad that you liked it. How do you feel about the question of co-existence in Britain? You are so much more mature and sophisticated than we are.

Benn: I think we realise, perhaps even more than you do, what utter destruction another war would involve for us. And we live in the hope of co-existence.

Stevenson: We are faced with a struggle with the Russians, which may go on for generations. I will certainly do all I can to negotiate with them, whenever the opportunity for genuine negotiations presents itself.

Benn: Well, next to the problem of military danger comes economic danger, and this really leads me on to ask you about another problem, which vitally affects us. What would you do if you were faced with another recession, big or small? For example, if the Korean War comes to an end and American defence expenditure levels off and there is a recession, we will be faced with a severe problem. Are you what we would call Keynesian in your approach to this? Or would the pressure for lower taxes become so acute that foreign aid would be cut down?

Stevenson: There is a lot to be said for lower taxes. With the exception of death duties, ours are almost as high as yours. And we certainly would not be Keynesian in our approach to foreign aid programmes during a depression, in that we should increase them simply to maintain our own level of production. We would continue to judge them according to their importance in the foreign policy that we were pursuing. What we should probably do is to have a programme of public works at home. This whole question is one that is very much in my mind, and because I do know that we shall have to face the question of finding opportunities for investment of the business capital that is available.

Benn: As far as Britain is concerned, the economic stability of the United States is far more important – if one can compare it, even – than the foreign aid programmes themselves. For example, three years ago before the devaluation crisis, a mere 3.5 per cent setback in American national output caused a 20 per cent reduction in the level of imports to America from Europe.

Stevenson: Well, I realise that that is the critical question that we have to face. We are, you know, the free trade Party. The Republicans in their platform have played to all vested interests in this matter. They say we should maintain our high standards of living at home by high tariffs. Of course, that is wholly inconsistent. But I have to face the same pressure groups. You see, here again we run into all this talk about treachery. A little Danish cheese is imported, and the farmers shout and shout and shout. I have these difficulties to face myself. Labour unions have something of a vested interest in this themselves. But they are much more wisely led now. The farmers I cannot make out. They seem to have everything, and to want everything. As you will understand, I am very liberal in my approach to all this. After all, if Europe cannot find markets in America, we shall have to give them more dollars, to buy our goods. With the world divided as it is now, and the barriers to trade from East and West, we must help you to build a new pattern that enables you to pay your own way.

Benn: On these various points we have been discussing and the policies behind them, how far do you think you would be able to carry Congress with you?

Stevenson: Well, this depends on the balance in the Election. I do not think that I shall have any difficulty in foreign policy, because in the past we have been able to rely on the eastern wing of the Republican Party to support the main lines of our policy. As you probably realise, I am very progressive on foreign policy – far more progressive than many – just about as progressive as some.

(The telephone rang: Benn's tip to go.)

Benn: Have you ever thought between the Election and your inauguration of coming to Europe? I could not presume to say that you might learn anything from visiting us, but you could teach us a great deal about

America by speaking as you have done here. And I know that it would be a gesture deeply appreciated. You see, it is very difficult for us to get here. Many Americans visit Europe; few Europeans visit here. I would dearly like Aneurin Bevan to come here, if any group would have the guts to sponsor him. I realise that you will be desperately busy in Washington after January, but would you be able to get abroad before that?

Stevenson: I had never thought of that. If I went anywhere, I think that perhaps I ought to go to the Far East.

Benn: Why not both?

Stevenson: You see, there are difficulties in this. As soon as the Election is over I shall be faced with a massive task of Government reconstruction. Unlike Britain, where only the Cabinet changes, I have a vast number of appointments to make. It is difficult enough in Illinois, and I shudder at the thought of it on the Federal scale. But this trip is an interesting idea.

Benn: Well, I must go. Thank you very much for sparing the time to see me.

Stevenson: By the way, what do you do? What brings you here?

Benn: Well, as a matter of fact, I am married to a Cincinnati girl, which is why I am able to come.

Stevenson: What do you do? Are you a newspaper man?

Benn: No, I am a Member of Parliament.

Stevenson: Labour or Conservative?

Benn: Labour; I succeeded Sir Stafford Cripps.

Stevenson: I had many pleasant evenings with him, talking, when I was in London. Do you by any chance know Kenneth Younger? He's a very able man. I had a charming letter from him only the other day. What do you feel about him over there?

Benn: He is very well regarded; and we in the Labour Party hope that when we get back to power, which we shall do very soon, he will have a very responsible position in framing our policy. Thank you very much again, sir. Goodbye.

I must say that I was very impressed by Stevenson. He looked rather tired, which is not surprising, but throughout the interview he gave his complete attention to answering the questions I put, which he did slowly and thoughtfully in a manner which suggested that he was looking at them afresh, and thinking out loud. At no point did he give the impression of quoting himself. He seemed to have a very deep sense of responsibility and a sure touch in dealing with such a wide range of subjects. If I were surprised at all, it was at the lack of twinkle in his replies, which I had been led to expect by the lightness of touch he regularly shows in his speeches. In fact, the only time he did smile was when I congratulated him on his Johnson quotation.

Thursday 24 September 1953

I am satisfied that my personal position in Bristol South East is secure. This is a great relief as I must admit that over the last three years I have worried about it a great deal. I am much more relaxed at meetings – for the very first time ever in Bristol I have made jokes. I am gradually escaping from the personality created for me by circumstances as a young Cripps, earnest, sincere, humourless and churchgoing.

I spent the evening working on Gaitskell's script for the TV broadcast on 15 October. Gaitskell realises its importance and is prepared to work hard, but he is intellectually arrogant, obstinate and patronising. I respect – but cannot quite admire – him.

Friday 25 September 1953

Today with Gaitskell was worse. He rejected our new script with all the indignation of an old virgin resisting an improper proposal.

It is a real problem.

Caroline and I arrived at Margate for the Party conference. We have a suite at the Rowan Court Hotel. Our co-residents are a very pleasant group, including the Stracheys, the Callaghans, the Youngers, Woodrow Wyatt and Tony Crosland. We all lunch at a big table and the conversation is amusing and we are mainly like-minded.

Professor G. D. H. Cole addressed the Fabian tea. He spoke with great clarity. He said we should nationalise the building industry, and we should never have gone into Korea or accepted German rearmament.

He was very stimulating.

Wednesday 30 September 1953

Watching and hearing a succession of speakers over the past three days, a few tips are worth noting.

(1) Don't shout: it is not a mass meeting.
(2) Don't lecture: it is not a debating society or a Workers' Educational Association classroom.
(3) Don't make jokes. Conference is sensitive about its dignity. A wrong step can never be rectified.

Two points well made are enough to do the trick.

Thursday 1 October 1953
General Impressions of Conference

This year's Conference did not want to fight. Most delegates are sick of abuse and threats and splits. Herbert Morrison's withdrawal from the treasurership was a fine start.

The right wing of the Party won almost every vote of importance. Land nationalisation and other more extreme proposals were all defeated by big votes.

A great deal of the friction between the trade unions and the constituencies arises from differences in the feelings between 'unpractical' people and the unions, with their huge roles.

It was a good Conference and one senses the great labour movement as a real living organisation, warm and generous, and dedicated. We can look forward to a good year in Parliament now and victory in a General Election.

Friday 2 October 1953
David Butler, who stayed on a further day, tells me that Gaitskell made a good speech on education ('abolish the fees in public schools') and was attacked by Jennie Lee ('he still wants an educated elite learning Latin verse').

Thursday 15 October 1953
Today the first Party TV programme, *Hugh Gaitskell: a Challenge to Britain*, was broadcast.

On Monday I had attended a script conference which greatly depressed me. The language was starchy and technical, the interviews phoney, the models ludicrous, with a moving wall to illustrate imports, a ladder against it to show exports and the ladder on a soap box to indicate invisibles and interest on foreign investments. There was also an apple tree in which were the golden fruits of solvency and independence. It was ludicrous and muddled.

Our great difficulty was Gaitskell. He resisted change with all his heart and it was only Tony Crosland who could make any progress. Tony Crosland finds his intellectual arrogance a trial even in economic discussion with him (Hugh thinks highly of Tony) and attributes his stiffness and sensitivity to the crisis of 1951 (Nye among other things). But basically it has its root in Hugh feeling that he has no charm or winning personality (which is true in part). So he puts up this front to protect himself.

We overcame some of the difficulties on Monday and more today. I said what I thought plainly though I got a sharp response at times.

The final programme as transmitted had many obvious defects. The ladder and wall were a flop. On the other hand the interviews went very well – and I say that having been against them all along.

Hugh himself was intense and urgent if a bit gloomy and confusing. Mrs Gaitskell thought his posture hideous and was furious with us all – a loyal woman but not a very helpful one.

In October 1953 the Progressive People's Party was elected to Government in British Guiana, a British colony, led by Cheddi Jagan in partnership with Forbes Burnham, Chairman of the PPP.

That victory was seen by America as a threat to American influence and interests in the area, and an alleged plot was unearthed by the British authorities, citing Communist conspiracies etc, leading to the suspension by the Colonial Secretary, Oliver Lyttleton, of the Guianan constitution. Jagan and Burnham flew to London to make their case here and win support from the Labour Party.

Tuesday 20 October 1953
On my own initiative I sent cables to Nehru and Nkrumah as follows:

Would you agree to nominate a suitable member of a Commission to go to British Guiana if asked to do so by British Government? I propose recommending this in Thursday's House of Commons debate if you are agreeable. Have sent similar request to Nkrumah/Nehru. Confident that Indian and African participation would greatly increase chances of success and restore confidence. An early indication of your view on this will enable proposal to go forward. Please cable Wedgwood Benn MP.

Each cable cost £2.15.0! Today I received a reply from Nkrumah:

If asked to do so by UK Government I should be prepared to nominate a suitable African member of the Commission. By making nomination I should want to know probable duration of Commission's duties. Nkrumah, Premier.

This encouraged me. However, I am in this difficulty. If I tell the Party leaders now I shall be thought very impertinent and presuming to correspond with heads of state. And Nehru may not reply at all, thus making me look a fool into the bargain. On the other hand if I just produce it like a bombshell in Thursday's debate it will get me into terrible trouble for seeking publicity – the more so if the idea is thought to be a good one, and I didn't seek to share it with my colleagues.

Wednesday 21 October 1953
In the evening a small group of us talked to Dr Jagan and Mr Burnham, the two PPP Guiana ministers who arrived today. They were very able and in a way attractive men, though slightly evasive on the major issues I thought. For example: question to Cheddi Jagan: 'Are you a Communist?'
'It's irrelevant.'
I recommended Jagan to say quite openly that he was a Communist if he was, or a Marxist or whatever, as it would be thought better of than an evasive reply. The following day he admitted he was a Marxist at his press conference.

Thursday 22 October 1953
This morning I had a letter from India House in reply to my telegram to Nehru. It was friendly in a courteous way but absolutely noncommital.

To the Commons. The debate on British Guiana was an awful flop from our point of view. Jim Griffiths was as weak as water and said he didn't support the PPP about fifty times, thus destroying the value of his few limited points.

Only John Hynd and I said anything positive. My speech contained the proposal on which I had worked so hard but Macmillan in winding up made no reference to it; neither did the press the following day. It was all very disappointing.

Monday 26 October 1953

Some while ago I had a letter from Dave Morgan, of the Bristol Communist Party, complaining that his mail was being opened by the GPO. Two letters had arrived in each other's envelopes. The Head Postmaster in Bristol refused to comment.

So I put down two questions for Wednesday – to ask why they were opened and under what general power, and how often it had been authorised in the last year.

Today I had a message from Gammans, the Assistant Postmaster General [PMG].

I went to ask Chuter Ede's advice; he explained the system. The Home Secretary signs a warrant for all letters to such and such an address to be opened. This lasts indefinitely and the Special Branch can ask for a renewal. Special Branch are responsible for all civilian counter-espionage.

Chuter advised that I should tell Gammans that I would be glad to talk things over with him but that I could not hear anything in confidence. I sought Gammans out and began with my caution. He was annoyed of course but was able to tell me the procedure as described by Chuter Ede. He then said he could not and would not answer the specific Parliamentary Questions. I could not pursue him as it was the Home Secretary who was in charge and he could shield behind the royal prerogative under whose authority the warrant was issued. Honours, mercy and the mails were the only prerogatives left and an MP could not query them.

He then tried (in the nicest but most patronising way) to discourage me by saying I was too young to query the decision of Home Secretaries, likely to get nowhere, only seeking personal publicity and only serving the communist cause. All this was bunk and I said so.

I asked the questions but my supplementary was rather rude, too long and not very well received. Radicalism has few friends.

Wednesday 28 October 1953

Last night I made a decision on a question that has caused me a great deal of thought: should I accept nomination for the Parliamentary Committee?

I pondered it carefully and decided to accept nomination. Jim Callaghan said at conference that I ought to think about it soon.

It really doesn't matter a damn one way or the other what you do. People will soon forget.

There were some comments in the House on my standing. I am a little embarrassed at my presumption. I shall be disappointed with less than 20 votes. I soberly expect 35. Jim Callaghan almost apologised for not voting for me. There was really no need for him to have done so. Churchill made a magnificent and brilliantly funny speech on the Queen's Speech.

Monday 2 November 1953
A complete session has gone by between 1952–53 virtually unrecorded.

Ever since 1950 when I was elected the peerage has been a constant problem. Various proposals for reform have been discussed in these last three years. Lord Simon's bill a year ago reopened the controversy and led to a Government proposal for an all-Party conference. But this was rejected by a small Party meeting in the spring.

I was approached by a group of Tories due to inherit peerages who asked whether I would care to talk it over with them. It came to nothing.

The story has been the same since 1711 when the first resolution on reform was moved in the Lords.

I decided I must make an attempt and so, although he was ill and away from work, I wrote a personal letter to the Prime Minister on 27 August in which I set out my problem simply and asked for his guidance.

On 2 September he replied in a very sympathetic way. I thanked him and dared to hope the Queen's Speech might deal with it.

Today the Queen's Speech was read from the throne and did contain a reference to 'Further consideration of the question of the Reform of the House of Lords'.

Thursday 5 November 1953
I must honestly say my 59 votes for the Parliamentary Committee exceeded my wildest dreams.

Monday 9 November 1953
Talking to Quintin Hogg on the telephone, he told me the Government were still discussing the matter: Salisbury and Churchill are very keen on reform, Butler and Eden don't care either way and there are some younger Tory ministers who are dead against any reform at all.

Trouble is brewing again in the Party. Cause: the Parliamentary Committee elections; the stand over British Guiana; the general inactivity of the Committee. What worries me is the obvious relish of the Bevanites at this turn of events. It depresses me beyond words.

Monday 16 November 1953
I am writing this in the waiting room at St Charlotte's. Caroline has gone off and I am to collect her suitcase and take it home.

It is a comfort to have her in hospital under expert care and attention.

Tuesday 17 November 1953
It is clear that they aren't going to bring the baby on early – so we must wait and wait.

Monday 23 November 1953
I sometimes reflect how appallingly badly treated are MPs. Free postage, stationery, secretarial help and proper desk accommodation is the least they could do for us.

Thursday 26 November 1953
Hilary James Wedgwood Benn born, 8lb 15oz, blond hair and darkish eyes. Caroline was wonderful. Not much time to do anything but wander dazedly.

Tuesday 19 January 1954
Parliament reassembled today and very depressing it is in prospect, though it may be the after-effects of the flu.

Wednesday 20 January 1954
First day back at the House. Haircut.

Talked at dinner to Fred Lee, who speaks of impending industrial crisis with more strikes and lockouts. We agree the Party must take a line soon. The trade union honeymoon with the Tories is over and they need us now – a good sign. The Minister of Labour, Sir Walter Monckton, is a sick man and is unpopular with those employers who really want a 'showdown' over wages.

Tuesday 2 February 1954
British Guiana Association meeting with Cheddi Jagan and Forbes Burnham back from their long tour. Jennie Lee made an impassioned plea to them not to desert the principles of democratic socialism. 'I take it that Cheddi and Janet Jagan are Communists – they have a right to be but it will be impossible for us (the Labour Party).'

The meeting went on for a long while – a struggle for the confidence and faith of two men who were going home probably to arrest and imprisonment.

We begged them to choose us and not the CP; to keep us informed frankly of their policy and to work constructively for a new constitution. They were evasive in part but we learned of their difficulty in not wanting to split the national front. Burnham is symbolic of the honest, nationalist colonialist leader, as yet uncommitted to extremism and with the supreme test ahead. Perhaps Nehru's advice on non-cooperation will win out.

Thursday 11 February 1954
At 8pm a very important meeting took place – to establish one body for colonial activity – the Movement Council for Colonial Freedom. It is what is badly needed at the moment for we are frittering away our energies in little tinpot groups with chronic money troubles and too great a diffusion of energy and skill. The four groups emerging to make up the nucleus are: Congress of Peoples against Imperialism, Seretse Khama Council, British Guiana Association, the Central African Committee. We want an income of £2,000 per year, a paid secretary and typist.

Tuesday 23 February 1954
Party meeting to discuss our attitude to the forthcoming debate on the Berlin Conference, a European Defence Community and German rearmament.

Clem read out the Margate Conference resolution: 'Conference urges that there should be no German rearmament before further efforts have been made to secure the peaceful reunification of Germany.'

He then put the Shadow Cabinet resolution to the meeting: 'That this meeting recognises that conditions laid down in the Party have been met and we should accept German rearmament in the European Defence Community.'

Harold Wilson moved his amendment to the effect that there should be no EDC because relaxation of tension is beginning.

Clem asked what were the alternatives. A neutralised Germany? A sovereign rearmed Germany? He said we must support an EDC.

Wilson said this was the most important decision for three years.

Wilf Messer made a brilliant speech. He said that German rearmament was the guncotton primer to a heap of gelignite. The logic of German rearmament is that we must bear a larger arms burden ourselves.

John Hynd believed that the Germans will rearm anyway. The US will rearm them.

Healey said we must catch the Germans now – while they are still on our side. German rearmament has been agreed in principle for nearly four years – so you can't say it isn't urgent.

Herbert Morrison said, Of course the Communists want to be strong and want us to be weak. But can we agree to that? You can't always regard Germany as untrustworthy.

In the vote, Wilson's amendment received 109 votes in favour, 111 against. This was achieved by making the Parliamentary Committee vote *en bloc* (Nye abstaining) and thus was not a true record of those present.

The motion was carried by 113 to 104.

Peers also voted on the motion.

Wednesday 31 March 1954

After fifteen years of pleasant slumber the Trade Union Group (of Labour MPs) have been seized in a most successful *coup d'état*. George Brown – thrusting, ambitious, unscrupulous – has ousted Sam Viant as chair.

The appalling power of the H bombs dropped in the current series of US tests in the Pacific is necessitating a completely new look at our whole defence and foreign policy.

Monday 5 April 1954

Commons debate on H bomb. Attlee made a superb speech, Churchill's mean Party attack misfired, Boothby walked out. Tory backbench embarrassment.

Tuesday 6 April 1954

This evening I was the guest of the Mirror Pictorial Group at the Savoy for dinner. Among those present on the Mirror side were Hugh Cudlipp, Sidney Jacobson, Philip Zec and Labour MPs Woodrow Wyatt, Ernest Davies, Jim Callaghan, Tony Greenwood, Kenneth Younger and self.

The journalists asked us what the Labour Party stood for and what we were doing and how they could help us. During the fascinating evening Jim Callaghan and Tony Greenwood emerged rather as traditionalists – 'nationalise and be damned'. Woodrow was an excellent and strong chairman. Hugh Cudlipp was dynamic, stimulating and unbalanced. Ernest Davies was leading us towards a new foreign policy in the H bomb age. I talked too much but hit upon a theme that I must develop: 'Socialism is a creed that must be based on the doctrine of liberation or the release of energy.'

We discussed foreign affairs. The age of the H bomb means a complete reassessment of East–West relations, and survival. The Cold War is dead, we must start afresh.

We agreed to meet again and see if we couldn't hammer out a real working policy, a theme and a basis for co-operation.

Wednesday 7 April 1954

This afternoon and evening I spent as usual with Hugh Gaitskell on his budget broadcast. Dora Gaitskell was there all the time too. I act as producer, script reader, personal private secretary, PPS and general bottlewasher – which is rather fun.

The most extraordinary thing was Hugh's amenability to suggestions. He accepted almost all the amendments with an appreciative air and was even humanly pleasant and grateful. It was by far his best radio performance yet and I told him so, which seemed to please him.

Thursday 8 April 1954
Earlier this afternoon I put a question to Churchill about whether the 1943 Quebec A bomb agreement[2] covered the use of the H bomb. He said it did, and I quoted Eisenhower and Truman to say it didn't and asked for him to withdraw the charge that Attlee had 'gambled with the national interest'. I thought it a good point but Attlee called me over at the Party meeting and said, 'Wouldn't it have been wiser to have consulted me before putting your question – after all *only I* know the whole truth.' This was stumbling into big things, so I apologised simply. I guess the truth cannot be told yet.

Friday 9 April 1954
Various efforts are afoot to get a national campaign going with a mass meeting at the Albert Hall, a petition based on today's motion and rallies all over demanding Big 3 talks on the H bomb. I am on the *ad hoc* Committee and we are hoping to get the thing moving.
   To Bristol – for a surgery 4.30–6 with only 2 visitors, one a council house tenant who wondered if I would help if the Housing Department would not agree to repair the dry rot in her living room.

Tuesday 19 October 1954
Parliament reassembled. Government changes announced yesterday – but Winston has not resigned.
   Statement on the dock strike, and on the London agreements on German rearmament.

Wednesday 20 October 1954
Eden made a KG.

Saturday 23 October 1954
To Bristol for a recording of a programme for the younger generation (15–25-year-olds).
   What emerged was

1. Great ignorance about Parliament and its work.
2. Cynicism about politicians and their sincerity.
3. Great gap between politicians and young people.
4. No inspiration of young people by politicians.
5. Healthy disregard of politicians' conceit.
6. Dislike of Party or intra-Party squabbles except as entertainment.

All very revealing and disquieting.

On 1–2 March 1955, during a defence debate in the House of Commons, Nye Bevan intervened to criticise Clem Attlee's stand on nuclear weapons, and he and 61 Labour MPs abstained on the Labour Party's amendment. This followed other public criticisms of the leadership in the preceding months and while the earlier Bevan crisis was rumbling on. As a result, Nye Bevan, the man who created the Health Service, was hauled up before a Party meeting with a view to disciplinary action being taken against him.

Wednesday 16 March 1955
Attlee opened the meeting and said that this situation was regrettable. It was a question of discipline and democratic principle. Nye's actions during the defence debate were a deliberate attack on the leadership.

They were taken in the presence of the enemy, which was a gross act of disloyalty. 'I have tried for unity,' Clem said, 'but have had very little co-operation. Whenever we find unity, it is upset.' He recommended withdrawal of the whip.

Bevan got up and replied. 'It is a personal matter. If I was ambitious, I am an ass. Look at the platform for conspirators. I never heard the charges until today, the only letter I received was when I was told the whip would be withdrawn. It is not very comradely that I should remain in ignorance. This was not an act of disloyalty – I was more lucidly articulating the doubts of other Members.'

He ended by saying he was sorry for Attlee, who had a difficult job.

Fred Lee said we want a face-saving formula. 'You'll martyr Nye and expel the trade unions and constituency Parties.'

Tom Fraser [MP for Hamilton] said the Party was sick of Nye's scheming. Withdrawal of whip is what is right for the Party.

George Brown said this was a long-continued course of conduct by Nye and talked about 'You and your friends'.

'Why not attack my friends?' Nye demanded.

'Because we must get the ring leader.'

Tom Proctor said he didn't believe Nye was sincere.

When asked if the vote was a vote of confidence, Attlee said if necessary it was.

The motion for Nye's expulsion was 141 for; against 112.

Notes

Chapter Three

1. (p.158) In the 1951 General Election, Lady Violet Bonham Carter stood as a Liberal candidate in the Colne Valley constituency. The Conservatives, under the influence of Churchill, who was a close friend of Lady Violet, decided not to put up a candidate against her, and Churchill even went to speak for her during the campaign. Despite his support the Labour candidate, Glenvil Hall, retained the seat.

2. (p.179) Winston Churchill, President Roosevelt and Canadian Prime Minister Mackenzie King met in Quebec in August 1943 to discuss the conduct of the war. It subsequently emerged that an agreement had been reached between Britain and America as to the development, production and use of Atomic weapons.

4
The Gaitskell Years
1955–60

June 1955
Why did we lose the Election? What do we do next?

For a while I have felt very miserable. I took the defeat personally and got too deeply involved. In the last two years I have remained a little more detached. But the rot spread to the constituency parties very rapidly. I could not help but feel that a Party unable to co-exist with itself was really unfit to govern and conduct international negotiations.

Now we are defeated again. The right will blame Bevan. The Bevanites will interpret it as the price paid for the right-wing policies and leaders.

But since 1951 the Tories have had good luck with the economic climate, people are generally better off and the end of most shortages has enabled rationing to be ended on everything but coal. There has been no unemployment. A family in a council house with a TV set and a car or motorcycle-combination on hire purchase had few reasons for a change of government. The Tories on a turnout 7 per cent lower than 1951 won a greater majority.

In Bristol, since my own meetings are so poorly attended I think my job should be:

(a) to attend each ward meeting once a year;
(b) to attend the annual GMC and one Executive Committee;
(c) to provide one surgery every three weeks in different parts of the Division;
(d) to go out canvassing armed with a 'Sorry I missed you' card, a 'Use your MP' brochure, and a 'Join the Labour Party' brochure.

It is still a very safe seat indeed and I needn't get panicky but I am frightened that the thing is disintegrating through the absence of a real livewire at its head. The old days of petitions, indoor meetings, 100 per cent canvasses and the rest, are probably dead and gone for ever.

Tuesday 7 June 1955
The new Parliament met.

Hugh Dalton's decision not to stand for the Shadow Cabinet, to 'make room for the younger men', has created the conditions for a shake-up in the leadership so desperately needed.

Dick Crossman told me Chuter Ede and Shinwell have also decided to stand down from the Shadow Cabinet. The big question is Willy Whiteley – we must get rid of him (as Chief Whip).

There might be six vacancies out of 12.

Wednesday 8 June 1955
Invited to Dick Crossman's cocktail party with Nye and the Bevanites plus the left of centre 'Keep Calmers'. Harold Wilson briefed us on the current position on the leadership.

Should Nye oppose Herbert for Deputy Leader? Should Jim Griffiths be put up instead? Do we really want Herbert or Hugh Gaitskell? What should Nye do about the Shadow Cabinet?

I found the atmosphere very depressing. The hatred for Morrison and Gaitskell is if anything stronger than their hatred for Nye. In the end it was agreed (almost) that Nye would not oppose Herbert but would stand for the Shadow Cabinet and that we should all plead with Clem to remain indefinitely. Pa advised me to steer clear of intrigues. They all sicken me.

Roy Jenkins cares desperately about getting rid of Morrison for the deputy leadership – to pave the way for Gaitskell.

Thursday 9 June 1955
Candidates for deputy leadership will be Griffiths and Bevan. I will vote for Nye as a last chance for him.

Party in goodish spirits and we have the Government (dissatisfied with Eden) on the run.

During the recess spent a lot of time with Gaitskell in connection with his first solo TV broadcast for Friday. He is far more amenable to advice than three years ago.

April 1956 – Trip to Israel for Independence Day Celebrations
Took the boys to Millbank to stay with Mother and Father, and they were received with great excitement. Home to pack. At 5.30 we were driven to the airport by the economic attaché and had the personal attention of the London manager of El Al.

Caroline and I crossed the coast of Israel at 3 pm and touched down at Lydda at about 3.15. The Chief of Staff, General Moshe Dayan, in an eye-patch, was there to greet his wife coming from New York. We were greeted by Mr and Mrs Yassol of the FO complete with a 1948 de Soto cab and David, our chauffeur.

We set off at once to Jerusalem along the Road of Valour and past the rusty wrecks of vehicles knocked out in the convoy actions to relieve the beleaguered Israeli garrison in Jerusalem during the 1948 War.

The most striking thing was the enormous growth of little white concrete settlement houses of immigrants that had mushroomed everywhere. The lower slopes of the hills were rapidly being cultivated and reclaimed in terraced agriculture and even the rocky bare upper slopes were starting the same way. We saw the water-pumping stations and a dam to get water to Jerusalem. The whole impression was of surging activity over which Mr Yassol enthused continuously.

We reached the King David Hotel at 4.40 and were collected again at 5 for the presentation at the Knesset of a giant Menorah to the Israelis, by Clement Davies. The simple ceremony in the sunken garden was moving, despite long speeches. At 6.30 the air raid sirens sounded. The stars were just out and the crowd were laughing and joking but underneath it all was the tragedy of 6 million dead in the gas chambers and the miracle of a home for the Jews after 1,900 years of pogrom and ghetto.

Gazing over the moonlit walls of the old city we could hardly believe that war was so close.

Monday 16 April 1956
Awoke to a clear bright morning at 6 o'clock. The old city was almost hidden by the sun on the low haze. Breakfast 6.30 and off to Haifa at 7. We were in a convoy of cars headed by two policemen on motorbikes with sirens screaming to get us through traffic that was pouring out of the city towards Haifa for the Independence Day celebrations.

Our route took us down the Road of Valour towards Lod and then northwards past Petah Tiqvah and Hadera. The early part of the journey on the slopes of Judaea showed us the old terracing for cultivation and the beginning of the new terracing on a much bigger and better scale. Great new afforestation schemes are changing the face of the land and bringing new topsoil and fertility to it. All the while the talk was of the land and the enthusiasm of the Israelis for the soil in which they feel rooted. The great new cultivation of the Vale of Sharon was another excellent example of this constant battle to get the new immigrants on to the land. The sand dunes with their scrubby grass were seen from that hopeless stage right through to the final rich agricultural state. First the sand is moved (used for cement and building) and then the trees and grasses are planted so that the process of fertilisation can begin. The swamps are drained with pipes and the planting of the eucalyptus trees which soak up all the water (and can then be used themselves for paper-making). All this takes about five years. The way it is tackled is to build simple cottages in concrete and then offer them to the immigrants who will usually jump at them after all the long years in the camps. They get a simple place of their own and the Government get a new agricultural settlement.

We stopped for orange drinks and finally reached Haifa at about 10.30. Places had been reserved for us near the saluting base on the row of seats just behind the Cabinet. It was a perfect spot. Behind us towered Mount Carmel crowded with people. There was a triumphal arch away to the left through which the parade passed and on it was inscribed 'Israel's Security is in her Military Strength'.

At exactly 10.59 a car drew up with the Prime Minister, David Ben-Gurion, in a blue suit and an open-necked shirt. The crowd roared. A minute later a bodyguard of police on beautiful Arab horses approached escorting the President of Israel, Mr Ben Svi. The brass band opposite us played 'Hatiqvah' and we all stood. The Colours were unfurled and the parade began.

The procession itself was most impressive. All the military units were represented. There was artillery of all kinds and tanks. The green-bereted border patrol got a special cheer and so did the paratroops. Overhead flashed the Air Force – Harvards, Spitfires, Mosquitoes, Meteors, Vampires and the new Mystères. At sea there was a line of destroyers and minesweepers as well as frigates and motor torpedo boats. The general impression of the show was that the Israeli Army could lick any and all the other Arab countries put together. The men were smart and tough and the equipment was very well maintained. The interest and knowledge of the crowd was also impressive. You could hear the comments and they showed how close the Army was to the life of the nation. Of course the Egyptian MIG-15s and the Ilyushin bombers are another story, but if these could be balanced or dealt with the Israelis would be in Cairo in about three days.

After the military parade there was a wonderful dance routine – there were cultural dances, agricultural dances (men with sickles and girls with bouquets of vegetables) and fishing dances (men with nets and girls with baskets); and thin emaciated Arabic-looking Yemenite Jews with their formal Eastern clothes and their shy diffident gracefulness and the Druzes with their arrogant and precise scimitar dance with its quick-stepping gaiety.

Afterwards we went for a trip to Acre. The villages and housing on the road were most impressive and we saw the new building for the heavy steel industry that is to be opened soon. Acre is a perfect walled town, never captured in battle until the successful Israeli attack in the war of liberation. The three walls and moats make it virtually impregnable. We walked to the mosque and through the Arab quarter. The filth and dirt of the slums recalled to mind the old city of Jerusalem, Jaffa and the general run of Arab urban squalor. The harbour was beautiful with its square and fishermen mending their nets and boats.

One impression of great impact today was of David our chauffeur guide. His grandfather brought him from Odessa in 1922 as a boy of eight. He worked as a land surveyor in the Negev in the Thirties. He speaks four languages, is an expert Old Testament scholar, knows a great deal of the history of Palestine and is a firm and informed Zionist with extensive knowledge of modern Israel. It could only happen here.

Tuesday 17 April 1956

We drove to the Degania kibbutz: Joseph Baratz (leader and 'father' of Degania and a former member of the Knesset) took us round. He was a man of seventy-two to -five with a kindly, worn, wise face. His granddaughter married in the kibbutz and she and her husband are building an enormous shelter deep in the ground in Negez. We saw an underground hospital costing £25,000 in the last stages of completion [in preparation for the threatened war].

When the Syrians advanced on Degania in 1948, Baratz and others were sent to Tel Aviv to seek help from Ben-Gurion. Yadin (Chief of Staff) could offer no help – 'You must stop them with your bare hands. We have no tanks or guns.' They suggested an assault with Molotov cocktails.

The Syrians attacked but as the first tank entered Degania the kibbutzniks jumped down from high trees on to it and threw petrol bottles. The tank caught fire and soon the others turned and went back.

After we had seen the tank, set in concrete, we drove northwards (half a mile from the Syrians) to Shaar Hagolan where I had danced so much on VE day eleven years ago and could not be made to get intoxicated! Some people remembered it.

In 1948 the Syrians blew up the water pipeline, the settlement was overrun for three days and the Syrians burned it down. The settlement began at once to rebuild – even while the war was on. Shaar Hagolan is linked to communities of 9,000 years ago. That's the staggering thing about Israel. Our guide David is the most wonderful exponent – he speaks one moment of Gideon and his men chosen by observing the way they drank from the stream, next of Orde Wingate and his Jewish patrols, and the revolt of the Maccabees.

We see the ancient flint arrows from the site of a Neolithic village, and pass a group of kibbutzniks digging trenches against air raids, next week perhaps.

It is nearly morning and I have sat up half the night to write this. Over the barbed wire half a mile away are the enemy forces in Syria and Jordan where the lights of their camps twinkle and burn.

The vast compass of history makes this day so short and unimportant. Perhaps the kibbutzim have the answer – stay rooted to the soil and pass it on more richly fertile than before to your sons and grandsons.

Wednesday 18 April 1956

Up at 7 and breakfast in the dining hall. We drove up the sides of the Sea of Galilee to the Church of the Loaves and Fishes, on next to Capernaum with its synagogue built by the money from the Roman whose boy Christ healed. Capernaum, quietly resting by the lake shore, is a perfect example of the way Israel handles the tourist trade – no placards or ice-cream stands.

We drove on to upper Galilee and had tea at the English kibbutz, Kfar Blum, where we talked to the English pioneers. I didn't like the people much, partly for the markedly different atmosphere there and partly because it aroused in me all the deepest doubts I have about the Zionist experiment and the cost to the Arabs driven out of their homes. But that is all over now – force has won and the only sensible thing is to build and think on the status quo.

Thursday 19 April 1956
To Caesarea, past the Roman aqueduct which brought sweet water down from the hills; alongside the ruins runs a modern pipe that does exactly the same thing. Caesarea is indescribably exciting. We could have stayed happily a whole day. When the excavation of the whole city begins it will reveal a complete settlement.

Friday 20 April 1956
Jerusalem. At 9 Lucien Harris (chief PRO of Hadassah and a contemporary of Michael Foot at Oxford) walked us over to the Hadassah Health Centre where we met Mrs Jaegar who took us around. It was obviously a showpiece and was excellently equipped. We were struck by the insistence that everyone pays something 'so that they are not getting charity'. This applies to most Hadassah organisations and may reflect the fears of the American supporters that they might be financing a 'socialised project'.

We hurried home to tea, a bath and preparation for the evening. A Foreign Office car took us to the Eden Hotel where we were the guests at dinner of Mr and Mrs Mordecai Shneurson, the Head of the Commonwealth division of the FO.

Others were General Yadin (fortyish, ex-Chief of Staff in the war of liberation and chief archaeologist in Israel) and his charming wife (thirty, one child and pregnant).

As we sat round after dinner a real political discussion developed with the men. They all pressed the Israeli claim for arms. I asked 'What do you do if Russia proposes an immediate embargo on all arms shipments to the Middle East coupled with a quadripartite guarantee of a new UN resolution establishing and accepting Israel and giving her access to Eilat and through Suez, enforced by Big Power agreement?'

This question disturbed them a great deal.

I said Israel is a natural ally of Arab nationalistic aspirations. I tried to get them to agree that Israel was a Middle Eastern country, neutralist, like India, and should develop independently of Western imperialism.

I asked what would happen if the Middle East went Communist.

Frankly they were rather woolly – Najar believing that a new Egyptian middle class would save the day with a Menshevik revolution. I think that to achieve the release of energy necessary to rebuild the Arab countries so much property will have to be redistributed that a revolution is inevitable.

Saturday 21 April 1956

To the Mandelbaum Gate and over no man's land with the Vice-Consul, Dawson, to Jordan.

He drove us to the Garden Tomb of Golgotha where the warden – Mr Matter – showed us the place of the skull, the wine press in Joseph of Arimathea's garden, and the tomb. Whether genuine or not, the lack of commercialisation made it all a great deal more devotional and natural.

Sunday 22 April 1956

To Beersheba along the main southern road – Beersheba is a real booming frontier town with a large military garrison and 1,500 people working on major construction. The old part of the City (population 200 in 1948) is now dwarfed by the great new neighbourhood area that has raised it to 20,000 and will lead to 40–50,000. The Mayor, David Tuvyahu (born in Lvov) speaks 7–8 languages and is a real Germanic type – close-cropped hair and red stocky neck. Beersheba is the greatest town in the Negev and is expanding to meet the needs of this booming area. Surrounded by desert it will have to be a main railway, mining and agricultural centre.

We went to the mosque, which is now a museum and shows the excavated areas with tools and coins from prehistoric and Roman times. Building for the future and digging for the past go hand in hand in Israel and the continuity of history encourages the drive for survival and development.

We stopped for an espresso coffee in the main street of the old city. It was full of soldiers and immigrants from Yemen and Morocco, pulsating with life and really romantic.

Monday 23 April 1956

Breakfast at 8.30 and towards Sedom along the new road. The first few miles were past kibbutzim and into the rolling scrubby desert. Parts of it were sparsely populated by Bedouin and we could see the women crouching to harvest by hand, the dark, brown-black Bedouin tents and the big and baby camels and black goats. We stopped to photograph three Bedouin children and some camels.

The Bedouins have been given water and attempts are made to settle them, but they are nomadic and wander freely along their old trade routes smuggling opium and hashish from the south and going by night in camel trains across from Egypt to Jordan with arms, and spying. It is hard to stop them for they know no frontiers and have friends and relations all over the Levant.

The desert grew bleaker and rockier and began to dip down sharply to the Dead Sea. The dust gave way to sharp red-brown sandstone crags jutting irregularly into the sky, eroded to reveal its stratification, cracked and bare.

The road swept majestically down in bends – a marvellous feat of engineering completed two years ago.

Lower still by the valley, south of the Sea, we were in salt rock instead of sandstone. Across the valley was Jordan.

Tuesday 24 April 1956
To excavations at Askalon where they are digging up a Roman house. Nearby is an AD 230 Roman tomb beautifully decorated with fish and wheat and grapes.

The fish and wheat were traditional symbols of fertility and the Arabs who lived in Askalon only ten years ago practised certain rites. Once a year all the women who wanted children used to bathe naked (with the fish) and an amazing record of pregnancies would follow. Perhaps not all the pregnancies could be attributed to the fish.

On to the Weizmann Institute where we saw Dr Weizmann's own room and laboratory and signed the visitors' book where we found my folks' signature from January 1938. This Institute was and remains the main scientific HQ for the conquest of the land of Palestine for development. Its dual purpose (pure and practical research) provides the country with a centre for advanced scientific study that compares with Princeton. All the buildings are a memorial to the first President and one of the greatest Jewish scientists of all time. If only Einstein had not been so modest as to refuse the Presidency, Israel could have claimed him as its own.

To Tel Aviv to the Histadruth (the Israeli TUC) where we met Reuven Barkatt, a quiet, very intelligent man, head of the political section. Our talk was much the most interesting and revealing of this trip.

He said that Israel had transformed the Jews from a nervous and unpleasant people, used to submission and persecution, into a brave confident people, facing danger and living close to death and attack without qualms. They are a self-reliant people – even the new immigrants who a few months ago were in the ghettoes of the Yemen or Morocco.

He said, 'We do not ask for help or troops or support but just to be allowed to buy arms to balance Egyptian air and armoured forces. The only thing the Egyptians will understand is force. Even with Soviet arms, Egypt will not win a war. We will utterly defeat Egypt. Nasser dreams of an empire stretching from Indonesia to Morocco. If Nasser does not defeat Israel he will fall.

'We would consider an alliance with Britain and a British base in Israel too if it would add to our security.'
End of Israel trip.

Monday 22 October 1956
Parliament meets tomorrow for the last ten days of the old session. It promises to be the most exciting year since I have been an MP.

The Government are in a terrible mess and they have lost confidence in Eden. The specific problems that confront them are Suez, the muddle over defence, the economic crisis and the awful bloodshed in Cyprus.

The Labour Party, on the other hand, is in better shape than it has been since I have been an MP. Hugh Gaitskell has done very well as Leader, despite the serious error he made at the start of the Suez crisis. Nye Bevan is Treasurer and has a real chance to make his contribution to the unity of the Party. The Parliamentary Party already shows signs of this rebirth and we must work to see that this spirit permeates to the constituencies. They are the weakest link in the chain at the moment.

For me the most exciting possibility this year is the prospect of Lords' reform. I have submitted my memorandum on the Privy Council idea to Gaitskell and Griffiths and it is being circulated to the little Committee that is looking into the matter. I think that it has a distinct chance of success.

Tuesday 23 October 1956
This morning I am going to a meeting of the Labour Party's Broadcasting Committee at the House of Commons. Nye Bevan has become Treasurer and will be a permanent member, and Tom Driberg has two years ahead of him as Vice-Chairman and then Chairman of the National Executive.

These two men will be very important recruits. Nye has shown himself to be very suspicious. He regards the whole set-up as being a part of a right-wing plot to keep him off the air. He also has the absurd idea that all publicity is unimportant and that all you need is the right policy. It will be interesting to see whether he is ready to alter his views about that. Of course his position in the Party will make it quite impossible to keep him off the air any more.

The first interesting development of the week will be the prospects for the elections inside the Party. Nye is unlikely to oppose Hugh for the leadership because he knows that he would be beaten.

The broadcasting meeting was rather a disappointment as neither Nye nor Tom was there.

I saw Lord Lambton and he had no real news on Lords' Reform but promised to try and find out before the Queen's Speech.

In the evening I went to the Movement for Colonial Freedom and we had the usual depressing financial report – being nearly £300 in the red. I suggested that we feed talks to the new broadcasting authorities of the ex-colonial territories so that they could have a regular flood of liberal comment from this country.

Thursday 25 October 1956

Had lunch with Francis Cassavetti at the Reform Club. He was of course London Editor of the *Bristol Evening Post* until a few weeks ago when he became Assistant Political Correspondent for the *Daily Express*. Far and away the most interesting story I heard from him was of his talk to Walter Monckton recently just before Monckton resigned as Minister of Defence. Monckton is willing to be quite indiscreet, as this story showed.

Monckton made it quite clear that he strongly disagreed with Eden's handling of the Suez crisis. He said that Eden was a most 'mercurial' person, always changing his mind and very obstinate. During the crisis he had behaved in a most curious manner. Monckton said it was unthinkable we could use force as a war would mean heavy casualties and the British people could not be made to believe that the differences with Egypt were great enough to justify a war.

The stories about Eden coming from the Conservative Party now are quite staggering. Lord Lambton, Selwyn Lloyd's PPS, was talking to me the other day about the developing chaos in our Middle East policy which he attributed in the past to Eden's decision some years ago to disband the Levant Service. This is all bunk, but it was significant that a criticism of that kind should have come from that source. Lambton is charmingly indiscreet and a week or two ago told me that relations between Eden and Salisbury were appalling. He said Eden had never forgiven Salisbury for resigning before him in 1938, thus taking the gilt off the gingerbread. And that since he had been PM he had taken it out on Salisbury by never listening to his advice – so as to prove to everyone that he was not dominated by Salisbury's more powerful character.

This morning the *Daily Mail* and the *Daily Sketch* reported that Lords' Reform was definitely coming in the new session. They said it would consist of seventy life peers, mainly for Labour, the exclusion of the backwoodsmen and a thousand pounds a year for the reformed peers. I rang Wakeford of the *Daily Mail* to find out where he got his information from. I think he knows less than I do about it because in certain respects he was flying a kite. But he said nobody had contradicted him and he knew for a fact that Butler was very keen on it.

Sunday 28 October 1956

To Newport last night for a conference. Harold Finch, the Member for

Bedwelty, met me and took me to his home, then into the miners' welfare institute where there was a crowded room of serious-minded people. I spoke for an hour about the challenge of co-existence. It was a wonderful audience to address and the questions were good and pointed. One old boy in a quavering voice asked, 'Can Mr Wedgwood Benn tell us what value he thinks the hydrogen bomb has as a detergent.' I sat listening to the miners talking of the bad old days – the soup kitchens, the struggles with the police, the terrible hunt for work and the agony and humiliation of destitution. It was very moving and more than history – for in the crowded smoky club room were many men gasping for breath from silicosis or limping about from some industrial injury.

Today's news is mainly of the Hungarian crisis reaching its climax. The spontaneous rebellion against the Communist Government has virtually succeeded. The Iron Curtain has risen and people are moving freely in and out of Hungary with supplies and relief. Mr Nagy, the Prime Minister, broadcasts further concessions every hour and the red, white and green have reappeared to replace the hated scarlet banner of the Communist government. Everyone in the world is breathless with hope that this may lead to a rebirth of freedom throughout the whole of Eastern Europe.

The family spent the day at Millbank – our last with the folks before they leave on their trip to Asia.

Monday 29 October 1956
The news came through this morning that Britain had raised the matter of Hungary at the UN. I decided to try to raise this as a matter of urgent public importance and get a debate on the adjournment of the House. I worked all morning (and most of last night) on this and phoned Gaitskell to ask him to take it up officially on behalf of the Front Bench. He asked me to come and see him immediately after lunch and I found that he had summoned a meeting of those members of the Party most concerned with foreign affairs. They decided that they could not be certain of getting the adjournment and feared that a failure might be interpreted abroad as a divided approach. They all feared that a debate might lead to the expression of damaging opinions from left and right extremists which again might harm our capacity to help. I greatly resented all this but on reflection they may well have been right. The Foreign Secretary made a statement and I had acquired for Gaitskell the full text of the Ambassador to the UN, Sir Pierson Dixon's speech which he used most effectively from the Front Bench. I asked whether the Foreign Secretary would make provision for the British people to send blood, relief and money to show their solidarity, without provoking the Soviet Union into a new policy of repression. This last phrase was almost drowned by Conservative boos.

Tuesday 30 October 1956

I heard on the early bulletin this morning of the Israeli attack on Egypt. The weekend news had been grave from the Middle East but I don't think anybody except those in the know had expected it to explode so rapidly and so seriously. I went to the House of Commons after lunch and heard the Prime Minister's statement announcing the ultimatum to Egypt and the decision to demand the right to occupy the Suez Canal. Rumours of this had been reaching us for a few hours and for a moment the Party was in a state of some uncertainty. Here was aggression and it had to be stopped. Yet we knew the real motives of Government policy – how could we say what we felt in a clear way?

In the event Gaitskell made a brilliant comeback following the Prime Minister's statement. The lead he gave us will certainly set the tone of the Party's attitude to this whole crisis. The House was in complete uproar. There was a Party meeting in the evening at which I did speak. I said that this ultimatum was an act of aggression because it denied Egypt's right to self-defence under Article 51 of the Charter and it violated the Tripartite Declaration, the 1888 Convention, the Suez Canal Base Agreement of 1954 and the Baghdad Pact. This was a bold assertion of the law from a layman but on further study it turned out to be absolutely correct.

It is impossible to see how this can now end without far graver disasters. But the impending aggression by Britain has touched a very deep chord in the hearts of every member of the Labour Party bar one or two. This is the same old struggle of collective security versus naked power politics. It has united Phil Noel-Baker and Konni Zilliacus who for twenty years have diverged so enormously since their joint struggles against Hitler.

Wednesday 31 October 1956

I rang the Movement for Colonial Freedom and asked them to book Trafalgar Square for a rally on Sunday afternoon. This they did at once and the meeting was handed over to the Labour Party the same day.

There was a Parliamentary Party meeting this morning of the very highest order. Hugh Gaitskell announced the following plan:

First, we should oppose prorogation of Parliament until the latest possible moment.

Secondly, we should put down a motion of censure in the strongest terms for tomorrow.

Thirdly, we should carry the fight to the country with an immediate national campaign in complete and utter opposition to this war. He warned us that we would be vilified and attacked as traitors but that we were bound in a solemn duty to do this until we had brought about an end to the war.

I may summarise the speeches as follows:

Denis Healey: Eden has broken every pillar of British foreign policy – the Charter, the Commonwealth, the Atlantic Alliance. The Israeli attack was a put-up job. It was a tragic blunder by Israel for Eden will use her and then destroy her.

John Strachey: We are committed now to the whole French policy in North Africa. We should back the UN resolution calling for a ceasefire and impose it collectively by force.

Fred Lee: We must bring in the trade unions and launch industrial action.

John Hynd: Be careful we do not leave our troops without arms. Political action is on the way.

Stanley Evans [MP for Wednesbury]: Opposing the Government will break up parliamentary democracy. The UN is no good; I won't support it.

Douglas Jay: We must oppose this war all out but by political, not industrial, action. The authority of the UN is everything to us. Eden has destroyed the rule of law which is our only protection. The Chinese have now a perfect precedent for an attack on Hong Kong. We have rushed to the aid of the aggressor.

Reggie Paget: Don't commit the Party to the UN and its Charter of disorder. Just attack the Government on policy grounds.

Maurice Edelman [MP for Coventry North]: This is an Anglo-French plan. We are at fault for not being tougher with Nasser. We must not oppose the war, but only seek to end it.

Barnet Stross [MP for Stoke-on-Trent Central]: Anglo-French intervention will not help Israel in the long run. A mixed UN force between Egypt and Israel is the only guarantee.

William Warbey [MP for Ashfield]: Israel's only hope is to extricate herself from the Anglo-French aggression. Gaitskell should urge Israel to withdraw and promise a UN force. This is an illegal war and UN law must take precedence over national law.

Dick Plummer: We must take direct action, make maximum Party capital and gain sympathy for Israel.

Leslie Hale: This is a tragedy. Eden is a pathological liar. The Party is 99 per cent united and we must recognise that by our dedication as men and women of the cause of world order we can make the Labour Party the hope of the world.

The Chief Whip announced there would be a standing three-line whip for the rest of the session.

The character and volume of the public protest now developing is most interesting. It has rallied round informed people of every political allegiance. The *Manchester Guardian* provides the intellectual leadership in the country and the Churches, leading figures in science, universities and among professional people are coming out solidly on this. For example, David Butler – normally most conservative – rang me urgently from Oxford to describe the horror with which the news had been received, to confess his feeling of helplessness and to give support.

Thursday 1 November 1956
This morning's news of the bombings added additional tragedy to the situation. The news contained an item that Egypt was contemplating withdrawal from the UN because of the failure of the UN to help her. I decided to ring the Egyptian embassy at once to urge them not to do this. I spoke to the Ambassador's Private Secretary and explained that the veto cast yesterday by Britain and France was not the end of the matter. Today the General Assembly meets and its decision is a foregone conclusion. I asked the Secretary to ask the Ambassador to send an urgent message to Cairo to get this decision reversed. I also added these words: 'Please convey this message to the Ambassador and add to them an expression on behalf of the vast majority of the British people of the feelings that he must know we all have.' The Secretary took this down verbatim. No doubt the telephone was tapped, which is why the exact words should be recorded. At any rate, very late tonight the Egyptian Government announced that the reports of its intended withdrawal from the UN were quite without foundation.

This afternoon, after Questions, the Prime Minister made a statement. Gaitskell asked him whether we were at war with Egypt. Eden would not reply. The House burst into uproar. I have never seen Members so angry. I appealed to the Speaker to act for us in ascertaining the legal position. It touched the royal prerogative and he was the spokesman of the Commons against the Executive. Silverman asked about the status of our troops if captured. Eden would not reply. The rage and passion reached such a climax that the sitting was suspended.

I wrote a note to Monckton asking to see him urgently and personally. Then later I phoned him and he told me to come to his room. Here is an account of the interview.

I explained that it was unprecedented for a backbench member to approach a Cabinet Minister (he is Paymaster General) with the request that I had to make. I said I did not know his view but I came to him as a human being whom I greatly respected and admired. The situation was so serious that it quite transcended Party loyalties of any kind. Only he could save the day. I told him that some Conservative backbenchers were so shocked and anxious that they had approached me today to ask what they should do.

I asked him outright to resign from the Government and make a simple statement that he could not support any policy so directly in conflict with the UN Charter. I said this would provide a focal point round which Conservatives might rally. I compared this action to Eden's action in resigning in 1938. I said that no one could doubt his loyalty or his deep sincerity. I did not ask for any answer but only that he should consider all these things.

Monckton was deeply moved. He said that our conversation must be in the 'confidence of the confessional'. Everything I had said to him was most immediately in his mind. The decisions he had to take were terribly difficult but he could assure me that everything I had said he should do, he was seriously considering. He could not tell me, of course, anything beyond that. But in a voice thick with emotion he said, 'I am thinking and praying that I may be given strength to do the right thing. I know that others are praying for me too.'

I rose to go and apologised for my impertinence in approaching him. He took me warmly by the arm and said, 'My boy, you have made me a friend of yours for life.'

Shortly after getting back into the House someone whispered that I would be called next. I had no speech prepared and I scribbled four headings on to a piece of paper. I spoke for over 20 minutes and it certainly was, from my point of view, the best speech I have ever made.

'The reason why our troops are in this critical difficulty tonight is that from nobody, neither from the Government Front Bench, nor from the back benches opposite, have we had a coherent argument to encourage our troops which will stand up even to today's test, let alone the test of time. It is because my right hon. and hon. Friends and I feel that to put troops in any illegal war of aggression is a crime against those troops that we have moved our motion of censure in the House tonight. These are bitter words. I make no apology for them.

'I want to say a word about British relations with Egypt; and let no one begin to accuse anyone here of being pro or anti any particular personality in Egypt. I say sincerely that no country has committed as many crimes against Egypt as this country has; and I say quite sincerely – and I hope that my words go out to Cairo, because unless some of us say what is in our hearts, we shall have no friends in Egypt in the future – that I am ashamed that within three months of evacuating Egypt, following seventy or eighty years' occupation, British troops should be going in again, provoked into it by the fact that Egypt was herself the subject of an attack.

'That is a very serious situation. Although Colonel Nasser is not a democrat – he was not elected by the majority of the people of Egypt – let it be remembered that for many years we imposed the Government of Egypt upon the people of Egypt. What speeches were ever made by hon. Members opposite protesting when a British Ambassador sent tanks to the palace, as happened during the war, when Lord Killearn sent tanks to compel a change of Government? Who, from the benches opposite, said that the Government of Egypt was not representative of the people?

'We did not care, because it was our Government of Egypt and was doing what we wanted. That has been the basis of Anglo-Egyptian relations since Mr Gladstone moved troops in temporarily – I repeat, temporarily – in 1882. That is the basis for the hatred of this country in Egypt. I bitterly regret it, but it is a factor in the Middle East which the House has to take into consideration.

'There is another element in the Middle East struggle which everyone in the House should at least try to understand. That is the element of internal revolution which, naturally, comes from the development and the distribution of oil resources. After all, in Saudi Arabia there is a primitive feudal community where slavery is still allowed. All hon. Members know that and I am not revealing anything. Slavery is still legal in Saudi Arabia. Saudi Arabia is running with oil and running with dollars and Saudi Arabia will one day explode, because one cannot maintain a primitive community when the wealth of the modern world is being distributed to the ordinary people . . .

'The odious hypocrisy of the new friends of Israel is an imposition not only upon the good sense but upon the intelligence of the House: the fact that we should suddenly be told that Anglo-French-Israeli interests have been united. The sad fact is that Israel, tortured and tempted as she has been, has made a tragic blunder which, for all I know, may cost her her existence. If Israel is to survive in the Middle East she must survive along with her Arab neighbours. Anything we do which worsens the tension which already exists between Jew and Arab is a fatal blow at Israel's chance of survival. That is the truth of the matter, and I say that without any desire to make party points. This is the real difficulty that we have to face if we are to have peace in the Middle East.

'I now come to the situation itself. Israel has attacked. I do not know whether she did so with the connivance of the British and French Governments, but she has been tempted enough to justify her doing it, and she was none the worse whether she did it with our connivance or on her own. She attacked, and a situation then developed which was quite extraordinary.

'My hon. Friend the Member for Wednesbury said that the United Nations was no good. He said that we should get out, and get on with the job of doing what we ought to do. That is an old-fashioned idea, but I respect him for putting it forward. He has had the courage to say it outright, but every hon. Member opposite has pretended that this action is something to do with the Charter of the United Nations. The one thing I hate is humbug and hypocrisy. I do not mind piracy or banditry, or anything else, but let us, please, not have the United Nations flag waved over every right hon. and hon. Member opposite.'

Friday 2 November 1956

This morning Guy Wint from the *Manchester Guardian* rang to say that he hoped I would make the meeting in Cambridge University tonight the kicking-off point for the national campaign. I promised him that I would think of a slogan and a symbol that would unite us all. The slogan, 'Law not War' which the Labour Party have adopted, is good enough but the symbol required a little more thought. I finally decided that the obvious symbol was the United Nations flag. And the colours white and blue were the colours under which we should fight. I therefore ordered four UN flags to be sent by special car from the manufacturer in Kent and these arrived within a few hours.

I then rang the UNA and asked them whether we could use the UN symbol.

The final job was a petition and within an hour of beginning to dictate it, 500 copies had been duplicated and given to me. The Party officials were so enthusiastic that they made the Party duplicator and the paper freely available.

Finally, I bought yards of blue and white ribbon and hundreds of safety pins, went home with the petition forms and waited there with the flag to go to Cambridge.

Kenneth Younger drove me to Cambridge and we went at once to the Union where the Committee was waiting. By now sixteen different clubs had united to sponsor the meeting. I sat with the Arab Society officials – two of them Egyptians. One of them, a graduate student of my own age, was crying through the whole of the dinner. He did not know what had happened to his family as all news had been cut off. It was a most awful occasion and I could not convey the shame and disgust that I felt.

The Union debating hall was absolutely packed tight with crowds round it trying to get in through the windows and jamming the entrance thirty deep. We struggled to reach our places. The UN flag had been stolen and there were wildly noisy scenes and shouts. Great posters hung from the gallery reading, 'Support Eden, not Nasser' and 'We are now committed and must support our troops'. The crowd of students laughing and screaming for war gave me an icy hatred of them. The uproar and noise and silly funny remarks when the world was on the brink of disaster was completely revolting, disgusting and shameful.

Kenneth Younger's speech was hardly audible, but he persevered patiently and quietly to the end. I decided to take it rather differently, by giving those people who took our view in the hall something to cheer about and I therefore attacked the warmongers at once. Then I tried to buy silence by promising to answer questions. This was moderately successful though it meant my speech was prolonged to over an hour. My notes were carried away by a rotten tomato and stink bombs, and lavatory paper was thrown all over the place. One did not mind that but it was the flippancy on such a grave issue that was so completely horrifying.

Dog-tired I dozed through the drive home and got to bed about 2 am.

Saturday 3 November 1956

Hugh Gaitskell rang me up this morning, said he was going to broadcast tomorrow night and told me to make all the necessary arrangements. He said he would give up the whole of tomorrow for this and I could do what I thought necessary and tell him. I therefore rang up Harman Grisewood, the Director of Sound Broadcasting at the BBC.

Grisewood was extremely short and sharp. He wanted to know what broadcast I meant. I explained that the Prime Minister was to broadcast tonight and that Gaitskell would want to reply tomorrow. He said this was an unwarrantable assumption as the PM was doing a ministerial broadcast. I said it would be controversial and we demanded to reply. He told me to do it through the usual channels and to make no announcement or assumption of any kind. The usual channels are the two Chief Whips.

I told Grisewood time was very short but that if he insisted we would proceed through the usual channels. However, I warned him that the Government would almost certainly say no, and we would therefore appeal for a BBC decision late tonight. 'That is quite impossible,' he replied, 'we shall all be in bed.' I told him that this was an intolerable situation and that he must make arrangements for the BBC to receive our request and give a reply that night. At this he became a little chastened and said that he would ask Sir Alexander Cadogan,* the Chairman of the BBC, to stand by. He then went on more cordially to say that he would have no objection to the hypothetical arrangements for a broadcast tomorrow being made informally with the Television Service.

I reported all this to Gaitskell and Herbert Bowden and we had a half-hour's discussion. While we were talking, Bowden contacted Edward Heath, Government Chief Whip, and asked for the right of reply. Heath replied that we could not know whether we should want one until we had heard the Prime Minister.

At my suggestion, we decided to put out a press statement as follows:

It is expected that following the Prime Minister's broadcast tonight, Mr Gaitskell will address the nation on Sunday at 10 pm. However, the Government have so far raised objections to this on the grounds that the Prime Minister's broadcast will be a ministerial statement and will not be so controversial as to merit a reply from the Opposition Leader. It is to be hoped that these objections will be overcome. It is,

---

* Sir Alexander Cadogan was Chairman of the BBC 1952–7; he was also a Government Director of the Suez Canal Company, 1951–7.

therefore, still expected that Mr Gaitskell will broadcast. The nation certainly expects it.

This statement was instantly taken up by the press and appeared in the ITA news flash at 6 pm. It was an exceptionally cunning move for whatever happened the headline was as damaging to the Government. Either it would be 'Eden gags Gaitskell', 'BBC gags Gaitskell', or 'Gaitskell beats Eden's gag', or 'Labour beats BBC gag on Gaitskell'.

But more – much more – was still to come. The arrangements were made as follows:

Gaitskell would watch the broadcast near his home in Hampstead.

Herbert Bowden, Chief Whip, would watch from his home in Leicester.

A courier would wait at Number 10 to take the script to Gaitskell by 11 pm. The Government Chief Whip would be at Number 11, Grisewood at the BBC and Sir Alexander Cadogan by his telephone. All was set.

Eden broadcast from 10 to 10.15 – an odious performance to me but effective. After it was over various people whom I had tipped off to watch it (Kenneth Younger and others) rang me with suggestions for the reply.

The Government kept Bowden waiting until 11.30, then they said that they regarded the broadcast as having been quite impartial but would not raise objection if the Party asked the BBC for the right of reply. Bowden, therefore, phoned Grisewood at 11.35 and requested a BBC decision in our favour. Grisewood rang Cadogan, who said it was too late to reach a decision that night. Grisewood rang Bowden and told him. Bowden rang Gaitskell. Gaitskell, in a furious rage, rang Grisewood and told him it was quite intolerable. After consulting Cadogan again Grisewood repeated to Gaitskell that a decision could not be taken until tomorrow.

Gaitskell insisted on Grisewood giving him Cadogan's number. By this time it was well after midnight and Gaitskell put through a call to Sir Alexander Cadogan. The phone rang and rang and rang but Sir Alexander refused to answer. He could not have been in bed for it was only a few minutes after Grisewood had spoken to him. It was the most monstrous discourtesy on his part and it had very unpleasant consequences. By delaying the decision until the following morning at about 9 o'clock, Cadogan denied Gaitskell the right to have his broadcast announced on the 8 and 9 o'clock programme parades.

Finally, after 1 am Gaitskell phoned me to tell me this. He was very tired and very angry.

Two footnotes to the day.

Fighting between Members of Parliament is now almost inevitable. I saw Ernie Popplewell [Labour MP for Newcastle-upon-Tyne West] almost come to blows with Sir John Crowder [Conservative MP for Finchley] just behind the Speaker's chair. And I was told that Gaitskell himself almost came to blows with a Tory MP.

The situation has transformed Gaitskell from a 'desiccated calculating machine' into a man of unusual fire and passion. I said to him that I thought the shouting by the Party in the House might be rallying the Tory waverers to the Government. 'You can't stop it,' he said very angrily to me. 'People are in a temper – I know I am myself.' And so to bed at 2 am washed out.

Sunday 4 November 1956
Bought all Sunday papers. Nutting, a minister in the Foreign Office, has resigned on principle.[1] Russia is crushing Hungary and has issued an ultimatum. A tragic, heart-breaking day with news flashes every moment that brought us all near to weeping. The last day of freedom in Budapest and the agonising goodbye to Mr Nagy in his dramatic appeal to the world. Then the Hungarian national anthem and total, total silence.

To Gaitskell's house at eleven where he was sitting at his desk beginning to think of his broadcast. Woodrow Wyatt joins us. For an hour we talk to straighten our ideas and work out a plan for the speech. The news is coming in so fast that it is necessary to have someone watching it for us. At my suggestion Gaitskell agrees gratefully that my brother Dave should be asked to go to the *Daily Herald* office and sit by the tape machine. This he does, phoning with news whenever it comes in. A wonderful service and greatly helpful.

By 12 we had sorted out the order for the broadcast. While we made arrangements to get a secretary for him, Gaitskell began dictating on to his tape machine. Woodrow and I talked and read the papers and I answered the phone calls that were flooding in. I really felt that at that house at that moment one was in the centre of the world. By 2.30 Gaitskell had completed his dictation and Woodrow and I lunched with him in the kitchen. Mrs Gaitskell cooked and fed us and washed up. It was a friendly and amusing meal: for 15 minutes we could forget the job.

After lunch we altered the script and recast it until there was a veritable pile of flimsy carbons with unrecognisable scribblings and scratchings upon them. At six we had finished. Woodrow went off and while Gaitskell changed I went on ahead by car to the studio.

Gaitskell arrived at 6.30 and we went straight on to the set. Gaitskell said a word to the assembled engineers, thanking them and apologising for their long frustrating stand-by.

We began together re-dictating the whole script with two secretaries and two reporters from the *Daily Herald* to take it down. Finally, at 27 minutes past 8 we had a script and were ready to go to the studio for a run-through.

It was a most impressive rehearsal. Absolutely solemn and obviously moved, Hugh went through the whole thing. What he had to say was so compelling that all the technicians stood completely silently and listened to every word. What a contrast to their usual lolling and whispering and hurried glances at the sports news from the evening paper.

At 9 o'clock that was over and we had to cut five minutes from the broadcast. This was done by striking out a single passage completely and it was most certainly the right thing to have done. At 9.50 I took the completed script and sat beside Hugh while he was powdered and brushed, in the long chair. The whole thing had an eerie unreality about it. At 9.55 he began reading it through to check for mistakes. At two minutes to 10 he sat down at the desk in the studio before the camera with the pages in front of him and just time to draw a breath before the red light flashed on.

I watched from downstairs in an easy chair. It was a very good broadcast, I thought, though I knew that I was far too involved in it by then to be able to judge. Certainly it set a precedent in every sort of way. It was the first ministerial broadcast which ever had a reply. It was the first time the Leader of the Opposition had demanded the resignation of the Prime Minister on the air and it was the first time that we had been able to test our capacity to put out a message to the nation with about 11 hours' notice. Afterwards we sat and talked for a little while and then dispersed. Hugh autographed his script for me inscribing it, 'A thousand thanks'.

Monday 5 November 1956
Thinking of positive ways we might help, I got on to the Red Cross this morning to see whether blood supplies could be sent to the Middle East from Britain. I spoke to Lady Limerick of the British Red Cross. The arrangements apparently are very simple. Anyone may get in touch with the local Health Service transfusion office anywhere and ask them to lay on what Lady Limerick called 'a special bleeding session'. This blood would then be bottled and sent to her in London. Of course it would be for the person who arranged this to see that enough donors came forward to make this session a success.

I went early to the House to check the final details of the petition which I presented today. Using the little-known Standing Order No.92, I asked that it should be read out by the Clerk of the House. This he did and as a result the petition got pride of place at the beginning of the day's business with a page of Hansard all to itself.

One other idea which I had been working on for two or three days came to fulfilment this afternoon. On Dave's advice I had made strenuous efforts to get access to the 'Voice of Britain' broadcasts from Cyprus. The transcripts were horrifying.

Limassol The Voice of the Allied Armies Command in Arabic To the Near East Nov 2 1956 1245 GMT

(The following was read by a non-Arab announcer – Ed.)

'O Egyptian People, your broadcasting station was destroyed. From now on you will listen to the voice of Allied Armies Command from this very frequency . . .

'O Egyptians, this is the first blow which has befallen you. Why has this befallen you? First, because Abd Al-Nasir went mad and seized the Suez Canal which is of vital importance to the world.

'O Egyptians, the seizure of the Suez Canal was against the interest of all the countries of the world which strongly demand guarantees for the passage of their ships through the Canal which is life's blood for these countries . . .'

Limassol Voice of Britain in Arabic to the Near East Nov 4 1956 0525 GMT

'Now listen carefully to us. You have hidden in small villages. Do you know what this means? It means that we are obliged to bomb you wherever you are. Imagine your villages being bombed. Imagine your wives, children, mothers, fathers, and grandfathers escaping from their houses and leaving their property behind. This will happen to you if you hide behind your women in the villages. You are soldiers and duty requires that you defend your villages and not bring destruction upon them. You have nothing with which to defend yourselves – no air force, nothing. We will find and bomb you wherever you hide.

'One thing which you can do is to wear civilian clothes. And go to your homes to see if any soldiers or tanks are concealed in your villages. Tell them to clear out before we come and destroy these villages. If they do not evacuate, there is no doubt that your villages and homes will be destroyed. You have committed a sin, that is, you placed confidence in Abd Al-Nasir and believed his lies.

'Now you are hearing the truth. This is the Supreme Allied Command addressing Egyptian soldiers, sailors, and pilots.'

Today I successfully raised it in a question to the Foreign Secretary.

It is impossible to give an idea of the feeling there is at the moment in the House of Commons – but one must try. I suppose one should go back to

2 August and the nationalisation of the Suez Canal to get the full flavour. Then, at short notice, Hugh Gaitskell made a speech of bitter denunciation of Nasser. He followed the Prime Minister in an emergency debate and he was wildly cheered by the Tories and heard in near silence by his own Party. I felt so sick as I listened that I wanted to shout 'shame'. I very nearly did buttonhole him afterwards and say that his speech had made me want to vomit.

Gaitskell's speech had only one saving grace. It ended with a phrase declaring that as a signatory of the UN Charter, Britain was bound not to use force without its authority. But the dominating impression of the whole speech was that British prestige and influence required really tough action.

At any rate throughout August it looked as if the Party was going to be deeply split. Aneurin Bevan – in a characteristically inexplicable lapse - began urging the merits of international control so that *Tribune* and the radicals came out against the Labour leadership and the campaign erupted in meetings and demonstrations all over the country.

But by then Gaitskell had been subjected to great pressure – of argument as well as numbers. I think he had genuinely changed his view and he put up a magnificent performance in the House of Commons.

This new situation had an electric effect on the Party. People began rallying round again and at the end of September came the Labour Conference at Blackpool, which from every point of view was most excellent. Gaitskell won the acclamation of the Party on his own merits. Bevan won the treasurership and therefore took his place in the hierarchy – secure, accepted and still very much loved, for all his mischief as much as despite it. The new policy statements were debated in an atmosphere free from rancour. All this was workmanlike and greatly encouraging. It came too at a time when the Government was running into all sorts of difficulties, and there were the first obvious beginnings of a loss of confidence in Eden.

The diary for the last two days will show how effective was the battle which we put up. But the temper of the Party is most important of all. The fact is that we were genuinely shocked and horrified by the decision to deliver an ultimatum. Here was no shadow-boxing. Here was no simulated uproar. Here were no rhetorical tricks. What we witnessed in the last week in the House of Commons was a very angry Party unable to control this anger. The shouting and the booing and the words of abuse that flew across the chamber were no doubt very reprehensible to the calm uncommitted middle-class middle of the road strangers watching from the Gallery. They may even have reacted against us because of our behaviour. But we could not control ourselves. That is the fact of the matter. It reminded me once more that politics is not a tea party, even in a parliamentary democracy. It is an orderly and disciplined struggle for power. The fact that the power changes hands according to a set pattern does not diminish the importance of that power nor weaken the bitterness of the struggle for it. Though our weapons were a point of order or a supplementary question, we were fighters for a cause just as powerfully as the marchers in Budapest this week.

The fact is that Parliament is not designed to cope with differences as great as have been in evidence this week. The sure sign of this strain is when the usual channels break down and when the personal relationships between Members on opposite sides become embittered.

Today I was sitting in the Smoking Room when George Wigg came in breathing heavily and sat down beside me. 'I've done a bloody silly thing,' he said. 'I've walloped a Tory. A few minutes ago in the Members' Cloakroom.' It turned out to be Leslie Thomas, the Member for Canterbury, whose father Jimmy Thomas was a Labour Cabinet Minister before the war. 'He said "Gaitskell's a bloody traitor." I said I'd rather be led by a bloody traitor than a f—ing murderer. He asked me to come outside and as we left the cloakroom, he swiped me. So I gave him one in the belly and two or three more and he went down like a felled ox.' George said he was going to see the Speaker to apologise – much as he would go to his commanding officer. And off he went, all 6ft. 4in. of him, an ex-Army colonel from the ranks – fifty-five and fit as a fiddle. A moment later Leslie Thomas limped in, 5ft. 9in. fifty-five, paunchy and pasty, breathing even more heavily and limping too. He should have picked on someone his own size!

This evening I did three meetings in Gravesend. They were not very big and rather confirmed what I had suspected: that ordinary people are not yet moved on this issue. Part of the explanation too may lie in the fact that every British soldier who has ever served in Egypt hates the Egyptian people.

Tuesday 6 November 1956
A really useful day – made possible by the fact that my secretary, the incomparable Mrs Small, was here all the time. She is going to be here all week, which is an enormous comfort.

This morning's news of a Russian near-ultimatum has made the situation far more grave and we could be within a few hours of a third world war complete with the hydrogen bomb. Very, very, very depressed as a result.

Spoke at University College London Labour Club on the situation. 200 very serious students – not by any means all Labour – who sat in perfect silence and asked the most penetrating questions. Lost control of emotions during my speech – as last night. I think it's the tension and strain that does it.

To the House of Commons at 7 pm where the Lobby was full of excited chattering members, talking about cease-fire. I do not believe it – it is too incredible. Two other members confirm it. It must be true. It is true. Feel like jumping in the air and cheering. Am engaged in a mild caper when spot Bessie Braddock. 'Bessie I want to kiss you,' I said. Bessie, with a huge smile, replied, 'Not now, dearie, with all these people about.'

Home at 8. Happy and very exhausted. But couldn't go to bed till 2 for trying to think out what all this means and what the lessons are. Will try to set down some first reactions tomorrow.

Wednesday 7 November 1956

Worked at home all morning, still on the diary and trying to catch up with the many jobs that I neglected in the last week. The situation is still somewhat confused in that one does not know exactly what the position is in Egypt. Rumours of Russian troop and naval movements into the Mediterranean are very alarming. There are reports that a quarter of a million Chinese have volunteered to help Egypt. The whole thing has the nature of a nightmare and one wonders whether we are not within measurable sight of a racial war.

To the House of Commons in time to hear a statement on Hungary. The first questions emerge, hinting at a desire to go to war with Russia over it. Some people's insanity knows no bounds.

The big news in the evening papers is of a major split in the Cabinet. From what I can find out (from Boothby and others) this is absolutely true. I gather that when the Russian ultimatum was reported to them a fairly substantial number – perhaps a majority – forced a cease-fire on to Eden against his will. He is apparently extremely angry about it and feels himself to have been betrayed. At 5 o'clock this afternoon there was a meeting of Ministers under the chairmanship of the PM to consider the situation. It did not include Butler, Monckton, Macleod and a few more. It looks possible that the Cabinet is now meeting in two halves and engaged in mortal combat.

I saw the Tory MP Peter Kirk in the Library and he asked me how I had got on in his constituency (Gravesend) on Monday. He was so cordial that I urged him to come and have a drink with me.

We went – by agreement – into the deepest recess we could find in the Lords' Bar which is the quietest place to go and where one has the best chance of a talk without being seen or overheard. However, our joint horror at the situation brought us very close together and we fell to talking with complete frankness. What he told me – under the oath of complete secrecy – was the inside story of the backbench Conservative revolt which we had all been hoping would take place.

On his return from Strasbourg last week Peter tried to make contact with those Conservative Members whom he knew to be opposed to this policy. David Price was one of them and the others were Sir Lionel Heald, Alec Spearman, Walter Elliot, and others. They wanted to act on the motion of censure last Thursday but felt that they could not do so for fear of endangering our troops. The fall of the Government on the eve of an invasion would, they thought, demoralise our soldiers at a critical moment. They therefore maintained contact with each other over the weekend and on Monday began making approaches to those Cabinet Ministers whom they thought shared their anxieties. It is significant that Monckton was not amongst them. Kirk said he did not know his view. Monckton certainly must have been very cautious if that was so – or perhaps he counts for so little in the Tory Party that the rebels did not think him important. In any case they discovered that James Stuart, the Secretary of State for Scotland, was a firm supporter and they were emboldened to compose a letter for the Prime Minister.

Kirk said he could almost remember the text of the letter verbatim and below I am reproducing my recollection of his recollection of what the letter contained.

Dear Prime Minister,

As it now appears that the objectives of the Anglo-French intervention have been attained, we are writing to urge that the policy of the Government should be

1. An immediate cease-fire.
2. That the Allied Forces in Egypt should be put under the technical command of the UN.
3. That a UN Police Force should take over the responsibility for policing to prevent a resumption of hostilities.

We, who have signed this letter, feel bound to ask for satisfactory assurances on all these points if we are to continue to support the Government in the Lobbies.

    Yours sincerely,
        (here followed the signatures of sixteen Conservative MPs)

On Tuesday morning Alec Spearman (I think) was deputed to take the letter to Number 10 Downing Street. He did not see the Prime Minister but Robert Allan, his PPS. Allan promised to convey this to the Prime Minister and there is no question but that he did so. No reply was received but at 6 o'clock that evening (yesterday) the PM announced the cease-fire in the House.

Of course a revolt of sixteen – even voting with the Opposition – would only have reduced the Government majority by 32, but that would have been a sizeable drop and Kirk rightly felt that had such a step been taken many more Conservative Members would have rallied to them and the Government would have been bound to take account of their views. Kirk modestly claimed therefore that this letter must have been one factor in the Prime Minister's mind when he reached his decision.

By now Peter and I were able to talk quite freely on both sides. We discussed the likely consequences. He said that Eden was now a paranoiac. He was so convinced that he was dedicated to the cause of British greatness that he was capable of anything. He agreed that in the present moment of crisis it was unlikely that the Cabinet would compel Eden to resign. However, he thought it possible that – like Hitler in his Chancellery bunker in Berlin – Eden might use his power to the full,

resign himself and ask the Queen for a dissolution. This would carry the
Conservative Party down to ruin and destruction and would be the Prime
Minister's way of getting back at his colleagues who had betrayed him.
Though all this is speculative, the situation is extremely fluid for one
simple, single reason. No one point of view in the House commands a
clear parliamentary majority. Thus the whole basis for the stability of
Government has been undermined. The Labour Party – united but for
four or five unimportant dissidents – is in a minority and the
Conservative Party is split at least three ways. There are the Suez Group
20 or 30 strong, led from within the Cabinet by Eden, Macmillan and
Salisbury. There are the 16 open rebels with perhaps 30 or 40 more who
share their view but not their courage, and there is the lump and mass of
the Tory Party which is leaderless and confused. They have lost their
faith in Eden, are suspicious of the ambitions of Butler and seek only to
save themselves and their Party from the ruin which immediately faces
them. Gerald Nabarro is credited by Boothby with the most penetrating
comment of all. When Eden announced the cease-fire, the Tories rose in a
body and cheered. One of them said aloud, 'What exactly are we
cheering?' Gerald Nabarro, who was beside him, exclaimed in a stage
whisper, 'We are cheering the last chance to save our political bacon, old
boy. That's what we're cheering and make no mistake about it.'

Kirk thought Eden could not last long and one must therefore be ready
for Butler to take over and for the economic consequences to hit the
country very hard. Not being an economist I do not know exactly what
these are. The emergency itself has probably cost £100 million. Aside
from the need for petrol rationing which is almost inevitable, there will
therefore probably be a severe balance of payments crisis and an Autumn
budget, with greatly increased taxation. The consequences of this are
very grave. Those members of the public who were not stirred by the
moral issue would almost certainly revolt against this Government when
the full cost of their folly became apparent. Kirk himself, of course, fears
an Election more than most. He only won last time because Dick Acland
was fighting Gravesend as an Independent Anti-H bomb candidate
against the Labour candidate, Victor Mishcon. Mishcon and Acland
together had a combined vote 3,000 greater than Kirk. Kirk reminded me
that if an Election were held now with a massive Labour landslide the
effect would be to sweep out of Parliament the young liberal element in
the Conservative Party. 'You would be left with the most ignorant and
reactionary section of the Party in Parliament,' he said, 'and I like to
think that there is a liberal wing which has some value and some part to
play.' I absolutely agree with him and confess to a growing admiration
for the man, though I never liked him at Oxford because he was thrusting
and rude. I do admire his independence of mind and his courage in the
Hanging and Suez controversies this year.

rafting an orange and lemon 'peace tree', Soviet
nion, 1960. The tree still bears 'Benn' fruit

Awaiting the result during the Bristol
by-election, 1961

tended family: Mother (standing left of TB), David Benn (standing second from right) and
roline holding Joshua, with Hilary, Melissa and Stephen at her feet, 1957

(right) With Nurse Olive and Father

(below) Boys will be boys – brother Michael carrying author, author carrying brother David (c. 1938)

Brother Michael (died 1944) and father in RAF form, North Africa

Stansgate – the fa home – pictured in 19

(*above*) On a 'jolly' to the pyramids during leave, April 1945 – author standing far left

(*above right*) Author proudly sporting the 'wings' in 1945, and (*right*) the real thing

(*below*) By-election victory of the Commons against the Lords, 1961

Financial Secretary to the Treasury Enoch Powell. Resigned January 1958 over his Government's monetary policy

(*below right*) Anthony Eden: Prime Minister 1955-7, architect of the Suez debâcle

(*below*) Young(ish) Rab Butler, Conservative Home Secretary

(above) Seretse Khama (left) and Ruth Khama and supporters Jo Grimond, Fenner Brockway and Arthur Carr

(left) Sir Richard Acland – leader of the socialist Common Wealth Party in the 1940s, formerly a Liberal MP, later Labour MP for Gravesend

clear disarmer and
ourge of the
itskellites: Frank
ousins, General
cretary of the TGWU
the 1950s

r father was Lloyd
orge: Lady Megan,
beral MP 1929 - 51,
ned Labour in 1955

Clem on the stump, during his premiership 1945-51

(below) Jennie Lee and Nye Bevan – fiery husband and wife team who led the 'Bevanites'

(*far left*) Sailor Jim –
later Lt Callaghan,
later still Prime
Minister

(*left*) Ernie Bevin –
Bristol dockers'
leader and British
Foreign Secretary,
1945-51

Oxford don, Labour
Minister, political
diarist – Dick
Crossman

On the set with tele-
vision 'personality'
and Labour MP
Woodrow Wyatt and
television-shy Hugh
Gaitskell

Oxford friend, later Cabinet colleague
Tony Crosland

(below) Malcolm Muggeridge, friend
and supporter during the peerage
struggle

The brains behind the peerage case,
Michael Zander

Someone told me that Jennie Lee was very cross at my *New Statesman* article about the House of Lords. I saw Jennie at supper and asked to sit beside her. It was a typical talk with Jennie. She had not read my article, except to convince herself by a glance that I must be saying the sort of things she would expect me to say. This was enough for her to set into motion her sacred socialist principle. She therefore began lecturing me in an intolerable way and I decided to hit back – and hit back hard. Her argument was roughly this: 'The Lords perpetuate class and snobbery. Your scheme is just another sort of Lords' Reform. It is very unsocialist. It will give great patronage to the leader. You are playing the Tory game.' Two well directed questions proved that she did not understand what I was suggesting. I even convinced her that my scheme involved the abolition of the House of Lords. The argument therefore proceeded from there on the technical case for a second chamber. She said that Privy Councillors were snob appointments. I asked her why Nye had taken one. She could not answer. She said that socialism meant electing everybody and not appointing. I asked if she was in favour of an elected Cabinet. She was not. She asked me how I could justify the House of Lords. I replied – quite rightly – that it was *Tribune* which was always arguing that you should leave the House of Lords alone. I reminded her that she had written an article opposing my Renunciation Bill and asked whether that was a socialist view. She did have the decency to apologise and to say that I had converted her to abolition as a practical as well as a theoretical desirability. I said I was delighted and now perhaps we could proceed to discuss the case for a second chamber on a technical basis.

Thursday 8 November 1956
Mrs Small all day again, thank God, and further progress with diary and letters.

Lord Salisbury's speech yesterday on Lords' Reform broadly confirms what Lambton told me in July and means I should be able to get out quite easily – if this Government lasts long enough to enact its provisions.

Gaitskell wrote me a very sweet note about the broadcast:

My dear Tony,
I should like to place on record my most grateful thanks to you for the wonderful help you gave me last Sunday. I do not know how I could have managed the broadcast without you. And if, as some think – including I believe almost all your friends – it was effective, this was largely due to you, both for the general plan which you suggested and for much of the drafting.
Yours ever,
Hugh

Today the Tory Party is breaking up, as I suspected it would. Jacob

Astor [Conservative MP for Plymouth, Sutton], Alec Spearman and others spoke in the House against the Government. The biggest news of all is of Edward Boyle's resignation from the Treasury. Reggie Paget saw him this afternoon and said a friendly word, at which Edward actually burst into tears in the corridor and Reggie had to stand very close so that three Tories going by wouldn't notice.

Therefore when I saw him after the vote it was with some trepidation that I clasped his arm and said, 'I don't want to embarrass you with my support, but I felt I must say one word.' He was terribly friendly and suggested we have a drink. In fact he came to talk to David, Caroline and me for almost an hour. He said he was sure history would prove him right and he felt a great sense of relief that it was all over. He decided to do it a week ago and was glad the announcement came after the cease-fire to prove that success or failure of the operation could not affect his judgement on it.

He confirmed – very tentatively – what I suspect may happen. Eden, feeling betrayed by his colleagues, may resign and carry the Parliament with him to an Election. It was a most charming talk with Edward who is an old, old friend, but who in the last year or two I have not liked to worry because he must have been so busy.

Monday 12 November 1956
I had a drink with Francis Cassavetti and we talked over the events of the last week. He said that rumour had it that Monckton had been bought off by a firm promise that he would succeed Lord Goddard as Lord Chief Justice in the New Year. I have no way of knowing whether this is true, although of course it has long been known that Goddard wanted to go and that Monckton wanted to succeed him. The difficulty up to now has been twofold. First, Goddard objected to the guilty party in a divorce case becoming Lord Chief Justice and Monckton had no direct claim on the job. It is a perk that goes to the Attorney-General if he wants it. The trouble is that the present Attorney-General is by common consent a complete clot and nobody can imagine how he could be moved up in this way. Goddard's private preference is said to be for Shawcross, but Shawcross appears to be *persona non grata* with simply everybody except the Bar Council and the yachting set.

What is interesting about this is the light it throws on Monckton's character and position. He entered politics too late to allow it to dominate his action and though not exactly a weak man, he wants above all things to be loved by everyone – a very human weakness but one that makes political leadership almost impossible. It is tragic that he who could have prevented the ultimatum said nothing and let it go on.

Wednesday 14 November 1956
There was really nothing to report from yesterday as I was at home all

day, catching up with letters and so on. Today I went into the Commons early for the Party meeting.

This evening there was an adjournment debate on the handling of the recent crisis by the BBC. This debate came on very early because there was a sort of plot to get the other business over quickly to allow this to become a major debate. I wasn't there but I gather that two or three Conservative Members had been given briefs to enable them to charge the BBC with left-wing bias. There were so few Labour Members there that George Wigg had to speak for two hours to keep the other Tory MPs out. Finally, the Assistant Postmaster General in winding up hinted at a redeployment of forces in the Overseas Broadcasting Service which suggests that there is something afoot.

I missed the debate because I was doing the first of my new television series, *Personal Column*, for ATV in Birmingham. It wasn't as difficult as I thought it might be and I was reasonably satisfied with it. There are only four in all, though I suppose they might ask me to go on.

Thursday 15 November 1956

David Butler who came to our party last night asked to see me urgently alone and so we came to the office for a talk. He has seen William Clark who was, until his resignation a few days ago, the Prime Minister's adviser on public relations. He's an exceptionally able man but an appalling name-dropper and snob. His story, as told to David Butler, was this.

Eden's personality underwent a complete change towards the beginning of the Suez crisis. Clark dates this at about the time that he collapsed with a fever when he visited Lady Eden in hospital. He is, said Clark, and I quote, 'a criminal lunatic'. Knowing what a middle-of-the-road, moderate, wishy-washy man Clark is, I was very surprised to hear such strong language used. However, he had more to say in confirmation. Evidently the Government were not themselves kept informed by Eden and various people were taken off the secret list for documents as the plan progressed. Clark himself was sent on leave (which he did not want) the day after he had explained to the PM what the likely public reaction would be to the use of force against Egypt. Clark thought that only an inner group of Cabinet Ministers had been told the plans Eden had made. Clark thought that there was no doubt about the charge of collusion with the French PM, Guy Mollet, and Ben-Gurion. He said that the final proof would come from the State Department in Washington. Apparently when the Israelis were building up for their attack a news blackout descended on London and Paris and consultation with the US came to an abrupt and sinister halt. However, the State Department intercepted and decoded messages passing between Paris and Jerusalem and discovered what was afoot. These messages are likely to leak out from the State Department and destroy the whole basis of Eden's case. Far from claiming the credit for putting out a small fire, he will be charged with having incited the Israelis to start it. This should surely produce more resignations from the Government and alter the whole position once more.

As Hugh Massingham said in Sunday's *Observer*, 'Meanwhile the little time bomb – the charge that there was collusion between Britain, France and Israel – ticks quietly on. If it goes off one day, a lot of beliefs and favourite figures will disappear in the ruins.'

Other items from Clark's story are these:

First, Mountbatten opposed the attack as did Sir Norman Brook, the Secretary of the Cabinet. Sir Roger Makins, Permanent Secretary to the Treasury, first read of it in the newspapers. Finally, the dirtiest thing of all was when Eden told Clark to tell the newspapers privately that Nutting's resignation was not on principle but because of personal difficulties he was in. Clark says he replied, 'If you want that put out, you must put it out yourself.'

One final titbit from today which might be worth following up. Shirley Catlin [Williams] of the *Financial Times* said that *The Times* itself had been secretly briefed of the Israeli attack and the British intervention four days before it took place. I wonder.

Monday 19 November 1956
Morning at work at home and to the Commons after lunch. Two questions for the Foreign Secretary. In the course of supplementary question I referred to the 'British aggression in Egypt'. At this the Tory MP for South-East Essex, Bernard Braine, began shouting 'Nasser's little lackey'. A terrific row developed extending over four pages of Hansard. It was all very silly but is indicative of the rise in feeling in the House. Had talks with various people about the situation. Undoubtedly the collusion story will break soon. It seems quite clear that the French have been secretly arming Israel over the last three months and that indeed the original attack on the Sinai Peninsula was assisted by three squadrons of Mystère fighters flown by French pilots. There is additional evidence which suggests that the French sold this idea to Eden around the middle of October and that at least three ministers – Eden, Selwyn Lloyd and Head – knew all about it. There is also evidence that the US was forewarned of this and brought what pressure they could on Britain and France. Thus Eden may be faced with a critical situation in Parliament which he cannot control.

Today's news is most revealing. The US quite clearly will not supply oil to Britain until we withdraw our forces from Port Said. This is partly because they feel that they have been the victims of double dealing, partly because they fear that the Arab states will cut off their oil if they do not press for the Anglo-French withdrawal and partly because they think that the danger of Soviet volunteers in the Middle East will remain high until these forces do leave.

Wednesday 21 November 1956
Saw Attlee in the Tea Room and smiled and he shouted 'Lackey, lackey, lackey' and burst into fits of laughter.

Thursday 22 November 1956
Was expecting David Butler and William Clark for a talk this morning. However, they were delayed and Clark had to go straight on. David stayed for a longer talk and retailed some of William Clark's stories. The ones I can recall are these.

First, the Anglo-French discussions all summer came to be known as the 'Pretext Committee'. At one time this Committee discussed the possibility of blowing up a British ship in the Canal and charging the Egyptian Government with having done it. Also the French brought pressure to bear by saying that the Algerian situation was so critical that they alone would be compelled to attack Nasser by the end of the year, even if Britain did not join them. Finally, the Israeli idea emerged from Paris and became the accepted plan.

It seems that there was a tremendous row in the Cabinet over the withdrawal issue. The American pressure and other factors had influenced a majority of the Cabinet to insist upon withdrawal. Eden became angrier and angrier and all the tranquillity which he has acquired from the drugs on which he has been living for two months disappeared. Finally he is said to have burst into tears and required a doctor there and then. Incredible as this story is, it fits in with all that one has heard about Eden's tantrums before the crisis began.

And now he is leaving for Jamaica without even a Private Secretary. William Clark said this was because all his staff were united by an intense loathing for the man but that is not the whole story. He has deliberately not made Butler acting Prime Minister, but only charged him with the responsibility for presiding over the Cabinet – a very significant difference. Butler is intensely suspect now. As one Conservative Member (Peter Kirk) put it to me, 'You all underrate Rab. When the smoke has cleared you'll find him there on top of a mound of corpses with his knife dripping with blood and an inscrutable smile on his face.'

Butler's skill was very much in evidence this afternoon when asked some pertinent questions on collusion. He answered by quoting Selwyn Lloyd and Eden, thus dissociating himself by implication from their answers. I rose on a point of order to emphasise this and ask the Speaker whether it was not a breach of collective Cabinet responsibility. He did not respond but my point is on the record.

Friday 23 November 1956
I wrote to Elath, the Israeli Ambassador, yesterday. The events of the last month have put a certain strain on relations between the Israelis and the Labour Party. Naturally enough, they feel that our support of Nasser represents a betrayal of them. This, of course, is quite untrue but that hasn't helped. I thought, however, that a little note of friendliness might be appreciated. Elath replied with a most friendly note inviting me to lunch with him alone on Wednesday. I shall certainly go. My guess is that he has not been happy about Ben-Gurion's policy and if we can keep it on the basis of two friends talking I may learn a great deal.

Monday 26 November 1956
This evening Caroline and I went as guests of honour to the Anglo-Israel Association annual dinner at the Savoy. I had been rather doubtful about whether they would want us to go. We were in the event put at the top table – the only Labour MP on it. There were a lot of Tory MPs sitting at the ordinary tables and they must have wondered what 'Nasser's little lackey' was doing there. Reginald Maudling, the Minister of Supply, made a very noncommittal speech about the needs of the Middle East. I don't think he mentioned the Jews or the Arabs once. Really he might have been speaking about the New World so little precision was there in his statement of the problem, or his answer to it.

He was followed by Elath, the Israeli Ambassador. Elath read his speech and it was really terrifying. He said that Israel had acted to prevent aggression and that if her rights were not recognised an even more dangerous situation was inevitable.

Tuesday 27 November 1956
The political situation changes hour by hour and it is very hard to know how it will all turn out. Eden's disappearance has undoubtedly put the Cabinet in a great difficulty. They are under enormous pressure from all sides: the UN and the Americans to withdraw; the appalling economic prospects; the many splits in their own Party; and the complete disintegration of British policy and prestige. Butler and the moderates in the Cabinet have put themselves into special difficulty by their decision to proclaim the Prime Minister as the effective Head of the Government even during his absence. This, of course, is designed to safeguard their own position in the future. However, it also means that they must pay particular attention to Selwyn Lloyd, who is Eden's mouthpiece. He is such a second-rate person in every way that the Cabinet are virtually guilty of dereliction of duty. One must not rule out the possibility that the moderates will carry the Cabinet and that Eden will resign. This could easily lead to a General Election.

Wednesday 28 November 1956

Lunch alone with Elath at his house in Avenue Road. He was a most charming and agreeable host and we had nearly two hours of solid talk. It is difficult to convey all that he said but it was most useful.

The Egyptian Army had turned out to be a complete flop. The bitter fanatical Arab nationalism had not proved itself to be much of an inspiration and the officers had run away. This was because Nasser had not made any serious efforts at reform in Egypt and had quite failed to create a new social base on which an Army must rely if it is to have something to fight for. The military defeat would certainly have led to Nasser's downfall if Britain and France had not intervened.

I formed the impression that the nature of the collusion had been much more complicated than I had at first supposed. Probably it went a bit like this: about April of this year the French came to the conclusion that Nasser would have to be destroyed if Algeria was to be saved. They, therefore, began supplying Mystère fighters to Israel with a view to building up Israeli strength. At any rate after the nationalisation of the Canal, the French began intensifying their arms supplies to Israel. They no doubt discussed the possibility of an attack on Egypt and Mollet undertook to see that the tripartite declaration was not invoked against Israel and probably promised to use the veto in the UN as well.

Again one cannot be sure how much Eden knew about these negotiations. Whether Mollet kept him informed of the plan is irrelevant. Eden must have known what was going on and it probably came as no surprise to him when Mollet finally said (as he must have done), 'Look here, there's a bit of trouble brewing between Israel and Egypt and if they do attack it will give us the excuse that we want to go in and seize the Canal under the pretext of protecting it.' Possibly under heavy French pressure, but more probably quite willingly, Eden agreed to this. Thus the operation began and the ultimatum was delivered.

The traditional anti-Israeli bias in the Foreign Office has already returned. They see that the only hope – a slender one – of rebuilding British policy in the Middle East is to give support to the Arabs against Israel. It is for this reason that Israel will be betrayed. She allowed herself to become the tool of Anglo-French imperialism and will have to pay the price.

Thursday 29 November 1956

This evening there was a meeting of the 1922 Committee at which Selwyn Lloyd, Macmillan and Butler spoke. Apparently Macmillan said that the economic outlook was very bleak, but the Party seem to have received the report without much protest. Then later a number of them got together and realised what was happening. A fresh revolt is therefore imminent. The importance of this revolt depends in part on the position of Eden.

There are rumours today that he and Butler have had a real showdown on the telephone and it might be that Eden would put himself at the head of a right-wing rejection of the climbdown. This is certainly the thing to watch.

Our Party meeting at 6.30 ended with a most touching little scene. Gaitskell announced the new Shadow Cabinet appointments under which Nye Bevan takes over Foreign Affairs from Alf Robens who is looking after Transport, Fuel and Power. Alf got up to say that he wished Nye all good luck and felt no bitterness at what had happened. Nye responded with a graceful little speech, contrasting our present happy unity with the acrimonious discussions of the past. The Party cheered itself silly in delighted relief at the formal recognition of the final end of all our splits.

Sunday 2 December 1956

Today was the third conference of the Movement for Colonial Freedom. It was held in the Bonnington Hotel in Southampton Row and was a much smaller conference than before. This, however, was itself a good sign. Only the representatives from area councils and nationally affiliated trade unions had been invited. So that everyone who came carried weight. The Fire Brigades' Union, Electrical Trades' Union, National Union of Railwaymen and the Miners from South Wales and Derbyshire of course represent hundreds of thousands of members. Our total strength is over 5 million and there are 109 Labour MPs amongst them. Jim Callaghan, who has just been appointed Shadow Colonial Secretary, sent a message of good wishes and this was very much appreciated. In short we felt that we were a going concern, as indeed we are. It is a fantastic achievement that less than three years after our foundation we should be so well established and so influential.

The greatest change in our policy statement this year has been the decision to urge the summoning of a conference from all the colonial territories as soon as a Labour Government is returned to office. With these representatives we should work out a specific timetable for our withdrawal and the transfer of power. This will achieve a psychological revolution and set the people free to work towards its realisation.

After some discussion we passed a resolution demanding the withdrawal of Soviet troops from Hungary. We, above all people, were entitled to do this, and it was supported by John Horner, the General Secretary of the Fire Brigades' Union, and other ex-Communists.

Monday 3 December 1956

Selwyn Lloyd made his statement this afternoon about the withdrawal of British troops from Port Said. It was a singularly inept statement in that it attempted to show that the operation had been 100 per cent successful, when everyone knows it has been a total failure. The phrases that must have sounded so good when they were being composed in the Foreign Office fell like a pancake on a wet pavement in the House itself. Indeed the derisive laughter from our side was in part genuine laughter at the words and phrases used. The Conservatives heard it in dead silence though our reaction to it united them behind their own dejected and defeated Leaders. It will be interesting to see what happens in the debate later this week. My guess is that few, if any, of the Suez group will actually abstain in the division.

Nye appearing as Shadow Foreign Secretary made a most effective intervention immediately following the statement. His phrase 'sounding the bugles of advance to cover our retreat' exactly fitted the bill and his decision not to interrogate because he didn't want to bully them at this moment was exactly right.

Tuesday 4 December 1956
This afternoon the Senior Broadcasting Committee met to consider our General Election plans. It was at full strength with its new membership. Nye and Tom Driberg had come for the first time and they transformed the scene. Nye was very scornful of TV generally, partly because he doesn't think he is any good at it. Being Treasurer he also was against any expenditure. Tom, on the other hand, was the great radio and TV correspondent and supported our desire to get good programme material. The most hopeful result of the meeting was the decision to consider the purchase of a closed circuit TV camera. This would enable us to rehearse at Transport House, and Morgan Phillips half promised a studio. Here we could get together all the equipment we need – such as our wire recorder, tiny cinema screen and the rest. It should enable us to do our rehearsals more easily and cheaply. However, as far as our general proposals for the Election were concerned they received very scant attention.

Wednesday 5 December 1956
There were more parliamentary questions today on collusion. We got an admission from the Minister for Defence, Antony Head, that an Israeli attack on Egypt had been anticipated for some time and that the decision to mobilise had been the first definite proof. Butler, however, continued to deny any knowledge of the matter and the Speaker began ruling that Members with supplementary questions could not quote French official statements or reports from the US.

Nye made the best speech I've ever heard from anyone. It was cool, calm and deadly – a most powerful piece of oratory that held the House in silence for nearly an hour.

Saturday 8 December 1956
I did a surgery this morning at Party headquarters – the first one for
some months. It was very busy. Quite unexpectedly I got a fresh piece of
evidence about collusion. A young woman came to ask me if I could get
her husband – a leading seaman in the Navy – home from Port Said for
Christmas. She told me that his ship HMS *Tyne* (the headquarters ship)
had sailed from Malta on 27 October – two days before the Israeli attack.
Apparently those on board had thought they were going to Cyprus but in
fact they had gone to Port Said.

This afternoon I went to the Hanham Labour Party children's party
and then looked in at the old people's Christmas Sale at Memory Hall.
Neither of these was really planned, but being in Bristol it was very nice
to be able to get to them.

Tuesday 11 December 1956
This morning I went to Granada in Golden Square for the showing of the
rough cut of the housing film that we are putting on as a Party political in
a month's time.

The film was not all bad, though the decision to use ordinary people
rather than actors – which was quite right – meant that there was a
certain stiffness and awkwardness about their performance. It is a
terrible thing that our political leaders should not by now have learnt
how to handle TV. Gaitskell can do it and so can some of the Second XI
who have appeared regularly. But we desperately need to run a television
training scheme to bring up the general standard. It is absurd that people
should be picked on the basis of their skill in this medium.

Thursday 13 December 1956
This afternoon the Party invited Anna Kethly to speak to us. She was, of
course, in Nagy's Government and is a famous Social Democrat leader
from way back. Considering the fact that she has been in prison so much
since the war and is sixty-seven, she is a most remarkable woman.
Despite her tough background, she is gentle and feminine as well as a
powerful personality. She spoke in Hungarian, which nobody
understood, and was translated paragraph by paragraph. She traced the
history of politics in Hungary since the war and particularly the pressure
put upon the Social Democrats by the Communists to fuse the two
parties. This had been done by arresting and gaoling most of the Social
Democrat leaders – about 14,000 of them. She then went on to describe
the miserably low living standards of the Hungarian people and their
falling confidence in their Government. She said the demonstration in
October had not been organised at all and was a spontaneous outbreak
which led to the formation of workers' and students' councils. She herself
was asked to join the Government at about that time but had refused

without a promise of free Elections. She pleaded for moral (but not military) support for Hungary and for the strongest diplomatic pressure against Russia. She feared that the deportations would rise above the 100,000 that have already taken place. She had photostatic copies of the letters dropped by these deportees from the trains leaving for Russia. Although she was very quiet in her presentation of all of this story and despite the time lag of interpretation, she made a very deep impression on us all. The agony of Hungary came home more clearly than it could ever have done by reading or even seeing films of the fighting. She said she wanted workers' delegations to go to Hungary and see what had happened there. She didn't mind if they were composed of British Communists or anyone, so confident was she that the facts would speak for themselves. She thought that there were only about 4,000 Communists left in the whole of that country and she did not believe that the Government would last one minute after Soviet force was withdrawn. What she feared was that by deportations and fear of deportations, Hungary might be absorbed into the Soviet Union as wholly and completely as were Lithuania, Latvia and Estonia.

Saturday 15 December 1956
Travelling to Bristol by train I found myself in the dining car with Sir Walter Monckton. After I had eaten he beckoned me over and we had an hour's talk. He was extremely cordial and most indiscreet. Among the subjects he mentioned were:
Mervyn Stockwood. Monckton said that Stockwood had been very kind to him from the first in Bristol. He, Monckton, had felt that his divorce had made it impossible for him to go to Communion, however Stockwood had said, 'Who am I to set limits to the boundless mercy of the Almighty?' Monckton thought Stockwood should certainly be made a Bishop and had personally urged this on Clem and Eden.
The Lord Chief Justiceship. Monckton said he thought Goddard would go in April when he was eighty. 'Of course, Shawcross is qualified for any legal post, including this, but I'm afraid he would be exactly like Goddard and I do think justice should be tempered with a little more mercy.' Monckton has suggested a peerage for Shawcross as he obviously isn't making the Commons his life. It was obvious Monckton wanted to succeed Goddard himself and he spoke of his resignation from politics in very definite terms.
Lords' Reform. Monckton is working on the final stages of the Lords' Reform plan at this moment. It isn't finished but must be completed for enactment this session. They have definitely decided on life peerages but Salisbury wants to extend it to cover other subjects as well. Monckton himself doesn't want to tinker with it too much. This was rather depressing news.

I told Monckton of my Privy Council plan. He said he would like to see it as soon as possible. I promised to send him a typescript at once as he told me that the middle of January would be too late for his purpose.
Eden. Monckton has not seen him since he got back from Jamaica but has heard he was still rather jumpy, 'which is bad news'. Monckton made it perfectly clear that Eden would have to go although the problem of the succession was a tricky one. Macmillan speaks of his retirement and Rab has behaved so oddly in the last two months that no one trusts him. He agreed that an Election was a remote possibility early in the New Year, though he said he would urge very strongly against it. 'If I were your boys I should prefer next summer as a large number of chickens will have come home to roost by then, and I don't just mean the Suez ones.'

He made his opposition to the Suez policy very plain. Evidently from the start Eden knew what his view was and when he wrote in September and said he wanted to resign the Ministry of Defence, Eden asked to see him and arranged for Head to come half an hour later so that a successor was planned from the outset. Monckton said he told Eden, 'I don't want to dodge this enterprise (presumably the Egyptian attack) but I thought it better to go now rather than later.' He resigned as Defence Minister and was made Paymaster General.

He quoted one incident in the Cabinet during a Suez discussion. 'Paymaster General, you are very silent,' said the PM. 'I am, Prime Minister, but I have heard that lawyers should only speak when they know that what they have to say will get a fair hearing and is likely to help their case. I am not sure of either of these things now.'

He spoke a little bit about Clarissa Eden, who is apparently a powerful force in politics and has a great influence on Eden. Monckton says that now she knows he opposed Anthony she won't have anything to do with him.

I asked about Winston and whether Monckton saw him. He said he saw him quite often but the old boy has had another stroke and said rather pathetically, 'I still have the ideas, Walter, but you know I can't find the words to clothe them.' He never will speak in the Commons again, partly because he just couldn't stand to make a speech. I asked what Churchill would have said of Suez. Monckton replied, '"I wouldn't have had Anthony's courage – or his recklessness."'

Monckton said he had been happiest at the Ministry of Labour under Winston. 'Winston wanted industrial peace at all costs and even thought on occasions that I was too tough. He once sent for me at 10.30 in the morning during a strike. He was in bed and he asked me what I proposed to say in the Commons that afternoon. When I had finished he said "Walter, you're handling this all wrong. You should give them the money. I can't have strikes."' He then developed this and finished up by saying "Are you going to take my advice or follow your own reckless course?"' Monckton said he would obey an order but would still prefer to keep the offer in reserve at any rate for the present. 'All right, my boy,' said Winston, 'you pursue your foolish course and I shall have the satisfaction of being able to say I told you so.' Eden apparently was much tougher than Monckton and on the famous occasion in May 1955 when he said in his broadcast that the railwaymen must go back before negotiations could start, he did it on the insistence of Clarissa and against the strong and urgent advice of Monckton himself and all the civil servants.

Finally, the train drew into Bristol and he went off to his meeting and I to mine. I was naturally most flattered that he should have been willing to talk so freely and I was delighted to get an inside glimpse of what is going on at his level in the Government. However, it's a great mistake to think of Monckton as a fighter. He has hawked his conscience round quite a number of people the last three months but I very strongly doubt whether under any circumstances he would have resigned from Cabinet altogether.

Tuesday 18 December 1956
On 29 October I had seen Hailsham, who had warned me cryptically that the Lords' Reform plan might not meet my problem. He suggested we talk after the Queen's Speech and I made an appointment to see him this morning at the Admiralty. There he was, like a happy bandit, in the glorious room used by the First Lord overlooking the Horse Guards Parade. I congratulated him on the robustness of his recent political utterances, although I said I didn't agree with any of them. He was obviously most pleased with life and enjoying himself enormously.

We soon passed to the subject of our interview – Lords' Reform. What he had to say was very simple and quite shattering. He said that the Cabinet had discussed the Lords' Reform plan in September and had definitely decided that it would not include the right for hereditary peers to stand for or serve in the House of Commons. He himself had urged this strongly and had been turned down flat. Apparently the final decision about what will be done has not yet been reached. This confirms the impression I had gained from Monckton on Saturday.

Hailsham said he had no right to tell me this but he felt he owed me a personal debt of honour to do so. There was only one possible ray of hope. The Cabinet might be willing to accept an amendment which allowed peers who renounced a writ of summons for life to come to the Commons or stay there. Hailsham thought that I should start lobbying very, very hard in the few weeks remaining so as to try to guarantee that such an amendment would be carried.

That was really all he had to say and as he explained, 'The rest is up to you.' I told him frankly I thought it very unlikely that the Labour Party would support such an amendment and that unless it did it could not hope to be carried since there would be opposition on the Government side. In fact I thought that the Lords were more likely to pass it than the Commons. He doubted this as the Lords would be very reluctant, he thought, to give up their young men – the only source of fresh blood. He suggested that I put it to the Labour Party in this way. 'If you really want to weaken the House of Lords, let the able young peers try for the Commons. All the good ones will prefer this and the Lords will be left with the second-rate people.' He said he thought this was an effective point and a sound one if used discreetly. I shuddered at the thought of pleading my own case and he suggested I get others to do it.

I saw Lambton at the House this afternoon and told him what I had heard under an oath of secrecy. At first he would not believe me until I revealed my source. Then he said it was an incredibly unjust thing and he felt he had been betrayed by Salisbury, who had assured him that this would be all right.

This news today has certainly been the gloomiest I have had. For if the Lords are reformed once, the chances of getting a change *again* will be slender in the extreme. Anyway the battle is not yet finally lost.

This afternoon there was a meeting to discuss the idea of an open letter to *Pravda* about Hungary. It was Dave [Benn's] idea and he got the cooperation of the MCF in putting it to various MPs. Only a very few came. Sydney Silverman took one look at it and said he thought the whole thing stank. Unfortunately he never thinks much of ideas that do not come from him. However, George Wigg, Barbara Castle and Fenner Brockway all agreed to sign. Later Dick Crossman added his name. Dave has done the job very thoroughly and he has enlisted the support of the *Pravda* correspondent in London as well as the Head of the BBC Russian Service, who has agreed to translate it.

The text is as follows:

Deeply esteemed Mr Editor

We, the undersigned members of the British Parliamentary Labour Party, who in the past have always worked for a better understanding between our two countries, are deeply distressed at the use of Soviet armed forces in Hungary. We therefore ask for this opportunity to express our view to Soviet readers and to put certain questions to you about the events in Hungary.

First of all, your newspaper has portrayed the Hungarian uprising as 'counter-revolutionary'. May we ask exactly what you understand by this expression? Does it include all systems of Government which permit political parties whose programmes are opposed to that of the Communist Party? If, for example, the Hungarian people were to choose a parliamentary system similar to those in Finland or Sweden, would you regard that as counter-revolutionary?

Secondly, you said on November 4th that the Government of Imre Nagy 'had in fact disintegrated'. Did you mean by this that it resigned or that it was overthrown? If it was overthrown with the help of Soviet arms, does this not amount to Soviet interference in Hungary's internal affairs?

Thirdly, do you consider that the present Government of Janos Kadar enjoys the support of the majority of the Hungarian people? Would it make any difference to your attitude if it did not? We ask this question because on November 15th, according to Budapest Radio, Janos Kadar said that his Government hoped to regain the confidence of the people but that 'we have to take into account the possibility that we may be thoroughly beaten at the elections'.

Fourthly, we recall that the Soviet Union has repeatedly advocated the right of all countries to remain outside military blocs. Does this right to choose neutrality extend, in your view, to members of the Warsaw Pact?

Finally, you have said that the Hungarian uprising was planned long in advance by the West and you have in particular blamed Radio 'Free Europe'. Are you seriously suggesting that masses of Hungarian workers and peasants were led by these means into organising mass strikes aimed at restoring the power of feudal landlords and capitalists?

We protest against the Soviet intervention in Hungary, because we think it wrong for any great power to impose its will on a small country for strategic or any other reasons. For this very reason we condemned the Anglo-French attack on Egypt. Both actions violated the Geneva Spirit and sharpened world tensions and have been condemned by the United Nations. We therefore welcomed the Anglo-French troops' withdrawal from Egypt in accordance with the resolutions of the General Assembly, and we urge you to do likewise in Hungary.

In asking these questions we emphasise that we think it imperative to seek a settlement of all differences between our countries on a just, honourable and mutually acceptable basis. Such a settlement must of course fully guarantee the security and national independence of all states including the Soviet Union.

For this reason we hope you will publish this letter.

Dick Crossman, George Wigg, Barbara Castle, Fenner Brockway, Anthony Wedgwood Benn
(Drafted by David Wedgwood Benn)

Wednesday 19 December 1956
At lunch time a group of us (Fenner, Barbara Castle and others) went to South Africa House to present a letter of protest to the High Commissioner about the Treason Trials.[2] He refused to see us but we left our message and there was a certain amount of publicity which is good for the MCF and helps to focus attention on what is going on. Our great scoop was to interest the Labour lawyers including Gerald Gardiner in

the trials and through them the Conservative and Liberal lawyers. Finally all three associations approached the Bar Council who decided to send Gerald as an observer to the preliminary hearings. He is on the point of leaving and his influence should be considerable.

Sunday 13 January 1957
To Waterloo air terminal at 10 for the flight to Germany. Tired and slightly sick in the coach to London Airport. The Viscount turbo-prop is a wonderful aircraft, silent and far steadier than a piston-engined machine. Tried to think of my speech on the challenge of anti-colonialism for the Deutsche–Englische Gesellschaft but could not make any progress.

To Frankfurt am Main in two hours. First impressions of Germany very mixed. The officials in uniform very reminiscent of the films. My Customs inspector looked the perfect Gestapo or SS Obergruppenführer – though very nice. It was a weird sensation of fear and hatred, no doubt accentuated by being a stranger and not very clear of where to go. By Pan American to Tempelhof and there a tall, fat smooth man came up and introduced himself as Mr Kulf, my host. My heart sank as he told me we were going to the opera and then on to dinner, I was so tired.

The performance was *The Marriage of Figaro* and it was most excellently done, the singing was beautiful and the staging superb, as was the design of the sets. The only trouble was that I was dog tired and dozed off fitfully.

Monday 14 January 1957
An hour's work on my speech after breakfast and some progress but still depressed at the prospect and suspecting more and more that it would be a terrible flop before a bourgeois English-speaking Union type of audience.

Mr Trevor Davies and Mr Dees of the British Educational Commission collected me by car and we drove through the Tiergarten, under the Brandenburg Gate and along the Stalin Allee to the Soviet Cemetery. As Dees said, the Soviet sector is like Salford during a strike; compared with the lights and shops and buildings of the Western sector, the East was unbelievably dreary.

The rubble from the bombing still remained and the people looked tired and cold and ill-fed and ill-dressed.

The Soviet Cemetery is a gigantic place, set in woods and marked at one end by a huge mound atop of which is a small circular chamber. The absence of individual headstones in the mass grave is a startling reminder of the victory of the monolithic state over the men and women who serve it.

Not even the symbolic sarcophagi which are lined up to flank the burial area and have bas relief stonework and extracts from Stalin's speeches can erase the dehumanisation.

At 8 to the Centre for the lecture. I was paralysed with fear and had taken a whole Benzedrine to induce confidence.

There were 300–350 people of all ages and various nationalities present. I was at a rostrum on a platform. I talked slowly and deliberately, and they were very attentive and could apparently understand what I said. I tried a joke or two and they worked so that proved the intelligibility to the audience. In fact it was a great success, and there was a lot of applause, a pause and a second round.

Tuesday 15 January 1957
At 9.30 Herr Kulf collected me from the hotel and we drove in his car to the Potsdamerplatz. There we got out and walked across the Iron Curtain to the East Sector. The devastation was terrible and the gigantic electric news bulletin machine stood out against the skyline of ruins as a grim reminder of the Cold War. Loudspeakers from each side blare out the news at fixed times and the black market in East and West flourishes.

Caught the 1400 plane to Hanover.

Dr Ronnebeck, the chairman of the Deutsche–Englische Gesellschaft, was at dinner and afterwards we talked in the hotel for half an hour. He feared that West Germany was mentally hypnotised by the boom. He thought that the heavy American investment in the Federal Republic had enabled the West Germans to escape lightly from the consequences of the war.

'Our children will have to pay for it,' he said. 'In the East at least the Germans are learning the lesson the hard way. Life is not easy for them. Now here we think we are the greatest nation again. The Americans are *nouveau riche*, the British are lazy, the French are stupid, we are hard-working respectable conscientious people.' This escapism and the apathy towards issues of personal freedom was a malaise.

Certainly the bright neon lights of Hanover and the enormous modern shops full of goods of all description gave an impression of prosperity that made Britain seem a very down and out country.

Thursday 17 January 1957
Bonn. Breakfast in my room and then to the Bundeshaus. I had to find Willy Brandt, the Speaker of the Berlin Parliament. We talked for nearly an hour in the spacious sunlit restaurant with its glass wall overlooking the Rhine (the aquarium, they call it). Brandt is young (39–42) and very intelligent. We discussed relations with East Germany and the frontier ('it can be negotiated at the right time'). I walked back to my hotel and was collected at lunch time for lunch given by the Secretary of the Anglo-German Parliamentary socialist group, Frau Hubert, a very charming woman.

Saturday 19 January 1957
Safely home by air from Düsseldorf to London Airport where a loving family was waiting *en masse* to greet me.

Monday 21 January 1957
The first working day at home after my visit to Germany. It certainly was extremely interesting though an exhausting visit. I am glad I went, for many reasons. First of all, there was a little cyst or boil of anti-German feeling in me which was lanced as a result of seeing the country. Obviously as an honoured guest getting the red carpet treatment, one cannot pretend to get more than a glimpse of a country or its political outlook. I was completely protected from the currents of opinion and the life of the average German. Nevertheless, by constant talking and careful looking one got an impression of the place which was not without its value. The bomb damage was phenomenal. The scale of the reconstruction was also interesting. The shops, hotels and petrol stations were so modern and impressive that the visitor might think the country better off than we are. Yet no doubt millions still live in very poor conditions. Berlin was particularly tragic. The total destruction was enormous and the division of the city pathetically obvious. In the West the bright shopping streets and the new architectural styles contrasted sharply with the poor and desolate Eastern sector. Of course, the Americans have poured money in to the West and the Russians are still taking it out of the East. One must make allowances for all that.

Now Parliament meets again tomorrow and we enter a new political phase. The resignation of Eden has thrown everything into the melting pot. In a few months one will know whether it really was health or not. The leading articles certainly regarded it as a minor factor compared with his monumental failure over Suez. Macmillan has shown just the right quality of drama in his opening days at Number 10. His Government is bold and his television performance was evidently a very dramatic one. His call for an 'opportunity state' has created interest and discussion just when things looked so soggy in his own Party. If he succeeds in making an impact it will call for great skill by the Labour Party to make a successful challenge to him.

Tuesday 22 January to Sunday 10 February 1957
Being three weeks behind with the diary it seems best to summarise the developments under different headings rather than to resurrect each day as it happened.

Defence
For some time Geoffrey de Freitas has been bothering me to take an interest in defence and particularly the Air Force. It's not at all my line

but as an ex-RAF pilot I suppose I must be one of the very few in the PLP who knows anything about the Air. My reluctance to take Air on is heightened by the fact that Geoffrey always recommends it as a sure way to get office in the next Government. That he should think that argument would convince me is intensely irritating and much as I would like office, the thought of the Air Ministry depresses me beyond belief. However, I promised I would watch it for the next few months and I have been attending the various committees.

Movement for Colonial Freedom

The North Africa Committee of the MCF is now bursting with activity. We have Algeria, Cyprus, the Canal and the Yemeni dispute to cope with so we must be the busiest committee of all. Our biggest leg-up comes from the arrival in London of the new Tunisian Ambassador, Taieb Slim. In the old days he was a member of the Congress of Peoples against Imperialism.

The Pravda Letter

On the 1 o'clock news on Sunday, 10 February, the BBC reported a reply by *Pravda* to our open letter last December.

This was exciting news indeed. It proved that the original idea had been a good one and it also got our views over to a tremendous audience in the Soviet Union. The circulation of *Pravda* runs into millions and its articles are regularly broadcast by radio stations throughout the USSR and are extensively quoted in satellite countries. We felt that we had succeeded where the Government and even the UN had failed: namely, the Hungarian issue was being discussed in both East and West on the basis of an exchange of correspondence fully publicised each side of the Iron Curtain.

Pravda's reply was printed in full in the *Manchester Guardian* today, Monday, 11 February. It began by saying we should have written to 'the appropriate Hungarian organisation'. However, it went on to give a detailed answer to our questions, repeating the charges that the rising was Fascist and counter-revolutionary. It concluded by resenting our parallel with Suez, but said that they value our interest in the matter and believe that by studying 'the facts' we could contribute to a better understanding.

I notified the other signatories and Dick Crossman was so interested that he came round last night to read *Pravda*'s reply and discuss the next steps.

My dreams of being efficient have been brought a little closer by the purchase of a beautiful four steel drawer cabinet and a suspension filing system to go in it. With all the lovely coloured plastic tabs I think it is the most beautiful thing I have ever seen. Everything now has a place and I find that there is no more enjoyable relaxation than standing looking at it with its drawers proudly pulled out and all the things I ought to do neatly filed away out of sight.

One thing leads to another and I have my eyes set now on the following:

an *Encyclopaedia Britannica*;
The Times on microfilm with a reader;
books on microcards;
Erskine May;
a minifon wire recorder (the size of 100 cigarettes with a wristwatch mike and a 6-hour spool).

All these are criminally expensive and most have been specifically banned by Caroline.

Tuesday 12 February 1957
To dinner this evening with Taieb Slim, the Tunisian Ambassador. He is a most cultivated, modest, and delightful man of thirty-four or thirty-five. He knew Fenner, Leslie Hale and others from five or six years ago, when he came here with the Tunisian nationalist leader Bourguiba in 1951 as his interpreter. Like all North African nationalist leaders he has been imprisoned by the French and tortured by them. French police methods against political prisoners are unspeakable. I have questioned many of them about their experiences and there is no doubt that appalling torture is used. They are always reluctant to speak of it. This is partly because the memory is so horrible, partly because they do not know whether you will believe them and partly because the experience is so degrading that it is damaging even to admit that you have undergone it.

So tonight as an Ambassador with a little dinner party in the most formal style, it was a pleasure to talk to Slim and see the world through his eyes. The Indonesian Ambassador and the Moroccan Chargé d'Affaires were there. The world we were discussing was a world that just did not exist twenty years ago. It was a world peopled with Asian socialists, Arab nationalists, involving countries and personalities who would never feature in Western diplomatic conversation.

Monday 18 February 1957
Caroline went to the hospital today. The baby is now two weeks late on the most cautious estimate. They have decided to bring it on on Wednesday.

Tuesday 19 February 1957
At home all day until 5 o'clock when the Senior Broadcasting Committee
met at the Commons.

   When I got home there were signs that the baby was arriving so I took
Caroline to Hammersmith Hospital at about 10.45, overlooking
Wormwood Scrubs. She was highly delighted to have jumped the gun on
Mr Morris, the Obstetrical Surgeon. Waiting in the darkened out-
patients hall in the prefabricated antenatal clinic was weird and exciting.

Wednesday 20 February 1957
Slept fitfully and called the hospital at 5.20 fully expecting to hear the
good news. Alas, the contractions had stopped and Caroline was sleeping
and would be pushed along the road as planned at 12 o'clock. The same
story at 7.50 and 10.15. However, they let me go there from 11–12 and I
sat beside her for an hour in a white coat and mask. The contractions
began again – and it looked as if she still had a sporting chance of doing it
unaided. As dawn had broken she saw the lights go on in the cells in the
Scrubs and the prisoners looking out through the bars at another cold,
clear morning. However, when I left at 12 things were well on their way
and I expected news by tea time. As it was, I rang at 1.50 for an interim
report and heard that Melissa Anne had been born at 1.35. Caroline was
delivered by Sister Tweddle, the Sister in charge of the Labour and
Delivery ward. After sending off all the appropriate telegrams and
messages, I was allowed to see them both at 3 o'clock and Caroline was
looking wonderful.

March 1957
I was forced to miss the annual meeting of the Party in Bristol by the
arrival of Melissa and I gather there has been some criticism there of the
rarity of my visits. This is partly my fault and partly theirs. However, I
shall have to devote more time to the constituency than I have been
doing.

Monday 1 April 1957
The debate on the Bermuda Conference. It was a severe test for
Macmillan but he exploited it very skilfully by probing us on our attitude
to the testing of the hydrogen bomb. Gaitskell was really not able to
answer satisfactorily and the speeches by backbenchers made us look at
sixes and sevens with each other. A Party meeting has been fixed for
Wednesday morning but we shall look very stupid until then. It was
something of a bankruptcy of leadership that we should not have had a
meeting earlier in time to forestall all this.

Tuesday 2 April 1957
The sense of humiliation at our trouncing in yesterday's debate was very

strong in the Party today. Nobody wants a row, but there is a strong body of opinion that feels the hydrogen tests should be postponed or abandoned. George Thomas has got the support of about eighty members and a motion has been submitted to the Shadow Cabinet.

There was a meeting of the Foreign Affairs Group and the Defence Group jointly tonight. George Brown was in the chair and Kenneth Younger opened with a description of past Party policy. He reminded us that the Party backed the decision to make the bomb. Between the two extremes of tests at all costs and bombs but no bangs, he thought there were various intermediate positions. He hoped we would put Party unity high in our minds as the disagreement was transitory in character. Healey argued that we should not agree to a unilateral ban on British tests, as banning would not stop others and we must prove we can make the bomb. Therefore, tests should be made public and the UN allowed to witness them. We should seek agreement to limit the yield of fission products.

Barbara Castle said that a clean bomb may be possible and may lessen the deterrent quality. Why make the bomb therefore except as a bargaining weapon? We will suspend manufacture until the next one is tested by the US or USSR.

The meeting broke up so as to allow the Shadow Cabinet to meet and hear our views. At this stage it was not clear what they would recommend though it was thought some compromise might be reached.

Wednesday 3 April 1957
The Parliamentary Labour Party meeting was held at 10.30 to consider the question of H bomb tests and was opened by Gaitskell. He moved on behalf of the Shadow Cabinet: 'That this Party meeting, conscious of the danger to humanity of the continuance of nuclear explosions, reaffirms previous decisions of the Party calling for the abolition of hydrogen bomb tests through international agreement and strongly urges Her Majesty's Government to take an immediate initiative in putting forward effective proposals for this purpose to the other Governments concerned.' He appealed to the Party to remember that we were in sight of a major victory and should approach the problem responsibly and primarily to maintain our unity. He traced Labour policy and rejected the two extreme views. He said it was impossible to reach a proper decision about the testing before we are in power. He was willing to admit publicly that it was a question we could not decide for lack of information. He reminded the Party this would give us all the opportunity of expressing our own views and said that difficulties on defence matters were inevitable. He asked that we should each give each other full credit for sincerity.

George Thomas moved a rival motion which read, 'That this Party, believing it to be in the best interest of mankind that there should be an immediate cessation of hydrogen bomb tests, calls on HMG to initiate a meeting of the three states manufacturing the H bomb with a view to reaching common agreement on this question and further urges HMG to give a lead to the world by abandoning the proposed tests at Christmas Island.'

In proposing it, George Thomas said, 'We naturally seek to avoid a clash but can't avoid moral issues. H bomb is a moral and physical challenge. Testing is not necessary for it to be deterrent. Don't trust scientists on detectability. Moral issues transcend all others.'

Strachey: I fully support the Gaitskell line. Disarmament by example is unacceptable. We must not 'snatch defeat from the jaws of victory'.

Herbert Morrison: The interests of our country must come before Party tactics. Stevenson failed to gain support in American Elections on this issue.

Jennie Lee: How can we meet the cost of our social programme if we go on making the bomb?

Maurice Edelman: I support George Thomas. This is a weapon not against man, but against mankind. The practical case against the bomb is overwhelming.

John Hynd: Let us halt the tests, at any rate temporarily.

Zilliacus: We need a compromise and the official resolution is no good.

At various stages in the meeting, points of order had been raised in the hope of getting Gaitskell to accept an amendment to the George Thomas resolution or an addendum to the official motion, which would have the effect of giving the Party the opportunity of voting for a postponement of the test pending negotiations. Gaitskell refused this on procedural grounds. However, it was pretty clear that there would be a bigger majority for a postponement of the tests to facilitate negotiations than there would be either for the unilateral abandonment of them or the uncompromising policy of testing.

The meeting actually ended with a vote of 78 to 58 in favour of adjourning the meeting till later so that other members could speak. This having been agreed to, it was pretty obvious that a further attempt would be made to reach a compromise.

All afternoon these compromise attempts went on. The most important stemmed from Christopher Mayhew and Lynn Ungoed-Thomas. They had an hour with Gaitskell immediately after the meeting and finally submitted an addendum to the official motion. The Shadow Cabinet could either accept this itself or stick to its guns and allow it to go as a compromise without official backing. Opinions varied as to what would happen. The MP for Smethwick, Patrick Gordon Walker, went round hinting darkly that Gaitskell would resign. There was no truth in this but it added to the general confusion. Rumours that George Brown would resign were thought to be double bluff by left-wingers. At any rate the feeling was quite good-natured and there was a genuine desire to reach an agreement.

At 7.30 the meeting reassembled and Gaitskell read the words of the addendum he was putting before us as a compromise, i.e. adding to the end of their own motion the words, 'meanwhile postponing the tests for a limited period, so that the response of those governments to this initiative may first be considered'. This was carried by acclamation after a short debate, notable for two speeches only. Billy Blyton, a miner from Durham, got up and asked crudely why the Shadow Cabinet had capitulated. He said he had never seen such a weak leadership as this. Gaitskell looked white and drawn. Ellis Smith, who has about as much tact as an elephant, and no sense of humour of any kind, said he hoped this would be a lesson to the Shadow Cabinet and they would learn from it that it was their duty on all occasions to give way to the rank and file. This crashingly inappropriate comment helped to make the meeting a little unpleasant. However, we had adjourned within seven minutes.

The lessons of all this are not hard to find. When there is a row blowing up, it is wise to anticipate it by a Party meeting so that the line can be clear before we are exposed to difficulty in a debate in the House. It also shows that a readiness to compromise by everyone is possible now that we have not got the personality battles of the last few years to bemuse us and particularly as we are on the brink of power.

My own views on this issue I feel I should in honesty set down. Since we are committed to making the bomb, it seems to me absurd that we should not test it. Our whole defence policy is based on making nuclear threats and carrying them out if we are attacked. That being so, I doubt if much moral leadership is available for a mere unilateral renunciation of the tests. To that extent I found myself very much in support of the platform.

However, the more one thinks about the implications of a nuclear policy, the more absurd and dangerous it all becomes. From a purely practical point of view, who in his senses would actually unleash a hydrogen war, even if one was threatened with invasion? Just as we thought survival was preferable to bombing Russia to stop her in Hungary, so I think it would be preferable to bombing Russia to stop her invading us. While there is life there is hope at any rate. The new missile agreement makes us more dependent on the United States because we cannot keep abreast of her technologically. That means we cannot have a military policy independent from America, although I think we could still pursue a different foreign policy. If this is true the only case for the bomb is that we would threaten to use it but not actually use it. This I think is both lunatic and impossible.

My mind is therefore moving in an anti-bomb direction as I think are the minds of many other non-pacifists in the Party. Sooner or later we must face this issue.

Tuesday 9 April 1957
Edward Boyle, finding me in the Library, asked me if he could talk urgently about a personal matter. Puzzled, I went with him to his room and this is what he asked me. 'The job of head Treasury representative in Delhi is going vacant. What do you think people would say if I took it?' I was so surprised I hardly knew what to answer. Edward anxiously added that it was not a dead-end job as the Washington post would come up later, that he liked India from his experience there as a Minister, and he thought they would get on all right with him. None of this I doubted. But the straight answer to his question was that a decision of that kind would be the subject of tremendous speculation. Would it mean Sir Edward had resigned again? Why was he leaving politics? Wasn't it a bit odd that he should go straight from a political to a permanent job? What was the real reason? I pointed all this out to him as best I could. What was the real reason, I asked? Then it came out. He was having difficulty with his constituency and he really wondered whether he would be able to carry on. That was one thing, and the other thing was a growing uneasiness about the present Government.

I went so far as to say that he seemed to me to be the person round whom the Conservative Party could and should rally when the Suez ghost had been exorcised. It was for that reason that I had hoped he would make a resignation speech and stay outside the Government. But that was all over now and the important thing was to see that his position was safeguarded for the future. If the Ministry of Education job meant that he would be able to avoid a direct clash with his constituency and stay in Parliament, then it was a very good thing he had taken the job. He should, therefore, I thought, work away at his departmental job, ease himself as far as he could with his constituency Party and look to the years of opposition ahead for fruitful thought and real leadership. He said that John Altrincham's attempt to build him up as a Prime Minister to replace Eden had been an embarrassment, but I think he was conscious of the truth of what I said. He told me that he had consulted no one else on this on either side of the House and I was naturally pleased that he should have sought me out. He seemed convinced, and I doubt if we shall hear any more of Sir Edward Boyle's unexplained disappearance from the centre of the political stage.

Tuesday 16 April 1957
Caught Quintin Hogg in the corridor and walked back with him to the Lords enquiring about Lords' Reform. It's a very confused picture but

the most accurate assessment is I think this. Salisbury had a plan which the Cabinet weren't very keen on. Now he has gone. What will happen? No one quite knows. Something will have to be put forward. If it is less than Salisbury wants, he will attack it in the House. 'Bobbity [Salisbury] is just looking for a chance to pull this Government down,' said Hailsham. If it is the Salisbury plan the Cabinet probably won't want to push it through. That's how it rests. Hogg is always very cordial. There will be a debate after Easter. 'I can't bring myself to say a good word for the hereditary system. Hereditary titles mean nothing, but hereditary legislators are ridiculous', said Hogg. I said that he would be bound to speak in the debate. 'If I do I shall walk on a tightrope, balanced between advocacy and belief.' I told him I could imagine him doing many things but certainly not walking a tightrope, and we parted.

18 April to 8 May 1957

Dick Crossman's party was on 1 May and we went along. No one quite knows what his political position is at the moment. Ever since he parted with Nye he has been a Gaitskell fan. He denounced the ending of the H bomb tests and has now come out against the H bomb itself. I'm afraid it has ruptured his personal relationships with other members of the Party but we seem to be on his 'new friends' list. He had a different crowd of guests than before but we enjoyed it very much. He told me afterwards that the little group who had stayed for a talk had voted Caroline 'the best wife for a leader of the Labour Party'.

9 May to 15 May 1957

On Friday we gave a tremendous party to celebrate Father's eightieth birthday. We sent out about 85 invitations only three days ago and over 60 people came. They included the Attlees, the Indian High Commissioner Madam Pandit, the Elaths, and an enormous number of MPs and showbusiness people, including Peggy Rutherford, Michael Flanders and Donald Swann, and Kenneth Horne. Father was in cracking good form. He certainly is regarded with tremendous affection.

This evening the American Ambassador came to a dinner of the British American Parliamentary Group in the Harcourt Room. John Hay Whitney is a wealthy man and something of a playboy – I would think. He's mainly known for the racehorses he owns and his appointment to London tells more about the size of his contribution to the Republican Party funds than about his ability. But I must give him credit for the straightest talk I ever heard from an American Ambassador. He dealt with Suez, the Eisenhower doctrine, the rivalry between oil companies and other Middle Eastern problems with crude bluntness. He approached us as if we were a lot of imperialists who needed to be reassured and said that we could expect American support at the UN against the 'new nations with their immaturity'. He was very plain about Communist China and painted the whole world in such a simple red and white way. I went up to him afterwards and thanked him for his frankness but told him that he should remember 40 per cent of the British people thought the US was right and we were wrong on Suez. He seemed disbelieving. But then he only meets the wrong sort of people, I would guess.

Now that the climb-down on Suez has come a motion of censure debate has been arranged for Wednesday and Thursday. The motion simply expresses concern at the loss of prestige and economic interests. I protested to Gaitskell, Bevan and Younger. Gaitskell was frosty but the real bogeyman is Bevan. I am afraid he has become too much the darling of the Tory Party to be able to think altogether straight.

Wednesday 15 May 1957
I had lunch today with Mr Narayanan, the First Secretary in the Political Department at India House. It was a most useful and enjoyable occasion for he is a highly intelligent and charming man. In accordance with my new hobby, I asked him all about himself and noted it down in my card index. It certainly makes it more pleasant having a game like this to play and moreover it is very useful as a political exercise and a memory trainer. I may not see Mr Narayanan again for twenty-five years and won't he be surprised when I ask him how his daughter, Chitra, is and whether he's been back to see his wife's family in Rangoon.

Much to my surprise, I got called in the debate on the Suez vote of censure. Very few Labour MPs had put their names down although 60 or 70 Tories were trying to get in. I hadn't really prepared a speech but being soaked in it and knowing what I wanted to say it went all right. In fact it had a most pleasing reception. The only actual note I got was from Edward Boyle saying that he agreed with almost everything I had said. He's become very friendly and we're going to have a meal together.

Thursday 16 May 1957
This evening I went to the Westminster Chapel to hear Mother giving a talk on her visit to China with Father recently. It was the Annual Congregationalist Conference and she was one of three speakers talking about the laity and the ministry. It was an extremely well-thought-out, well-delivered speech and the 2,000-odd delegates were more than delighted by her vivid imagery and the authentic, perceptive and encouraging report she was able to bring back from China.

The Suez debate concluded tonight and Nye wound up for us. It was an alarming speech.

Saturday 18 May 1957
This evening we went and had dinner with Dick and Janice Taverne.

They live in 'an improved industrial dwelling' just off Charing Cross Road. They have a nice little flat and only pay a pound a week. But they have no bathroom and the block is just as gloomy as can be. Dick is struggling at the Bar and Janice is helping to keep them afloat financially. She has just got her doctorate as a research biologist.

Monday 20 May 1957
Mervyn Stockwood to tea at the Commons and for a long talk. In two years at Cambridge he has done brilliantly well in reviving the University Church of Great St Mary's. Thirty people attended his first ordinary service and he now has filled it to up to 2,000 on big occasions. He has worked with tremendous energy and has become a highly controversial figure in the University. His decision to go on the City Council as a Labour Councillor and his sermons on Suez help to ensure that. He ought to be our first Bishop when we come back to power and I think there's a reasonable chance he will be.

To East Ham North with Barbara Castle for the by-election. Eighty people.

Tuesday 21 May 1957
A Party meeting this morning on the new National Superannuation Plan. Dick Crossman introduced it with all the lucidity that he commands. It is such a complicated new idea that it will take weeks for the Party to understand it and years for the local Parties and the general public. It is certainly the most exciting thing that has happened since the Beveridge Report. Dick Crossman will undoubtedly be the first Minister of Pensions after the Election and will find a haven for his talents after the storm since 1945.

This evening Nye Bevan spoke to the Commonwealth and Colonies group of the Party. It was a joint meeting with the Foreign Affairs group and he kept us enthralled for 50 minutes. He described his talks with Nehru and the significance of the Communist victory in Kerala. He had told Nehru that India's pro-Egyptian attitude had annoyed a lot of people in England and 'if India didn't use its influence to compel Nasser to yield on the Israeli points, American/Indian relations would deteriorate'.

He spoke of the hatred and failure of Pakistan and came out with an entirely pro-Indian view on Kashmir. He dealt fleetingly with the problems of Persia and bitterly attacked the Baghdad Pact as a waste of money on a project that meant nothing and simply diverted attention from the real job.

The brilliance of the word-spinner captivated the audience, who listened with rapt attention. But on reflection I was more than disappointed with what Nye had said and the way he had said it. As in his speech in the House last Thursday night, he took a much more anti-Egyptian line than is reasonable and became an advocate of *realpolitik* with a certain zest. The doctrine that backward countries could not nationalise their industries for fear of losing foreign credits was, I thought, a very dangerous one. Nye will have to be watched for fear that he become not only the darling of the Tory Party – which he is already – but that by his speeches and actions he deserve that title.

Saturday 25 May 1957

Last night canvassing in Hanham and today at the Carnival in Bristol. Not many people stood round our lorry. But the interest in the new Labour pensions scheme is tremendous. As it affects everybody the questions are coming quickly. This evening to Tony Crosland's party. His divorce came through two days ago and this must have been some sort of celebration. I only knew two people there – Hugh Dalton and Roy Jenkins. The rest were a sort of rootless crowd of nondescript men and rather sulky women between twenty-five and thirty-five. Tony is, of course, a very unhappy person. I've known him for eleven years and at one time we were very close friends indeed.

The main trouble is his strict Nonconformist background. His parents were Plymouth Brethren and against them he has been in constant revolt. His years in the war gave him the excuse for thinking that his youth had gone and he has been trying to catch up since 1945. At thirty-nine it is rather silly. But he is in fact a very kind man. He taught me economics as a favour in the evenings and we went to the cinema together. Without his recommendation I should never have got Bristol SE and without the redistribution in my favour he would never have lost South Gloucestershire. He is unusually gifted as an economist and has a very clear mind with a very great faith in the power of reason. But the proof of his unhappiness is his curious death wish, which he showed when in the Commons, and which now takes the form of affecting to be bored with current politics. If he gets back into Parliament he will get high office. If he does not, then his life could be a very tragic one.

Friday 31 May 1957

This evening Caroline and I went to Hampstead to a party given by the Gaitskells. Adlai Stevenson was the guest of honour and he had been there for dinner. It was very crowded and we stayed from 9.30 until about 1.45. It was amusing to see who had been invited. Nye was not there but most other members of the Parliamentary Committee were. The only trade union leader was Frank Cousins with his wife.

There was dancing in one room and people got slightly tight. In many ways it was a little depressing to see the Leader of the Party half-way to being sozzled. But it might have been a great deal worse and certainly

Winston always looked that way from lunchtime onwards so it can't be a complete bar to a successful premiership.

Monday 3 June 1957
Hard at work on the plan for the week's campaign in Bristol. It has developed along these lines. Each day I shall be painting the office during the period of my surgery, and the lunchtime will be taken up with a factory meeting followed by afternoon and evening canvassing and an At Home at the Grand Hotel. The idea is to give some dramatic impact to the work of the Party and try to get over the feeling that the Labour Party is on the move again.

Wednesday 12 June 1957 .
Off today down to Blandford to help in the North Dorset by-election.

18 June to 21 June 1957
In many ways this is the busiest week in my life. I was up at the office at 9 and worked solidly through then till midnight with just a sandwich snatched. I've been frightened of Bristol SE ever since I've been an MP. I've always had the idea that in some way I wasn't quite measuring up to the demands they were making on me. In fact I have been rather on the defensive and responding only to initiatives from them. I imagine they knew what was going on.

In fact this has been absolute nonsense. Certainly since we lost our agent, Ernie Collett, just before the last Election there's been no effective central direction to the Party at all. It has been a loose federation of ward parties – some good and some bad. Therefore, when I began the card index system a year ago it amounted to a piece of central organisation. It meant the compilation of information on the constituency which did not exist before.

Saturday 29 June 1957
The new car (a two-year-old Ford Consul) was delivered today. I went down to the Fabian School at Wiston House, Steyning. Dick Crossman is the Director and they are a most delightful crowd of young people. I think sociology may be something to do with it but the interest in human beings is growing again. The stick-in-the-mud bureaucratic planner is being cut down to size. It's all to the good.

Tuesday 2 July 1957
The first of a series of discussions about the Party political broadcast on Labour's new superannuation plan to be shown this Friday. Dick Crossman, Jim Griffiths and Anne Godwin (General Secretary of the Clerical and Administrative Workers' Union) are taking part. Jim is a

dear old fuddy-duddy now. He's really past active politics, though only in his late sixties. His perorations have eaten into him so that he's always on the brink of tears. Not for nothing have his tough old trade union colleagues nicknamed him 'Old Bleeding Heart'. Anne Godwin is a very nice woman, though a little bit dried up after years in her union. Dick Crossman has chosen this broadcast to demonstrate his extraordinary capacity for being bloody-minded.

I am a great admirer of Dick's. He has the most brilliant intellect and his clarity of exposition is unrivalled in British politics. He can hold the House of Commons with rapt attention. Admittedly he changes his mind, but that is his right and better to do it honestly than stick to an outdated viewpoint for the sake of consistency or, worse still, have no opinion at all. All this said, he is generally thought to be on his way to office in the next Government, probably as Minister of Pensions. If his behaviour today is anything to go by he would be a most intolerable colleague. He is rude, touchy and obstructive in a most persistent way. It is impossible to talk aloud lest he takes offence at the hint of a suggestion which one was merely airing. He shouts and argues over minor technicalities, and then when you are at your wits' end, he gives way and says that if you just want him to take orders he'll do or say anything you require, and he knows his place and is sorry that he has spoken in the first place, but he wished he'd been told he was just asked as a mere mouthpiece, etc., etc. By this time exasperation had gone beyond tragedy to comedy. After boiling rage all afternoon, it was a real job not to giggle.

This is the season for parties. Today we went to Mrs Pandit's Garden Party in Kensington Palace Gardens. We shook hands with Nehru and had a short talk before he was swept away.

We also met Sardar Pannikar, who is a most distinguished Indian politico-diplomat. He looked like Leon Trotsky with shrunken cheeks, gold-filled teeth and a goatee beard, but there was a live twinkle in his eyes, magnified by the steel-rimmed spectacles he wore. He was Ambassador in Peking at the time of the Korean War, having continued on from being Ambassador to Chiang Kai Shek before the revolution. Last year he was Ambassador in Cairo and played an important part in the Suez negotiations.

I told him that Adlai Stevenson told me in 1952 that the Chinese intervention could have been avoided if they had accepted Pannikar's advice on this subject.

Sunday 7 July 1957
To dinner at the Garrick Club tonight as the guest of Dingle Foot. He invited four of us to an intimate little gathering with Kwame Nkrumah. I was looking forward to it enormously and was indebted to Dingle for having thought of asking me. His other guests were Kenneth Younger,

Lynn Ungoed-Thomas and Jim Callaghan – three of the nicest and ablest members of the party. Nkrumah was alone.

I perhaps should set down my feelings about him before this dinner. I naturally admired his wonderful leadership of the Gold Coast into independence. I regarded him and his Party as the great lights in a dark continent. But on three things I had reservations. First of all I wondered whether he was a bit of a crook in the political sense. The charges of corruption against him by the Opposition have not stuck personally but have obviously touched those pretty close to him in the Cabinet. Secondly, I wondered how far Nkrumah had allowed the cult of the individual to develop. There were some rather disquieting reports of the statue to himself which was erected in Accra and now of the decision to move into the Christianeborg Castle, plus the new stamps and coins with his head on them. Thirdly, I wondered whether he would be willing to listen. Thus moderately encumbered with preconceptions, I sat waiting for him in the smoking room of the Club.

In the event he turned out to be an absolute charmer in every way. He was modest, cordial, and immensely receptive to what we had to say. If his face wreathed too readily in smiles when you called him 'Prime Minister', it was from shy embarrassment rather than arrogance or self-satisfaction. He was willing to talk and keen to listen. He was well informed but cautious in his judgements. He sensed his role in Africa but did not seek it as such – rather leaving it to us to thrust it on him.

From the many things we discussed, some items stand out. He wanted to know about Gaitskell and Bevan and our likely line in our relations with the Russians. I think he found new leaders and personalities on the scene since his last visit and he was anxious to catch up.

He spoke of the tremendous job to be done in his own country and, tempted by our frankness, he became frank himself about his own position. He admitted that for various reasons he had to carry ministers who could be no more than passengers. This was obviously an indiscretion but a very interesting one. It showed the play of democratic forces in Ghana and dispelled the idea that it was just Nkrumah and his pals in power. Third-rate colleagues forced upon you by circumstances must be the lot of many Prime Ministers. Third-rate colleagues by choice is a very different story. He also spoke of his own unassailable personal position and indeed he is life Chairman of his Party. He said that he could always appeal above the heads of his colleagues direct to the Nation. But this was an assessment of political power rather than an admission of personal conceit. In fact I would accept as perfectly justified his decision to move into the castle and change the stamps and coins.

Jim Callaghan put to him the very important point that he should have a proper public relations man in London. He even suggested an interview with Beaverbrook on the offchance that the old man's heart might be won by a friendly chat. But whether this would work or not, the general point was very important. Nkrumah agreed and said this would be set in hand.

On African problems generally, Nkrumah spoke of his intention to hold a conference of independent African states – that is to say, those countries from Egypt to South Africa which are not under the control of an imperial power. He said he had had a meal with Mr Louw, the South African Minister at the Conference. Louw had been most friendly and had tried to persuade him that apartheid was good for the African. Nkrumah smiled as he told it, but there was no bitterness there – or none evident.

I think it suited his book to let us press him on it rather than be laying down the law. Anyway it did us no harm in his eyes to be urging him to champion African nationalism more vehemently. I think we gave him a lot to think about.

After Nkrumah had gone the four of us stayed for a talk, and Dingle reminded us of the history of Nkrumah, with his years in America studying and then his return to Ghana less than ten years ago as organising secretary of the United Gold Coast Party. Within four years he had founded a new Party, been imprisoned for sedition, won a landslide victory in an Election, and had been released from prison to become first Chief Minister. It is an amazing achievement. Dingle remembers him as a red revolutionary. Now he is established and wiser and more experienced. He did not think Communism held out anything to Africa. I ventured to disagree with him at dinner but he resolutely asserted that nationalism would win.

One of the most encouraging things about the evening was to discover how sound our colleagues were on African affairs. It gave me tremendous comfort.

Monday 8 July 1957
This afternoon the MCF presentation to Nkrumah took place at the House of Commons. Nkrumah had muddled his dates and was 45 minutes late so a large gathering had moved on to the Strangers' Dining Room when he arrived. Bertrand Russell was ill and couldn't speak so it was Fenner Brockway, Lord Hemingford (his old headmaster from Achimota), Lord Attlee and myself. We presented him with an album and he was very moved to get it.

Of Nkrumah I said a few words. I said no man had had a better preparation for high office than he. He had studied sociology, education, law, economics and even theology. He would need them all. The Gold Coast was famous in our encyclopaedias because the sovereigns minted there on examination turned out to be worth a guinea. Dr Nkrumah himself was like that extra shilling in the pound – a bonus from Africa. His father indeed was a goldsmith and no finer coin could he have minted.

Wednesday 10 July 1957
Felt lousy all day with tonsillitis or laryngitis or something – a hell of a
sore throat but a temperature of 95. Decided to miss the Vietnamese
party but we did go to dinner with Vejvoda, the Yugoslav Ambassador.
The invitation to dine with him had come as a complete surprise since we
had never met him and could not understand why he should have asked
us.

After dinner the ladies retired in the best Victorian style and the men
stayed to drink and talk over brandy and cigars. With the exception of
Hajek, who is a shrivelled up Communist youth leader in his early forties,
they were a charming bunch. We discussed the changes in Russia, which
they all thought very significant. The Yugoslav Minister was very
disappointed with Selwyn Lloyd's response, which he thought had been
most negative. They saw in the disappearance of Molotov a wonderful
sign for the future.

But it was when we got off politics that the conversation became most
revealing. Vejvoda is an art collector in a small way. He had a lot of
pictures by a young Yugoslav painter called Prica (Pritska). I admired
them and he took me up to show me more. I began asking about socialist
realism and some of the other Marxist phrases which are current in
modern Soviet controversy. Vejvoda was contemptuous in the extreme.
As far as that was concerned he had no time for this nonsense. He himself
graduated as an architect before the war and is very interested in things
artistic. We talked about architecture, furnishing and industrial design.
Once freed from the confines of politics, it was so easy for us to jump
backwards and forwards across the Iron Curtain. The Ambassador
admired Scandinavian architecture and also the work of Corbusier.
Contemporary design also pleased him. He recognised the superlative
quality and design of machines in the US, particularly cars. It was a real
pleasure to feel for a moment that one was a member of a world
community and could admire without political discrimination the
achievements of any country.

Thursday 11 July 1957
All the trade union MPs are now blazing with anger against Dick
Crossman. Apparently he said in his *Daily Mirror* column that only four
TU MPs were any good – Griffiths, Robens, Brown and Nye. The TU
Group are up in arms and there is real resentment.

Saturday 13 July 1957
The Anglo-Scandinavian Labour Youth Rally was held in Hyde Park
this afternoon. I suppose between 1,000 and 2,000 people were there –
although I am not very good at estimating. For some reason the thing
absolutely lacked any zip. Great drops of rain soaked the duplicating

paper on which Harold Wilson's speech was written. It began to disintegrate as he hurried through it. The loudspeaker van was behind the platform so we could hear our own voices. It's absolutely infuriating and completely wrecks any chance of making a good speech. I had laryngitis and was very crabby anyway.

Monday 15 July 1957
Although I have forgotten to mention it in the last few days Lords' Reform is coming back into the news.

Father and I agreed that it would be worth asking for an interview with Macmillan. Accordingly I rang his Private Secretary, and asked whether the PM could spare a few minutes of his time. He said that I would hear in due course. Today I had a message to go and see Ted Heath, the Government Chief Whip. He is a most amiable and friendly soul whom I have known casually since very early 1951. I had then been in Parliament about two months and he about eight months. He has done brilliantly well to have risen to his present position of eminence within such a very short period.

Anyway that is all by the way. He told me that the PM was too busy to see me before the Recess and was in any case doubtful about forming a precedent in agreeing to see an Opposition backbencher on a point of policy. He would, however, be glad to receive a letter from me 'which would then be sent to the right people'.

Wednesday 17 July 1957
To the Speaker's party. It was as dull and grim as the Speaker's parties always are. No one quite knows why. Some say it's because there's no booze and others because it is just MPs. But yesterday there were quite a lot of outsiders, including the Archbishop of Canterbury and a number of ambassadors. The absence of booze wouldn't affect me and even *I* think them awful. I think it's really because the whole thing is like tea with the headmaster and the crush is awful.

Thursday 18 July 1957
To the Buckingham Palace Garden Party this afternoon. What an occasion it is. The spacious royal park with its ornamental lake and bridges and the splendid front of the Palace dominating it. There in the private enclosure are the Royal Family surrounded by the Diplomatic Corps and the 'distinguished' guests. Outside promenading on the lawns are 9,000 more guests. The occasional Bishop, the invariable Sultan with his umbrella, the sprinkling of turbans, saris and white duck jodhpurs, the grey toppers and the flowery dresses with the wide-brimmed hats. The two Guards bands under their tents blowing for all they are worth in their scarlet tunics. The whole pattern is like a gigantic ballet – a Cecil B. de Mille crowd scene.

There is a secret way of eating two teas. One at the beginning when the Royal Family are arriving and everyone is crowding for a peep, leaving the tea tent deserted, and the other at the end when they're leaving and the same thing happens. In the middle when everyone else is jostling, pushing and shoving, you promenade yourself looking disapprovingly at those who seem 'only to have come for the food'. Actually Joe Lyons and Co. do quite a good job with the catering, though the bridge rolls were soggy.

But like the story of Cinderella the romance evaporates. At the end hundreds of people were waiting for their cars to be called over the loudspeaker. You could see the guests still immaculate, if a little tatty. And you would hear: 'The Town Clerk of Little Chippings' – that tall figure whom you thought was a central European Ambassador (at least) scuttles away to get into his Austin 7 driven by his son. 'The Chairman of the S.W. Area Gas Board' the flunkey announces . . . and so it goes on. Now we know the secret and we slip out the back door and catch a bus.

Saturday 20 July 1957

Caroline and the children came with me today to Bristol by car. The bus strike had increased the traffic congestion and it rained solidly. It took us five and a hours to get there, including a short stop for lunch. That was an hour and a half late for the Fête. Herbert Rogers made his usual introduction which begins, 'We don't see enough of our Member but we're very, very grateful when we do get a glimpse of him . . .' I know this game of old. It is a perfectly monstrous thing to say as I go to my constituency regularly. It's much better to stand up to him. We got home at 11 pm after nearly ten hours on the road. The boys were so good.

Monday 22 July 1957

This morning's papers were full of the new crisis in Oman.[3] Apparently the Sultan, faced with a rising from the religious leader, the Imam, has appealed for British help. We have responded and it looks as if there may be trouble.

I tried to put down a Private Notice Question but was scooped by Jo Grimond, the Liberal Leader. I sought an assurance that troops would not go into action without further consultation, and the Foreign Secretary flatly refused. I then tried to move the adjournment of the House and this was rejected. The Speaker's ruling was monstrously unjust and a number of people came up to say that they would be willing to support me in a motion of censure on the Speaker. It seemed a bit much but the idea was planted in my mind.

I went to see Hugh Gaitskell for 15 minutes and was infinitely depressed by his pedestrian mind. He claimed to know all about it as he had read a book by James Morris called *A Sultan in Oman*. This he felt gave him a special understanding vouchsafed to no one else. His line was patronising, tight-lipped, but kindly. 'I suppose you know what this is all about,' he said frostily. 'I suppose you realise this might mean having to pay for our oil in dollars.' That was as near to a passionate *cri de coeur* as you could ever get from an economist. 'What would you do?' he asked. 'Have you thought about that?' He went on to say that he thought it was quite wrong to try to precipitate a debate before the Party line was known and that the Foreign Affairs Group ought to get together about it.

I felt handicapped by my own ignorance. I saw Denis Healey, who took exactly the same view – that you must close your eyes while British jets do their dirty work and hope to God they do it quickly so that you can open them again and pretend you haven't seen anything nasty going on. Such a view is I think quite indefensible. This whole business is dirty in the extreme and oil cannot be secured if it isn't acquired on a proper basis.

There is one other complication and it is that the rank and file left-winger has got firmly into his head the idea that this is an oil rivalry, pure and simple, and that when it comes to the showdown (hideous as this is) he's on the side of the Iraq Petroleum Co. in preference to Aramco (the Arabian–American Oil Co.). This, coupled with a dislike of the American Government, the Eisenhower doctrine and the rest, leads them to the view that Selwyn Lloyd should be permitted to continue to fight his dirty little war. I had a huge row with Barbara Castle about this and within two seconds we were calling each other the most hideous names. It depressed me very much but was very interesting. Her line is likely to be the official Party line and that became clear in the course of the day's proceedings.

Tuesday 23 July 1957
This morning was really a helluva morning. The last-minute arrangements had to be made for Melissa's christening – the time of which had to be advanced by half an hour to permit Dad and I to get to our respective Houses for the statement on British action in Oman. News came through that the RAF was in action and I rang Reggie Paget to ask him whether he still thought that a motion of censure against the Speaker might be a good thing. He backed me up to the hilt.

Wednesday 24 July 1957
At work all day on chores beginning with a rush article for *Tribune* on the situation in Oman. They collected it by messenger at 10 am and I did my best with very little knowledge to be up to date and accurate.

This afternoon I went into the Commons especially to have tea with Dad and St John Philby. Philby is a great Arabist whose knowledge and experience goes back to before the First World War. He must be nearly seventy and looks exactly like an Arab chieftain, with wrinkled skin and tiny beard.

His history is that in the First World War when T.E. Lawrence was backing the Hashemites in the North, he was interesting himself in the Saud family. Since then he has really sold himself in heart and mind to them. He wrote the biography of the great King Ibn Saud and has a house and property in Riyadh, the capital. He left his English wife and children when he became a Muslim and married an Arab woman with whom he has been living for many years. He is a complete and utter cynic but that doesn't much matter. He is well informed, and without taking his view one can learn from what he has to say.

The family connection with him goes back many years. Benn Brothers published his book and my dad has known him for thirty-five years at least. The Foreign Office hate him because they say he is sold to King Saud. He frankly admits that there is not a Government in the whole of Arabia which commands any popular support at all. He is himself very right wing and that is of no concern to him at all. The bombing of Oman certainly did not shock him at all.

Father thinks that during the war he was pro-German, which is quite likely.

The rest of the day largely spent on the telephone and in conversation about the motion of censure.

I gathered from the Chief Whip that Gaitskell is angry with me for tabling it.

Jim Callaghan is a real friend.

The only two members of the Committee who openly backed me, Jim Callaghan told me, were Nye Bevan and himself. They argued that one should not damp down backbench adventures. If one wanted to keep any sort of spirit in the Party, one should welcome them. Nye said that whereas some of the present leadership had got to the top without backbench experience, others (and, of course, he meant himself) had come up the hard way.

I am shaking in my shoes at the thought of the Party meeting tomorrow, and more especially terrified at the prospect of Monday.

Monday 29 July 1957
I have never been more pleased to see a day dawn. All weekend was absolute hell because of the motion on the Speaker. Worked on the speech almost continuously and polished phrases as never before. Happily in all the uncertainties of this, have never doubted that it was the right thing to do.

Full notes and all quotations typed out and memorised this morning and thus armed, with sinking heart to the Commons. The family had all established themselves in the Gallery, and the whole scene began to assume the aspect of an execution. The Statement on Oman delayed proceedings until 3.45 pm when the Speaker called me.

I have never felt such an icy atmosphere as when I stood up. Not a single person even whispered 'Hear Hear', and the House was completely silent, although quite full. The three-line whip which the Government had issued had brought a lot of people in, and curiosity kept them in the chamber.

Being free from the embarrassment of notes, I was able to keep an eye out for the reactions in the House. Mutterings of discontent came early on, but once the introduction was over, the detailed examination of the precedents came up and the House began to listen.

This was the first milepost. People like to hear about themselves and the House enjoys references to its own past if they are not too complex or long drawn out. Indeed at this point, there were even some cheers from Labour Members. The ice had melted on our side and this made all the difference.

The next section of the speech was the plea for backbenchers; it was in a sense a breakthrough at every point. It prepared the way for the peroration. I have never felt so completely in command of a speech, nor do I ever think one has come out as neatly. It was tremendously exciting, and one felt about it as an artist must feel when he has finished a canvas.

July 30th

Wedgy –

A great Parliamentary performance. I was proud of you.

Barbara.

The debate took exactly the right course, and justified the decision to hold it. Butler was very friendly, and Gaitskell indescribably shifty. Of course, he has never sat on the backbenches of the House of Commons, so he does not understand.

The Parliamentary Recess – August–September 1957

Following the debate, I had a number of congratulations, including one from Barbara Castle [*see previous page*]. In the *Spectator* Bernard Levin wrote a very complimentary account.

At this time of the year my mind always turns to office reorganisation. There is so much to do to make the filing system efficient. The new steel cabinet has kept my papers in order and is a real godsend.

For a long time the problem has been to get an efficient reference library that could be readily used and could provide me at home with most of what I need for political purposes. For twenty years Dad cut *The Times* and filed it and this is undoubtedly the most effective way of keeping up to date. But it involves so much work and is so expensive that I cannot possibly manage it. He has become too much a librarian and this has reduced the amount of time he could spend on active politics.

The Inter-Parliamentary Union [IPU]

The Forty-Sixth Inter-Parliamentary Union Conference opened in London on 12 September. It was my dad's last conference as President. He is retiring this year after ten years in the job. He has done an enormous amount for the IPU, building it up from a primarily Western organisation into a truly world organisation representing Communist, Arab, Asian and now African countries.

The opening ceremony in Westminster Hall was superb. There were 2,000 delegates and visitors and it was a first-rate royal occasion. The trumpeters of the Household Cavalry and the Beefeaters stood against the south window to provide a lovely backcloth against which the Queen opened the Conference. Father had been in bed with a temperature of 102 a few hours earlier but he got up to do this. He greeted the Queen when she arrived, presented her to the Executive and introduced her to the Conference. He looked so tiny and old and his feet so shaky that we really wondered whether he would manage to carry it through. He forgot his opening remarks but it was a very human touch which contrasted sharply with the formality of the Queen's read speech and Macmillan's speech following.

The Conference has been the excuse for a rash of parties at various embassies as well as receptions at St James's Palace and the Guildhall. The one party that we enjoyed most of all was nothing to do with the IPU at all. It was given by the Chairman of Granada, Sidney Bernstein, in honour of Charlie Chaplin. Heaven knows why I was asked. The invitation only arrived in the afternoon and was for that very evening at the Savoy. Although it didn't start until 11 pm we thought it would be well worth while.

So it was. I've never seen such a glittering collection of people from the stage, literature and politics. Charlie Chaplin and Oona and most of their children were there, as well as Madame Pandit, T.S. Eliot, Graham Greene, David Low, John Mills, Victor Gollancz and the cartoonist Vicky. These are only the names of those I can recollect off hand. There were about 400 people there and a full three-course dinner was served at a cost that must have run to £2,000 or £3,000. There were two bands playing and we sat and talked and danced until 2.30.

Tuesday 24 September 1957
To Manchester today to take part in a programme for Granada TV. It was called *Youth Wants to Know* about the House of Lords. Opposite me was Lord Killearn, a former Ambassador to Egypt, who was a charming old boy. The Granada Studios are wonderful modern studios decorated throughout in the best contemporary style and running on sound principles of joint consultation. The director, Denis Forman, took me round and showed me the place. The programmes Granada are doing are the most imaginative being done by the commercial stations. It's an outfit full of drive and social purpose. The only trouble is that Sidney Bernstein drives everyone crazy by interfering ceaselessly in the affairs of the station. He's got lots of ideas but devolution is not one of them.

Wednesday 25 September 1957
To a special meeting in Bristol to consider our local financial crisis. The Party is nearly £3,000 in overdraft and is running an annual deficit.

The Labour Conference – 30 September to 4 October 1957
This week at Brighton was a very exciting one. Everyone thought it was going to be the dullest Conference ever, but they turned out to be wrong.

The elections offered no surprises and Jim Callaghan displaced Sydney Silverman from the National Executive. I stood for the first time. I missed election by two places and 48,000 votes. But to get 517,000 on first standing was wonderful.

The first day we spent in condemning the Government's economic policy and bringing forward our own emergency resolutions on rents. Of course all this can only work if there is cooperation between the trade union movement and the Labour Government. What has to be got across discreetly to the public is that this cooperation will be forthcoming without any binding undertaking on either side.

We then reached two very important decisions on pensions and public ownership. After excellent debate the national superannuation scheme was adopted. The new policy of share purchasing in place of nationalisation was also overwhelmingly adopted after an important speech by Hugh Gaitskell. Finally, in a day full of drama the Party decided to continue with the manufacture of the H bomb, although it expressed its readiness to suspend tests unilaterally.

The Party thus can claim to have reached firm decisions about important matters and to have done so in an atmosphere of unity. The decay of this Cabinet and the prospects of a Labour Government within a short period has helped to bring us to our senses again in our personal relations. The triumphs of individuals are worth recording. Harold Wilson delivered two speeches: one on the economic situation which was well received, and one on public ownership which was less well received. I admit I never find him very convincing although he has great ability. Nye Bevan cut away his left-wing support by his cruel wording during the speech on the H bomb. Though I think he was right in the line he took, it was a very unhappy speech. It earned praise from the *Daily Telegraph* and the *Daily Worker*. Neither of those is a good indication of his talent and I still distrust him profoundly.

Dick Crossman was probably the greatest personal success. After his difficult change of front over the years and the rage he had stirred from the Bevanites he had then annoyed the trade unionists with his unwise article in the *Mirror* saying that only a handful were fit for high office. Therefore when he rose it was to a polite handclap. But so brilliant was his speech and so lucid his exposition that he sat down to a thunderous ovation that carried him to the inner councils of the Party.

Saturday 19 October 1957

Travelled to Bristol by train with Hugh Gaitskell who agreed to open the Hanham sale of work. He was in a very talkative mood.

He has an intense personal aversion to Macmillan stemming from a most offensive speech the PM made about Hugh when Hugh was Minister of Fuel.

We discussed Hailsham. The head prefect pomposity annoys Hugh. We agreed Hailsham would go too far one day.

We discussed public relations of the next Labour Government. Hugh is very conscious of the need for this. He doesn't want to be bothered with it personally.

At Hanham he made a very friendly speech and wandered round amongst the local workers with interest and enthusiasm. The only embarrassment was when Frank Jones, the chairman of the Party, said, 'We welcome the next Prime Minister and shall expect him to put our MP in his Government.' Ted Rees, the Regional Organiser laughed: 'That's real village politics,' he said. 'And if you do get in the Government everyone here will say that it was Frank Jones what done it. He told him straight.'

21–28 October 1957

Not much news on the political front. I gather that tentative attempts are being made to form a new left inside the Labour Party. Nye Bevan's defection has left some people rather leaderless. Michael Foot, Barbara Castle and Kenneth Robinson are, I know, engaged in discussions. I don't quite know what to think about it all. Certainly you could form no effective left wing simply on the basis of the unilateral renunciation of the H bomb. The total failure of Nye Bevan to offer constructive thought for generous personal leadership has destroyed the group and relegated him to the position of captivity in which he now finds himself.

Tuesday 5 November 1957

The trouble about a personal diary is that it is entirely subjective. It is not a history, nor has it any value except such as it gets from the personal slant it shows on events. But of course these events are the framework on which the thin personal story is woven. Every now and again one has to step back a little and assess the changes that are taking place outside.

This is particularly true this autumn. The staggering news of the launching of the Russian satellites, Sputnik I and II, has really changed the course of world history. It shows the brilliance of Soviet technology, alters the balance of military power, and more important than either of these two, it marks the beginning of the space age. As long as recorded history exists, 4 October will be remembered and remarked upon. It is far more momentous than the invention of the wheel, the discovery of the sail, the circumnavigation of the globe, or the wonders of the industrial revolution.

Looking at the political situation there are not so many momentous events to report.

The Government is losing popularity steadily. Despite this Macmillan remains confident and Lord Hailsham wanders about the country making ebullient speeches. What drift there is against the Government is not coming to Labour but is going to the Liberals.

The Labour Party on the other hand is in really good shape. Hugh Gaitskell has emerged as a popular Leader in Parliament, although he lacks certain dramatic qualities and loses effectiveness thereby. Nye Bevan is determined to be Foreign Secretary and is touring the world making speeches and influencing people. Whether he is winning friends is another question. His Russian talks were evidently cordial and he is at this moment engaged in lecturing the Americans about their own affairs and policies in a way that is causing a lot of excitement, but not a little interest. Americans like people who 'talk turkey'. There is none of the diplomatic hypocrisy about Nye Bevan. I do not altogether trust him, for I think he lacks the qualities of self-confidence, serenity, generosity and personal loyalty, which are desperately necessary for high office. On the other hand he has energy, imagination, the gift for good human relations, directness, courage, vividness of expression, a wide view, a good political sense, a colourful personality, most lovable faults and a lot of other things which are missing in those who possess the qualities he lacks.

This morning the Queen opened Parliament. I watched from the Gallery of the Lords. It was very colourful and bright though the whole ceremony is so formalised that it is beginning to become a bit stale. The speech from the throne contained nothing of any interest except the Life Peers proposal that would enable hereditary peers to convert to life peers, which Father could then take advantage of.

Wednesday 6 November 1957
With Ken Peay to the Design Centre in Haymarket to look out the furniture for the Labour Party TV studio. Then back to Transport House to see the studio under construction. It is going to be the most amazing addition to our resources. It will probably mean more hard work for me but I am very excited about it.

Thursday 7 November 1957
Last weekend Hugh Dalton wrote and offered to nominate me for the Parliamentary Committee. I wrote back accepting as a great honour. However, as nominations close at 3.30 today and I had heard nothing from Hugh, I asked another Member to nominate me – just in case. This afternoon a note from Hugh arrived:

Dear Tony,
Oh, ye of little faith! You are now well and firmly and doubly, if not triply, nominated.
    Good luck when the electors ruminate this weekend.
Hugh

This evening to the Soviet embassy for the cocktail party celebrating their 40th anniversary. In a fit of enthusiasm I wrote my name in the visitors' book, and added 'Congratulations on everything.' As soon as I had done it I regretted it. Would those who followed list me with Mr Kadar as a butcher of Budapest? Would MI5 photostat the book and put it on my dossier? Such are the things one worries about when one hasn't enough else on one's mind. I don't think I shall try to slip in and steal the volume and destroy it. Perhaps no one else will notice! Perhaps the intoxication of two sputniks and the anticipation of two tomato juices will be held to be just cause for this display of recklessness.

Friday 8 November 1957
Today the 'London Last Night' column of the *Evening Standard* reported what I had written in the visitors' book. So now everyone knows!

Monday 11 November 1957
This afternoon HOC for meeting of the Public Information Group at which Sir Robert Fraser, Director-General of the ITA, gave the statistics about ITA.

In 4.5 million homes with choice 75 per cent prefer ITA, 25 per cent preferring BBC if you include children. Excluding children the figures are 70/30.

He created an appalling impression; remembering Labour's attitude during the debates on ITA he should have tried to deal with our anxieties. Instead he laughed his way through in a most arrogant fashion and the atmosphere during his speech was the iciest I can remember. It was the worst Public Relations job he could have done.

Thursday 14 November 1957
Lunch with Mary Adams of BBC TV. We discussed the psychological impact of commercial TV's competition on the BBC. She said they were absolutely defeated and in a complete dither. Her very mild comments on the benefits of competition had earned her a rebuke. My article on breaking up the BBC had apparently been circulated to the higher executives. She spoke of the new technical developments and we talked about the problem of televising Parliament. She is interested in this and it will be interesting to get the BBC to put on a film show showing how it is done in other countries.

Friday 15 November 1957
To Bristol University for a Parliamentary debate. The subject was: 'That socialist equality is unnecessary, unnatural and undesirable.' Opposite me was Sir Toby Low, the Tory MP for Blackpool North, who is a most attractive character. Unfortunately it ended with a vote against us of 104 to 90, with 25 Liberal abstentions. The Liberals came out of the debate in a most unattractive light with real Poujadist tendencies showing themselves most clearly.

Monday 18 November 1957
A meeting of the Public Information Group of Labour MPs to consider the future policy of the Party towards television. I had put in my views and was asked to open.

The reception was extremely frosty. Mayhew, who followed, wants to nationalise the commercial programme companies. He is a little better than Scholefield Allen [Labour MP for Crewe], who does not even have a television set. Dick Plummer also spoke in favour of a second nationalised corporation.

Thursday 21 November 1957
I heard this morning that I had been elected to the Executive of the

Fabian Society. This is the first time that I have stood. I did so at the suggestion of Bill Rodgers, the General Secretary.

From 5.30–6.30 there was a meeting of the Senior Broadcasting Committee to consider our recommendations for future Party broadcasts. It was most unsatisfactory in every way. Our proposal for 'countryside questions' was ruined by the proposal that amateurs should be used and by strong prejudice against even a professional chairman. Nye Bevan was the cause of all the trouble and his whole attitude to TV is absolutely heart-breaking. He is frightened of it himself and completely anti-professional in his outlook. Probably the stupidest thing was his boast that he had turned down two invitations by BBC and ITA to go on the air to describe his recent visit to America. He thought that was very wise so that the public wouldn't see too much of him. He also raised strong objections to our request that we should have a three-month experimental trial with an audience measurement service.

Coming away I had a word with Hugh Gaitskell and I thought he was very depressed too. The constant rejection of our technical recommendations does make our position very difficult.

Saturday 30 November 1957
Annual General Meeting of the Fabian Society. It was the first one I had been to. They are an impressive crowd in a way. They are heavyweights and serious. But at the same time they have that stick-in-the-mud appearance which I suppose is a spiritual inheritance from the Webbs.

All evening on my accounts, now seven months late. What a chore!

Monday 2 December 1957
All day on accounts. Then the Chief Whip rings up telling me to speak on the Air Force order from the Front Bench tomorrow as John Strachey had had a heart attack. Knowing nothing about it means a late night's work.

Tuesday 3 December 1957
Spoke for 20 minutes on the Air Force Continuation Order. A perfectly routine and ordinary performance to a very empty House.

Thursday 5 December 1957
To Robin Day's party. He was voted TV personality of the year yesterday. It is a tremendous honour that he richly deserves. He was celebrating by producing a girlfriend who was Miss Great Britain – a not very glamorous blonde. All our Oxford contemporaries were there.

Saturday 7 December 1957
Drove to Oxford for the Nuffield College dance. Caroline came down by

train from London and we had dinner with David Butler beforehand in his rooms. Nuffield is vigorous and forward-looking. It has absolute equality between men and women and close camaraderie between teacher and student. It draws its Fellows from a wide social background. There is no snobbery about it at all.

Monday 9 December 1957
Went to the Lobby lunch at the Savoy as a guest of Tony Barber of the *Bristol Evening World*. Harold Macmillan was the guest of honour.

His speech was off the record, which was flattering to the Lobby since they got a private briefing on the way his mind was turning. His opening light-hearted remarks were very amusing and centred on the incredible interest in all his doings by the press.

He then went on to speak about his approach to the NATO meetings in Paris. He outlined the alternatives of a loose NATO which would make disengagement feasible and a greater integration than ever before. His next sentence made it clear that his mind was made up in favour of a more friendly integration even than hitherto. He compared disengagement to appeasement and reminded us that during the war many counsels of despair had almost turned us from courses of action which were just beginning to bear fruit. It was a terrifying speech.

Thursday 12 December 1957
Worked at home all day. What a lot of jobs one postpones. I've learnt one lesson from my filing system. Although there must be a special place for everything, there ought to be only one file or tray for Jobs to be Done. I have tended to have half a dozen different places labelled, Letters to be Answered, Bills to be Paid, Articles to be Written, Memoranda to be Drafted, and so on and so on. And unless all these different things are gathered in one file. I just manage to forget them all. Of course a filing system ought to be a conveyor belt to speed up the work to be done and not a treasure hunt where all the clues are concealed.

Despite this personal rebuke the office is working extremely smoothly at the moment. The new filing cabinet bought in January has been an absolute godsend to me. Everything has a place and I can go to each committee armed with all the relevant papers, without searching everywhere for them. Of course they tend to get over-full but a quarterly pruning will keep that in check.

Saturday 14 December 1957
Drove to Cheltenham in the afternoon to speak at a meeting of Party members. The H bomb issue is a big one and I really must decide once and for all whether I am in favour of unilateral renunciation or not. I have funked the issue because it is so very difficult and the arguments are so evenly balanced. But it can't be postponed any longer.

Drove home through the night but made very good time and in bed by 11.

Monday 16 December 1957

Mrs Small here all day, and what a pile of work she got through. The sight of her poised with her fingers above the typewriter has an electric effect on my lazy mind. She is coming again for two and a half more days this week and I should be absolutely cleared up before Christmas. This system suits me perfectly. I just couldn't manage someone whole time. Similarly, the Peter Jones Bureau suits Mrs Small for much the same reason.

Wednesday 18 December 1957

Meeting at the House of Commons this afternoon to discuss ways of financing Felicity Bolton as Parliamentary Secretary for the MCF. We've decided to appeal to all MPs to make a contribution. We also hope to find a room.

Also the first meeting of the Fabian Executive to which Roy Jenkins was elected chairman. He is a caricature of an up-and-coming young politician in a Victorian novel. We discussed co-options and Tony Crosland uttered a caveat against John Murray 'because he hasn't got a Fabian background'. Considering John Murray is one of the most original people in Labour politics, this was a curious comment. However, Crosland did vote for him when it came to the show of hands.

To the BBC this evening for the recording of *Frankly Speaking* in which Lady Violet Bonham Carter was grilled for half an hour by journalist John Connell, Margaret Lane (the Countess of Huntingdon) and myself. I quite enjoyed it although I didn't feel that my questions had contributed much to 'bringing Lady Vi out'. Although she is effusive, overpowering, goody-goody, and so much else that is awful, I still like her and admire her. She has a tremendous vitality and an unparalleled enthusiasm for life. She belongs to the 'couldn't care more' brigade in contrast to so many of the bored people of today. She is still active in public life to a degree which is remarkable in a woman of seventy.

Obviously the real key to her personality lies in her childhood. Her mother's death when she was very young, her own two years in bed with polio in her early teens, her father's second marriage to the brilliant, arrogant Margot Asquith and a central position in the political life of Britain from the time she was fifteen until she was thirty have made her what she is. Her devotion to her father and his memory is most intense. In the whole evening, and the broadcast, all of which was devoted to her and her life, she never mentioned her husband once. He clearly has played no role of importance in her life. In fairness to him, it is hard to see how anyone who had to live with Lady Violet for forty years or more could retain much influence.

Thursday 19 December 1957

This is perhaps a convenient moment to set down the latest moves in the House of Lords question.

After the meeting at which it was decided to wait until the Bill reached the Commons before a final decision was made, the Committee stage began in the Lords.

The Lord Chancellor committed himself to the view that the relief of heirs was a matter for the House of Commons and opinion should be tested by means of a Ten-Minute Rule bill. I think he knew that such a bill had no chance with the Conservative majority and was quite safe. But in the future it might be a convenient weapon to use against him with a Labour majority in the Commons.

Today my dad rang to say that Herbert Samuel (aged eighty-seven) had written urging him to continue the campaign with a newly drafted bill which would give power of renunciation to any peer. I have, of course, among the dozen bills that I have drafted got one tailored to fit Lord Samuel's proposal. I think I shall suggest Father send it to him and hope that he may be encouraged to try it out.

The Movement for Colonial Freedom is going through a difficult period. It is a perpetual financial headache and is not run at all efficiently. However, it is doing a vital job of work. My particular concern is the Mediterranean and Middle Eastern Committee. We have now drawn into the work of this Committee a number of enthusiastic young Arab students, good Algerian contacts, Cypriot representatives, and others.

Tuesday 7 January 1958

Today's sensational news of Thorneycroft's resignation has reawakened everyone to politics again with a bang. I wrote about it for my *Bristol Evening World* column:

The resignation of Mr. Thorneycroft, Chancellor of the Exchequer, and his colleagues exploded like a hydrogen bomb over the Westminster testing ground on Tuesday morning. No hint of trouble on this scale or on this issue had leaked through to the press. Those long Cabinet meetings over the weekend had remained a closely guarded secret.

First of all one must pay tribute to anyone who resigns on principle. Though I profoundly disagree with the ex-Chancellor, I admire him for his courage in carrying his convictions to the point of resignation. It is not an easy decision to reach for any man. For the pressure to remain despite disagreement is always powerful. Everyone in politics agrees to give up something of his own independence to achieve the greater good that can only come

through working with colleagues. Every party of three hundred MPs is a coalition of three hundred elements. When can one break that coalition? Is it too soon to justify a resignation? Or is it too late to have anything worth saving?

In the last seven years we have seen four major resignations. Mr Bevan and Mr Wilson in 1951 and Lord Salisbury in 1957.

These examples are proof enough that integrity and independence remain despite the Party system. Just as there are many courageous lone voices on the back benches in both major parties, so there is no lack of toughness and conscience on the front. Let us not forget Mr Nigel Birch and Mr Enoch Powell who have gone with their leader into the wilderness.

The political implications of this resignation are not hard to see. The question at stake was whether the Government's economic policy should be carried to the point where the fabric of the welfare state was to be partially dismantled. The Prime Minister and most of the Cabinet shrank from a course of action which would have such grave political consequences. Mr Thorneycroft was willing to wield the axe even against the Social Services.

Inside the Conservative Party therefore, this is a left versus right struggle. The Butler wing have won a tactical victory over the wild men of the City. We should all be grateful for small mercies but the consequences for the Conservative Party need to be assessed.

There is already a nucleus of disgruntled right-wingers inside the ranks of the Tory MPs. They first appeared in 1954 as the Suez Group. During the war against Egypt in November 1956 they thought they had captured the Prime Minister. Then came the sell-out and the humiliation of the evacuation. Eight of them resigned the whip and decided to sit as Independents. They are still there in open opposition.

But Suez wasn't the only issue on which they wanted a fight. They were adamant for toughness in Cyprus. They received a distinguished recruit in the person of Lord Salisbury. Although *his* resignation fizzled out like a damp squib, he remains the only man of real influence in the House of Lords. At any moment he could embarrass Macmillan very gravely.

Now Thorneycroft, Birch and Powell are thrown up as real leaders of this dissident group. The financial issues on which they have resigned will attract the support of the Independent Conservatives. And the Cyprus problem looms up right ahead ...

It is at this very moment that Macmillan is leaving for his important Commonwealth tour. It is a cruel blow to him, for his

team will have no real leader in his absence. Mr Butler is a spent
political force who has not one chance in a hundred of succeeding
to the premiership. Lord Hailsham is not taken seriously and
cannot be effective as acting Leader. Who then is the man to watch?
Mr Derick Heathcoat Amory, the new Chancellor of the Exchequer.

He has everything in his favour. The Treasury gives him a
position of dominating power, which he well knows how to use.
The controversy that will rage round his policy will itself make him
into a major political figure. And his background and record offer
the only formula for a Conservative recovery. He was known to be
against Suez, although he remained a member of the Government.
He has shown himself to be against a major assault on the welfare
state. From this position to the left of the Conservative centre, he is
the obvious successor to Mr Macmillan. Mr Macmillan must be
wondering about this as he wings his way away from the confusion
of his own Cabinet on his world tour.

How long more have we got to put up with this crowd? That is what
75 per cent of the people of this country are asking themselves this
week. When a Government gets itself into this sort of a mess, it has
a duty to take the issue to the country and let the people decide.

Only one thing of particular interest came from the recess and that was
the Hartley Shawcross speech just before Christmas.

Hartley, the former Attorney-General, speaking in his constituency of
St Helen's had urged consultation between the Government and
Opposition before great decisions on foreign policy. He was reported to
have said, 'How can it be thought that British foreign policy should
influence events when foreign powers know that if a Government of
different political composition should come into power the policy might
be reversed?'

Too much parliamentary time, he said, was occupied by sham fights
on matters irrelevant to real problems and he referred to a speech made
by Clement Davies, the Liberal Leader, who had said that since 1945
nobody of real achievement or distinction in any outside activity had
gone into the House of Commons. He went on: 'A public opinion poll the
other day disclosed that 30 per cent of our people want a coalition
Government. I do not favour a coalition, but I do say that on some
matters of vital importance we shall not progress until Government and
Opposition Parties try to find out not how much they can exaggerate
their differences and sabotage each other's efforts but how much they can
make common cause.'

This made me hopping mad and I know had the same effect on a large
number of other people. Then Charlie Pannell rang me up to say that he
had written to Shawcross telling him his private view of the matter.

As Attorney-General created by Attlee, his talents should have had an opportunity to show themselves. Since our defeat in 1951, he has been making these speeches continuously which pour scorn upon the Party and its activities. He has been combining this with moaning to his friends that he is not understood or liked or used or wanted. But when they try to do something about it, he is always too busy.

Friday 10 January 1958
This afternoon I went to Oxford for the Nuffield Conference on Political Broadcasting. The idea originated with David Butler, who persuaded the College to sponsor it. It was decided to invite the leading figures on both sides, political and broadcasting, not as representatives of their Parties or of their broadcasting organisations, but as individuals with a special knowledge of and interest in the subject. Those who attended were:

Alan Bullock
David Butler
Rt. Hon. R.A. Butler, MP
D.N. Chester
Geoffrey Cox
Sir Robert Fraser
Rt. Hon. Hugh Gaitskell, MP
Harman Grisewood
J. Grimond, MP
M.H. Harrison
Rt. Hon. Edward Heath, MP
Maj.-Gen. Sir Ian Jacob
R.T. McKenzie
H.G. Nicholas
K.C. Wheare

Armed with documents, including my background paper, all the representatives headed for Nuffield for dinner.

Hugh Gaitskell drove by just after 5 to collect me. I thought he looked rather tired. We arrived last of all the guests, just before dinner was to be announced. The others were all in a most amiable mood and we settled down along the long table in the Fellows' Dining Room.

I was right opposite the Director General of the BBC, Sir Ian Jacob, with Geoffrey Cox of ITN on my left and Jo Grimond on my right. David Butler was on Sir Ian Jacob's right and Bob McKenzie on his left. It was rather a dismal meal. Sir Ian Jacob had been angered by one of the papers circulated and he was in his most bureaucratic mood. One felt he was lusting for blood and the best thing was to let him get it out of his system. He felt the BBC was under fire – quite wrongly – for having knuckled under to the Parties. One famous criticism is that the BBC kept Sir Winston Churchill off the air during the 1930s. This is an often repeated charge. Sir Ian was able – with obvious relish – to point out that the occasion took place in 1931 when the Secretary of State for India asked the BBC not to let Churchill broadcast his views on India just before the round-table conference. The Secretary of State was none other than my Dad. This caused much amusement.

Meanwhile Bob McKenzie was deep in conversation with Rab, which Bob retailed later. Rab was being wildly indiscreet about the Cabinet crisis. He could scarcely forbear to cheer at Thorneycroft's disappearance. 'Nobody seems to have spotted,' he said, 'that this is a great Butler victory. Of course I shouldn't rub it in myself, don't you agree? It wouldn't be right for me. Would it? No, I'd better not gloat, had I? I probably look very tired, but I shall soon feel better. It has been a wonderful week.' This quote comes via the fertile imagination of Bob McKenzie to me and must not be taken as verbatim. But undoubtedly the egocentricity, the indiscretion and the jubilation were all in evidence.

After dinner we gathered round the fire for coffee. It was rather exciting to think that the Deputy Prime Minister, the Leader of the Opposition, the Liberal Leader, the two Directors-General and three Heads of Oxford Colleges should be meeting together at this particular moment. No publicity has been given to the meetings and nothing has leaked to the press. But what a wonderful news story it would make.

After we had settled down, the Warden opened the discussion by describing the function of Nuffield College at this conference. It is to provide facilities for the academic discussion of important political topics. We then began to talk. No official record was kept and no decisions of any kind were reached.

Finally we broke up at about 11 and scattered to our various hotels and colleges. One interesting tailpiece was that Rab told David that he was in favour of televising Parliament – a powerful recruit.

Saturday 11 January 1958
This morning we talked from 9.45 till nearly 1 – still in the wide circle round the Senior Common Room. At lunch we went on talking broadcasting and then did a conducted tour of the College. We began again at 2.30 until 3.45; finally, we had tea and broke up. Jo Grimond gave me a lift home with Ted Heath. One nice Churchill story I heard was from Ted. When in January 1951 he was made an unpaid Assistant Whip, Winston said to him, 'It will be hard work, Heath, and it is unremunerated, but as long as I am your Leader it will never go unthanked.'

So finally home again just over twenty-four hours after leaving – feeling very exhausted and sick, and worrying in retrospect lest I had talked too much. For on reflection I wondered how I had had the temerity to speak at all in such a glittering gathering. Such thoughts, alas, had never troubled me during the meetings themselves.

Tuesday 21 January 1958
Parliament met today after the Christmas recess. I didn't go as there was nothing much doing and I was busy. Dick Crossman gave a party to which Caroline and I were invited. It was quite fun as it was largely non-political. Denis Healey and Hugh Gaitskell were the only other MPs. Gerald Kaufman of the *Daily Mirror* was there and so was Hugh Massingham, the *Observer*'s political correspondent. I met Cecil King, the chairman of the Mirror Group, and had a fierce argument with him about the future of television and parliamentary procedure. He was very gruff and tough and tycoony, but I stuck to my guns. He said we must continue it over lunch – an invitation I don't propose to slip.

Thursday 23 January 1958
Economics debate. Gaitskell was not bad but I still think that tactically it is wiser for us not to attack the Government too hard at this moment. The people are sick of the Government anyway, don't need to hear it from us and don't much want to. What they want is a clear answer to the question: 'What would you do, chum?' We have an answer and should give it clearly and without any more knockabout than is absolutely necessary.

Thorneycroft made a brilliant speech. Abhorring recriminations, he talked simply and powerfully about his own view of our problem. The House took it very well and he established himself again as a big figure. Enoch was really touched that I had phoned him the day he resigned. I felt hardly anyone else had bothered, even on his own side.

Monday 27 January 1958
I took the morning off to do electrical jobs. It was pure escapism but very restful. I began by throwing an aerial over the roof and then brought up my old radio to the office and connected it with the wire recorder and the 'Fonadek' for the telephone. I can now:

– play the wireless ordinarily, through earphones
– record on the wire recorder through the microphone
– play gramophone records through the wireless
– play the telephone through the wireless, or record it through the wire recorder

Quite a successful morning.

Wednesday 29 January 1958
Following my meeting with Cecil King at the Crossmans' party I had

invited myself to lunch with him. So off I went to the *Daily Mirror* at 1 o'clock. As I left the taxi a man dashed up and said, 'Are you lunching with the Chairman?' Then the butler hurried out and it was the hall, the lift, the outer office, and the inner sanctum before you could say 'knife'. The tall, lumbering, kindly figure of Cecil King moved forward. The sherry was there. The table in his office was laid with crystal and silver and we were soon sitting down to the most superb meal of smoked salmon, breast of turkey and hot apple pie, silently and rapidly served by the butler. It was tycoonery at its best. What a tycoon Cecil King is. A word about West Africa? 'I own a chain of papers there.' Australia? 'Of course in Sydney we have the most successful of the commercial radio stations.' Television? 'You know, we are half owners of ATV.' All this and the 4 million a day *Mirror* and *Sunday Pictorial* not to mention a vast Canadian paper company with its own forests and pulping.

Still, he was absolutely charming and we had a most interesting talk about Ghana, Parliament and its procedure, radio and television, and all sorts of other things. Having virtually asked to be told when to go, I felt not too worried to have stayed an hour and a half in all.

To a meeting in Gillingham, Kent for Gerald Kaufman. He made a most amusing speech which included the results of some research he had done on relationships inside the Tory Party. No fewer than 40 per cent of the Cabinet are actually relations of the Prime Minister and 39 per cent of the Tory MPs are too. Some of it is distant but it's all proved through *Debrett* and *Who's Who*. So also are Sir Arthur fforde, the new BBC Chairman, and Professor Trevor-Roper, the new Oxford history professor – both Macmillan appointments – and to think *we* were accused of jobs for the boys.

Home 11.30 and worked till 2, including a quarter of an hour of perfect reception from Radio Moscow. I recorded it all.

Wednesday 5 February 1958
Lunch today with Gerald Kaufman and Keith Waterhouse. The *Mirror* toughness and freshness is very healthy for a politician. We get a bit rarefied, and benefit by contact. The lunch was about the future of television, on which Keith Waterhouse is writing a pamphlet. The fantastic profitability of commercial TV is going to precipitate a fresh crisis when the figures are published.

Thursday 6 February 1958
Peter Shore of the Research Department at Transport House to tea at the Commons today. He is being sent to Rochdale to observe the effect of TV on the by-election. I found him very receptive to the general theme that television is the greatest, best and most important thing that has happened to British politics. The facts are so overwhelming once you present them.

This evening to Transport House for the first television training course. I introduced it. Ken Peay described the facilities available. Woodrow trained them, then they all practised. We discovered two stars in MPs Sidney Dye and Fred Peart. Kenneth Robinson – full face – is also very good.

Friday 7 February 1958
Jeremy Isaacs from the Gallup poll came to quiz me for half an hour for a world leadership survey. It is being done in European, Asian and American countries and the results will be published by Princeton University. The questions were very intelligent indeed.

Sunday 9 February 1958
The news of the bombing by the French of Sakhiet, Tunisia was a terrible shock today. I rang Taieb Slim, the Tunisian Ambassador, and put myself at his disposal. At 11 o'clock at night he rang me and I went to see him. He had not been to bed and was very tired. We went over the story together and he told me of his talk with Selwyn Lloyd and of what his brother, Mongi, was going to say to Hammarskjold at that very moment. He and I went over the map of Tunisia to pinpoint French posts. I promised to get the matter raised in Parliament and to speak to Nye Bevan about it tomorrow.

On all this I worked late into the night preparing the case against France.

Monday 10 February 1958
I rang Taieb this morning and told him what I had been able to discover about the NATO treaty and the Mutual Defence Assistance Agreement, both of which France had violated. He was most interested, as he knew neither of these things. I felt it justified my filing system just by itself.

Nye promised full Front Bench support on Wednesday. I arranged for a group of us to telephone our sympathy to Bourguiba and put down a motion on the order paper. This concentrated on the important points of the UN, NATO, Red Cross aid and efforts for peace in Algeria. Taieb Slim is very grateful.

Tuesday 10 February 1958
To Lime Grove for Nye Bevan's TV party political programme. Nye arrived a bit late and was just impossible for the first three-quarters of an hour. He launched into an attack on the BBC for bias, distortion and discrimination against himself and all the rest. It was an ignorant attack, so easily refuted by the facts. The atmosphere was extremely tense and I was unhappy since I could not support him. The programme was going to be terrible if this went on. To make it worse, Nye wouldn't drink anything before the broadcast so he was on edge even more.

Then between the steak and the cheese we got on to farming. Nye, the farmer, mellowed before our eyes. On grazing and pigs and subsidies he found common ground with Gerald Beadle. He began to laugh and do imitations of Tom Williams, who was our Minister of Agriculture, and by the time he came up for the first run-through the tears were running down his cheeks with good humour and giggly laughter. *NOTE:* Nye must never do another broadcast without having some of his intimate friends there beforehand to keep him sweet.

The show itself was very good, I thought. Reckoning the limitations we had to face, a talk with a lot of young people was undoubtedly the best projection of his personality. The *Daily Telegraph* next morning said it was the best Labour Party political yet.

A long talk with Leonard Miall afterwards about the future of television.

Wednesday 12 February 1958
The Party meeting first of all discussed the establishment of a benevolent fund for Members' families in distress, like Wilfred Fienburgh's.* We agreed unanimously to contribute 5 guineas a year each towards the establishment of such a fund. We then discussed life peers.

I went from there to sit in the car in New Palace Yard to hear Father as Guest of the Week in *Woman's Hour*. He was brilliantly relaxed and amusing. His choice of a tune was 'My old man said follow the van', sung by Marie Lloyd. As soon as it was over he hurried back to the Lords to make two speeches – one on Spain in NATO and one on Tunisia. Then he came and sat in the Commons Gallery for two hours waiting for me to be called in the Life Peers debate. I met Taieb Slim, the Tunisian Ambassador, and Messaoud BenMohammed of the Algerian FLN in the Central Lobby and put them in the gallery of the Commons. There they listened to my questions. Then they moved to the Lords and heard Father in action. Taieb was absolutely delighted at what we had done for him.

Home at 11.30 too tired and excited to sleep. I knew I would toss and turn, so up to the office to work till 1 and to hear the result of the Rochdale by-election on the wireless. The Labour victory is encouraging but could have been better. The fact that the Liberals came second is very annoying, though worse for the Tories than for us. There is no real chance of a Liberal revival. This will probably help us in the next Election considerably.

Saturday 15 February 1958
Seretse Khama came to dinner tonight – the first we had seen of him for eighteen months. He was much slimmer, fitter and tougher in every way.

* Labour MP for Islington, 1951–8, died in car crash February, 1958, aged 38.

It was difficult to talk about Bechuanaland with a big party, but we did exchange a word about it. He made it pretty clear that the Bamangwato were not sufficiently politically conscious to worry about the problem of incorporation of the Protectorates in the Union. This could be an issue one day. Of course nowadays Seretse is a member of the Establishment. With Rasebolai and Tshekedi, he now rules the tribe. And from a suburban existence in Croydon he has become a massive cattle-owner living on a big scale. His personal household staff is nine, having been reduced from twelve because the others did no work.

Thursday 20 February 1958
Had a talk to Frank Barlow at the Commons. He told me that some sections of the Party (Jim Callaghan, Tony Greenwood, Alf Robens and Nye) were sick to death of my campaign on the peerage and were being very rude about it. This plunged me into depression.

Nye Bevan opened the debate today. Apparently he made a most appalling speech – his worst flop yet. He tried to explain what he had said at the Conference at Brighton about the H bomb. All he succeeded in doing was alienating his new friends as well as his old ones.

Friday 21 February 1958
To dinner with Cecil King at the Dorchester, with a lot of commercial TV tycoons. I must say they thoroughly irritated me. Here were these extremely powerful men who were not interested in programmes as such but only in making money. The whole conversation was on a financial carve-up of the world. I came away feeling that the public accountability issue is a really important, live one. Couldn't all public companies be put in the same position as nationalised industries and made subject to directions from a Minister in the public interest? I shall do some work on this.

Wednesday 26 February 1958
Messaoud BenMohammed, the FLN representative in London, came to see me this morning to finalise the plans for the Algeria meeting on 1 April. Public interest is high and we should do well.

Lunch with Taieb Slim and Cecil Hourani. (He is a Professor of Politics at the American University in Beirut, now working for Bourguiba.) We carried the discussion a great deal further than when we last met. They hope to launch a Maghreb Federation very soon and then to summon a conference on the Algerian problem thereafter. Only with such a federation could you give the French the sort of guarantees about the *colons* [colonists] and defence that they would need to settle. It is a most imaginative idea. The Foreign Office realise that sooner or later France must accept defeat. They are seriously worried about a right-wing *coup d'état* in Paris or Algiers, or both, and so are listening seriously to the proposals put forward.

To the Cyprus Conciliation Committee. Clem Davies in the chair, Sir Harold Nicolson and others. We heard that Archbishop Makarios wants to come to London and would like an invitation from this Committee. It was decided after discussion that his intentions should be probed and that a delegation should see the Prime Minister.

Monday 3 March 1958

At 7 o'clock in the Division Lobby I saw Geoffrey de Freitas and asked for a word with him privately. He knew what it was about before we had sat down in the Members' Lobby. I asked to be relieved of the responsibility of being No.2 on Air matters. I explained that I had had many anxious hours of thought about it (as indeed I have) and that I had come to one definite conclusion: under no circumstances would it be right or sensible for Britain to use the hydrogen bomb. I said I did not know yet in my own mind what the right course of action was, but I could not conscientiously be the spokesman of a policy with which I was in disagreement.

Geoffrey was very sweet. He said he absolutely understood my view and the motives that had prompted it. He said he wished he could be relieved of the burden of the Air Force but there was nobody willing to do it. I pointed out that it wasn't reluctance to do the donkey work that influenced me, and he understood that. We left it that he would tell the Chief Whip that I was from that moment discharged.

Without making too much of this it was, of course, a tiny resignation and may not be popular in high quarters. But I really can't help that. If one allowed oneself to be dragged along doing something one thinks is wrong, it would be hopeless.

Tuesday 4 March 1958

Jim Callaghan buttonholed me. He has had a letter from a wealthy man who has retired to St Helena. Shocked by the poverty of the people, he has offered to pay for a good Labour Party man to go out, study the situation and report back with a view to action being taken in the House. Jim consulted Hugh Gaitskell, who suggested me. So it is a great honour and would be a challenging task. The report could cover everything from constitutional through to social, educational and political questions. I asked for twenty-four hours to think about it. The trouble is it means nearly two months away.

This evening mainly at Millbank talking to Tappa and Dave about TV and politics. Also watching a bit of TV. Work till 1 o'clock on St Helena.

Thursday 6 March 1958

This evening to the Cambodian reception at Claridge's. I had a very

friendly talk with a chap from the Chinese embassy and was hailed by a
man with a familiar face whose name I couldn't place. It turned out to be
Mr Joseph Godson, who is First Secretary at the American embassy and
Labour attaché. He asked me why I was not going to be the Front Bench
spokesman on air this year. I was staggered that he should know this.
Next week's business was only announced today and the Party
spokesmen from the Front Bench are not named until the Party meeting,
which was taking place at the moment we were talking. Someone must
have mentioned it to him: it shows how closely the American embassy
watch British politics. I am told they have three or four people working
full time on each Party.

Friday 7 March 1958
To Bristol this evening for a meeting in support of the South African
Treason Trial Defence Fund organised by the MCF. About a hundred
people turned up in the Grand Hotel to watch the film *African Conflict*
made by Howard Smith for CBS. We raised £25 for the fund. More
important even than the money was the feeling that a little group of
Bristolians who had never been to South Africa were expressing
solidarity with these people on trial for their beliefs.

Saturday 8 March 1958
Home on the early train and Seretse Khama to lunch.
    In between and after talking to him the children came in and Seretse
was just as sweet as he could be with them. Hilary asked him point blank
about his blackness, and we had a good old laugh. Seretse was missing
Ruth and his children a bit and, I think, enjoyed himself.
    This evening we went to dinner with Enoch Powell, who resigned with
Thorneycroft over the estimates. Tonight he and I had a long post-
mortem on Suez. As he was a member of the 'Suez Group' at the time of
the Canel Zone Base Agreement in 1954, I naturally took him to have
been a violent supporter of Eden in 1956. But as it turned out I was quite
wrong, and for a most interesting reason. His argument ran like this. 'To
be a great Empire, sustained by military strength, requires military bases
at strategic points. In 1954 Eden tried to pretend to us that we could still
be a great military power without maintaining by force a base in Egypt. I
said then that that was hypocrisy and humbug. When Nasser
nationalised the Canal I was proved right. But by then it was too late to
get it back. World opinion would not have it, and militarily we could not
do it. I therefore watched with amused detachment the outbreak of
hysteria from July to October which had come two years too late to be
effective. I didn't think it was right or could be successful to attempt to
invade and get back what we had lost. As far as the position now is
concerned, we have given up the means by which we can maintain our
Empire by force.'

This is not an exact quote, of course, but a précis of his argument.

Wednesday 12 March 1958
To Torrington for the by-election this evening. The first meeting drew in six people. The chairman said it was because of a Methodist film show in the village hall. It was a more original excuse than the weather, which is always too bad for people to come out or so good that they're gardening. I just sat and got them to put questions to me. Then to Okehampton for the second meeting, where quite a big hall was booked. It was crammed to the doors with over 200 and a large number standing at the back. This so encouraged me that I let fly for fifty minutes on my H bomb theme. They seemed very interested!

Back to Exeter by car dog-tired, and to bed at once without a meal.

Friday 14 March 1958
Still extremely depressed. No particular reason, but on the trade cycle theory of ups and downs, a down has been due for some time.

Sunday 23 March 1958
All day at the MCF Annual Conference at the Cora Hotel. There must have been about a hundred delegates and observers there and I found them an impressive lot. They ranged from bearded anarchists and what Dick Plummer used to call 'bicycling Christians' (by which he meant athletic, though elderly pacifists whom he suspected had cycled from Liverpool in plus-fours in order to be there) to trade union officials and other delegates, with one or two Africans.

The annual report showed a year of solid achievement, which justified all the work put into the MCF. It touched off a debate on the future of the organisation in which Felicity Bolton and I suggested closer relationships with the Labour Party. We were both badly mauled in the subsequent debate but it had planted the seed which may later grow.

We also had a debate on whether our policy should include the word 'immediate' to qualify self-determination. On a vote, this was rejected. We also debated whether we should walk out of 'Settler territories' before democracy was established. This was rejected by 34 votes to 15. I found myself in a majority on both these issues, which was some consolation for the general feeling of hostility. But in the elections for the Central Council I came top with 41 votes.

Tuesday 25 March 1958
This evening in the Commons we had the Committee stage of the Life Peers Bill. I hadn't been able to decide whether I would be able to speak or not. Recent fears that the Benn case had received too much publicity tended to hold me back. But when we came to it, I just couldn't keep out

of it. I must say it was a most amusing four hours. Leslie Hale's speech showed him at the top of his brilliant form. His description of the creation of peeresses in their own right had the House in helpless laughter. He went through the women friends of George I who were thus ennobled; 'She was one of the King's most trusted and intimate counsellors, as history records, and took her duties so seriously that she was on duty day and night.' Butler's laughter could be heard above the rest, but Leslie ploughed through it all deadpan, as he always does.

Wednesday 26 March 1958
Tea with Megan Lloyd George,* who is so friendly and such a tremendous admirer of Father's. I wonder if she is really happy in the Labour Party yet. It must be a bit of a come-down after all those years in the Liberal Party. The Life Peers Bill speech she made on second reading was, as she confided to me, 'the happiest moment since I got back into the House'.

Saturday 29 March 1958
Surgery in Hanham this morning, but few people came.

Lunch with Fred Newman of USDAW who has agreed to be agent for an Election, which is a great weight off my mind. I am doing a lot of the groundwork of organisation in my office and will be able to hand him quite a useful file when he starts.

This afternoon I opened the one-thousandth council house in Kingswood. It was all very homely and pleasant.

Sunday 30 March 1958
To Mary Adams' retirement party at the BBC. Had a long talk to Gilbert Harding whom I have known for eight years, long before he was famous in broadcasting. He used to broadcast for me when I worked for the North American Service.

Despite the fact that he was very drunk I had a most interesting talk to him about Cyprus, of all things. He was a schoolmaster there in the 1930s and knows the island well. He was also at Cambridge with Sir Hugh Foot and keeps in very close touch with him. He told me that he had seen Mac (as Hugh Foot is known) on both his recent visits to London. 'I have no time whatsoever for the Turks,' he said. 'But I warn you that the problem of Cyprus will be with us to nag us for years like a boil on our scrotum' – as he most vividly put it.

Also talked to Frank Pakenham. He said Father was the most popular Member of the House of Lords without doubt, and he gave three reasons. First, his war record and decorations. The Tories looked on him as a

* Lady Megan Lloyd George, daughter of Lloyd George and Liberal MP for Anglesey 1929–51. Labour MP for Carmarthen 1957–66.

serving officer with funny ideas and would take anything from him. Secondly because of his age, which gave him an authority and a status which was quite impregnable, and thirdly because he was far and away the wittiest and best speaker in the Lords. The House loved his jokes and the kindly way in which he hit about him.

I have known this for a long time, but it was nice to hear Pakenham say it. Pakenham really is a very kindly man, although he looks such a wet. And indeed what could be more like him than to have given up alcohol before 7 pm as his fast for Lent. Always a compromise: hence that impression of the reasonable man.

Tuesday 1 April 1958
Messaoud came in a great state of excitement to finalise the resolution for tonight's meeting in the Caxton Hall, which was a tremendous success. The Tunisian, Moroccan and Libyan Ambassadors were there in person and also various other Ministers from Afghanistan and the Lebanon and so on. About 600 people crowded the hall and there was a small overflow meeting of about 50. The speakers were not really all that good and the meeting flagged a bit until Barbara Castle gave it a fillip at the end. But we collected £305 for Algerian relief and this in itself justified the meeting. I did the appeal and felt rather pleased.

Tuesday 8 April 1958
To watch the Party political programme on education at Lime Grove. But the real television news of the day is the invention of VERA, the recording on to tape of TV broadcasts by a relatively cheap machine. It will revolutionise TV and looks as if it will be cheap enough to be in general use.

Friday 11 April 1958
To lunch today with John Whitney, the American Ambassador. Also present were Godson, Kidd and Rendle of the embassy and the Labour MPs Shinwell, Bellenger, Peart, Mayhew and Mellish.

I believe the Ambassador is one of the ten richest men in America and has never had to do anything in his life, but he has tried hard and has a fair record of public service behind him. What stirred him into activity was when I asked about Truman. How he hated him. Something of the wealthy Republican aristocrat's detestation of this thrusting demagogic haberdasher came to the fore. We moved from that to the future of the Republican Party without Ike. Whitney is a 'citizens for Eisenhower' man. He was interesting on this.

But the object of the lunch was revealed and achieved half-way through the pear melba when Godson said to one of us, 'Did you go on the Aldermaston march?' This started Mayhew off. 'They're just a lot of

Communists and fellow travellers and pacifists and cranks and do-gooders and they haven't got a leader and they're splittable because they don't fundamentally agree.'

I said I thought that the official Labour Party was just as deeply divided on the H bomb as the Aldermaston marchers. Mayhew said, 'Rubbish', but was proved wrong. This is a summary of the position taken up in the hour's discussion.

Shinwell: Bitterly opposes disengagement.

Bellenger: Believes a world war without the H bomb is possible – and likely.

Mellish: Accepts the current Party line and would certainly use the H bomb.

Peart: Reluctantly accepts the current line but admits the strength of the neo-pacifists.

Mayhew: Says he would keep the Russians guessing about whether he would use the bomb. Is pro-disengagement.

I took the simple view that under no circumstances would we ever use the hydrogen bomb, but that unilateral renunciation would not solve the problem.

Throughout all this the Americans listened intently, contributing little. I don't think it did them any harm to see the mood. But coming away in the car we agreed that the Party was at sixes and sevens and really in no state to take over office at the moment. We also agreed that there should be a lot more meetings on this.

Tuesday 15 April 1958
Parliament met today and it was Budget Day. I didn't go in at all as our new baby showed signs of arriving last night and really seems imminent. I missed the vote on the budget as a result and am in trouble with the Chief Whip!

Wednesday 16 April 1958
Polling day for the London County Council, and I took Stephen and Hilary with me to vote. We collected the ballot paper, chose the right names, marked the cross and dropped it in the box. They really found it exciting, with a policeman at the door and a hushed, church-like atmosphere. But it was the runners on the way out who were collecting the numbers that brought it home. I explained they were the soldiers in the war without any shooting. This really went home to them and they understood that if you could vote there was no danger of bad men governing you. All the rest of the day they played elections, with ballot papers and candidates. Then we had the declaration of the count and spoilt papers and the returning officer spinning a coin to decide a tie.

To the Commons, where Dr J. Shaer, the President of the Arab Students' Union, came to see me. He is a man of about thirty-five, completing his work for a fellowship at the Royal College of Surgeons. He founded the Arab Students' Union, which now represents 3,000 Arab students in England. These young men are intensely excited at what is happening in the move for Arab unity. They are mainly Ba'athist socialists and none of them support Iraq and Jordan. Shaer felt that there should be better contact with British socialists and particularly some clear thinking about Israel.

He rejected the idea that Israel must be destroyed and said that a settlement was bound to come sooner or later. Nasser would welcome it, but whenever he made any sort of a move in that direction Baghdad Radio condemned him as a pro-Zionist. This was the only weapon the Iraqis could use to counter the charge that they were imperialist stooges. Moreover, it was a most useful weapon for the West generally against Nasser.

Thursday 17 April 1958

Today was a hell of a day all round. First, Hugh Gaitskell pulled me aside as I was going into the Party meeting and said, 'Look here, you'd better drop the Cyprus meeting in Trafalgar Square. We know more than you do about it and it would be better if you left it.' I said that the meeting was no secret. The first person I had told had been Jim Callaghan and I'd also written to notify the Colonial Office about it. Hugh was a little taken aback and said he thought I had better see Jim Griffiths about it.

So I buttonholed Jim Griffiths at the end of the Party meeting. Of course he always takes the line of least resistance. To begin with it was paternalism: 'Now look here, Tony, I should drop it if I were you. There are things going on you may not know about. And what's the point of having a meeting anyway? Have you thought what would happen if the Turks tried to break it up? You might have a knife fight.'

At 8.15 Mr Moreas of the Greek Orthodox Church came to see me. He is rather a puffy and sweaty man in his mid-forties whose nervous disposition does not make negotiation easy. He began by protesting vigorously at the fact that the left-wing members of our Sub-Committee – notably Pefkos – had released news to the Greek press about the first meeting. He said the Archbishop was dead against any Cypriot participation and thought a simple British meeting would be the best thing. However, he swore me to secrecy about the source of this opinion.

At 8.30 the Sub-Committee met. I realised at once that I was in an impossible position. The Labour Party was against the meeting and the Greek Church was against the meeting and I could not say this to those who were present. For if I had, it would have made trouble on a monumental scale. I had to argue it round as best I could. In the end – with Fenner Brockway's help – we agreed that the Trafalgar Square meeting should be all-British and that in addition there should be indoor meetings for the Mayors of Nicosia and Limassol, who should also go round the country. The petition continues.

I left the meeting in a fit of black depression, fearing that the situation might get more serious unless somehow it could be brought back to reality. It was a really sleepless night.

Friday 18 April 1958
This morning a very offensive letter came from Sir Vincent Tewson, General-Secretary of the TUC, in reply to my invitation to him to speak at the meeting in Trafalgar Square. So now the TUC is against it as well.

Went to Bristol today for two meetings. The first was the introduction meeting for Michael Cocks, the new Labour candidate for Bristol West.

Saturday 19 April 1958
Cyprus still the main headache in life. I rang Tom Driberg and he told me that he could not come on 18 May as he is the delegate from the Labour Party to the German Social Democrats. But I give him full credit for not running away. He is a real enthusiast on Cyprus. He could so easily have said 'Well, old boy, you've made your point and if I were you I shouldn't go ahead.' Indeed he had every excuse for saying this as Tewson had protested to the Labour Party about the meeting and Morgan Phillips had discussed it with Tom, Hugh Gaitskell and Jim Griffiths.

I rang Fenner Brockway, who said the Trafalgar Square Rally was now dead without Tom Driberg.

Tuesday 29 April 1958
Caroline went into hospital this morning with labour pains. It's quite a relief to have her under close medical attention though I shall miss her daily judgement on affairs very much. Our half-hour survey of the day each evening is always the stabilising and comforting part of the day.

To Lime Grove for the Party political broadcast. Hugh Gaitskell was friendly and Frank Cousins extremely cordial. Of course, he's up to his neck in the bus strike, and all the evening papers were streaming with headlines about his latest effort to settle. Alan Birch is a quiet, thoughtful and competent man, whom I also like. Bill Pickles took the chair for the programme and the two editors taking part were Harold Hutchinson of the *Herald* – an old friend of mine – and Hugh Cudlipp, editor of the *Daily Mirror*. John Grist produced again and he did a really first-rate job with the last-minute changes upsetting his camera plans.

In the event, we thought the programme went extremely well.

Certainly the editors saved it from total disaster. Hugh Cudlipp's little speech in which he said, 'We know this Government are no bloody good, but on behalf of the public I doubt whether you'll be much better!' was a very frank, representative and useful approach. Honestly, the subject was a terribly difficult one to get over. For those in the know, it was of first-rate importance: 'What are the terms of an agreement between the unions and a Labour Government?' But what is full of drama for the economist or the trade union leadership may be as dull as ditchwater to the ordinary man.

I thought Cousins came over extremely well. And his appeal for a policy which was fair to the whole community, as the only basis for industrial peace, was extremely compelling.

After the show Hugh Cudlipp invited us back to his house in Cheyne Walk. It is the most charming place, overlooking the river. His wife, Eileen Ascroft, is the fashion editor of one of the evening papers. She's a rather catlike creature – an impression strengthened by tight black slacks and a leopardskin blouse. We stood around and talked and listened to gramophone records. Hugh Cudlipp conducted his favourite pieces from opera and kept insisting that we should hear just one more side. It bored me stiff after a time, but although everyone else felt the same no one had the courage to go first. So I decided to leave at about 12.30. But no bed till 2.15, for Dave was here for the night and there was lots to talk about.

Wednesday 30 April 1958
Home working all day.

This evening to the Libyan party given in honour of the Libyan Prime Minister. When I was announced the Ambassador clutched me warmly by the hand and said he had heard me at the Algeria meeting. He then told the Prime Minister in Arabic all about it and the three of us stood with our arms clasped in warm embrace while the queue of guests built up behind. It is well worth while showing friendship in these cases, for Britain stands pretty low at the moment in Arab eyes.

As soon as I had shaken hands I nipped out of the back door and was away within four minutes of entering the building. It was hospital visiting time.

Later this evening to the St Marylebone Labour Party to talk about the future of television. For a Constituency Labour Party general management committee, it was pretty distinguished. Lord Lucan is the Membership Secretary, Lady Ungoed-Thomas is a committee member; Bill Rodgers of the Fabian Society and others were there. Home and early to bed, which was much needed.

Today was a really lovely, sunny, cloudless, hot spring day. It was good to be alive.

Wednesday 7 May 1958
Tonight the Tories broadcast a Party political for the local government
elections. It consisted of stories of socialist inefficiency described by the
Tory MP Geoffrey Rippon and illustrated by film, interspersed with little
moral lectures by Lord Hailsham, and a repetitive film sequence of
polling station notices followed by a slogan YOU CHOOSE. This was
repeated about five times.

Hailsham was simply odious. His little smirks and sneers and the
controlled hysteria with which he spoke made him look like a nanny at
the end of her tether who was giving us all one more chance to behave.
Rippon, on the other hand, gave the impression of great confidence and
competence, although he did look a bit sweaty, and just like the QC who
is prosecuting must look to the man in the dock. The programme was
wholly negative in its approach. This must have been to rally Tory
doubters, since it could never win over floaters or Labour supporters.

It was badly done but I've no doubt they had the advice of an
advertising agency with its tame psychologists. This is a technique we
must investigate.

After the programme it made me despair that none of our Party leaders
have television sets. They are totally unaware of these great
developments that are going on which are influencing the minds and
thought of the voters. How can one lead a great Party unless one keeps in
touch with the people?

Friday 9 May 1958
Working at home this morning with the usual round of chores: reading
The Times, answering letters, sorting my papers and the rest. The phone
rang: 'This is Hammersmith Hospital. Your wife has had a beautiful
baby boy.' And so after ten days of waiting, all is well. Caroline wouldn't
let them tell me that they were inducing it today. She didn't want me to
worry. But, of course, not having paced the room for three hours meant I
didn't earn my relief.

I rushed over to the hospital in time to see her wheeled in on a trolley
from the labour ward to her room. She was very well and happy. Later
that evening I met Joshua. He looks just like the others, with straggling
waving crinkly fingers which are always exercising in front of his face.
Once he opened his eyes and closed them again with an expression which
reminded me irresistibly of Gilbert Harding.

In between two visits to hospital I went to see the Sultan of Lahej. He
is a very well groomed man of thirty-six who speaks perfect English and
has an aristocractic bearing; he is the direct descendant of a line of
Sultans of Lahej going back 250 years.

Not knowing exactly how to begin, I simply asked if he would explain
the situation that had arisen. He began talking and we weren't able to get

away for two and a half hours. We frequently interrupted him with questions, to which he gave a frank answer.

Tuesday 13 May 1958

The Foreign Affairs Group met to discuss the situation in Aden and the trouble on the Yemen border. Two MPs, Reg Sorenson and John Dugdale, have just returned from a visit to the Yemen where they were the guests of the Government and met everyone. Reg described the history and gave his impressions of the present absolute theocratic monarchy which came from a fairytale book. Public executions, slavery and mutilation as a punishment for theft still survive. All chiefs have to send a son to the 'School' in the capital so that the Imam has hostages in the event of trouble. Reg detected an undercurrent of hostility to the regime, partly no doubt Palace jealousy and partly the rising tide of Arab nationalism.

He recommended that Britain face the fact that the Protectorates may want to join the Yemen. We should offer a United Nations supervised plebiscite which the Yemenis would accept. Meanwhile some boundary commission should be established.

John Dugdale attached more importance to the Russian and Chinese missions. Particularly the Russian aid of $60 million and the technicians to build the port. He thought a United Nations force should be based on the frontier and that we should support the Nasser bid to control the Yemen as being preferable to the Russian and Chinese bid. He also hoped that we would develop Aden and the Protectorates so as to make them independent.

Nye Bevan was contemptuous of the Sorenson line. He began his characteristic philosophical waffling, full of phrases like 'in the problem of succession of power we are the contemporary culprits from an evolving imperialist transmutation. . .'. It was all quite meaningless and included some grave factual errors. For example Persia is not in the United Arab Federation. He then launched into an attack on me for my support for Arab nationalism: 'It is a sham and an eruption of hysteria against Zionism and the West. The Arabs are incapable of running anything with Islam round their necks. We should give this stretch of desert to Nasser, even if only to prove what a failure he is.' He then turned at me and said I was a romantic to think that this hysteria could lead to progress. I said that he was a romantic himself and had proved that when responsibility came romantics sometimes changed their mind and became quite practical. It took him a little aback and at the end of the meeting he went out of his way to be polite again. But I was full of contempt for his performance.

Talking to people afterwards I found a unanimity of view on this. Reg Sorenson was in despair. Sidney Scholefield Allan compared him to Ernie

Bevin in his early days. Denis Healey said, 'Nye's absolutely hopeless.'
The feeling against him is really much stronger than I had realised. It is a
terrifying thought.

Wednesday 14 May 1958
Lunch with Anthony Howard. He is a brilliant young man of twenty-
three who was President of the Oxford Union some years ago and then
did national service. While in the Army he wrote some articles for the
New Statesman, as a result of which he got taken on by *Reynolds News* as
their political correspondent from absolute scratch. To land a political
column at that age and with no journalistic background is outstanding.
He has done it very well for four months and told me that the *Express* now
had offered him 'Crossbencher'. He asked my advice. Of course the
money is fabulous and to be personally summoned by Beaverbrook – as
he was – is very flattering. I discouraged him on the grounds that it was
rather mean to *Reynolds*, that the Beaver bought people body and soul,
that it was really incompatible with a Labour candidature, and that it
would prevent him being a serious journalist. Anyway the offer is bound
to remain open. I would guess he would go too.

Wednesday 21 May 1958
Walked for an hour and three-quarters up and down the terrace talking
to Kenneth Robinson. He really is a very nice man. We talked about the
general state of the Party and exchanged family news. There is a sort of
malaise over politics at the moment which it is hard to explain. The
traditional basis on which Parties have drawn their support is altering.
The problems that divide us are new and different. People are rather sick
of the old arguments which get more intense just as they are becoming
less relevant. I know I feel this way myself.

Friday 23 May 1958
Jim Callaghan rang me up today. Curly Mallalieu, the MP for
Huddersfield East, had written an article in today's *New Statesman* saying
that Callaghan had been negotiating with Sir Hugh Foot and had
committed the Party to the Foot plan on Cyprus. Foot had been
empowered to tell Callaghan the details of the plan since he, Foot, had
advised the Cabinet that without Labour support the plan had no chance
of success. In this way Mallalieu claimed that the Party had been steered
into bi-partisanship by Callaghan's craftiness.

Obviously Jim had rung me partly to sound me out on this article and
its implications and to clear himself. In fact he confirmed what Mallalieu
had said. He did have lunch with Sir Hugh Foot last Monday and Foot
did explain his plan. Jim did say to him 'I will recommend to my
colleagues and to the Party that we accept it.' No doubt Foot told Lennox

Boyd this and it was the last piece of the jigsaw to fit into position. Now Lennox Boyd, Selwyn Lloyd, Foot and our Ambassadors in Ankara and Athens are selling the plan as one that has the united support of both Parties in Britain.

What is the Foot plan? Well, it seems to be a reversion to the earlier ideas of self-government. But unlike the earlier Tory policy it does not exclude self-determination (or even partition); it is simply silent about the ultimate and no doubt concentrates on the immediate. Perhaps it associates Greece and Turkey in some way. I don't know.

Jim justified his support of the plan by saying that we must trust Hugh Foot. Civil war is imminent and if we do not support the Foot plan and it breaks out it will be our (i.e. my and Brockway and Robinson's) responsibility. After this I had a tremendous row with Callaghan on the phone. I pointed out that the Foot plan seemed as if it was contrary to all the Party had said about Cyprus in the past four years, in Parliament, at Conference and through the NEC. I pointed out that belief in self-determination was incompatible with the Foot plan and if we had changed our mind we should say so. This is not the Foot plan but the Cabinet plan. It was also quite wrong that the Party's position should have been prejudiced by a prior commitment to Foot by Callaghan.

Jim got very angry and said that 90 per cent of the Party would support him and he would welcome a showdown. We ended with genuine and cordial personal exchanges.

This is obviously a big crisis point for the Party. Our leaders have panicked and are inviting us to abandon our view in a vain effort to stop the fighting. With the background of the present French crisis it is particularly unhappy.

Jim's phone call thoroughly depressed me and I resolved to spend the next two or three days digging out all the Party had said about Cyprus so as to be armed with the necessary material.

Tuesday 27 May 1958
The French situation is now critical. Civil war seems quite likely. On top of this de Gaulle issued a statement today saying he was forming a Government but a lot is going on under the surface. One does not know whether de Gaulle is coming in by a coup or whether by abject surrender of the politicians. It looks as if the lights are going out in France.

Tuesday 3 June 1958
Messaoud BenMohammed caught me on the phone and came to see me. He told me his real name and a little bit about his history. I ought first to say what his official status had been up to now. Known as Messaoud BenMohammed, he came in as a student on a Moroccan passport and was here studying something or another. I knew, of course, he worked for the FLN but really not much more.

He now told me that his real name is Mohammed Messaoud Kellou and that he is an Algerian and is the chief political representative of the FLN in England. He is in fact a fully qualified lawyer who has practised in Marseilles and did postgraduate work in Paris. He came to London to take on the job which he now does. He has really created it from nothing and I must say has done it extremely well.

He said that when he came to England first both he and the FLN had expected to find Britain almost universally hostile and pro-French in their attitude to Algeria. They had expected the same rigid domestic control in the interests of colonialism and imperialism. Instead he had found real freedom. Britain must be 'the freest country in the world,' he said. 'Why, you can go to Hyde Park and hold a meeting demanding the British withdrawal from Kenya and Cyprus and all the rest without anyone interfering.' Also he had discovered that there was a fund of goodwill and friendship for him and Algeria; he felt that he had such a good and useful job to do that he wanted the FLN to send him someone else.

I discreetly asked how far his work was really underground since I didn't know whether he was engaged in buying arms on the quiet. But he told me he wasn't and that the Army command operated quite separately. This sounded quite reasonable although it wouldn't be likely that he would tell me he was buying arms, even if he was!

All the same I was touched by what he had said and felt it justified the work we try to do.

Wednesday 4 June 1958

To Television House for a run-through of a new programme I've been asked to take over on an experimental basis. The idea stems from *My Fair Lady* and *Pygmalion*. Does accent really betray background? ATV have got together two members of the Faculty of University College, London: Dr Fry, the Head of the Phonetics Department and Mr Trim, a lecturer. They have added a woman called Dr Eisler, a psychologist doing research at UCL. I am the chairman. The idea is to play over a one-minute recording of a voice and then for seven or eight minutes the Panel discuss it and say all they can think of about it: what region, what origin, what occupation, what age, what build, what height, what features, what sort of clothes, everything. A cartoonist draws as the team decide and finally the person appears. Then follows a post-mortem.

We had a run-through with about five recordings and then met the people. Two were absolutely spot on. It was almost uncanny. Two were pretty wrong and one was half and half. But it was tremendous fun to do and what pleased me was that I was almost as good as they were. They are a very nice crowd.

Thursday 12 June 1958

Cyprus came up at the Party meeting and I urged that we delay our decision on the Foot plan. Jim Griffiths pledged that we might have another Party meeting if we did not reach a decision next week. That is something.

Jim Callaghan was very angry with me. He knows he is in a corner and is turning nasty. This is going to be a very tough battle. I am sure I shall lose but I have never been more certain that it was right to fight it. If the Labour Party is going to run away from its policy just because there is a local disturbance – however serious – then we might just as well invite the Turkish Government to draft our Cyprus policy. There comes a time for firmness. This is it.

Thursday 19 June 1958

I had another futile argument with Callaghan, then a more cheerful talk with Dick Crossman. Hugh Gaitskell had said to Dick, 'Tony is a very able chap but he has no judgement.' I was somewhat comforted by the feeling that this view would be roughly what Hugh would feel about Dick. It would also be much milder than what Dick and I would feel about Hugh.

Sunday 22 June 1958

My anxieties over the Cyprus debate reached a climax as it seems the Party will accept the Foot plan. Tappa came over this morning and I confided in him my determination – if needs be – to divide the House alone. He was very sympathetic. I had alerted *Reynolds News* through Anthony Howard, and they had a very cautious piece.

Monday 23 June 1958

To the Commons for another Foreign Affairs Group meeting on Cyprus.

Nye opened to say he had no recommendations but wanted just to hear the views of the meeting. I asked if our pledges on self-determination and negotiations for self-government still stood. He turned a blistering attack upon me in his most hectoring way. 'We are not messenger boys from the Conference to Parliament,' he said. I left it at that.

To dinner with Mr and Mrs Edward Sieff and the Tynans. He is 'Mr Marks and Spencer'. Ken Tynan is a contemporary of mine from Oxford. After dinner when the women had gone, we sat for an hour talking politics. Ken was a real 'eighteen-year-old Red'. Of course I don't keep up with these things but I gather that he is a leading Angry Young Man. He pressed on me afterwards the view that young people were looking for a new lead. He thought they were sick of both Parties and really wanted something that took them outside themselves and made them feel there was something worth worrying and thinking about.

This conversation set my mind on to the general political problem that faces this country. The population of the world will be 7,000 million in the next forty years – far and away the greatest part being in Asia. That fact and the tremendous industrialisation in China and India will turn Britain into a little Denmark. How are we to adjust ourselves to this new world without becoming wildly frustrated and defeatist and bitter and apathetic? This problem of power contraction does threaten our political system. Someone said the Angry Young Men were a symptom of the shrinking pains of the British Empire. The answer probably lies in two things – a widening of Britain's horizons so that we can get satisfaction from the achievements of others, and a domestic revolution to modernise ourselves. It presents a serious psychological problem for politicians.

Thursday 26 June 1958
To the Party meeting on Cyprus. Nye was anxious we should not get the blame for the Government's mistakes.

He then said that he proposed to criticise the plan because it meant spiritual partition and because the Turkish and Greek commissioners could not be a permanent feature. But Labour could not impose self-determination and it must grow out of accepted self-government. For me this speech did not go far enough and I asked about self-determination and whether it would be mentioned by name. Nye was rather cross. The plan was very much criticised and it did the Party a lot of good to hear these criticisms. I spoke fourth and said I thought that we had to be extremely careful about our previous pledges.

This brought Nye to his feet to ask how his speech was incompatible with our pledges. I said, 'Don't try to bully me, I am developing the case as best I can.' Then I went on to argue that this plan meant neither self-determination nor self-government, nor was it negotiable. I then went on to say that it was unworkable and would leave us with the responsibility of continuing to impose colonial rule.

The speech had a curiously quiet reception and I think I had got rather too excited. My hands were shaking, for I was very nervous. Anyway I was very depressed for the rest of the day although in the event the Party meeting turned out to have been immensely worth while.

Though I wasn't called during the debate, I sat through it and to my amazement Nye, and to some extent Jim, went far further in criticising the plan than had seemed possible even this morning. In fact there was no fault at all with Nye's speech. It criticised the Government's handling of the problem, declared the key elements in the new constitution to be unacceptable, and called for negotiations with flexibility on all sides. When you compare this with what Jim Callaghan told me on the telephone – that he would recommend the acceptance of the Foot plan – it is a remarkable advance.

I saw Nye in the corridor afterwards and felt constrained to grasp his hand and congratulate him on his speech. He apologised for what had happened this morning. 'I wasn't meaning to bully,' he said. I brushed it all aside but came home thinking that no one ever loses by standing up for himself.

Couldn't get to sleep for hours reviewing the Cyprus nightmare, which has now, temporarily at any rate, gone away.

Wednesday 9 July 1958
Today Stephen and Hilary came to the Houses of Parliament. The trip had been long planned and as luck would have it the weather was simply super. Their hair had been specially cut and they looked very tidy. They behaved simply beautifully. We saw the Speaker's Procession and then went to the Lords to await Tappa (Father). Black Rod put us in the Diplomatic Gallery and then waved to the boys. We met him later in the Lobby and he was so friendly. The boys had seen him on television and were very interested in his buckle shoes and nylon stockings. Then we went to the Commons where they were put in the special gallery behind the peers. Father sat in the row in front and I took my place. Those tiny heads with the hair so short just poked above the back of the seat and looked like two little eggs all ready for a Humpty-Dumpty fall. We met a lot of people and went over to the Jewel Tower before we had strawberries and cream on the terrace. They were so excited. I was so proud. We also went to the Control Room and watched the Commons through the periscope. I almost forgot. Wherever they went Father said, 'These boys, father, grandfather and both great-grandfathers have sat in the Commons.' It's quite something.

Friday 11 July 1958
I collected Peter and Liz Shore and we lunched on the Terrace. This problem of making the Party effective is in everyone's mind at the moment. Douglas Jay agreed about it, and said he had urged it years ago. I have written a memo which I gave to Crossman this morning, to look at.

Just before I left for Bristol I rang Dick, who said Hugh was very interested and had read my memo.

Saturday 12 July 1958
I rang Peter Shore and Ken Peay of the PLP. They agreed to come along at 7 o'clock tonight to discuss the memo. This they did and stayed till midnight. It was a bit of a douche of cold water but we hammered out ideas on strategic publicity, tactical command and selling the Leader.

Each had specialised knowledge in different problems. After they had gone I stayed up rewriting the memo until getting on for 4 am.

Sunday 13 July 1958
At 9.30 I rang Dick Crossman in the country and read him the revised memo. He made helpful suggestions. Then Miss Blanchard arrived at 10 o'clock to type it. When the first draft was ready I read it on the phone to Ken and Peter and revised it again. At 3.15 it was ready and I rang Gaitskell to tell him I would drop it in. He invited me to talk about it. At 3.45 I reached his house and stayed an hour and a quarter. He was very gloomy and worried. He read it through three times and agreed with every recommendation. Of course it remains to be seen whether things actually get done but the way is clear.

I felt that all the fantastic effort had been worth while.

This evening to Michael Flanders' and Donald Swann's for a party to celebrate their 500th performance. They are dear friends of ours and we stayed till 11 o'clock sitting round in a circle talking and listening and laughing.

Tuesday 15 July 1958
Tappa had Paul Robeson and his wife to tea at Lords. I didn't know what to expect. I wondered if he would be an embittered Red, but my doubts were dispelled in five seconds. I have never been more quickly attracted to a personality than I was to his. He is a giant of a man, towering above us all, and has a most mobile face and greying hair. He was immensely easy to talk to. You only had to mention a song of his (or of anyone else's) for him to begin singing very softly. It was just too tempting for us to go through the ones we liked best, and it was irresistible for him to sing them. I thought it might be embarrassing to have him singing in the Lords' Tea Room but he did it so naturally and so softly that it was only properly audible a few feet away. Beyond that it must have reverberated like some tube train passing deep beneath the building.

Afterwards I took him to the Commons Gallery for a moment and through the lobbies down to the Terrace. It was a journey of triumph. Everybody gathered round – MPs, police, visitors, waitresses from the Tea Room – for unlike most celebrities who make you want to stare, Paul Robeson made you want to shake him by the hand. Two negro women from Florida were almost ready to embrace him. A jet-black Nigerian was touched as if by a magic wand, and nearly split his face with a smile. You just couldn't help feeling that he was a friend of everyone there. He greeted people as if he knew them and those he really knew he remembered. There was no hint of embarrassment, whoever it was who came up. Herbert Morrison shook him by the hand on the way out and as we marched down St Stephen's Hall the crowds queueing for the

Strangers' Gallery stood and lined the route as if it were a triumphal march.

Thursday 17 July 1958
I did a very rare thing for me nowadays and went into the Smoking Room for a drink and a gossip for an hour and a half. Nye was there and Dick Crossman, Dingle Foot, Curly Mallalieu and Sir Tom O'Brien.

In the other corner was the Prime Minister sitting and gossiping with his cronies. At the table next to him was Winston, looking much as ever but a bit more shaky. It really is exciting to feel that one is in the middle of events and the Smoking Room after a great debate has an atmosphere that is very thrilling.

Sunday 20 July 1958
Party at Mrs Pandit's to meet Mrs Indira Gandhi. Nothing very exciting really, but she is such a gracious hostess and it is always fun to look in and see who is about.

Thursday 24 July 1958
The Speaker himself came to give evidence before the Procedure Committee this afternoon. It was really quite impressive. The isolation of his office and the wig and high position do make a Speaker into a demi-god. One really trembles before him – perhaps the only headmaster figure who continues into adult life. I was particularly nervous as a year ago I moved my motion of censure on him. He did not look at all pleased at the time.

What a very majestic figure he is. His jutting jaw, bushy black eyebrows and snowy white hair would stand out in any crowd. He has great height, good voice and a delightful sense of humour. Twice he had us contorted with laughter, particularly when he said that 'however little the lawyers know, they have an unlimited facility for uttering it'. For all this we were each of us struck by the way in which the Speaker has aged. He looked very frail and was obviously much worried by his deafness. Charlie Pannell remarked to me that a Labour Speaker would be a necessity as well as being overdue.

August 1958
Parliament rose on the 1st and we went off to Stansgate and stayed through till the end of the month. It rained most of the time and I caught mumps but otherwise it was a very pleasant change from politics.

Not that politics stayed still. In August several crises began to develop, and to occupy attention.

The Sino-American crisis over the offshore islands moved to flashpoint and threatened to bring a major conflagration.

The Iceland fishing dispute has moved into a new stage with the decision of the Iceland Government to arrest vessels that trespass inside its new unilateral 12-mile limit. The Admiralty sent the Navy in to protect our trawlers.

Race rioting in Nottingham and Notting Hill at the end of the month loomed suddenly and unexpectedly on the scene.

The Government's decision to impose the Foot plan on Cyprus against the wishes of the Greek community and the Greek Government moved the island one stage further towards a hopeless futile bloodbath.

And so back to London again on 30 August.

Monday 1 September 1958
For the second night running last night the race riots went on in Notting Hill. A very ugly situation is developing. I drove through the streets this evening and it was extremely sinister to see everyone standing out in front of their doors in the hot sultry air just waiting for something to happen. The crowds of young people gathering on street corners indicated the outbreak of some new attack.

Tuesday 2 September 1958
The trouble continued on an even bigger scale last night. I toured the area before breakfast and saw the debris and the corrugated iron up behind the windows of the prefabs where the coloured families live. The use of petrol bombs and iron bars and razors is appalling. There is a large area where it is not safe for people to be out. I saw Chief Inspector Simmonds at Notting Hill police station for a short talk. He is confident that the police can handle it.

This afternoon I toured the area again by car and even at 5 o'clock there was an ugly atmosphere and people hurried along the streets. The Labour Party really must say something about this.

Wednesday 3 September 1958
Saw Gaitskell this morning and we had two hours discussing Party political broadcasts. All the agreement we thought we had reached last July appears to have been forgotten and he was in a most obstructive mood. I think the Gallup poll which showed the rise in Macmillan's popularity and the Government's general recovery depressed him a bit.

I urged a Party broadcast on the race riots and that he should visit the area personally. He said he couldn't tour without Butler's permission and later said that he was advised that it was unsafe. I came away very dejected. What is wrong with the Party is that it is inactive. We ought to be offering a constructive daily alternative on a wide range of issues. We are just not doing it.

Saturday 6 September 1958
To Bristol for the Kingswood Community Association Horticultural Show and the St George E. garden party. Felt lousy and collapsed in bed on returning home.

Friday 12 September 1958
To Bristol to discuss Election arrangements and to the St George West Social evening in the Walter Baker Hall. There were some new young intelligent people there, but one must face the simple fact that 90 per cent of those who turn up at Party socials are women over sixty. I think this is partly a reflection of the changes of political thought and campaigning. But it is worrying.

Wednesday 17 September 1958
This evening to a film première. Heaven knows why we were asked, but we enjoyed gawking at the famous no end. Olivia de Havilland was there and we saw the Duke of Bedford and one or two others. Afterwards I got the Attlees a taxi. He looked so frail and old. As he threaded his way through the crowd people pointed at him and you could almost hear them saying, 'It can't be . . . yes, it is . . . well, I never.' He was touchingly grateful.

Tuesday 23 September 1958
Barbara Castle's statement about roughness by British troops in Cyprus is headline news. But Barbara's main contribution has been to bring back from Athens news that Makarios is willing to ban Enosis. This is staggering news that transforms the whole situation. Only the Vice-Chairman of the Party and a firm supporter of Cypriot freedom like Barbara could have got this interview and helped to shape this new policy.

But today she went to see Gaitskell (as well as Bevan, Griffiths and Callaghan). He saw fit to issue a statement afterwards in effect repudiating her. Without paying tribute to her diplomatic achievement with Makarios, he concentrated on the object of the press hunt (i.e. British troops) and thus encouraged it. I was so sick that the Leader should have repudiated a colleague who was in difficulty. It was such a poor demonstration of the Gallup poll mentality defeating ordinary instincts of personal loyalty and leadership. Whatever his faults, Macmillan has never allowed a colleague to be downtrodden without rising firmly in his support.

I conveyed this feeling of revulsion in no uncertain terms to Roy Jenkins when he happened to ring this evening. I have no doubt they will be conveyed upwards to Gaitskell.

Tuesday 30 September 1958
By train to Scarborough this morning for the Labour Party conference.
Everyone in the related fields of politics, journalism, television and
diplomacy are all in one place at one time. That's what makes
Conference such fun.

Wednesday 1 October 1958
Harold Wilson made an excellent speech today in the economics debate.
He is certainly Number 3 in the party and Jim Griffiths is fading quietly
into the background. Hugh Gaitskell also made a good speech, which
earned him a standing ovation. This is the second of three major speeches
he is making at Conference. Quite rightly, he is taking command of the
Party, consciously and deliberately.

Tribune meeting. It really was rather pathetic. I missed Donald Soper,
who apparently made a wonderful speech. Michael Foot was a pleasure
to listen to as a craftsman. He is a real master of the open air technique.
But the audience didn't take to him all that well. Nye, speaking last,
made one of the very worst speeches I have ever heard him make. It
rambled. It was self-contradictory. It was repetitive. It had neither
information, thought nor uplift. In fact it was like someone sitting down
at an organ and trying all the most stirring chords in turn, with no one
pumping to give them voice and no one in the choir to accompany them
with responses. I came away completely dejected and feeling he had
nothing to offer.

Thursday 2 October 1958
Nye Bevan opened the Foreign Affairs debate today with a speech as
good as last night's had been bad. He struck just the right note. It was
serious, helpful and with as much uplift as was reasonable in the
circumstances. The foreign policy statement is very good and Conference
received it well despite the renewed H bomb debate. I wasn't called,
which rather disappointed me. But that is the luck of the game.

Friday 17 October 1958
Drove to Bristol this afternoon loaded with equipment in preparation for
the Election. And it worked beautifully. The volume of the amplifier in
the wire recorder is quite adequate to activate our big loudspeaker horn.
So I can either use the mike or broadcast what is on the wire or play
gramophone records on the car. The only remaining test is to get a
synchronous motor vibrator so that the wire recorder can be operated by
a 12-volt battery. That achieved, I can do loudspeaker work all day
without losing my voice. Kenneth Younger with his guitar can record a
signature tune and our street meeting can include a message from
Gaitskell and my daily speech. Mrs Small suggests (while dictating this)

that Donald Swann and Michael Flanders might write a special signature tune for the campaign. It's a frightfully good idea.

Saturday 18 October 1958
Went to Barton House – the new 14-storey skyscraper of modern flats – this morning. A man from the Housing Department and Mr Solomon, the caretaker, took me round. It was a perfect autumn day with the sky blue and a shimmer of sunshine, on the whole of Bristol. We went right to the roof and visited various flats. To see the bright airy rooms with the superb view and to contrast them with the poky slum dwellings of Barton Hill below was to get all the reward one wants from politics. For this grand conception of planning is what it is all about. The people were happy, despite the grumbles about detail.

Dora Gaitskell arrived to open the Hanham Sale of Work in Bristol. She was very nervous but did a good job and was very well and warmly received. But for me the best part of the day was driving her home from Bristol to Hampstead. It took three and a half hours and we talked the whole time.

She is a most intelligent woman. She is Jewish and was actually born in Russia, coming to England when she was four. She is as sharp as a needle and altogether an extremely good influence on Hugh. She is 100 per cent loyal to him against all comers, which is as it should be. But she is also very critical of him in private and I know that's a good thing too. There are only a few people who can speak absolutely frankly to him. She is also an extremely perceptive woman and her comments about people are very much to the point. This is probably her greatest asset. You can't take her in and she forms very strong impressions, which I would think are usually correct.

We talked about people most of the time. About Clem and Vi, about Morgan Phillips and other Party figures. She detests Morgan but thinks he is very able and competent. She loves Sam Watson. She is very anti-Hartley Shawcross, who she felt had betrayed Hugh. About him and others she was very critical of what she termed their being 'too fond of money'. She said this about Frank Soskice with his work at the Bar and about Dick Crossman with his column on the *Mirror*. I think her motives were that she thought that any sincere socialist should devote himself 100 per cent to the work of the Party and should not combine it with other occupations, and that a simplicity of living conditions was an essential element of the leadership of the Labour Party. She took real pride in the fact that she has no help at home other than someone to do part of the cleaning. She cooks and washes up and does the housework herself. And whether it's the American Ambassador or Clem or anyone else who is coming to dinner, there is nothing fancy laid on. 'I'm a very good cook,' she said 'and they must all see us as we are.' I admired her greatly for this.

But when it came to the Royal Family and social distinctions I found her curiously insecure. She said how she had admired Hugh for his easy way with people (!) and how difficult she had found it to overcome her nerves. This was very human but it was coupled with a sort of feeling for the aristocracy as if it still had some meaning and as if she felt on the outside. It wasn't envy so much as quite inappropriate respect. This did really surprise me.

But the time passed most delightfully and rapidly and her anecdotes were amusing. She talked very frankly about her first husband who was a Communist psychiatrist. She said she thought my current *I Hear, I See* series was probably explained by telepathy, in which she took a great interest. And she touched my heart by saying how devoted she was to Caroline and admiring her for the way she ran the house and brought up four children without any fuss.

Monday 20 October 1958
I Hear, I See this afternoon, and it didn't go too well. I think I'm talking too much in the programme and will try to shut up more.

Wednesday 22 October 1958
This afternoon to the Grand Hotel Bristol for the Bristol Women's Annual Rally. I tried out the material from the new policy statement Dick had sent me. It went over well. Arthur Bottomley was the guest. The Chairwoman introduced him as 'one of the less well known Members of the Party – but not to be thought less of for that. He is on the Shadow Committee,' she said, 'or what we call a backbencher.' Arthur took it very well. He then described how he had overheard a woman leaving one of his meetings at Walthamstow last week saying to a friend, 'What we must get over is that Labour looks after you from your infancy right through to your adultery.'

Home at 7.

Monday 27 October 1958
Lunch with Gaitskell in a private room at St Ermin's to discuss his interview on TV tonight by Kenneth Harris. It was a most delightful meal, very relaxed and everyone in excellent spirits. We discussed Attlee and his control over the party when Prime Minister. Hugh described how he had said to Attlee that he thought it was a pity Dick Crossman had never been given a job. 'Not at all, not at all,' said Clem. 'I've known him all his life, and he's totally unreliable.' I think Dick is one of the few people Attlee really hated.

I had to go to do my ATV programme *I Hear, I See*, and then rush back to Lime Grove for the dinner preceding the broadcast.

Gaitskell was as quarrelsome as hell, just as Nye Bevan had been when we did his programme on 11 February. He and Dora (who have not got a TV) started a huge argument about something. Finally the storm passed and Hugh went up to have his make-up done. We took tremendous care to obliterate his double chin and remove the bags and even to shorten that long upper lip. It was quite a new thing, but I think it was right.

The programme itself went very oddly. Harris asked nearly twenty questions in 15 minutes and so the thing had pace and life. But he would get on to his hobby horse about trade unions running the Labour Party and this annoyed Hugh. He didn't show it in his answers, which were agreeably and well given. But he was angry afterwards. Even so it was a success because he came over as a nice man who hadn't been ruffled by that aggressive Kenneth Harris.

Wednesday 29 October 1958
To Dick Crossman's party. He has gathered round him a bright group of young people. Brian Abel-Smith and Peter Townsend of the LSE, Peter Shore and a lot of others. He could be the great intellectual centre of the Party in the years ahead. He is a brilliant exponent of the Party's case, both in speech and writing. He has immense imagination, terrific drive. He gets on well with Hugh and now is one of his principal advisers.

Thursday 6 November 1958
Phoned Dick Crossman. He is likely to be co-opted on to the Election Campaign Committee and will thus be in a key position. Between us the whole field of publicity will be under review. He is starting a new weekly lunch at his house on psychological warfare.

On my way home from the House there was a message to see Dick so I called at his house at 8 o'clock. It was a frantic three and a half hours deciding the slogans we should use in the commercial plug for the Party's pamphlet on 25 November. He was in his most bloody-minded mood and abused me up and down. I've seen this before and it doesn't affect me any more. It reduces some people to tears. If you argue back things get so tense the conversation has to stop, so I just sat and giggled quietly, which is really best.

Anne gave me a meal and I stayed until 11.30. We had by then pretty good slogans.

Friday 7 November 1958
Desperate last-minute effort before breakfast to get the title of the pamphlet changed from *What Labour Offers You* to *The Britain We Want*. Rang Dick at 8.45. He was very rude again but really agreed.

Wednesday 19 November 1958
At 10.30 to the House for the morning committee of the Election campaign.

The most important item that came up was the Gallup poll figures showing that of all British institutions the trade unions were the most unpopular: 26 per cent take an unfavourable view of them and 11 per cent a very unfavourable view. This I raised as a major problem for the Labour Party. To my surprise everyone agreed, including the trade unionists. Apparently the Trade Union Group are very concerned and are engaged in some sort of study of the question. In the end it was agreed that I should prepare a memorandum on the subject setting out very briefly how the public relations of the unions might be improved.

Took a party of schoolchildren round the House of Commons, which took nearly an hour and a half.

Thursday 20 November 1958

The porter at the hotel in Bristol forgot to wake me at 3.30. It was 12 minutes to 4 when he rang the phone. This left six minutes to dress and get to the station. I caught the train by 30 seconds, still wearing my pyjamas under my clothes and looking like an escaped criminal.

The results of the Elections to the Executive of the Fabian Society were published today. I have moved from third place last year to top of the poll 100 votes ahead of Roy Jenkins, Tony Crosland and Denis Healey. Heaven only knows why, since I have not been particularly active. But it's very gratifying.

Sunday 23 November 1958

To Gaitskell's house at 8.30 and was there till nearly midnight with Woodrow Wyatt working on his script. Finally in bed just before 2.

Monday 24 November 1958

Looking through the weekend press for the morning meeting I noticed that the trade unions were panned in every newspaper. It confirmed our talk of last week. Everyone agreed something had to be done. The best way forward is to tackle it at every level at the same time.

First, Hugh must try to get in touch with the union leaders and acquaint them of our concern. In fact I mentioned it to him last night and he said there ought to be a lunch with some of them at which the matter could be discussed. This could give an impetus from on high. Secondly, we must try to work through the Trade Union Group in the House of Commons who are very concerned about this. They have a special role here.

Tuesday 25 November 1958

I had a talk to Harold Wilson in the course of the evening and he hinted that possibly Sidney Jacobson might recommend me to fill the post of Director of Publicity which he thinks should be created. Of course, if it were offered to me (which is very unlikely) I would not take a penny for it, but I would want a room and proper assistance. It would be a tremendous challenge and I feel I could do it. In fact I am doing a lot of it now.

Tuesday 2 December 1958

Charlie Pannell told me today his delightful story of his visit to Anglesey to speak for Cledwyn Hughes. Throughout his speech he was much struck by an old man who sat there impassively with his head on his stick. Charlie said he couldn't keep his eyes off him, and after the meeting asked Cledwyn who he was. Cledwyn said he was an old, old man well over ninety who had been a friend of Lloyd George.

'Go and talk to him,' said Cledwyn. 'He'd be delighted.'

Charlie moved to the back of the hall and sat down beside the old man. 'Sir,' he said, for he couldn't address him in any other way, 'I understand you knew Lloyd George.' The old man raised his head slowly and spoke. 'Lloyd George,' he said, 'had a prick like a donkey.'

Charlie was taken aback. 'Ah, well,' he said. 'He was a man of many parts.'

'I know he was,' said the old man. 'And he'll be remembered more for that part than any other.' He gave a deep chuckle.

Thursday 4 December 1958

Dick told me that on Wednesday Hugh Cudlipp, Sidney Jacobson, Harold Wilson and Hugh Gaitskell had come to lunch with him. The *Mirror* boys had urged the need for proper co-ordination of information. But Hugh had simply nodded and chatted and gassed, without appearing to be aware of the urgency of it. As Dick said, he will neither assert himself and take firm decisions, nor will he delegate to others. Dick feels particularly strongly about this as he is the obvious candidate to be Director of Publicity, but feels they do not trust him. He also told me that nobody had ever thanked him for his work on the pamphlet. This is absolutely characteristic of the lack of imagination in high places.

Sunday 7 December 1958

The family called in at 40 Millbank (where I was born). The last time the children will probably ever be there. It really was sad to see it looking such a shambles before Mother and Father move to Great Peter Street (just round the corner.)

So Sunday really meant time off from 6.15 to bedtime.

Tuesday 9 December 1958

Collected Dick Crossman at his home this morning. He was sunk in deep despair about the future of the Labour Party and even the future of democracy. I have days like that too and his tummy trouble probably hadn't improved things. He said he wondered whether we were not just spectators at the funeral of democracy. But he then cheered up and said he thought Mr Khrushchev probably had the same problem in the Supreme Soviet. Most people in politics were, he thought, essentially third rate under any system of Government.

Thursday 11 December 1958
My usual morning coffee with Peter Shore. It's the best part of the day and he always stimulates my mind immensely. He is thinking of writing a book about modern mass society and it really stimulated me to do the same. If the information side of the Party is going to pot, I might just as well prepare myself by writing out how future policy should shape. I have never dared to think of writing a book before but all the themes in which I have an interest do marry up into quite a reasonable unity.

Wednesday 17 December 1958
The Fabian Executive Committee met at 5 and after the routine business we came to a paper written by Brian Abel-Smith. He was arguing that the Fabian Society had lost its zip as compared with the *Universities and Left Review*. They got five or six hundred to their meetings and we were completely missing young people. He therefore made a number of proposals. We should publish more controversial pamphlets. We should provide a platform for controversial speakers. We should redesign our literature. We should meet in a coffee house instead of in large bare halls. We should go all out for young people. We should have debates with *ULR*. It was a very sensible document.

Tony Crosland opened the attack. He said that he could see nothing of interest in the *ULR* except that 'there's a man who seems to be able to run a coffee house'. He thought that political activity under the age of thirty-five was not of great interest to the Fabians and, referring to the Labour pamphlet *The Future Labour Offers You*, he affected to forget its name whilst describing it as the worst thing he had ever seen produced by any Party. All this was said in a most bored and offensive way and was greeted with a titter of laughter.

A number of other people were asked to comment. I forget who they were, but they agreed with Tony to a greater or a lesser extent. Then I was called. I admit I was by now in a high temper and began by saying that if Tony's view was the Fabian view – then I certainly wasn't Fabian in any sense. But for the life of me I couldn't see how you could run any political organisation on the assumption that the political views of people under thirty-five didn't matter. And when Crosland was seventy were the views of those under sixty-five to lose their importance? 'Boredom seems to me to be unforgivable. But an affectation of boredom is quite incomprehensible and lunatic in a political organisation.' We should certainly stimulate controversial activities and take a lot more trouble about presentation. We were after all concerned with convincing people. And the question we had to face was whether we had anything relevant to say in the modern world.

After I had finished I felt I had gone much too far – and that this would finally rupture my relations with Crosland. But I later heard from Roy Jenkins that Crosland had admitted it was a most effective intervention that had blown him out of the water.

To a dinner where we met Jim and Audrey Callaghan. Jim and I drove to the House for the 10 o'clock vote. He said he wished the Party would take a strong moral line on Central Africa. I could not but be a bit cynical, remembering the Cyprus controversies of last summer and the repudiation of Barbara in September. I have hardly seen Jim in the last few months. I am afraid my relations with him are not what they were.

Friday 19 December 1958
It was announced that Kenneth Younger was giving up his Grimsby seat to go and run the Royal Institute for International Affairs. I rang him to say how sorry I was. He sounded a bit low. He told me of his interview with Gaitskell. Only as he left did Gaitskell say that he was sorry but supposed that Kenneth had already made up his mind. In fact the interview confirmed what Kenneth feared – that he did not have a future in high office under Gaitskell. It is very sad to lose him for despite his defects we have too few good people to be able to do without anyone of his calibre.

This evening there was a dinner in honour of Fenner Brockway. About 250 people from politics, journalism and public life turned up to hear the speeches and help him celebrate his seventieth birthday. Nye was a bit defensive. Michael Foot was very aggressive. Fenner was intolerably long-winded and showed all his strength and weakness in his speech. Jim Callaghan proposed the vote of thanks and Bob Boothby said a word. It had all been run by Leslie Hale, as usual. With messages from Nehru and Nkrumah and many others it was an historic occasion. In the future Fenner will be remembered as one of the greatest men of his time.

Tuesday 30 December 1958
At 8 o'clock this evening there was a dinner at the Charing Cross Hotel in a private suite for us to meet with Donald Baverstock and Cliff Michelmore of the BBC who had expressed readiness to give us their advice on the series of TV party politicals. On our side it was a very high-level affair: Gaitskell and Barbara Castle, Herbert Bowden and Morgan Phillips. Woodrow, Ken Peay, Chris Mayhew and I completed the party.

After coffee we talked for a couple of hours around the programme and

Baverstock said some extremely sensible and helpful things. He also expressed a readiness to undertake the production of the programmes during an Election if the BBC would release him. This is exactly what we want. Meanwhile he has agreed to join in private talks with us to hammer out the structure of the programmes so that we can really sort it out.

Michelmore agreed to train whoever was appointed as chairman. When asked for his opinion he said he thought the chairman should be me. Baverstock was not so sure that I was the right man. It will require a lot more thought.

Looking forward into the New Year, I think I should make some slight change in my own activities.

First I must keep up with activities in the chamber. It will help Bristol if I keep a lot of questions going and try to help them with unemployment. Secondly I enjoy it and have a contribution to make as a debater in attacking the Government and encouraging and helping our own people. Thirdly I am not as happy as I should be with the 'do-nothing' policy of our Front Bench.

My main job will be the television and radio. It is a gigantic responsibility that could decide hundreds of thousands of votes. It is clear I shall hardly get to Bristol at all in the Election and must make it up as much as I can. I am sure they will understand. This means cutting down still further on MCF, other committees and all speaking outside my own division. It also means fewer articles and broadcasts even if they are offered.

This policy will have to be reviewed again immediately after the Election. And that should come in March or May.

Tuesday 6 January 1959
Lunch with David Ennals, Head of the Overseas Department at Transport House. He is a very intelligent fellow and far better quality than we have any right to expect at the salary we pay. Apparently internal communications at Transport House are as bad as ever. There are no weekly staff meetings and Morgan has not summoned him in three months since he started.

Wednesday 7 January 1959
Felt very sick this evening but had to go to dinner with Audrey Callaghan in her new house in Blackheath. It really is modern and is very effective. Also there were Margaret, her daughter, now at Oxford, Peter Cox, son of Geoffrey of ITN, and Julia Gaitskell, who is the spit image of her mother.

Monday 19 January 1959
We had a very pleasant dinner party tonight with the Crossmans, the

Enoch Powells, David Butler and Dave. Dick was in a very mellow mood and everyone got on very well. Enoch is really very depressed. His resignation now looks to have been fatally ill-advised. He was urging an even tougher policy than the policy which has now led to unemployment, so he is in the wilderness of wildernesses as far as the Tories are concerned. And there is the added bitterness of the resignation on the eve of Macmillan's Commonwealth tour. He wonders how the future will shape for him. But I told him that I thought his sheer ability and lucidity would carry him upwards. As a working-class Tory he has the social barrier to overcome. He has not been offered any directorships since his resignation and he has taken a heavy fall in his standard of living. But he was as nice and friendly as ever.

Tuesday 20 January 1959
To the Campaign Committee to present the paper on Election Broadcasting. It was embarrassing to introduce as it included the recommendation that I should be chairman. But it was accepted without a murmur. Nye Bevan said he thought there ought to be a woman in the programme and suggested Michael Foot's wife, Jill Craigie, but he was quite well disposed towards the general idea. Now that is agreed, we are well away.

Herbert Bowden reported on the BBC Election plans. These are to put on two Party political discussions before an invited audience in each of the seven regions during the campaign. The Party headquarters would thus pick two candidates from each region for this purpose.

Several points arise. There is a danger of saturation; a problem of BBC-engineered squabbles; and a danger of sheer boredom through bad technique. We have the headache of picking our people. Nye asked me outright if we had trained any MPs or candidates. Morgan Phillips in his press conference had announced that we had. I had to say in his presence that we had not, which was rather embarrassing.

Wednesday 21 January 1959
Day largely devoted to christening Joshua. Pouring with rain and very chilly, but the service went off all right and we had a riotous tea party. Hilary said thank you very loudly after Canon McLeod Campbell had pronounced the Benediction; Melissa pointed and said, 'You' and 'Baby' several times during the service. Hilary also asked the battery of photographers, 'Can't you click your cameras together? I can't smile for each of you separately.'

Saturday 24 January 1959
Went to visit Bedminster Down Comprehensive School and was shown over by the headmaster, Mr Simmons. It certainly is superbly situated,

designed, built, equipped and decorated. In sixteen acres of grounds, it has all the facilities for grammar school standard education plus scientific, engineering and other equipment. There is even a swimming bath. The headmaster was as proud as punch and spoke with boundless enthusiasm about the benefits of this type of education. I was very impressed.

Thursday 5 February 1959
Long and bitter discussion in the Smoking Room with Dick Crossman, George Wigg and Ungoed-Thomas about Wilfred Fienburgh's novel *No Love for Johnny*. Kenneth Robinson had told me earlier in the afternoon that Wilfred told him, at the Brighton Conference in 1957, that Johnny Byrne (the hero) was an amalgam of the worst characteristics of himself (Fienburgh), Desmond Donnelly and Jim Callaghan.

The novel gives a totally cynical view of Labour politics and has stirred colossal controversy in the Party. Dick Crossman regarded it as a piece of pure betrayal, and George Wigg – as one would expect – described it as an epitaph not only on social democracy but on the parliamentary system.

Tuesday 10 February 1959
Usual morning meeting of the Election campaign committee with nothing much to record.

Lunch with Boris Krylov, a Reader in Law at Moscow University who is in Britain. He had written to suggest a meeting, and I invited him for a meal. His first remark as we met was, 'I have been reading *No Love for Johnny* and it seems as if it is your *Dr Zhivago*' – which may very well be so. I showed him the House of Lords, and we had a long and delightful talk. He knows a great deal about the British Parliament and his visit here is to collect information for a book.

Wednesday 18 February 1959
David Ennals sent me the note on youth organisation in the Party. I dictated a memo suggesting it be renamed 'The Activists', and that some literature be produced of a controversial nature. Their main work should be canvassing young voters and trying to build a working organisation. But this was too revolutionary. I doubt if anything will come of it all.

Worked late into the night on Oxford Union speech and reading Khrushchev's seven-hour speech to the Communist Party Congress; all in preparation for the trip with Krylov tomorrow to Oxford.

Friday 20 February 1959
Spent the day in Bristol with Boris. We had a long talk. He was astonished by the following things:

our press – which was terrible and made no attempt to give the facts
accurately;

our courts – which were harsh and distant in their treatment of the
criminal; except for the juvenile courts, which he liked;

the fear of retirement among old people, for whom it meant a drop in
living standards.

On balance he said that his Communism had been strengthened by what
he had seen in England. The capitalist ethic appalled him and the
absence of a uniting sense of purpose was very noticeable. But he told me
what his father had said to him before he came to England.

'When you come to the West,' he had said, 'you must not be
disappointed. Do not make up your mind against it too soon. There is
much good there.' It was rather a remarkable statement as it was guiding
him against the error of being too critical – rather than the other way
round. The father, of course, was an old-stager. Young Boris is a very
skilled Marxist philosopher.

Boris said he had been pleased to find so little cynicism in England. He
was really surprised to find that people were so keen and believed in what
they were doing. The rottenness in our society has obviously been much
overplayed in Russia.

Secondly, he was very interested in the idea of Parliament as a safety
valve. He even wrote this down. In the light of our later discussions on
Hungary I could see why.

Thirdly, he was pleased to see so much good in England in the way of
rebuilding and the development of good things in our society. 'I am
happy that there are good schools like this one,' he said as he left one in
Bristol in the afternoon.

In Bristol we also paid a visit to the Party HQ and then I took him on a
very rushed tour. First to the worst slums. I insisted that he take some
pictures of them with his movie camera. He was a bit surprised. We also
visited an old smoky school with overcrowded classes and no proper
playground. Then I showed him the prefabs, the horrible, dull red brick
pre-war council houses, and finally the new housing.

I took him to Barton House, the 16-storey block of flats in the centre of
the Barton Hill redevelopment. We went to the roof and then knocked on
a flat door and were shown round by a railwayman and his wife. It was
lovely and they were very happy.

Then we went out to Hartcliffe estate – a 50,000-people new suburb. It
really is a lovely place, well laid out and planned with different types of
houses and the finest school I have ever seen anywhere in the world. I
spotted it in the distance, not knowing what it was. But we walked in the
front door bravely and asked if we could look round. It was Withywood
Comprehensive School and the headmaster insisted on taking us on a
tour. We started by going up in the lift to the top and walked down and

through the beautifully equipped laboratories and classrooms. The school has enormous playing fields, two gymnasia and lovely design in aluminium and glass. It really knocked Boris sideways.

Saturday 21 February 1959
Up early and we set off for London via Bath at about 9 o'clock. A broken fan belt delayed us in Reading so we had five more hours of political discussion. This time we got on to Hungary and the real reason for the Soviet intervention came out quite clearly.

Boris began by asserting that it was the Americans who had caused the Hungarian uprising. He admitted that there was a lot of gunpowder about in Hungary. Then he said, after a discussion, 'We could never permit a hostile Government again in Hungary.' That I think was the honest reason for the intervention. And it is much better than pretending that Kadar now enjoys the support of the people. I asked Boris whether he thought he did. He didn't reply, except to say that things were quite different in the Soviet Union. I am sure he is right.

Yesterday at the Co-op clothing factory, which we visited on the way back from the school, he met a number of Poles – the remains of General Anders' Army. They were all very friendly to him and he expressed great sadness that they should have been driven out.

We also had a word about Israel. He thought Zionism the most reactionary creed in the world, being based upon national superiority. He could not believe that there was any good in Israel.

Wednesday 25 February 1959
Taieb Slim, the Tunisian Ambassador, rang up to invite me to go with him to the Independence celebrations on 20 March. This I think I will do.

Saturday 28 February 1959
Home by mid-morning and spring has really arrived. Joshua sat up in his cot unaided at 4.30 am and played happily. The whole family to Holland Park and Father arrived by bus to visit us. All these are irrefutable signs that winter is over.

Tuesday 3 March 1959
Stonehouse was arrested this morning in Nyasaland and put on a plane for Dar es Salaam.[4] Decided to raise it as a matter of privilege.

Wednesday 4 March 1959
The Stonehouse debate was absolutely brilliant. Jim Callaghan opened in superb form with exactly the right tone and power. Dingle Foot followed and Barbara Castle also spoke. Lynn Ungoed-Thomas wound

up for us. It was a moral, political and intellectual victory for us. The Party is magnificent on this issue. Gaitskell deserves special credit.

Monday 9 March 1959

Worked all day at home. It is such a struggle keeping ahead of Mrs Small, who types like a machine-gunner. It takes me at least five hours to prepare material for her and about two more to sign and clear up. But it was very good to do those jobs that get forgotten.

Wednesday 11 March 1959

At home all day and must have made 25 to 30 phone calls in quick succession, on lining up people for our Election testimonial films. I rang Bertrand Russell in North Wales, but he wouldn't do it. 'I'm rather dissatisfied with the Party over this nuclear business,' he said. 'I don't think I can do anything to support it.' I reminded him of the developing African crisis and the Party's role. 'Yes, yes, well, well, I know,' he said rather more sympathetically. 'Even so, I think I won't.' Compton Mackenzie, on the other hand, was far more jovial. 'Well, dear boy,' he said. 'The Tories are simply terrible and they have been the same all my life. But you know I'm mixed up with the Nationalists up here and there'd be an awful stink if I came out for the Labour Party – though, of course, I admire your line on these things.' He paused. 'No – damn it – I will do it. After Cyprus and now Malta and Central Africa, I must do it. But I don't guarantee what I'll say.' I jumped in and arranged to fly to Edinburgh the week after next with a film unit to get him to do it before he changed his mind.

Thursday 12 March 1959

To Transport House this morning for two more testimonial filmlets from writers. C.R. Hewitt (C.H. Rolph of the *New Statesman*) was the first, and Ritchie Calder. It is a lot easier doing it in the studio but what a slow business. Two hours' hard work for one minute of material. And the cost, probably £60.

Friday 13 March 1959

To Swindon for BBC *Any Questions* at the Vickers Armstrong works. Gerald Nabarro, Ralph Wightman and Jacqueline Mackenzie were on the team. Nabarro is a very decent chap and we agreed that if Parliament was to be made effective proper facilities had to be put at the disposal of MPs. The present amateur set-up is quite hopeless. Jacqueline Mackenzie was rather nicer than I had expected. Like so many young people, she was fed up to the teeth with the sedate stick-in-the-mud pace of British life. She would really like to emigrate, I think. All this gets me down – partly because I'm sure it's true.

Sunday 15 March 1959
Did ATV's *Free Speech* with Boothby, Foot and Brown. The usual decadent table talk from which only one interesting fact emerged: according to Boothby, five members of the Cabinet were under the care of psychiatrists during the Suez crisis.

Wednesday 25 March 1959
Flew up to Edinburgh today to make the film with Sir Compton Mackenzie at his house. We only wanted 25 seconds of him saying why he supports the Labour Party.

I arrived at 31 Drummond Place at 2.15. Sir Compton was still dressing, and he appeared in a few minutes in a bright blue tweed suit looking twice as large as life. He remembered having met me before, and beckoned me into his room where he kept me talking until 4 o'clock when the film unit was ready.

The unit – the Elder Film Corporation – was headed by Mr Elder, the Managing Director (and also the cameraman); his wife did continuity, and other members of the family handled the lights and sound. They were tremendously excited to be working with Sir Compton, and all crowded round and shook his hand. He of course was completely composed, and gave a superb dramatic performance. This is what he said for our film:

'I have never voted Tory in my life, but I shall vote against them with greater zest now than ever. They never learn from experience. And as I approach advancing old age I feel less inclined than ever to entrust my future to such a lot of boneheads.'

This was delivered so amusingly that the film crew began laughing and ruined the take. So we did it again. Afterwards we all shook hands again, and they took photographs, got autographs, and hurried away.

Sir Compton took me round his house and showed me a huge empty room being redecorated in the basement. 'I am opening a Ladies' Hairdressing Saloon,' he said. I thought he was joking. But he wasn't. His secretary has a sister who is a hairdresser, and he said he thought it would be a nice idea if she could practise. He seemed much amused too.

I knew he was a busy man, and kept trying to get away, but he insisted on my staying, and regaled me with stories and anecdotes until 7.30, when I had to catch my plane home.

It was a most amusing day. For him it was the beginning. He gets up after lunch, dresses, and starts work after tea at 4 o'clock. He works from then till 7, when he has dinner. He watches TV from 8 to 10, and works again from 10 to 2 am. He then goes to bed, reads and does crossword puzzles until 4 am, when he goes to sleep.

He was full of anecdotes.

For all sorts of reasons Macmillan has disliked Bob Boothby. One of them was Bob's great popular success as contrasted with Macmillan's more diffident manner. 'You see, it wasn't until he had that successful TV interview with Ed Murrow last summer that he felt he had caught up with Bob. A few weeks later he gave him a life peerage.'

'At last I've discovered the real reason why the Beaver [Beaverbrook] hates Dickie Mountbatten. Dickie was the adviser to Noel Coward in the film *In Which We Serve* and in one of the opening sequences it showed the sailors trooping aboard the destroyer. The camera tilted downwards as they crossed the gangplank to show a copy of the *Daily Express* floating in the dock. It had a banner headline: NO WAR THIS YEAR.'

'The Beaver is the devil himself, and I tried to persuade Malcolm Muggeridge to sue him for libel for his tendentious extracts from his article on the Queen. I told the Duke of Edinburgh that I would just love to get the Beaver in the box, and he was simply delighted with the idea. But Malcolm wouldn't do it. And knowing English judges, he may have been right.'

'You know what Winston calls the Foreign Secretary, don't you – cellu-loid.'

There were also some particularly scandalous stories about other people. Some of them were not new, but with his wagging goatee beard, twinkling eyes, his expressive hands and his deep chuckle, everything acquired a special quality of their own.

Finally I left him and flew home to London in an hour and a half.

Monday 30 March 1959
Took the boys to watch the Aldermaston marchers as they came in. They were 1,500 strong at Trafalgar Square, and had Frank Cousins amongst them. This movement is a force to be reckoned with.

A representative of the White Defence League was there with some Fascist propaganda. Mosley is standing in North Kensington constituency at the next election.

Wednesday 15 April 1959
Filming again this morning and afternoon. We concentrated on education and visited a new primary school and also Bedminster Down Comprehensive. The headmaster was absolutely delightful and showed us round so that we could film anything we wanted.

Finally home by 6.30. We have completed it all except for some studio work which will be done next week.

At a quarter to eleven this evening David Butler and I (dressed in boiled shirts and tails) and Caroline went off to the American Ambassador's house for a dance. There must have been 300 people there and it was every bit as much fun as we had hoped. The only other Labour people there were the Gaitskells, the Soskices, the Gordon-Walkers, the Youngers and the Healeys. I guess I was asked because of my lectures to the American wives on the British constitution.

There were quite a number of Tory MPs there. Rab Butler, Maudling, Boyle, Christopher Soames and so on – fifteen in all. There were no journalists, no showpeople (except Joyce Grenfell) and a lot of rather undistinguished people of middle age. I would have been really puzzled if Susan Soskice hadn't recognised a Duke and three Duchesses. It was London society mixed with racing people – which constitutes the Whitneys' private group of friends.

He, of course, is a multi-millionaire, and his pictures on the wall must have been worth many hundreds of thousands of pounds. He also owns the *New York Herald Tribune* and no doubt a lot of railways as well.

It was all very decadent and passé. Somehow to see gathered together such a lot of non-producers of anything was slightly revolting. One wondered how a society led by these sort of people could possibly withstand the thrust and dynamism of the Chinese communes working away so feverishly and seriously on the other side of the world. Look at it how you like, the triviality and irrelevance of private ownership is really going to condemn it to obsolescence.

This is not to say we didn't have a whale of a time. We did. We danced till nearly 3 and sat and gossiped and chatted and commented on everyone who went by. It was the brightest and best party we'd been to in years. Bed 3.30.

Monday 20 April 1959
To Broadcasting House this afternoon to pick the music for our Election programmes. We chose a phrase from Holst's 'Jupiter, the bringer of jollity'. It is strong and powerful, and conveys exactly what we want.

At 7.45 pm Alasdair Milne came to discuss our Election series. He is running *Tonight* and struck us as being extremely competent. Ken Peay was there. Among his useful suggestions were a filmed sequence for Vicky cartoons. He also thought a magnetic board for announcing big meetings, with a girl to control it, would be a good idea.

Saturday 25 April 1959
To Bristol again this afternoon to speak at the Annual Dinner of the Boot and Shoe Trade Managers' and Foremen's Association. It was the first time I had ever made an after-dinner speech in Bristol.

Tuesday 28 April 1959
Sent out letters to the group of people who might possibly become sponsors of the 'Algeria Committee' that I am forming. It is really to please the Algerians as much as anything, but I think it is a useful job of work.

Caroline and I went to lunch with the Crossmans. The only other guests were Hugh and Dora Gaitskell. Dora is, of course, a very easy person to get on with. She's bright and sharp and amusing and we all like her. Hugh can be very crabby. But in fact he was extremely relaxed and friendly.

We discussed all sorts of things at lunch – all revolving round politics. Desmond Donnelly's name came up and Dora was very contemptuous. 'You didn't get people like that in the Labour Party before the war,' said Hugh, 'but I suppose that when you win a majority it is inevitable that people like that turn up.' It was much more perceptive than I would have expected from Hugh. We also discussed Randolph Churchill; the Royal Family; and the sort of people that gather round the Leader of the Labour Party. Dora complained that she was left alone a lot and said, 'The only people who ever take me out are rich homosexuals.'

Sunday 3 May 1959
Didn't go to the May Day parade in Bristol. I've worked clean through the last four weekends, and ten hours away from home just to sit on the platform with Barbara Castle was, frankly, not worth it. There just comes a time when the claims of the family must have priority.

As it was, we had a gigantic clear-out of the house. Complete ruthlessness descended upon us and we went through cupboards and drawers and files, bunging out old papers and toys and candle ends and linoleum and wallpaper until we had accumulated such a tremendous dump that we may have a special estimate made for it to be removed. It somehow makes you feel a lot better.

Monday 4 May 1959
To the Commons this afternoon for the first meeting of the committee set up by the Fabian Society to consider the publication of controversial pamphlets. I was moved into the Chair and we had a very useful meeting. Roy Jenkins, Tony Crosland, Brian Abel-Smith and others were there. There was a general agreement on the need for this series. We drew up a list of possible subjects. Perhaps the most interesting were those which dealt with the labour movement. We agreed we ought to look into the question of a Labour Youth Movement, liberty in the Labour Party, the LCC machine, the relations between the trade unions and the public, the constitution and working of the Labour Party and Transport House. All these things have got to be faced after the Election, and if the Fabian Society really does face them, it will be doing a most valuable job.

We also decided on titles dealing with the welfare state, the exportability of the parliamentary system, ugly Britain, the future of TV, the H bomb, the coming crisis in Africa and Britain without an Empire. It was very very stimulating.

Monday 11 May 1959
To Liaison Committee this morning. We agreed that it was time to do some serious stock-taking. The Party's standing is very low and the loss of 292 seats in the municipal Elections is not a satisfactory conclusion to the 'Into Action' campaign.

We must also face the fact that attendance at the House of Commons has now fallen off drastically. People turn up for a big vote but otherwise not at all. And they just don't sit in the chamber, even for important debates. One begins to wonder whether the national apathy isn't spreading to Parliament. This malaise hangs over British politics and is quite incompatible with our assertion that we are on the eve of a great victory.

Tuesday 12 May 1959
To the Campaign Committee for an hour and a quarter.

The simple fact is that they had not thought out tactics for the next months at all and were just muddling through without proper documentation or briefing. There was no co-ordinated plan of any kind and everyone was junking in with their own schemes. Gaitskell wanted to make pensions the big issue; Barbara Castle thought we needed more fire. Nye Bevan wanted leaflets and public meetings. Harold Wilson thought we ought to be more anti-American. It was all very unfortunate.

Friday 15 May 1959
I had just mowed the lawn and was dripping with sweat in a dirty shirt, with Melissa and Joshua to look after and the lunch to watch while Caroline was collecting the boys from school, when the front doorbell rang. It was two Chinese who had called to visit 'Sir Wedgwood Benn'. One was a Mr Chi Kuo, an MP from Formosa, and the other Mr Chen, the Director of the Free China Information Service. They had been put on to me by some American friend.

Lissy screamed, Joshua bounced, the lunch burnt while they drank sherry and I tried to converse. They left after ten minutes still doubting whether they had met the real Sir Wedgwood.

In May 1959, Caroline and I took up an invitation to visit Tunisia, to celebrate the promulgation of the Tunisian constitution. While there I had a talk with President Habib Bourguiba plus African leaders who were in Tunisia for a Pan-African Congress.

At that time the situation was very tense with the colonial war in Algeria continuing and Tunisia finding itself drawn in. Algerian soldiers of the FLN were based inside Tunisia and relations between Tunisia and France were affected, with France bombing Tunisian towns.

Britain and the USA were reluctant to interfere in a part of the world that was

regarded as being within the French sphere of influence, indeed were secretly
supporting the French Government.

Wednesday 27 May 1959

All the domestic arrangements for our departure were completed this morning. Thre is someone coming in to cook and look after the children. So we could leave with a clear conscience.

We flew first to Paris, changed at Orly and then down to Marseilles and over to Tunis. All air terminals are wildly exciting. This was the first time we have heard 'Aeroflot announce the departure of their flight AE 106 to Moscow.' The Iron Curtain is getting a heavy hammering from all directions.

It grew dusk as we flew over the Mediterranean and the deep green of the sea below merged with the grey mist on the horizon into the azure, gold and red of the sunset. Beneath were the twinkling lights of Bizerta and, beyond, Tunis itself.

We were met by Abdellaziz Meheri, the Chef de Protocol at the Foreign Office, got VIP treatment and were driven to the Tunisia Palace Hotel. Bed, very tired, after a short walk.

Thursday 28 May 1959

Breakfast at 7 o'clock and Taieb Slim phoned to say that Bourguiba would receive us at 11. Walked about a bit and then by car to the Presidential Palace. The guards in their light blue uniforms and sub-machine guns saluted us as we went in and up the splendid staircase to the Presidential suite where the Chef de Protocol was waiting. Superb ceramic tiling was everywhere.

At 12 we were ushered in to see Bourguiba and we were with him for just over half an hour. His office is large and spacious but simply furnished. Behind his desk was the red silk Tunisian flag and a map of Tunisia was on the wall. He was dressed in a light grey tropical suit, which was a little too big for him. He came forward and shook us warmly by the hand as Taieb introduced me as 'the son of Lord Stansgate, a great friend of the African Peoples, and his wife who is a journalist.' Bourguiba has a magnetic smile and tremendous animation. He said he remembered Father in Cairo as a great friend of the Egyptians at the time of the negotiations. 'He was very important and I was an exile looking at him from afar.'

Our conversation was conducted entirely in French, which I speak very badly. However, it did make it more direct and doubled the time which was available.

He is an absolutely fascinating man. All his life he has dedicated himself to the Tunisian cause and has suffered terribly as a result. He has regularly been imprisoned by the French and was about to be shot by them in 1940 when the Germans reached the prison where he was held. That morning he saw his coffin coming into the prison, yet even this did not stir him to collaboration with the Nazis. He is really pro-French and exercises a very restraining influence on his Party on this question. He is certainly a man of the people who moves about freely mixing with them.

The routine he has imposed on himself is remarkable. He goes to bed at 10 o'clock every night and gets up at 3 to work for several hours before breakfast – often sleeping again before he goes to the office at 9. From about 11 when his routine work is finished he sees people all day. He rules Tunisia with his voice, preferring the spoken word to any other. Every Thursday he broadcasts for an hour, reporting to the people what he is doing and why and commenting on world affairs generally. These broadcasts are the main instrument of the political education in the country and are not demagogic but informative. He uses a mixture of classical and colloquial Arab which is understood by everyone. He talks quite freely and there are no diplomatic secrets in Tunisia. He tells everybody everything.

There is a cult of the individual in Tunisia, but it is genuine public affection. We saw the crowds clapping him and heard the things they said. Probably the most comparable leader is David Ben-Gurion in Israel. The people regard both men with affection, amusement and respect.

We were driven by car sixty miles to Hamamet where a lunch had been laid on for the delegates to the Pan African Conference. There was a Palestinian Arab refugee who appealed to their delegates to remember the plight of him and his people, who have no home and live in tents, waiting.

Talking to Joe Murumbi, Nkomo and other African delegates I got the feeling that they had no confidence in the Labour Party whatsoever and were in a much tougher mood than ever before. They feel that they have been betrayed by the Europeans and must fight for their own freedom. I certainly intend to see that these top men get access to British opinion. It is vital.

At the same time their personal relations with me were very good and it is invaluable to me to be here during their Conference.

Friday 29 May 1959
We visited Angus Malcolm, the British Ambassador; Eton and New College, had a little moustache, a floppy bow-tie, light grey tropical suit and co-respondent shoes. He was terribly chi-chi and had I been the chief gossip writer for the *Tatler* he would undoubtedly have been the best contact anywhere in Tunis.

Tom Mboya and James Miumie from Kenya arrived today and Kanyama Chiume from Nyasaland also appeared. We all dined at the Strasbourg Hotel and Tom Mboya and I had a great argument.

He was saying how careful an African had to be in England not to be wooed away from his basic beliefs. They do not trust the Labour Party and stress that things are moving much more quickly than we realise. Mboya said, 'We have put up with enough injustice and we will not put up with it any more. We are not children to be given freedom when they think we are ready.' I said I thought they were winning and Mboya replied, 'We had a foot on our heads. Now it is in our backs. Do you call that winning?'

After supper Caroline went to bed. I walked to the Bourse but the Conference had adjourned. There were festivities in the streets with flaming torches and bands in anticipation of tomorrow's promulgation of the constitution.

I sat about in the hotel until about 11.30 waiting for Tom Mboya. The Conference ended this evening, but when he arrived he said he was too busy for a talk, but I hung about and caught him as he was going out to a night club. I told him that the Fabians wanted him to write a pamphlet on the Pan-African Movement. I also conveyed Nye Bevan's greetings. He arranged to see me in London this coming Saturday.

From 12 to 1.30 talking to Gavin Young of the *Observer*. He thought the Egyptians were tiring of the Algerian campaign. At 1.15 a man rushed into the lounge with a copy of the constitution for each of us. It was the beginning of a great day.

Monday 1 June 1959

To the National Assembly at Bardo this morning for the promulgation of the new constitution. The streets were lined with people, and the route was guarded by the Youth movement wearing red track suits. The steps of the Assembly were flanked by the magnificent Spahis with drawn scimitars, which they clanked from a salute down on to their scabbards. The scene was one of tremendous brightness and excitement. We sat in the front row of the Gallery beside the Ambassadors. Below us were the press in a box, and the MPs. The British Ambassador came in with his white topee and a spike, for all the world like someone playing the role of the British Ambassador in an Ealing Comedy film.

The curtains on the stage drew back to reveal steps, up which came Bourguiba and the President of the Assembly. Bourguiba was dressed in tails, with a broad ribbon and what looked like a mayoral chain. He was lauded in an introductory speech, then took the rostrum. As he did so, a servant brought him a tray of tea and he sipped tea throughout his two-hour speech in Arabic.

He is a wonderful orator, gesticulating and electrifying his audience. But the hot room, the unending Arabic and the loud snores of the German commercial delegation sitting beside me, all produced a nightmare effect. I dozed and woke, and dozed again, until the Arabic translated itself into hilariously comic English sentences, and then back again into gibberish.

At last it was over, and a very dramatic day it had been for Tunisia. Their nationalist movement was created to achieve a constitution and independence: today their victory was complete. I believe Bourguiba's speech was in fact a history of constitutional development in many countries, and was really worth listening to.

After the ceremony we were received by Bourguiba again, and drove back to the hotel. Cecil Hourani, Bourgiba's Adviser, collected us and drove us back to his house at Carthage, where we had lunch.

To the Presidential dinner at the Beylical Palace at Lamasa tonight: 350 people were entertained at this banquet. Crowds lined the streets again, holding lighted torches, and we drove under the triumphal arches that had been built. The splendid military guards were there again, and in the central hall of the Palace was a glittering array of brilliance: the Diplomatic Corps and their wives, and hosts of others.

We were seated at the President of the Assembly's table. I was between the French Minister, M. Jean Pierre Benard, and the wife of the American Minister, Mrs Stratton McKillop.

Mrs McKillop had the usual gripes about the servants and primitive Tunisian ways. She was critical of the regime, and said that many opponents of it were in jail. But on the FLN she was much more forthcoming. They see the Yazids socially, and are not under the ban imposed by the British.

Mr Benard was much more political in his comments. On the question of contacts he denied the French embassy had any in Tunis. De Gaulle's policy was for the FLN to give up, and for elections to be held which would throw up leaders with whom de Gaulle would work. I asked if these elected leaders could demand independence. Benard shrugged, and said he hoped the *colons* would permit a solution. De Gaulle will not meet the rebel Government, nor did he think that a Bourguibist solution was practicable, if independence were expected to come out of it.

He was a very intelligent man to talk to, and I felt awfully sorry for him. France has been defeated so many times in the last ninety years. He was infinitely more realistic than the British, and somehow the absurdity of his case made it seem unkind to press him.

Monday 22 June 1959
At 3.30 to the FO to see Profumo, the Minister of State; I delivered my report on Tunisia. He was interested, having served there in the war. He agreed Tunisia was important and said money for cultural work would be made available. He also promised £13,000 for the refugees and would like to do more.

He thought the Pan-African movement was important and hinted that Yazid might be able to come if I asked him in the autumn.

Saturday 27 June 1959

To Bristol for the most dejected, depressing, inadequate, badly run, deadbeat sale of work that I have ever attended. If that is the Labour Party's image, then something is wrong.

Monday 29 June 1959

Cocktail party this evening at Transport House for all those who have worked and are helping and might help us in TV. They all appreciated the invitation very much and it was certainly the nicest thing Transport House had done for a very long time.

Caroline and I had dinner with Dick and Anne Crossman, as well as Megan Lloyd George and Stefan Arski from Poland.

Monday 7 September 1959

Filming all morning, this evening to Lime Grove to see *Tonight* go out. It was interesting.

Prime Minister has left for Balmoral. Announcement expected any day.

Tuesday 8 September 1959

Editing film all morning at Transport House. We just don't know how the chain of command is to work out. We are determined to insulate ourselves from interference by the General Secretary Morgan Phillips.

Polling Day October 8th is announced. Tea with Peter Shore; both very pessimistic about outcome. His chances in Halifax are slightly better than average.

Rush of work begins in earnest.

Wednesday 9 September 1959

John Osborne the playwright came in to do a 'testimonial' film. The production unit (Mayhew, Woodrow Wyatt, Alasdair Milne and myself) is now meeting regularly to review progress. Our current headache is: who will be in charge at Transport House during the Election? Will it be Dick Crossman? And, if so, will he interfere with us? We feel we must write orders for ourselves to safeguard ourselves.

Thursday 10 September 1959

Worked on my Election address for Bristol. It incorporates one important phrase:

'But this does not and can never mean that I, as an MP, surrender my independent judgement and freedom of action to you, to the Labour Party, or to anyone else. If you elect me again, I shall go on trying to do what I think is right, whatever the consequences may be. If I were to do anything else I would be betraying the personal responsibility which a man assumes when he offers himself for Election to Parliament.'

Sunday 13 September 1959
Russian rocket hits the moon. Socialist economies are certainly overtaking capitalist ones now.

Monday 14 September 1959
Mrs Small hard at it all day.

David Butler predicts a heavy Tory victory.

Rang Dick Crossman this evening and he told me that he definitely is going to be in charge during the campaign. He got extremely unpleasant and said that he would look at our plans in due course and 'if you can make out a case for a magazine format for Election broadcasts, you'll find me very reasonable'. Of course this is no damn good. We have been working for eighteen months on the magazine format and he has not got the power to change it. I explained this and he became increasingly peremptory and wouldn't let me finish a sentence. So I lost my temper and said 'Shut up' several times and we had a flaming row. I think in the end I rang off.

Tuesday 15 September 1959
At 10 o'clock I phoned Hugh Gaitskell to appeal for his help against Dick. I said that he was behaving in an impossible way and he couldn't have the technique reopened at such a late date. I said the question was did he really want our scheme or not, because it hung together.

Hugh said 'Of course we want your scheme but you must not build yourselves up.' He then went on to ask why I had been away for two months, and that I had made things very difficult for him. He was extremely crabby, but I hit back and said that I had worked like a black on programmes for a year and I was very sorry a long-arranged trip to America had had to take place. If he didn't like my work, he could appoint someone else. Hugh said, 'Don't be silly' and calmed down a bit.

He then told me the MPs that we were to build up – Nye, Harold Wilson, Jim Callaghan, Jim Griffiths, Dick Crossman and George Brown. They are the inner circle. 'Don't worry about the second eleven, but go straight on to the younger people – the up-and-coming generation – Crosland, Jenkins, Healey, and you can include yourself in that category.'

So the phone call ended in quite a friendly way.

Caroline's advice was, as always, the most sensible: 'The most important thing is that you should be seen to be an easy man to work with.' This was prompted by Hugh having described Dick and me as a couple of prima donnas.

Thursday 17 September 1959

Worked at home and at 2.15 went to a showing of all our Election material for Hugh, Dick, Tom Driberg and David Ennals. It lasted for three hours and most of it was approved. I had to fight to keep Donald Soper in. Woodrow's pieces on Suez and his build-up for Gaitskell were totally unusable because they consisted of 95 per cent Woodrow. Rather sad. Chris Mayhew, on the other hand, won full marks for his comprehensive schools piece.

Sunday 20 September 1959

To Lime Grove from 2 to 8 for the first rehearsal of *Britain Belongs to You*. The set is superb and Alasdair was able to knock us into shape. Tom Driberg is our resident political commissar and fairly easy to deal with. I was rather wooden and stilted. Just could not go to sleep for worrying over tomorrow's live 'Opening Night'. So I took some aspirin.

Monday 21 September 1959

To Lime Grove after lunch and rehearsing all afternoon. Cliff Michelmore looked in to watch over us. Gaitskell and Crossman arrived to take part. So the first edition of *Britain Belongs to You* went on the air.

Tuesday 22 September 1959

Woke about 4.30 and couldn't get to sleep – a sort of reaction. The press reports on the programme are really rave notices and we have scored a tremendous advantage. The Tory ones were so dull and dated.

Left by car for Bristol before breakfast and drove like a madman to be there for a lunchtime factory gate meeting at Strachan and Henshaw.

Canvassing all afternoon in the car, and it works like a dream. I have recorded a ten-minute speech on the issues of the Election (the Summit, pensions, housing, education, and Africa) and this lasts just long enough for me to go round to the houses with window bills. I got lots of them up completely single-handedly.

To the Colston Hall where Hugh Gaitskell is addressing a big meeting. 600 were turned away. The size of the crowd and the tremendous reception given to Gaitskell surprised us all. He was on top of his form and made a really grand, clear, forceful speech. It included a most friendly reference to me among the other Bristol MPs. Afterwards police with linked arms had to hold back the crowd to let his car go back to the Grand Hotel.

I had dinner with Hugh and Dora, John Harris (Hugh's political adviser), and the regional organiser, Ted Rees. We are now frankly much more optimistic about the outcome of the Election. The tremendous meetings, the successful TV, and the Gallup poll showing a shrinking margin, have got us to the point where we think that the Liberals holding the balance with us only just behind the Tories is now a distinct possibility. Walked round Bristol talking to John Harris until very late. His appointment is the best thing that has happened to Hugh for years.

Thursday 24 September 1959
Herbert Rogers had brought a black woolly cat and arranged for some kid to give it to me to make a good publicity picture. But the kid screamed so hard that its mother had to give it to me instead.

Lunch with the six Bristol candidates and immediately drove back to London. To Israeli embassy for goodbye party to Eliahu Elath and his wife, who are returning to Israel.

Monday 28 September 1959
We have definitely got the Tories on the run. It is agreed that Tom Driberg will interview Nye Bevan for tonight's broadcast. Nye refuses to be interviewed by Chris, Woodrow or me. Tom, being an old jellyfish, was quivering at the thought of the great man. It is a ghastly interview – but it only lasts two and a half minutes! This was the tightest, slickest show we have done: thirteen people in fourteen and a half minutes.

Thursday 1 October 1959
Transport House this morning. The pledge that there would be no income tax increases that Hugh gave in his speech, coupled with the purchase tax pledge released by Morgan, has upset us all. We feel the Tories have now got us on the defensive. This is partly true but partly a question of counter-attack. They are now attacking and we are bound to feel the effect of this. Of course the purchase tax thing is just a muddle by Morgan and stems from old material that was hanging about the office. The income tax pledge was done to forestall an anticipated scare that there would be 2s.6d. on the income tax to pay for Labour's programme. Neither of these was discussed with Crossman before release.

Saturday 3 October 1959
Liverpool. To the Adelphi Hotel and breakfast with Hugh, Dora and Harold Wilson in Hugh's room. Dora in her nightie is quite a sight. Hugh was a bit frowsy and looked like the man who used to be on the Bovril bottle in his pyjamas. We were all cautiously optimistic about the outcome of the Election. Hugh has had a gigantic reception everywhere (20,000 people at Trafford Park yesterday) and the Gallup poll still suggests that we are on the up-grade.

Spend the morning writing Hugh's broadcast, which he then rewrites and I rewrite, etc. We then walk to the BBC studio and record it.

Sunday 4 October 1959
David Butler phones. 'The Election is wide open,' he says. He will even

admit that it is possible Labour could win. At my most optimistic I now think there could be a Labour majority of 30, but it is more likely to be 15 with a Tory victory by a tiny majority also pretty likely.

To Transport House for the last campaign and many discussions about the tactics tomorrow. Tom Driberg gets very cross because we are not dealing with nationalisation in our programme. Dick gets angry with Tom. Frankly I think Dick is right. The campaign is coming to its conclusion and it is quite sad that our happy set-up at Transport House should be moving to its end.

Monday 5 October 1959

All is now sweetness and light. The clouds have blown away and it is possible to see the tremendous contribution Dick Crossman has made to the campaign. He has a brilliant clarity of thought and he concentrates the attention at a meeting on what is relevant to the exclusion of every-thing else. Morgan's press conferences, Hugh's speeches, our TV content and the campaign notes have all reflected the steady pulse of his thought. It shows how efficient the Party can be when your Leaders are away. Without the NEC and the Publicity Committee and the Shadow Cabinet everything works fine. I am sure there are lessons in this for the future.

You'll get a lift in life from Labour!

The modernisers' General Election appeal, 1959.

Tuesday 6 October 1959

Set off for Bristol very early by car and straight to HQ after breakfast at the Grand Hotel. Put rostrum and placards on the car and to lunchtime meeting and the Robertson's jam factory.

More loudspeaker work and seven meetings this evening. The schedule was so tight that I was about 40 minutes late at the last one. Frankly, the campaign has lost some of its impetus. There is not quite as much enthusiasm here as I had expected and the number of workers has not been as great as I had hoped. Also I noted that quite a lot of the window bills which I had personally stuck up in council houses had disappeared. This, despite the very warm welcome given me when they were put up.

Wednesday 7 October 1959

Loudspeaker work all day and then joint meeting with the Conservative candidate, Malcolm St Clair, at Kingswood Old People's Home. We discussed pensions and he said that the Conservatives would give the 10 shillings increase within two months, a wholly unauthorised pledge badly received by the pensioners. St Clair is a drip anyway and one always dislikes one's opponent in a fight.

Caroline arrives from London for the last few days.

Thursday 8 October 1959

Up early and a perfect day. The Gallup poll suggests that the enormous 'don't know' group may be inclining to the right.

The usual senseless and exhausting visits to 36 polling stations and 30 committee rooms. Shaking hands with the policemen, asking the returning officer how many people have voted, nodding at the clerks, and heading off for the next.

Finally the usual loudspeaker 'knocking up' and a rather quiet end to the day. People were voting earlier. Then to Unity House when the polls closed to remove all the Election equipment from the car, and to the Grand Hotel for a bath and tea and sandwiches.

Just about 10 the first results begin coming out and it is clear within a short while that the Tories have won and increased their majority. We have gained a bit in Lancashire and Scotland, but otherwise are out. The count is thus very depressing with the crowing Tories and our people very dejected. Indeed my result looked like being in the balance at one stage, and I thought I might have been beaten. But my vote is up 1,000 even though my majority is down 2,000 with a 3 per cent swing.

The arrangements for the count were appalling, inefficient, long-drawn-out. Back to the Grand Hotel too depressed to watch TV.

Saturday 10 October 1959

Dick Crossman rang up and we discussed the state of the Party. We both agreed that Hugh had come out of the campaign with tremendous prestige and could do more or less what he liked for a bit. We also agreed that we must not lose the impetus that the campaign had given us and we should begin making people work before they had time to get defeatist and depressed.

The Tory majority is 100, and the Party will really have to reorganise itself.

Spoke to Hugh on the telephone and he invited us up for drinks tomorrow.

Sunday 11 October 1959

To the Gaitskells'. Hugh was tired but mellow and said he wanted a holiday, which he deserved. He says it would be a good idea to have a meeting next weekend to review the work of the Election and this will presumably take place under Dick's auspices. I then proposed that a number of changes should be made, including a political permanent Vice-Chairman, a new Secretary, a Shadow Leader of the House, new whips and John Harris on a permanent basis.

I said that I thought Harold Wilson would be the obvious Shadow Leader of the house if that wasn't an insuperable difficulty – taking him away from finance. 'Oh no, not at all – in a way it would suit me nicely,' said Hugh. He said he intended to appoint younger men to the Front Bench but thought I would get elected to the Shadow Cabinet anyway.

He also said several times, 'I'm not prepared to lose another Election for the sake of nationalisation.' He laid great stress on the disadvantages of the name Labour, particularly on new housing estates, and said, 'Of course Douglas Jay is going to urge us to adopt a new one.' I reminded him that the prune had been resuscitated without a change of name by clever selling.

Hugh also thought we must review our relations with the trade unions especially the need for greater freedom and in local authorities.

Dora was bubbling with hate of left and right. She is game.

Monday 12 October 1959

To Manchester for a Granada *Searchlight* programme on the next five years with Keith Kyle (who was Liberal, was on the Tory candidates' list until Suez, campaigned for Liberals in this Election, and joined the Labour Party last week), and journalists Bernard Levin and Paul Johnson, a very defeatist, rootless young man who was saying that we must drop nationalisation, end links with the trade unions and join up with the Liberals. I said that morale was high and that what we wanted was to revitalise the Labour movement by modernising its constitution, driving its policy thinking forward, creating a new Youth Movement, and making the Opposition more effective.

Flew home to London and saw Roy Jenkins on *Panorama* advocating very modestly that you should drop nationalisation, watch out for the dangers of the union links and not rule out an association with the Liberals.

He dropped in here on his way back home and we had a flaming row. As a matter of fact I was very calm and collected and he got into a semi-hysterical state. Usually it's the other way round. 'We must use this shock to drop nationalisation entirely at this forthcoming Conference,' he said, and I concentrated on the dangers to our integrity if we were to be so reckless. In the end he half apologised for his temper and went off with Jennifer.

Tuesday 13 October 1959
I rang Dick Crossman and told him that Roy was very definite against nationalisation. Dick said he thought we'd have to drop it, but not now. And I was a bit surprised to find myself on the left in this argument. Hugh is going to stay with Dick tonight at Dick's Farm. Dick would like to be Vice-Chairman on a permanent basis in charge of Transport House. I think that that's right too.

We ended up with an amicable recollection of our Election rows. These are now quite past and indeed he has asked me to be the godfather of his daughter, Virginia. You couldn't have a nicer tribute than that.

Thursday 15 October 1959
Telephoned Barbara Castle. We discussed the desertion of the Party by the *Daily Mirror* after the Election. Hugh Cudlipp took the result as a personal insult to himself, sacked Dick, killed 'Jane,' the strip girl, and removed 'Forward with the People' from the front page in a burst of absurd pique. Actually Dick was told in August that whether we won or lost he would not carry on.

Spoke to Jim Callaghan, who wants Bevan to be Deputy Leader and thinks we must rethink our nationalisation.

Wednesday 21 October 1959
Tea with Harold Wilson, who is extremely bitter. Hugh certainly has failed to keep us together.

To Barbara Castle's flat this evening where she, Ted and her sister Mrs Mackintosh entertained Mikardo, Michael Foot, Dick Crossman, Kenneth Robinson, Paul Johnson and Peter Shore. There was a general inquest on the campaign and we all agreed that if the constitution and working of the Party was to be reformed full evidence should be submitted. It was also agreed that Hugh Gaitskell had cooked his goose – or that Douglas Jay had cooked it for him by raising the Clause 4 issue. There was great bitterness about the general position and Dick suggested putting out feelers to Nye and Harold, who are both lonely, and to try to re-form the Bevan group. The others were not keen as they do not much care for them. But it was agreed to try and get a lunch to talk with Nye.

Peter Shore and I got very depressed and broke in about the urgent need for reorganisation in the Party and for it to be coupled with more political activity by the Party. This focused attention on the job to be done and led to a more fruitful discussion. The re-formation of the Bevan group would be disastrous.

Monday 26 October 1959

At work on lecture tour material. Associated Rediffusion have asked me to be the commentator at Churchill's funeral whenever that might be. I accept.

Sunday 1 November 1959

To London Labour Party Youth School. They all agree that trade unions, local councils and nationalisation had harmed us in the Election but none of them wanted to break with the past. They all wanted to modernise and bring up to date the work we do. I was encouraged. Niall MacDermott, who lost his seat in Lewisham, is Director and I formed a more favourable impression of him. A guy who does that is not just a Labour lawyer on the bandwagon.

Monday 9 November 1959

At 12.30 went to see Hugh at his request. He was cautious and pessimistic. He then asked me if I would be the principal spokesman on transport from the Front Bench. This is, of course, a real honour but I was a bit knocked sideways and must have sounded rather crabby asking questions about it and whether I was still to be free to speak from the backbenches on other questions. He said 'Yes.' It will be a big challenge.

I phoned Dick Crossman. He is carrying on in Pensions and envies me my job. The more I think of it, the more important it seems.

Tuesday 10 November 1959

Peter and Liz Shore, Gerald Kaufman and Ivan Yates came to dinner tonight and we discussed the idea of a 1964 Club to be based on the simple objective of doing to the Party what we know has to be done – modernise and overhaul and make it a vehicle for progressive action in our society. We would include in it only those who were young and also had some contribution of a positive kind to make – by virtue of their position in the Party. It's a sort of colonels' revolt, with no objects save that of revitalising the movement.

We thought we might include in the Club: David Ennals, Peter Shore, Tony Howard, Ivan Yates, Gerald Kaufman, Shirley Williams, and Reg Prentice and Dick Marsh, as trade union MPs.

Sunday 15 November 1959
Spent the whole day preparing a lifetime diary from 1925 to 2025, with a separate page for each year on which I have glued a calendar for that year culled from the front page of the New York telephone directory which prints a perpetual calendar. It is a most interesting project which will provide an index to all my past records and a pointer towards the future – focusing my attention on it.

Friday 20 November 1959
Father is sick with bronchitis. What a misery this is in the English climate. But he's got such fantastic powers of resistance – most of them psychological – that he never looks like being within a mile of being even sick.

Worked on my accounts for 1958–59 all day. I hate doing them, always leave them six months after the last possible date and can only attribute it to a reaction against the absurd systems Father has adopted.

Thursday 26 November 1959
First appearance on Front Bench at 3.30 when the Minister of Transport, Ernie Marples, announced his Pink Zone plan to reduce parking in Central London. I had forced him to do this by threatening to raise it in the House if he didn't. Then I got a bit too excited and he rebuked me for showing 'anger'. But it was really just anxiety.

Saturday 28 November 1959 – Conference
After lunch Hugh Gaitskell delivered his long-awaited speech. It was over an hour long and surveyed the whole field. I agreed with most of it and it incorporated many ideas in my memorandum. But it was a ghastly failure because it was constructed in quite the wrong way and without regard to the needs of the Party. In effect he asked, 'How much of what we once believed will the electorate now stomach?' The answer he produced was not surprisingly, 'Very little.' But that is not the question you should ask.

If he had said, 'Here is the modern world full of causes for us to take up. Here is what we must do. Here are the changes we must make in ourselves to do them' the Party would have risen to him to a man. But he is quite incapable of inspiring people. I spoke in the debate. I said the three issues were peace, colonial freedom and modernising Britain, and that the Party had to get on with the job. Since I didn't mention nationalisation one way or the other it was a bit outside the stream of debate which reached its climax with Michael Foot's stinging attack on Hugh.

Nye and Jennie came to dinner at our hotel with Shirley and Bernard Williams. Nye turned on me most viciously at the beginning, attacking the campaign, TV, and the idea of surveys of public opinion. He was really a bit touched, thought Bernard Williams, who sat opposite me. Unfortunately I am like a red rag to a bull to him. Perhaps he knows that I don't trust him at all. Or is it because I am young and middle class?

Couldn't sleep much tonight for nightmares about the National Executive election. I got elected to the Executive in bottom place – ousting Ian Mikardo. My vote had risen from 483,000 to 566,000 and Mikardo had dropped from 646,000 to 554,000. I am sorry it was Mik, and he said at lunch, 'I'm glad it was you' which was very sweet as he has lost the chairmanship, his seat, and this, all in two months.

In the debate Shirley Williams made a brilliant speech and won universal applause. Nye's speech this afternoon was witty, scintillating, positive, conciliatory – the model of what a Leader should do. He didn't knock Hugh out but he gently elbowed him aside.

Monday 30 November 1959
Heard from Sir Winston Churchill, to whom I wrote for added support in my latest plea to Macmillan for a change in the law to permit me to get out of my peerage. He won't write me a new letter but has given me permission to make further use of his earlier one. Today is his eighty-fifth birthday. He certainly is a wonderful old boy.

Tuesday 1 December 1959
Lunch with John Altrincham today, which I much enjoyed. He is an intelligent and kindly person with lots of guts. We discussed the Labour Party, his romantic royalism, and his idea for a London statue to Gandhi. I promised to think about this further.

Wednesday 2 December 1959
Lunch with the American Ambassador, Whitney, at his residence. Also there were Morgan Phillips, Gordon-Walker, Arthur Bottomley and Charlie Pannell. Then Brewster Morris and a lot of pasty-faced middle-aged Labour attachés whom I didn't much care for. I didn't say a word but I was rather shocked to hear all the other people being publicly disloyal about Frank Cousins, Dick Crossman and others. Hurried away as quick as I could.

Saturday 5 December 1959
Up Big Ben with the boys. What a climb!

To the Fabian Annual Meeting this afternoon. There was a lot of criticism of the complacency of the Society. My amendment to alter the aims and objects was accepted, and the following words were added.

'It also aims at the implementation of the Charter of the UN and the

Universal Declaration of Human Rights. It seeks the creation of effective international institutions to uphold and enforce world peace.'

This is the first time the Fabian has ever taken official notice of the international situation.

Tuesday 8 December 1959
Dinner with the American Ambassador, about forty of us in all. Present were various Cabinet members. It was rather high level all round. The only other Labour people were the Gaitskells. James Symington played his guitar after dinner. It was so unlike the Communist dinners where everybody splits up to talk politics. This was gracious living at its height. I cannot but feel Western civilisation has reached its peak and is now slowly declining before the upsurge of pressure from the more serious societies.

Thursday 10 December 1959
Opened debate on traffic congestion. It went off all right. Father and Mother and Caroline were in the Gallery.

Friday 11 December 1959
To Bristol to speak at the College of Technology. On the way, thought of a Traffic Control Bill to give Marples the power he needs.

Wednesday 16 December 1959
To first meeting of National Executive at Transport House. Not a very impressive example of democracy in action. It is too big, and the seating arrangements with their back-to-back overlap are really awful. Also the trade union and constituency people sit on opposite sides.

We discussed the Youth Movement, and it was all referred to another sub-committee. We just had time to get on to the Transport House reorganisation point, and this was then referred to the Salaries Sub-Committee. Most of the items were referred to sub-committees.

But we did agree to support the boycott of South African goods, and to launch an African Year. This is well worth while.

Friday 18 December 1959
Home, and saw Herbert Morrison on *Face to Face* being interviewed by John Freeman. He said he thought Attlee had lingered on to keep him out of the leadership. It was a very fascinating half-hour. TV certainly permits everybody to be in on the secrets once reserved for the inner group.

Saturday 19 December 1959
Dinner with Pam and Enoch Powell.

The Powells relaxed a bit about politics and I learned that they really cannot bear Macmillan, which is interesting. There may be more discontent with him in the Party than is generally realised.

Monday 21 December 1959

Dinner as the guest of the Fire Brigades' Union at the House of Commons – an intimate little group of only three MPs and perhaps a dozen others. Why did John Horner ask me? I don't know. Audrey Callaghan had a theory that they might be looking for some MPs to sponsor. What should I do if such an offer were to come to me? I don't know.

Monday 28 December 1959

Dave's wedding this morning at Caxton Hall. Also his thirty-first birthday. He and June went off to Rome on their honeymoon.

Saturday 1 January 1960

Tony Howard of the *Manchester Guardian* came to see me about an article he is writing for the paper on the trade unions and the Party. I tried to dissuade him from attacking the trade unions as such and focus on the need for the unions to modernise themselves and extend the limits of their own support. This is in contrast to the Jenkins–Crosland school who believe that it must all be done by weakening the traditional links.

Monday 4 January 1960

I phoned Dick Crossman in Manchester. We discussed the new danger of a split in the party due to Nye's illness.

Wednesday 20 January 1960

We heard that Nye is critically ill and today looks as if he may not last.

Thursday 21 January 1960

To the House of Commons to talk to the 1944 Association – a group of Labour businessmen. It's also known as the queue for peerages. I gave them a talk on 'The Future of the Labour Party' and it really got a pretty frosty reception as they were all welcoming the spread of unit trusts. I'm afraid I didn't go down very well.

Saturday 23 January 1960

To Bristol where I spoke at the Republic Day celebrations run by the India Society. There were lots of Indians there and lovely dances performed by dance groups and singing of Hindu songs. There must have been nearly a thousand altogether and it was certainly the most colourful and enjoyable do I have been to in Bristol for ages. Britain is far too inbred and what we need is some foreign influence to make us more interesting. American culture has detribalised us to some extent and we shall be better off still when we get the full blast from Russia and China.

Sunday 7 February 1960
Whole family to Hyde Park and played football in the icy cold by the Serpentine. Joshua nearly fell in.

Tuesday 9 February 1960
We gave a dinner party tonight for Alexander Surkav, the Secretary of the Writers' Union of the USSR, and Tikhomirov who is also with him, on a visit from the Great Britain–USSR Association. We invited to meet them Bill Hessler of the *Cincinnati Enquirer*, Kanyama Chiume of the Nyasaland African Congress, Messaoud Kellou, Barbara Castle and a few others. It went extremely well. We discussed China and Surkav said, 'I am not responsible for what happens on the Indian frontier. China is in the restless stage of her revolution. Do not isolate her from the international community as you isolated Russia. That is the cause of much of the trouble.'

Tuesday 16 February 1960
Melisssa came to the Houses of Parliament today, at the age of two years eleven months and three and a half weeks. She stood and watched the Speaker in the Central Lobby and then went in the Serjeant-at-Arms' private gallery with my folks while I asked a question. Father was ticked off for talking too loud – not Melissa. Then we went and she sat with me in the Diplomatic Gallery at the house of Lords and waved at Father, who waved back with his order paper from the Front Bench. She looked at the Lord Chancellor and said, 'There's another Speaker.' Then she talked to a policeman – at her own request – just by the Cromwell statue and came down for tea in the Members' Cafeteria. This was the high spot of the day. Finally she met Kenneth Robinson as she was leaving. Earlier she had met Dick Crossman and as we drove home she said, 'Dick Crossman is a nice guy.'

Thursday 18 February 1960
Had 45 minutes' talk with Hugh Gaitskell this evening in his room. He was very cordial and we discussed transport problems, broadcasting and then finally Clause 4. This argument is raging in the Party at the moment[5] as we approach the meeting on 16 March. Hugh asked me what I thought about it and I told him I was 100 per cent in favour of modernisation and additions but I had a strong feeling we should not delete the famous phrase about 'common ownership of the means of production, etc.'. He was a bit surprised. I explained that I thought the

whole thing had been represented in a very negative way from Blackpool onwards. However, it was a perfectly cordial evening.

Saturday 27 February 1960
The whole family went on the march from Hyde Park to Trafalgar Square to launch the boycott of South African goods in March. The Shores came with us and on the parade were Gaitskell, Altrincham and Father Trevor Huddleston. It was a tremendous occasion which we shan't forget. The boys carried placards and Melissa walked a lot of the way. At Trafalgar Square Sir Oswald Mosley and his thugs were circling in big lorries. It was alarmingly like the pre-war demonstrations.

Wednesday 2 March 1960
Spoke this morning at the Conference of American Women's Activities in the UK attended by 300 or more wives of American Air Force personnel. It was amazing to hear them introduced as 'Maxine Taylor, wife of General Taylor, Commander of East Anglia', etc. etc. Here is an Army that has divided the UK up into its areas and commands. We know nothing about it. I talked about the power behind the pageantry in Parliament.

Hugh Carleton Greene, new Director-General of the BBC, spoke to the public information group on the future of TV. He was terribly unimaginative and cautious and Third Programmy. It was Auntie BBC at its best and worst. He was really under the thumb of the establishment. But as a public service man he wasn't just on the make like the vulgar, thrusting profit-rich ITV tycoons.

Wednesday 16 March 1960
Left early for Transport House for the long-awaited meeting of the National Executive at which we are to rewrite Clause 4. Got there so early I had a chance to look in and see the folks at the flat. It's so very nice to be able to get Dad's advice with all his tremendous experience of political rows over sixty years. Caroline said, 'Keep your mouth shut today.' Dad said, 'Don't get involved.' I think it is all very sound.

Walking to Transport House I saw an enormous crowd of journalists and photographers. There were even ten or fifteen Trotskyites wearing placards announcing that they were from 'The Clause 4 Defence Society'. The flashbulbs popped as I approached and it really was extremely funny to see – I couldn't help laughing.

We were in the tiny committee room on the fourth floor and as I arrived Bessie Braddock looked out of the window and claimed to have spotted a journalist on the roof so we pulled the curtains.

There was some question raised about the leakages of Gaitskell's draft which had appeared in *Tribune* last week.

Finally Gaitskell opened. I kept my notes written at the time in my book. He really went over the ground of his Blackpool speech again. In the subsequent discussion it was clear that nobody wanted a great row. The tone was extremely good and it was a very interesting debate. Walter Padley gave an impassioned defence of Clause 4 as it stands and Sam Watson reminded us of the two Irish labourers arguing about the ownership of a cow which was standing quietly in the corner being milked by a lawyer.

It soon became clear that people were looking for some way of bridging the gap and Jennie Lee suggested that the words 'commanding heights of the economy' might provide such a bridge.

Dick Crossman suggested we wanted an amplification and somebody said surely it was a clarification too. Finally Charlie Evans of the NUR said 'Why don't we reaffirm it?' So that's how the three key words – reaffirms, clarifies and amplifies – came into Gaitskell's draft. We accepted this by 22 votes to 1 with one abstention – Harry Nicholas of the TGWU on Frank Cousins's orders. I said it was like saying that we 'accept, reject and explain . . .' We then paused for sandwiches before we went on to discuss the detailed amendments to Gaitskell's draft. This went through fairly smoothly with some toughening up. I tried to get World Government specifically written in. It was defeated. I tried to get the UN Declaration of Human Rights written in. It was defeated. But I did succeed in getting an explicit repudiation of colonialism with the words 'rejecting the exploitation of one country by another'. This is in line with the Tunis Resolutions, and I felt was well worth while doing.

The press were still pouring round the building as we left it, catching us with movie cameras as we walked away. But news of the compromise had reached them and we were able to be all smiles.

Thursday 17 March 1960
All this week I have had Dick Crossman's dismissal on my conscience. Barbara Castle and I planned to write to Hugh but the difficulty was we couldn't think of a way of doing it without making our own resignation from the Front Bench inevitable.

So I decided to raise it at the Party meeting. I didn't tell Dick or Hugh but I asked Frank Barlow as a pal and he advised against it. Nevertheless I went ahead.

I said I recognised the difficulty of transitory Front Benchers and didn't doubt the Leader's right to sack, but I said it was wrong to ask for a pledge of good behaviour which I couldn't possibly myself have given. I said that no one had contributed more than Dick Crossman to the Party in the last two or three years, with his pensions work, the two pamphlets he wrote and his campaign leadership. I referred to George Brown's abstention in the Lebanon landings in 1958, and urged for a new start now that Clause 4 was all behind us.

There was a deadly silence and Iorwerth Thomas of the Rhondda got up and said I was pleading for special privileges for intellectuals. One or two others got in too. John Hynd said that if it was in order to speak about the merits of Front Bench spokesmen he would have a word to say about the Transport spokesman. Gaitskell then stopped the discussion and he definitely had the majority of those present with him.

I was conscious of a very icy atmosphere but one or two people did come up and say friendly things, which I much appreciated. I didn't greatly care as I felt I had to do it whatever people thought. I was more worried about Dick Crossman's reaction. After a flaming row on Algeria on Tuesday, we are not really on speaking terms at the moment. I thought this might make it worse.

Friday 18 March 1960
Dick Crossman rang this morning to say how touched he had been by my speech last night at the Party meeting. He said that my point about his contribution had evoked from Gaitskell his first public admission that Crossman had done anything worthwhile.

Tuesday 22 March 1960
The Sharpeville shootings are headline news and there was a flare-up in the House of Commons. I asked a very stiff question as to why no one had the courage to speak out against such brutal repression.

Thursday 24 March 1960
Set off for the Königswinter Conference, near Bonn. These Conferences are a German initiative to restore Anglo-German relations after the war – and are attended by parliamentarians, academics and journalists.

Our delegation had tea with the SPD to discuss the visit of some of our colleagues to East Germany. The SPD are very angry about this and it was rather a sharp exchange. Dick Crossman came under very heavy fire for his article envisaging the possibility of recognising the East German regime.

Both the SPD and the others agreed that there were some things they could say publicly and others which could only be said privately. I joined in the debate by arguing that we could only understand the European situation in the context of the wider *détente* which is developing. I thought the Summit would produce some results and that the German problem would then have to take its place among a number of unsolved problems. But this would mean normalising relations between the two sides, which would inevitably involve recognising East Germany. I thought that a reduction of tension was the greatest weapon available for getting German unity.

This evening we went to a reception given by the President in Bad Godesberg.

Sunday 27 March 1960
The day was taken up with a general discussion and very little agreement was reached. The West Germans are physically so close to the Russians and are so frightened of them that they are really terrified the West is prepared to sacrifice them as part of a deal in Central Europe. The West, on the other hand, welcomes the thaw in the Cold War and does not want the German question to prevent this leading to a real *détente*. Indeed the German integration into the West as an ally within NATO was never very warmly welcomed except as a sheer necessity arising out of the Cold War. So there are few regrets at finding the German alliance less necessary. However, Germany is now the most powerful military and industrial force in Western Europe and is in a position to dictate her terms on the German question – all of which serves to irritate Britain even more. Our isolated position outside the Common Market is an additional irritant.

Monday 28 March 1960
Arrived home and Caroline and I went this evening as guests of the Anglo-Israel Association to a dinner at Quaglino's in honour of Arthur Lourie, the new Ambassador. Looking back over my feelings about Israel I must admit that Suez did make a big difference. And also my close contacts with the Arabs.

Tuesday 29 March 1960
Spent two hours after lunch at the British Transport Commission archives doing research on Harold Macmillan's period as a director of the Great Western Railway. It was very rewarding and is ammunition for future use.

Went to drinks with Mervyn Stockwood – first time I have seen him since he was made Bishop of Southwark. He looked awfully pale and drawn. He doesn't enjoy good health. Had a long talk with Stephen Spender before I realised who he was. Also met John Betjeman, whom I felt I knew well through TV. He is terribly funny and, with that inane toothy grin, he talked about 'friends of friendless churches', and spoke bitterly about this and that bishop or rural dean who had ordered the closure of some 'lovely, Victorian, Gothic monstrosity'.

Afterwards persuaded Tony Crosland to come and have a meal in a pub and back for a drink. He is the most complex character and it takes half a bottle of whisky and immense tact to penetrate his susceptibilities. We had bucketfuls of self-analysis but finally did have a reasonably intelligent discussion about rebuilding the Labour Party and what Hugh should do now. I felt it had done something to bridge the gulf between us over the last few years.

Saturday 9 April 1960
At home all day and David Butler to tea. South African Prime Minister, Dr Verwoerd, shot. The South African crisis is deepening.

Wednesday 13 April 1960
At home all day working on my speech for this evening. Big row in the House over the end of the Blue Streak rocket launcher for British atomic bombs. It will precipitate the growing crisis in the Labour Party on nuclear weapons. Many trade unions are now supporting unilateralism and the Party will be under heavy pressure on this subject. There is general talk of Gaitskell being forced out of the leadership.

This evening's debate on the railways went quite well. My folks and Caroline were in the Gallery and I had quite a good House. It certainly did something to re-establish me with the Transport Group. The Macmillan research came in handy much sooner than I expected.

Sunday 17 April 1960
To church this morning: Easter.

The Aldermaston march is a stupendous triumphant success and is getting massive and sympathetic publicity. I am not a unilateralist but I am glad this is going well because present nuclear policy is mad.

Wednesday 27 April 1960
Peter Shore and I had lunch together. He feels the Party leadership is facing a really big crisis and that if we don't establish links with the younger generation we may not be there for them to use when the day comes for a change from the Tories.

Sunday 1 May 1960
To Bristol for the day with Stephen and Hilary for the May Day march. The boys marched stoutly and sat on the grass listening to the speeches. They behaved extremely well. Geoffrey de Freitas and Harry Nicholas were the other speakers, and we came back in the train with the Archbishop of Canterbury's Chaplain who advised Hilary on his rummy game with Stephen. Hilary turned to the other people in the compartment and said, 'This man is a real expert at cards; he must play a lot.' When Stephen heard he was the Chaplain to the Archbishop he said, 'Oh you mean Geoffrey Fisher.'

Thursday 5 May 1960
Now the AEU have gone unilateralist, people are seriously talking about the Party breaking up in October. Dick Crossman came out this morning with an article on a non-nuclear Europe which seems to make the best sense.

Road Traffic Bill Committee, and having a lot of fun on it.

To Mrs Pandit's house for a garden party to meet Nehru. The saris in the sunshine under the marquee were beautiful. I didn't meet anyone particularly interesting. Ladies Vi Bonham Carter and Megan Lloyd George were talking to each other – quite a sight.

Friday 6 May 1960

Up early and by taxi for Princess Margaret's wedding. It was a glorious, hot summer day and we drove down Constitution Hill and past the Palace, down the Mall where the crowds had been sleeping all night and through the Admiralty Arch into Whitehall. The Guards in full dress and the general air of expectancy with all the decorations, and the streets empty of cars reminded me of the 1937 Coronation. We were terribly early and sat on the terrace of the Commons until we walked over to the Abbey.

Every pillar in the Abbey had a closed-circuit TV screen and during the service we saw ourselves singing a hymn lustily. We also saw most of the Commonwealth Prime Ministers and other visiting celebrities. Afterwards we had lunch at the Commons and I went off to Bristol to canvass in the local elections.

Tuesday 10 May 1960

Met Jim Callaghan on the bus to the House of Commons. I think he has got his eye on the job of Shadow Foreign Minister. He let slip some remarks which made this very clear. The colonies are shrinking and he doesn't want to shrink with them!

Monday 16 May 1960

The Summit news is very grim.[6] Khrushchev has issued an ultimatum to Eisenhower.

Caroline and I went to the party given by the High Commissioner from Ceylon – another colourful garden party.

Tuesday 17 May 1960

I gather that a new defence policy for the Party is slowly emerging based on the idea of NATO with some political control over American atomic striking power but no independent European deterrent.

Saw the hovercraft demonstrating in the Thames and it is really fantastic. Home to work. The Summit has now clearly failed after the most grotesque day. Mother said on the telephone that it just proved you couldn't do anything without China.

This seemed so obviously right that I decided to send a telegram to Mr Khrushchev. After all, if ordinary citizens can send resolutions to Number 10 Downing Street about matters of national politics, why shouldn't MPs appeal to heads of government? At 12.19 am I sent the following cable:

> Premier Nikita Khrushchev, Soviet Embassy, Paris.
> You can still save the Summit from disaster. Can you propose that Chou En Lai and Pandit Nehru be invited to come to Paris as soon as possible for a fresh attempt to solve outstanding world problems by peaceful negotiation. Such a Soviet initiative would win the support of peoples everywhere.
> Anthony Wedgwood Benn,
> House of Commons, London.

It seemed to offer a better issue on which the Summit could disagree than the U2 spy incident, and who knows: the implanting of such an idea at the right moment might have been useful.

Wednesday 18 May 1960
Spoke on the Finance Bill tonight about the measurement of urban congestion using my new unit the *Block* – which is the 'square foot hours of road space occupied per passenger mile carried.' I made it up myself and it's a real winner.

Home 12.45.

Wednesday 25 May 1960
Lunch at the Athanaeum with Dick Crossman today. There was nothing particular to talk about, but he's such a warm friend of mine that we really ranged over the whole state of the Party. He is deep in the new Defence Statement and is thoroughly enjoying it. It means postponing his holiday, which is not very popular with his wife, but of course it is a job he does supremely well.

We talked about Hugh Gaitskell and Dick said he was 'accident prone'. He doesn't like the Party and doesn't understand it and everything he does and says upsets them. Clause 4, and now defence, are two current examples. I asked Dick whether there was a move against him. Dick said 'no'. But he thought that Hugh would get into one mess after another and there would come a time when his colleagues would not want to save him. There is no intrigue but George Brown has decided that he does not really have confidence in Hugh. This represents an important erosion of strength. We both agreed it would be totally wrong to engage in any sort of intrigue.

Dick is now out of the wilderness again and back in the saddle – the shortest exile since the original Lent!

Thursday 2 June 1960
Andrew Hake came to breakfast. I hadn't seen him for three years, since

he went to join the Christian Council in Kenya. He's a wonderful man who has made a great impression – first as industrial adviser to the Bishop of Bristol and now in Nairobi on inter-racial work. He told me a lot of interesting things and was strongly in favour of the release of Jomo Kenyatta from jail in Kenya. His problems in the CCK come more from the very reactionary and numerically most powerful fundamentalist, bible-bashing American Methodists. I had no idea that they were as numerous as he said – 500 in East Africa.

He spoke of the African National Movement as being poised between forward-looking political organisations (Mboya, etc.) and backward-looking tribalism (Kenyatta, etc.). This unfortunately is overlaid with another impending tug-of-war between Mboya's American-orientated students and the Communist-trained students from behind the Iron Curtain who will flood back in when Kenya is free. The tussle may then be between Communist and non-Communist-trained leaders – both agreeing only on the need for some sort of authoritarianism. What the African desperately needs is some guidance as to how to run a political system that is as free as possible but still meets the needs of his community. Here Britain is pitifully inadequate: exporting hothouse parliamentary systems intact is no guarantee of successful transplantation.

Saturday 4 June 1960
Went to Stansgate for Whitsun. My folks were there and we had a quiet time.

Friday 10 June 1960
This afternoon the Ford Motor Company put on a demonstration of the Levacar, a rail vehicle held above the rails by magnetic repulsion, at my request. I had fixed all this up so that Labour MPs could see it. Only one turned up. The BBC TV filmed it and the British Transport Commission sent some engineers, but they were so incredibly negative and stick in the mud. Of course there are tremendous difficulties and the whole idea is in its earliest stages. But instead of concentrating on the development possibilities, they were chattering about the snags and difficulties and technical problems until one could have throttled them all.

Saturday 11 June 1960
The Party is in a deplorable state. Woodrow Wyatt's speech attacking Frank Cousins as 'the bully with the block vote' has disheartened members.

Afterwards drove to Oxford for the Nuffield dance. Jim Callaghan was there. Caroline has almost convinced me that he should be the new Deputy Leader.

Monday 13 June 1960

To Bristol for the General Council. It was the first I had attended since the Election. They passed a unilateralist resolution for Conference despite my appeals to them to think again. The pattern of thinking of the Cold War years has now been replaced by a desire for peace which no Party is utilising properly. If only we could give a lead which would be constructive I am sure we would win over most of the unilateralists to a more sensible policy.

Sunday 19 June 1960

Took the family to tea with the Mayhews in Wimbledon. Chris is really out of sympathy with the Party as it now exists and thinks we must gradually break loose of the trade unions and become a consumers' Party. It all sounds very reasonable. But politics is about power and if we are not firmly linked to the working-class movement, then we shall never be anything at all except a lot of Liberals with bright ideas.

Wednesday 29 June 1960

A Party meeting this morning to discuss the state of the Party and pass a vote of confidence in Gaitskell. The really important thing was the fact that all the trade unionists who spoke in support of the motion were strongly critical of Gaitskell and particularly attacked his assault on Clause 4 and 'his little coterie of friends'. Manny Shinwell gave a tragic performance of senile egomania and Sydney Silverman really lost his grip. Finally we passed a vote of confidence in Hugh.

This evening we debated changes in the homosexuality laws. Kenneth Robinson opened and I voted with the 99 who wanted to legalise homosexuality over the age of 21.

Thursday 30 June 1960

To Broadcasting House to see Newby, the head of the Third Programme, about the idea of a series of broadcasts on great speeches. He was unbelievably negative about it all and thought of every difficulty that could possibly be imagined. The only thing he forgot to say was that it might be ruined by people rustling their scripts. I doubt if much will come of that.

Wednesday 6 July 1960

Nye Bevan died this afternoon.

Sunday 10 July 1960

Took the boys to Trafalgar Square for the demonstration against the Spanish Foreign Minister Castiella's visit. They stood on the plinth with me listening to the speeches and watching the great crowd. Hilary clapped vigorously whenever he could detect a punchline. He even did this when the Spaniard spoke in Spanish. As we left the plinth a man came up and asked him why he had applauded. 'Because I agreed with what he said,' replied Hilary, 'and with the way he said it.'

Tuesday 12 July 1960

This evening to the dance at the American embassy. There were 700 people there and we stayed until dawn was breaking. I haven't danced all night since I was an undergraduate. It was without exception the most fabulous party I have ever attended.

There were artificial trees with real fruit wired on to them. By using enormous plastic bags, four artificial swimming pools had been created in the garden which had been filled by the London Fire Brigade. Between and around them were gigantic candelabra wired for gas; from these tremendous candles burned continuous jets of flame.

The guests were the establishment *in toto*. We danced round beside the Armstrong-Joneses and saw the Queen Mother and Bob Boothby gazing at each other rather balefully across the champagne bottles. R.A. Butler, Lord Salisbury, the editor of *The Times*, David Niven, several dukes, Alf Robens, Frank Soskice, Osbert Lancaster, Joyce Grenfell, the Gaitskells, etc. etc. Name them and they were there. We had no really close friends but knew an enormous number slightly. Though we enjoyed every minute of it, we felt a bit like the Roman Senators must have felt the night before the Huns and the Goths arrived to sack Rome. Such splendid extravagance carries with it an inevitable taste of decadence.

Wednesday 13 July 1960

With two and a half hours' good sleep behind me, I went to Transport House for the special Executive on the state of the Party. The whole of the morning was again taken up with what to do about Clause 4. It was finally agreed that we would drop the idea of a constitutional change and recommend our new statement of aims to the Conference as being a fresh presentation worthy of consideration by the movement.

Wednesday 20 July 1960

Seretse and Ruth came to dinner tonight on the eve of their return to Africa. He is better but showed us a scar on his tummy from hip to hip, rising in a great semicircle above his navel after a recent operation. He and Ruth are very anti-African nationalism and if the wave of modern political activity reaches Bechuanaland, then I think Seretse will be on the wrong side of the barricades. He is, after all, a Chief and said that even his daughter, Jacqueline, said 'Daddy looks like a servant.'

Wednesday 24 August 1960 – USSR trip

Boat train from Liverpool Street to Harwich where we caught the *Prinses*

Beatrix to the Hook of Holland. The Moscow coach was in the siding – heavy with polished mahogany, bright brass, thick curtains and plush stuffed decoration.

Dinner in the wagons-lits as we passed through Utrecht and to bed as the train moved into West Germany. A Thermos, some Nestea, condensed milk in a toothpaste tube and saccharin provided that comfortable feeling of home as we headed for the Iron Curtain. We are the guests of the Inter-Parliamentary Group of the Supreme Soviet.

Thursday 25 August 1960
Woken at 2.30 am by East German police and dozed till 7 when the train went through shining, flashy, opulent West Berlin towards the East Sector.

Tonight we went to bed in our clothes and at 11.30 the Polish police and soldiers call as we passed into the Soviet Union. At midnight two Red Army soldiers, a Customs official, a girl from Pest Control, and an Intourist girl came in. Changed money at Brest and the wheels changed.

Woke late and had breakfast of ham and eggs and tea in the Russian restaurant car.

At 2 in Smolensk and rolling across western Russia all afternoon. At each level crossing stood a girl or woman holding a yellow flag in one hand and a silver or tin horn in the other. They were symbols of patient, loyal Russian people doing their duty and watching the great technology of Soviet power as it went on its way.

At 8.50 met by Nicolai Kutchinsky, who is to accompany us. We went to the Sovietskaya Hotel and then drove round Moscow up to the Lenin Hills and on the Metro. We are definitely getting VIP treatment and will get on well with Kutchinsky. Comment on Russian society by him: 'I didn't want TV but my mother-in-law and the kids did. There's too much violence and shooting with all the revolutionary and wartime films.'

Breakfast in our room and drove to see new housing development. Big posters said 'Eat More Cheese'.

To Lenin's office and apartment and then to the Cathedral in the Kremlin, the Armoury Museum and the Palace of the Soviets. It was all very beautifully restored and well kept.

Lunch at 4.30 at the hotel, by which time we were really knocked out. Kutchinsky is very anti-Molotov and we discussed the 20th Congress.

To the Park of Rest and Culture to see Obratsov Puppet Theatre. Lots of English and Americans in the audience. Dinner 11.30–12.30 in hotel; big lumpen Mongolian delegation at next table. Band playing in 1930 style with young male singer singing 'I Love Paris'. Discussed China, de-Stalinisation, Hungary and British colonialism. Kutchinsky is very agreeable and ready to talk frankly.

Monday 29 August 1960

With Alexander Prosorovsky of the Planning Department to see a housing research project. Prefabrication is going ahead and we also heard about the operation of 'Comradeship Courts' which operate in blocks of flats and neighbourhoods to check bad behaviour by children, nagging wives, unfaithful husbands, etc. Sunday School has nothing to teach them!

This afternoon with Alexander Sirotkin to see the Moscow Metro, which is extremely impressive.

Russians are anti-American, to us anyway. Worried about China, pro-Macmillan, anti-Stalin and said the BBC is clever propaganda but its Russian Service is run by 1917 émigrés who are ignorant, or later émigrés who are hostile.

Tuesday 30 August 1960

Woken at 5.45, breakfast at 6, and porter comes to collect baggage at 6.15. Caroline's in her nightie and I'm in underpants. No possibility of making myself understood. Porter withdraws and man in raincoat and trilby hat appears to remove baggage. He rings on the phone and has long talk in Russian to operator who understands him, but it doesn't help. I speak to girl with help of phrase-book but page flips over and I read the phonetic translation of phrases that have no meaning like 'I'm sorry your mother has been ill' and 'How many hectares of wheat are there on this collective farm?'

To Moscow Airport and talk to Kutchinsky about the Institute of World Economy, which is doing objective research on world events and is used by the Soviet Foreign Office. Kutchinsky is a research worker at the Institute.

Kutchinsky said: 'The reports of Soviet Foreign Office officials abroad are sometimes tendentious and reflect what they expect and want to see. Our reports are highly valued and Khrushchev might get notes from us when making his speeches.' It is quite clear that the Soviet Government 'does not believe its own propaganda'; this is a factor of the greatest importance.

We discussed Truman and MacArthur and Kutchinsky says he wishes there could be two Chinese delegates at the UN!

By plane to Sochi where we had a suite and balcony overlooking the incredibly beautiful Black Sea.

In a speedboat along the waterfront to see the enormous palatial sanatoria built by the trade unions for the workers. In the evening to the Opera with a stage the size of La Scala to hear *Traviata* sung by the Siberian Opera Company. It is all so fabulous and surprising.

Supper from 11 to 2 am in our room and a long and most intimate political talk which represented a complete breakthrough in personal relations. From then on we were on first-name terms.

Wednesday 31 August 1960

Bathed before breakfast and at breakfast discussed U2. Was it a hit? Did USSR really want Summit? Kutchinsky doubtful.

A couple of hours of talk over supper in our room again: Kutchinsky says there are few political prisoners in Russia today and it is much easier than under Stalin.

'I would open the frontiers and prove Russia is confident of its system.'

Then he added, 'Collectivisation was a tragic error and Stalin a disastrous leader. If Lenin had lived it would have been very different. Khrushchev is absolutely honest and straightforward and gets no special privileges.'

'The Labour Party needs discipline, should abolish the block vote, should know who it intends to represent, especially white-collar workers and technical people, and must be more concrete. The Campaign for Nuclear Disarmament is a protest but not a practical idea. It is isolationist, anti-patriotic and dishonest.'

Friday 2 September 1960

By boat across the lake to breakfast in a restaurant and then drove through the mountains back to Adler Airport. Kutchinsky explained how the constitution of the USSR worked and how the CP representative really controlled every organ at every level. He explained how candidates are selected and how polling takes place. He said he would not be opposed to allowing the public to choose between two alternative 'approved' candidates. But, of course, once you give the voter even that limited power, it reorients the whole political system in such a way as to shift the power.

The plane was late and we flew to Moscow via Stalina and didn't get to bed till 2.30 am.

Saturday 3 September 1960

We try unsuccessfully to telephone the British embassy. The operator says it has no phone. Kutchinsky says it is very stupid and compares it with the refusal to publish a street map of Moscow as a hangover from Stalin.

To the Bolshoi Theatre to see *Ivan Sussanin* by Glinka – magnificent patriotic opera.

Sunday 4 September 1960

To the Tretyakov Art Gallery: lots of socialist realism and rather dull.

Boris Krylov collected us by car for dinner at his flat. Mme Krylova and Krylov's mother-in-law live with the family – very crowded. Great family smiles and jokes and tremendous meal with enormous good will all round. They are so affectionate yet serious, good-humoured yet courtly and we felt immediately at home with them. Of course they retain the pre-revolutionary attitude to the outside world and look forward to the relaxation that they know is coming. But what a terribly tough forty years they have had.

Off to the Bolshoi again with Nick. But only stayed for one act of *The Taming of the Shrew*. Long talk over coffee at the hotel.

Monday 5 September 1960
Up early working on speech and to see Barker at the British embassy. He was very intelligent and described the siege life of the diplomats. He thinks the seven-year plan is everything to Khrushchev, who has ruled the idea of war out. Relations with the Russians are good; analysed the Russian–Chinese conflict.

From there to the American embassy where Mr Freers gave us some film for our camera. He is a great Soviet expert and regrets that the Camp David spirit evaporated. He thought they should have recognised China in 1949 but could not now do so.

To the Institute of World Economy where we were greeted by Professor Lemin and about thirty others. I spoke for half an hour in English on co-existence and said that a new generation was born who believed in co-existence but that we must recognise that some honest and sincere men in both camps did not believe in it. I also said that co-existence must mean more than a sullen acceptance and that I thought the effects of co-existence would change both systems profoundly.

The Institute – with 400 people, 150 of whom are research workers – was established in 1956 and is the most important body for the study of foreign countries; it has six people in its British Empire section alone. We saw the reading rooms, and it is a sort of political wing of the Central Intelligence Agency cum Chatham House.

I asked if it influenced Soviet policy: 'Stalin asked how many battalions the Pope had – how many have you?' There was loud laughter. Lemin said it was an apocryphal story and Kutchinsky said they had half a battalion. We walked round the Institute and met Volkov, another British specialist. He had begun a major book on the effect on the British economy of the break-up of the Empire but abandoned it when he found it made no difference.

Shvetsov and Kutchinsky apologised for the poor discussion and I think I spoke too fast and was not ideological enough in my presentation.

At 6 o'clock to the Praha Restaurant for a private dinner with Jacob Paletskis, a full member of the Central Committee. He is a rank-and-file leader and an old guard Bolshevist. For an hour at dinner we have the most cordial talk, exchanging pictures of his grandchildren and our children, and I thought it was all going to evaporate like that. Then, all of a sudden switching to Russian, he turned to Kutchinsky, who later translated, 'Gospodin [Comrade] Wedgwood Benn, you have a very progressive record, except on one question, the question of Hungary.' It was a direct head-on challenge that I could ignore or take up and I decided to take it up. For an hour and a half we had a fierce argument through Kutchinsky.

Still, the conversation ended with many expressions of friendship. Paletskis pinned a medal on my lapel from the Supreme Soviet and I thanked him for the other presents of perfume, records, books and the Sputnik music box.

To the station to catch the Red Arrow to Leningrad. As the train pulled out, Caroline with a new bouquet waved goodbye and we settled into the comfortable sleeper to drink tea and eat biscuits while the bells of the Kremlin rang through the radio in our compartment, followed by the 'Song of Moscow', which traditionally followed it. As usual we had another talk with Kutchinsky.

'I hope that there is no war,' he said, 'because the Russian people have suffered so much and have worked so hard for so long that it would be very tragic indeed if they were, at the last minute, denied the fruits of their sacrifice.' And as he left he turned and said to me, 'You are an idealist underestimating the forces against you and you will be due for disappointments.'

Tuesday 6 September 1960
Early this morning the woman brought us caviare and tea to wake us up. Met at Leningrad Station, and to the Astoria Hotel.

For a couple of hours we drove round Leningrad with an Intourist guide, who pointed everything out. We saw the Admiralty, the Winter Palace, the Kirov Stadium, the Aurora, and drove up and down the main streets. At lunch Kutchinsky said I should have been in the Tory Party, would have made better progress, and could have done more for my country. I said that he should have stayed an optical engineer – which was his job before he became a research worker in foreign affairs.

Just after midnight Nick and I decided to go for a walk and Caroline went up to her room. About 30 seconds after we had left the hotel we heard an enormous explosion behind us, turned and saw a column of flame rising 30 feet into the air right outside the front door of the hotel. We rushed back and saw a truck on its side blazing. Thinking of the man in there frying, and wondering if there was more petrol still to explode, we forced our way round it and into the hotel. Our room overlooked the site and Caroline, hearing me bang on her door, thought it was someone to say that I was in the accident. We watched the truck blaze until the fire brigade put it out with foam, and the ambulance – complete with a doctor, as is usual in Russia – had arrived. It was then that we discovered that no one had been killed. The truck had been stolen by a fifteen-year-old boy and it had skidded and turned over, leaving him a couple of seconds to get out before it blew up. Flash-photographers and police gathered, then the truck was towed away.

Not one word appeared in the Leningrad papers the next day. 'We don't believe in sensationalism,' they explained.

Wednesday 7 September 1960

At breakfast Nick asked two personal questions. He wanted to know our family history and how rich we were. He has hinted that he will be making a report on our visit and these may be for inclusion in it. We answered both questions fully.

Caroline goes on to discuss anti-Americanism, which we have noticed in its most virulent form. We say that the propaganda goes beyond the policy differences, embracing all aspects of American life and constituting a sort of McCarthyism. Nick is very indignant but finds it hard to justify himself.

Thursday 8 September 1960

We visited the Russian Museum and then at 12.30 went to the Cazana Cathedral which is now run by the Academy of Sciences. It is a museum of the history of religion. Our guide Nina Nosovitch, aged about twenty-five, was an atheist theological student, writing a thesis on a reform movement in the Russian Orthodox Church.

One section was on the history of the origins of Christianity and we were assured we could ask questions. Here are a few:

Q: Do you accept the historical fact of the man Jesus Christ living and dying aside from his claims?
A: No. He never lived. There is no evidence of his life. He was fabricated later by others and the story of his birth, life, teaching and death is without foundation. However, the Dead Sea Scrolls suggest that there was a cult – the Essenes – 100 years earlier who taught similar things.
Q: Have you any exhibits showing the persecution of the Christians in Rome?
A: No. They were greatly exaggerated and were touched off by the incredible wealth of the Christians in Rome who offended the Emperor.

The exhibits were designed to show that Christianity came from earlier cults. The Lamb of God, the cattle by the manger, Peter the fisherman and other symbols linked the religion with pagan faiths. A glass case contained extracts from Christ's teaching showing how it strengthened the slave owner by undermining the resistance of the slaves; for example:

'Turn the other cheek.'
'If a man takes your coat, give him your shirt.'
'Blessed are those who suffer.'

'Love thine enemies.'

On our walk round the Museum more and more people had gathered to listen to these question and answers and by now we had twenty or more around us. Nina attempted to disperse them but soon they were edging back.

We saw an exhibit of a German bomb in 1914 on which was painted 'God, King and Country', and yellowing photos of two bishops who had left the Church to become atheists. Finally there was a photo and oil painting of Hewlett Johnson, the 'Red Dean' of Canterbury.

Q: Why is he here? He believes in Christ.
A: He is a progressive working for peace.
Q: Could he join the Communist Party?
A: Not in the USSR, but he could in England or Poland.
Q: What would happen if a member of the CP became converted to Christianity?
A: Someone would try to dissuade him.
Q: And if he persisted?
A: He would be expelled from the Communist Party.

As we left Nina shook us firmly by the hand, thanked us for being so interested, and said that the younger generation now didn't seem to care about anti-religious propaganda. Maria said afterwards, 'Unfortunately there is no systematic anti-religious propaganda except at Christmas and Easter.'

Kutchinsky realised that we didn't like the exhibition and couldn't understand why. We joked with him about items we would put in an anti-Communist museum. He said he would complain about its lack of objectivity.

In the evening attended a farewell dinner at the Restaurant Metropole. Everyone was so warm and friendly and they drove us to the dock and put us on board the *Estonia*. The wind was blowing and the rain bucketing down and we felt that winter was closing in on Leningrad and would hold it tight until the spring came to melt the ice. We had no real chance to say goodbye – just a warm handshake on the wet cobbles at the quayside. And then warm and comfortable in our cabin in this lovely new ship we edged out into the sea, our Russian trip over.

Tuesday 13 September 1960
Maurice Thorez, the Secretary-General of the French Communist Party, is on the ship with his wife and three sons. He is half paralysed with a stroke and was sitting in a deckchair in a dark flannel cap with a white golfing cap and a smile half kindly and half capable of hate. One of his sons, Jean – a teacher – interpreted and I introduced myself and asked some questions about Algeria, and French politics.

Afterwards I got up, thanked him very much and said how much I enjoyed meeting him and his sons (who were very charming and pleasant) and said how secure we all felt that the ship was under the control of the French Communist Party. Thorez smiled broadly and shook my hand with his left hand as I said goodbye. He is known as a Stalinist and the French Communist Party, under him, has been very bad about the Algerian War.

Sunday 18 September 1960
Dick Crossman phones. Hugh Gaitskell is ready to fight it out on defence and the Conference will be a big showdown.

Monday 19 September 1960
Catching up with all my letters and phone calls to David Ennals, Dick Crossman and Peter Shore. Build-up for the Conference.

Tuesday 20 September 1960
Dick and Peter to dinner and we discussed the Conference. The left is determined to crush Gaitskell and the right is determined to crush the left on the defence issue. We represent the centralists and hope that the crisis can be averted by the Brown–Ennals formula which would allow the Executive to accept the TGWU resolution,[7] instead of making a fight of it.

Sunday 25 September 1960
Gaitskell's Battersea speech yesterday threw down the gauntlet. He is sticking firm. Cousins has similarly given a press conference.

Monday 26 September 1960
I decide that it may be necessary to resign from the NEC at Scarborough in an attempt to make peace.

Tuesday 27 September 1960
Tell Peter and David that I am thinking of resigning.
To Fabian Executive where I discover that a pamphlet by Michael Young suggesting the formation of a new consumers' Party has been printed and is ready for publication on the eve of the Conference this Friday. I lose my temper, say it is 'sharp practice' and after an acrid debate we defeat the idea by 6 votes to 5.
Tonight I issued a press release saying how anxious people are that the Scarborough Conference may become a personality clash between Gaitskell and Cousins.

Wednesday 28 September 1960
Phone Hugh this evening to ask if he is likely to come round to our idea of

a compromise. He says he will not and if the NEC accepted it, he would not speak in the debate.

Thursday 29 September 1960

To King's Cross to catch the special train to Scarborough.

I distribute the galley proofs of George Brown's article 'The Road to Trust' which is appearing in tomorrow's *New Statesman*. Gaitskell glowers as he gets it. I talk to Jim Callaghan. Jim says, 'I'll join the bandwagon after the Conference.' I lunch with Dick, Peter and Barbara Castle and test out my resignation statement.

Caroline warned me last night that it would be fatal to resign. I thought her very unsympathetic indeed and we had rather a row. It seemed to me that the earlier I could resign the better so as to carry the fight to the Conference.

Dinner with Harold Wilson, Barbara Castle and Dick. Harold is busy composing his speech for Sunday night and frankly all he's interested in is turning the situation to his own advantage. He thinks Gaitskell can be dislodged. My opinion of him drops the more I see of him.

Phone Caroline and she's relieved that I am not resigning. Bed 10 pm.

Friday 30 September 1960

Up early and breakfast at no fewer than four different tables in the hotel trying to win people round to the benefits of peace-making.

This morning's NEC meeting was routine business in a jovial atmosphere. The left have joined the peace-making moves with the *New Statesman* flat out for us and *Tribune* not against us. The *Spectator* and *The Times* are bitterly hostile. The real issue is that Hugh and Frank won't have it, each being anxious to destroy the other. We must try to strengthen the middle and make its pull irresistible.

Long walk and talk with Barbara Castle. Talk to John Harris, Hugh's Adviser, who thinks a split is inevitable. Frank Barlow says to me: 'Being who you are, there is nothing you can do about it, old boy.' Jim Callaghan says, 'Don't worry, old boy. After this week we'll pick up the pieces.'

Despite this discouraging advice I decided I would have one more go, so I caught Gaitskell as he was going up the stairs to bed and asked if he would agree to meet me the following morning. He looked very wooden and gave me the wateriest of smiles but finally agreed and told me to come to his suite at 10 o'clock.

Saturday 1 October 1960

For the last day or two I had been talking quite openly with the press about the peace-making efforts. John Cole of the *Manchester Guardian* had been interested but sceptical. My line had been one of unlimited optimism and I had claimed repeatedly that the centre was responding well to my peace-making approaches. I told them that everyone I spoke to wanted peace-making to succeed, even though many thought it was too difficult, too late, or hopeless.

Today I had planned my interviews with Gaitskell and Cousins to see what sort of reception I would get from the two extremes. At exactly 10 o'clock I knocked at the suite of Room number 1 and Hugh opened the door and beckoned me in. He was wearing a dark blue shirt with no tie and blue trousers. He looked dejected and bored and had the longest face, which regarded me with intense distrust. I knew it was going to be a most unfortunate and unhappy interview – as it was.

I told him that I was very worried about the split, which I thought was unnecessary, and that he knew that I had worked to prevent it. I still thought there was time, with a little good will.

He replied most unsympathetically and said that under no circumstances would he be dictated to by Frank Cousins. 'Frank Cousins is *not* the only trade union leader,' he said. 'You seem to forget that.'

He then went on to attack Cousins in extremely personal terms and went so far as to say that Mrs Cousins was 'very left indeed' and to hint that she was a fellow-traveller. It was clear that on this point he was quite irrational. He said that he had underrated the strength of the campaign by the nuclear disarmers and the Communists and that it was clear that he would have to make a stand and fight on this.

'This is a much better issue on which to fight than Clause 4. On Clause 4 the PLP didn't care one way or the other, and the trade union leaders were tied by their own constitutional provisions, which pledged them to support a specifically socialist party. But here, on the defence issue, I have got the support of the trade union leaders and the majority of the PLP. This is a much better issue on which to have it out.' It was clear that he was obsessed with the necessity of purging the Party of the Left and didn't much care on which issue he would fight.

I then raised the history of the last year. He fully admitted that his policy on Clause 4 had been a tactical error.

On the merits of the defence issue I pointed out that Dick Crossman had been sacked for advocating the very policy that he, Hugh, was now making an issue of confidence. He was very angry with me and said I should have troubled to find out the facts, which were that the Shadow Cabinet had forced it on him.

I then raised the question of George Brown. Hugh smiled grimly and said that George had behaved disgracefully by trying to circulate a paper without consulting him.

I then asked Hugh why he thought that I, who had always supported him, should have got to feel so utterly hopeless about his leadership. He looked very grim and said, 'You are a very talented young man, but you have no political judgement and you don't realise that sometimes silence is golden.'

I moved on to his differences with Cousins. He said that if Cousins was in favour of NATO why didn't he say so? I agreed. I raised the question of whether our statement would permit us to purchase Skybolt. 'It would not be excluded,' said Hugh. I then pointed out that we pledged ourselves not to purchase these weapons from the USA. Gaitskell picked up this statement and pointed out that the actual phraseology was as follows: 'We are opposed to the *spread* of nuclear weapons, either by independent manufacture or by purchase from either of the two great nuclear powers.' 'So,' said Hugh, 'if Britain bought Skybolt it could be argued that it would not involve the *spread of nuclear weapons*, because Britain has nuclear weapons already.'

This was the finish for me. It was this sort of trickery which had made Frank Cousins so rightly suspicious and had driven him towards his own extreme resolution.

I left after 50 minutes, pretty despondent.

It was now pretty clear that my plan for a compromise had foundered. Over lunch the idea formed in my mind that if we couldn't get agreement between the official side and Cousins we might actually have talks to clarify the points of disagreement and invite Conference to accept a common interpretation of what these differences were and ask them to decide.

I drafted a memorandum along these lines, discussed it with Barbara Castle and got the Party office to type me out several copies. Armed with one of these I waited in the lounge for Frank Cousins to come in. He arrived with Harry Nicholas and some others and I was summoned over imperiously.

Frank was breathing rather heavily and was obviously on the top of his high horse having just come from the Compositing Committee. I said I had an idea for some talks to try to avert the crisis. He began breathing more deeply and said, 'If you think that you can save that man in this way, you've made the biggest mistake of your life.' It was clear he regarded me as an emissary from the Hampstead set, anxious to do anything that would save Gaitskell from defeat.

I tried again. 'Well, will you read my memo. . .'

'No, I won't,' he said.

'Well, how will you know what I've proposed if you don't read it?' I said bravely.

'I don't care. I won't agree. I won't read it,' he said. Harry Nicholas blushed scarlet at the way in which he was mauling me. I didn't give a damn, although it was a little disappointing. Frank seemed to realise that he'd gone too far; he grabbed the memo from my hand and looked at it. His eyes lit upon a sentence which said that 'when Conference has reached its decision the whole Party should accept it.'

'I certainly won't agree to that after the rigging and fixing of the vote which that man is out to achieve. If I defeat him, he must accept it; but I won't accept it whatever happens.

'I've always wanted to form a trade union political Party and I've half a mind to put up against that man in his own constituency of South East Leeds. And as for you, you've burned your boats now and you've no future with that man,' he said menacingly, implying that I was finished unless I worked with him on his own terms.

Anyway he eased up a little bit after that and I explained that I would be putting this proposal informally before the National Executive tomorrow and that I hoped he wouldn't turn down the idea of talks out of hand. He stuffed the memo into his pocket saying, 'All right, all right, I won't say no now,' and with this half a victory I got up and left him.

It was now pretty clear to me that both sides wanted a showdown and that Cousins and Gaitskell were completely irrational about each other. Frankly, I agreed with both of them in their assessment of the other.

I ought to add a word about the atmosphere in the Royal Hotel among the Executive. Harold Wilson thought of nothing but how he could turn the developing crisis to his own advantage. For him his speech on Sunday night at the Eve of Conference Rally was to be his great bid for the leadership and he had concocted a lot of phrases which were full of significance but took no stand. My contempt for him grew each time I met him and I don't think he has one-tenth the character of Gaitskell. Tony Greenwood is not ambitious; he just wants to be popular and he was managing the most superb double act. This evening he and Jill managed to get Frank and Nan Cousins to have dinner with them at a private table to the unspeakable rage of the left and Keep-Calmers who, as usual, had taken a long table. Tomorrow Tony and Jill are lunching with the Gaitskells and the Archbishop of York, who is coming to preach the sermon for the Conference. Dick Crossman has dropped out of peace-making a bit and the most important thing for him is that he should be Chairman of the Party next week. George Brown is due in Scarborough and everyone wonders whether he will pursue his line.

I drifted into the wide circle round Frank Cousins after dinner and he made some slightly disrespectful remarks to me so I replied very tartly, 'You may have been in the movement before I was born, but I shall still be in it long after you're dead.'

He was a bit shaken by this and went out of his way to be friendly. I wanted to get it quite clear that he wasn't going to bully me.

Just before going to bed this evening I saw Ray Gunter, who cursed me up and down in the sweetest possible way. 'You're crucifying Gaitskell,' he said. 'As you know, I'm no Gaitskell man but there are decent ways of doing this sort of thing.' I went to bed quite clear that I should resign tomorrow if the Executive refused my proposal for talks.

Sunday 2 October 1960

I canvassed the *Times, Guardian, Herald* and *Daily Mail* correspondents this morning with my plan for talks and gave a copy of the memo to John Harris.

I also heard that Harry Nicholas would be authorised to accept the suggestion of talks if the NEC put it forward at this afternoon's meeting. I therefore went to the meeting waiting for the moment when I should have to make this proposal, having firmly decided that I should resign if it was rejected.

As we met, the CND parade led by Horner, Mikardo, Canon Collins and others tramped by the hotel shouting 'Ban the Bomb! Gaitskell must go!' It almost drowned our proceedings and introduced an element of mob violence into our affairs.

When we came to the defence resolutions, including the TGWU resolution, I moved that we initiate talks. My proposal was backed by Jennie Lee, Dick Crossman and a lot of others but was bitterly opposed by Gaitskell, Gunter and Sam Watson. After the vote on it was taken I raised a point of order. I said I had tried to bring peace ... At this, the Chairman, George Brinham, interrupted me and said it was not a point of order. I raised my voice and shouted that he should hear me out and I then said I thought this was a disastrous piece of action and I proposed to resign from the Executive forthwith. I had got too excited and as I walked across the room to the door I heard George Brinham saying, 'Anyone can resign from the Executive, that is not a point of order.'

I went upstairs and saw George Brown. I told him what I had done and he said, 'Don't do anything else until you've spoken to me.' I summoned a press conference for 5.45 in the billiard room and telephoned Caroline to tell her the news. At 5.45 I read my statement to a gigantic press conference and answered questions.

I gather that I had caused some consternation after I left. I got some pretty grim looks from colleagues who later emerged from the meeting but Walter Padley (who is not a unilateralist) clutched me warmly on both shoulders and said with tears in his eyes, 'What's your personal position now? Are you going to stand again? That's all that matters.' All the secretaries from the Party were also very tearful. They are CND and were very sorry to see me go.

I rang Caroline and my dad and he was wonderfully encouraging. Caroline was sweet as could be but she thought I shouldn't have done it.

To bed but couldn't sleep till about 3.

Monday 3 October 1960

I had an excellent press this morning with full statement printed but a very cold reception from colleagues and hardly anybody said they thought I had done the right thing. Someone quoted George Lansbury's advice: 'Never resign', and somebody else hinted that it was just a stunt to get re-elected on the Executive and avoid an inevitable defeat by Mikardo. Lots of other delegates were puzzled.

For the first time in my life tonight I had a sleeping tablet and it was a relief to get a few hours of rest.

Tuesday 4 October 1960

The results of the Election for the Executive were announced this morning and I have been knocked off by Mikardo. I rang Caroline to tell her and was very dejected indeed. Hugh came out of a door unexpectedly and had to shake me by the hand with the popping of flashbulbs. Lots of delegates came up and said they thought I was not standing again and had not voted for me though mandated to do so.

I spoke in the debate but it got a rather chilly reception. This afternoon we debated the constitution and this evening I had a flaming row with Roy Jenkins and Woodrow Wyatt. The atmosphere is terribly oppressive as it builds up for tomorrow.

Wednesday 5 October 1960

The long-awaited defence debate was opened well by Sam Watson and sustained a high standard throughout. George Brown recanted, Noel Baker cheered for his Nobel Prize, declared himself a multilateralist, Denis Healey said Khrushchev used to murder cats when he was a child and Michael Foot shone like a torch of radicalism. Finally Gaitskell in a magnificent defence of multilateralism that captured the Conference threw the whole lot away in his final minutes with his attack on 'unilateralists, pacifists and fellow-travellers' and by his declared intention to 'fight, fight and fight again'. In the vote the platform was totally defeated but the left was dejected and the right wing exultant at this 'moral victory'. Bob McKenzie, Ivan Yates and the rest are plotting the new non-socialist radical Party that they would like to see emerge.

To the *Tribune* meeting to hear Soper, Mikardo and Foot and to bed very late, very depressed and feeling that I had made an absolute fool of myself by resigning. Caroline was comforting on the telephone.

Thursday 6 October 1960

Still very depressed but was cheered up by the Chief Whip, who told me this story.

He said that after the result of the NEC elections had been announced in the morning session he was walking up the hill back to his hotel for lunch, feeling rather depressed at the state of the Party. In front of him were two old ladies with white hair – obviously delegates from their constituency Parties – talking keenly together. They walked rather slowly and he overtook them. As he passed by he could just hear one saying in a squeaky voice to the other 'I just didn't know which way to vote. I wanted to kick that little shit Wedgwood Benn up the arse and then that bastard Mikardo got on.'

The Chief Whip is a great friend of mine and the tears rolled down his face as he told me.

I went to the Fabian Tea today where Crosland and Crossman debated their rival approaches. It was very cordial and each was an outstanding advocate of his own point of view. The Labour Party would be mad to create conditions in which one or other of them was driven out.

John Horner asked me to his annual FBU Dinner which gets bigger every year. After the meal I was called on unexpectedly to speak – having had no idea it was coming. All I could think of was the Chief Whip's story and it went down like a bombshell.

At 11 o'clock to the Boilermakers' party where comradeship was lubricated with beer and I had a lot of really pleasant conversation. I had a long talk to Jim Matthews, another even more affectionate with Walter Padley and quite a talk with Frank Cousins. Also got into a huddle with Harold Wilson who sees the whole business entirely as a way of getting him the leadership or deputy leadership. The left have really lost confidence in him.

Dan McGarvey of the Boilermakers' Society sang some songs of the Irish Rebellion and Hugh Delargy, the Thurrock MP, swayed and wept like a child. Then came some 'Non-con' hymns which drew gigantic choruses and proved how much stronger the chapel is than Marx in our traditions.

To bed at 2.30 feeling much more cheerful.

Friday 7 October 1960
Home on the early train.

So glad to get back again after the hectic and anxious week in Scarborough. Caroline was rather cross with me for having resigned but though it was probably a mistake no one ever achieves anything without mistakes, and people forget.

Saturday 8 October 1960
Ring Peter Shore and we agree that Gaitskell can't really ever lead a united socialist Labour Party.

Kenneth Robinson, on the other hand, rings to say that Gaitskell seems to be the only man who comes out of Scarborough with honour.

To Beryl Mishcon's party. Met Eric Estorick, the most successful art dealer in London. His clients include Paul Getty, the oil man, and many Hollywood stars.

Tuesday 11 October 1960
Harold Wilson rang up to ask me to go and see him and to ask if I had

still got all those copies of George Brown's article, 'The Road to Trust'. I bought 2,000 but they became irrelevant and I left them in Scarborough in their original wrappings.

I'm keeping out of everything at the moment but it's nice to think that people want to know my opinions.

Dick did a broadcast tonight which was a brilliant exposition of the constitutional position and a plea for sanity.

Sunday 16 October 1960

To Bristol for the weekend. Worked in my hotel room this morning and at 2.30 to the Walter Baker Hall for an emergency meeting of the General Management Committee at which I could report back from Conference. It was quite full and included left, right and centre.

I spoke for 45 minutes describing everything that had happened and the way ahead I thought we should follow. There were a lot of questions and comments and in the end the chairman proposed (quite unknown to me) a vote of confidence in me which received unanimous support. A 'Gaitskell must go' resolution was ruled out of order and I was tremendously encouraged to think that they are really behind me.

Back to London.

Monday 17 October 1960

This evening an hour on *Panorama* about the American Polaris programme. In three years there will be 45 of these nuclear submarines roaming the seas, each with 18 Polaris missiles with H bomb warheads. Foreign bases will disappear. This gives us our great chance to feel our way through to independent foreign policy.

Wednesday 19 October 1960

Sydney Silverman's letter to Gaitskell threatening a Party within a Party and the right-wing manifesto were published today. They threatened a major split if conciliation doesn't take place.

Lunch with Frank Pakenham at the National Bank in Old Broad Street, at his request, to discuss peace-making. He said that he believed Communism was the greatest evil in the world and could not support what he called my 'moral neutralism in giving priority to the need for a *détente* between Moscow and Washington'.

To the House of Commons, where I typed out my own manifesto and had fifty copies of it duplicated.

Saw Harold Wilson just before the Shadow Cabinet meeting and he said he was going to make a really tough speech on Friday night. 'Better to be disliked than despised,' he said to me rather oddly.

Thursday 20 October 1960

Dick rings early. He spent till 2 am this morning trying to persuade

Harold to stand and to persuade Tony Greenwood to stand down in favour of Harold. Harold and Tony are meeting at 10 am this morning for final talks.

Tony is proving to be very tough and trying to impose conditions on Harold. He feels that he stood out first and doesn't see why he should be overtaken by someone who is not a unilateralist, but Dick is hopeful.

At 11.40 am Dick rings again. The talks were a success. This afternoon Harold is giving a press conference and announcing his decision to stand. He is coming out strongly in favour of defence for Britain but saying that the differences can and must be bridged. He has been promised full support from the Bevanite left, and Tony Greenwood is issuing a most helpful statement saying that despite his differences with Harold he is prepared to support him. This is exactly what is required as it makes Harold a centralist and does not smear him with the left-wing label. Dick says Harold has stiffened a great deal and is ready to make a fight – though not a personal one.

George Wigg tells Dick that a poll by a Wolverhampton paper shows an overwhelming majority of local Labour MPs are against the Gaitskell policy of fight, fight and fight again.

Dick says that he thinks everyone should now come out openly in support of Harold – except himself as Chairman of the Party. I agree. If Harold is defeated and Hugh stays on we must form a centre and left-centre parliamentary opposition of our own operating from the back benches for a year and showing how the Government can be fought without going out of our way to humiliate Gaitskell.

Friday 21 October 1960
Rang Audrey Callaghan. She said Jim was very depressed, but had come back from Czechoslovakia convinced that socialism does work.

Thursday 27 October 1960
Dick rang again to urge me to come out for Harold. Caroline is dead against it. I wrestled with my conscience and them both, but decide I won't as I have said enough already, have little confidence in Harold and am rather sick of the whole business.

Friday 28 October 1960
Dick wrote this morning a sympathetic and rather touching letter saying he understood the mixed tangle of motives that led me not to come out for Harold, but by this morning I *had* decided to come out and issued a statement saying why I couldn't support Gaitskell and putting it on constitutional grounds. I also wrote a personal note to Hugh, telling him – in sorrow more than in anger – why.

Big talking point nowadays is *Lady Chatterley's Lover*. The case is filling the papers.

House of Commons,

London. S.W.1

31st October, 1960.

PERSONAL.

Dear Tony,

Thank you for your letter of
the 28th October. I appreciate the'
spirit in which it is written, but
I don't propose to reply.

Hugh

Anthony Wedgwood Benn, Esq., M.P.,

Saturday 29 October 1960

Issue press release saying Harold Wilson is right to work for an independent foreign policy. This seems to me to be the key issue and not unilateralism.

Thursday 3 November 1960

At 2.30 the House met and for an hour the Labour Party was in public shambles: Members denounced each other and Sydney Silverman publicly repudiated Gaitskell. We cannot survive as a united Party if this goes on for more than a week or two.

Another fierce argument at tea with Strachey, Strauss, Douglas Jay and Kenneth Robinson – alas in the wrong camp.

To the Party meeting to hear the result of the vote. It was as follows: Gaitskell 166 and Wilson 81, with 7 not voting.

Hugh thus commands just under two-thirds of the PLP – a severe jolt. For Deputy Leader, George got 118, Fred Lee 73, and they will fight it out on a second ballot when Jim Callaghan's 55 votes will be the decisive factor. From our point of view it is a perfectly satisfactory result.

Saturday 5 November 1960

Worked in the office this morning. Guy Fawkes fireworks this afternoon.

Report of Hugh Gaitskell being shouted down at a meeting when he spoke on defence.

Sunday 6 November 1960
Hugh shouted down again yesterday. The Party now at its worst.

Tuesday 8 November 1960
I nominated Harold Wilson and Fred Lee for the Parliamentary Committee. The left is against their standing, but a rebel group on the backbenches working all year would achieve nothing because it would have no cohesion. I am under some criticism for agreeing to stand as well.

Wednesday 9 November 1960
Up at 6.30 and watched the TV reports from America. Kennedy is beating Nixon though it is going to be a close thing.

Wednesday 16 November 1960
Father rang this morning to say how glad he was that my name was not starred in this morning's *Times* as an 'approved' candidate for the Shadow Cabinet.

To the Commons for a Broadcasting meeting. At 4.45 a messenger came in and said 'Lord Appleby' wants to see you urgently. I said I had never heard of him and was busy. Five minutes later the messenger came back with a note from Lord Amulree (who is a doctor): 'Sorry to bother you, but your father is in the House and not very well. I think he should be taken home and got a doctor. It is very difficult to decide what is wrong.' I left the meeting at once and met Amulree in the Commons Lobby. We hurried to the Lords' Lobby where Father had been sitting, but he was gone.

We found him in the Peers' Guest Room, lying down in a deep armchair. He said he felt dizzy and had a neuralgia pain. 'I won't talk,' he said, 'I'll have a bit of a rest. Ma's coming for tea.' His pulse was very weak and he was cold, sweating a little. I went to phone Mother to get Dr Pitts to come.

When I went back to Father he was almost unconscious and so we got a wheelchair and carried him down the stairs where he waited in one of the little dining rooms in the Harcourt Corridor. He had his coat on and hat and began breathing very heavily so that I thought the end must be very near. We decided instead to get an ambulance to take him to Westminster Hospital. Finally this arrived and we wheeled him out into it. He was now completely unconscious and I held his head in my arms as the ambulance went out under the arches, through the courtyard, past the Speaker's House and through New Palace Yard.

It was very obvious that he was leaving the Palace of Westminster for the last time. The ambulance rang its bell to get through the busy traffic and at 5.45 we got to the Casualty Department of Westminster Hospital where Mother and Dr Pitts were waiting.

At 6.45 the result of the electrocardiogram showed that he had a coronory thrombosis. Dave and June arrived and we saw Dr Lloyd, the specialist, who said it was extremely serious. Lloyd said Father would talk but he didn't seem to hear when the doctor told him that he must be as quiet as a mouse. He said the next two days were the most dangerous and the question was, had he the reserves of strength to recover? Father said to me, 'What's the news? I'm not staying here, you know. You can't bully me.'

Thursday 17 November 1960
Mother and Father's 40th wedding anniversary. News of Clark Gable's death. Mother phoned at 9.45 to say that Father's blood pressure was up above the danger level.

I went to the Commons for lunch and then to the hospital at 12.30.

Dave came to the hospital and at 2.30 the sister told us that Father was very seriously ill and could go at any moment, although he was just holding his own. I looked in to see him and he said, 'Hello James. Where's Ma? I certainly did have a thump. I can't understand it. How's Caroline and the children?' He looked very, very pale.

At 6.45 Dr Lloyd said he thought Father was rallying a bit, but Pitts said it was touch and go.

I went back to the flat for a few sandwiches and then to the hospital where I sat for half an hour holding Father's hand. He was pretty much unconscious. But his mind was going back. 'Father used to say "Boys, I never take an engagement on Sunday for money"' and, 'That was in 1919' and, 'Old boy, you're absolutely right.'

He took my finger and used it as a pencil, writing away.

At 9.15 Mother was whispering in his ear, 'Don't worry' and he said, 'It's no good without breath.'

At 9.30 Dave and I were talking and the sister hurried in and said 'Come at once. He's very distressed and I'm very worried.'

Notes

Chapter Four

1. (p.201) Anthony Nutting, Minister of State at the Foreign Office, resigned in early November 1956 in opposition to his Government's actions over Suez; he subsequently wrote *No End of a Lesson* (1967) exposing the collusion and the disreputable conduct of Eden and the Government.

2. (p.223) On December 5, 1956, in dawn raids by the South African police, 140 prominent opponents of apartheid were arrested and subsequently tried for treason or offences under the Suppression of Communism Act.

3. (p.244) When the Speaker refused to grant an emergency debate about the use of British forces against Omani villages I took the only course open for challenging his ruling by tabling a motion of censure on the Speaker. This had not been done since Father moved a similar motion against Speaker Whitley in the 1920s. By convention such a motion has to be debated. On the day of debate I moved a censure motion but announced that I would not press it to a vote.

4. (p.300) John Stonehouse, the MP for Wednesbury, always took a strong interest in African affairs, and was manager for African Co-operative Societies in Uganda in the early 1950s. In February 1959 while visiting Nyasaland he was ordered to leave on the grounds that his continued presence amounted to an incitement to the Africans to civil disobedience. The Labour opposition tabled a motion of censure against the Government for failing to support him.

5. (p.324) Clause Four of the Labour Party Constitution, which includes Labour's commitment to 'the common ownership of the means of production, distribution and exchange' was adopted in 1918 and has been printed ever since on every Party membership card. After Labour's Election defeat in 1959 Gaitskell wanted it removed as part of his modernizing strategy. He failed to win the support of the NEC for this plan and Conference re-affirmed Clause Four.

6. (p.330) On May 17 1960 a 'Big Four' summit, in Paris, to which Eisenhower, Khrushchev, Macmillan and De Gaulle had gone to build up east-west rapprochement, broke up in disarray after three days. It was overshadowed by the shooting down over Soviet air space of an American U-2 aircraft before the Summit began. The 'U-2 spy plane' was piloted by Gary Powers, who had baled out and was imprisoned for spying, and in 1962 was exchanged for a Soviet spy imprisoned in America. The Americans claimed that Powers had 'strayed off course' while carrying out weather research.

7. (p.342) Frank Cousins, General Secretary of the Transport and General Workers Union, was prime advocate of unilateralism in the Party. At the Conference of 1960 the TGWU resolution rejected any defence policy 'based on the threat of the use of strategic or tactical nuclear weapons' and called for the cessation of manufacture, the banning of aircraft carrying nuclear weapons, and nuclear bases, the admission of China to the UN and the reopening of international discussions to secure world disarmament and peaceful coexistence.' This motion was carried narrowly by 43,000 votes and the NEC policy statement on defence was defeated. Hugh Gaitskell pledged to 'fight, fight and fight again' in his speech supporting the NEC motion.

5

Into the Wilderness
1960–62

Because my Father died suddenly I did not have the opportunity I had anticipated to discuss with him how to handle the constitutional consequences to me. At the moment of his death, in constitutional law and practice, I succeeded to the peerage, and was automatically disqualified from the House of Commons. All the earlier efforts to avert this situation had failed, and the chances were non-existent or very slight that at this stage another effort would succeed.

Therefore on the night of 17 November when he died in Westminster Hospital, I found the House of Commons door shut to me.

At this stage the diary ceases because of all the circumstances of my grief over my father's death, the renewed campaign to avoid disqualification, my constituency case work and political activities in Bristol which I continued voluntarily, and the need to earn a living. By then, also, I had four children.

It was not until 28 July the following year that I was finally and completely removed from the Commons by the Election Court which seated Malcolm St Clair, the Conservative candidate whom I had defeated at Bristol in 1959, in my place.

The only glimmer of hope that remained was that a joint Select Committee of both Houses, which had been announced by the Government, might issue a report that would allow MPs who were sons of peers to remove their disqualification from service in the Commons. The Government was of course mindful of the fact that two peers – Lords Hailsham and Home – were potential contenders for the Conservative Party leadership and that legislation to help me would also free them to enter the Commons.

During this period of limbo, my old friend David Butler, a Fellow of Nuffield College, came to do a series of interviews for an oral history project which he had launched. He interviewed me in a very penetrating way and the resulting transcript recalls in some detail the story of that crucial year from the death of my father to the final clanging of the gates at the Palace of Westminster.

It is from these interviews that the following extracts are taken.

Father had been suffering from bronchitis, and he broke a couple of ribs in the summer of 1960. When you're eighty-three, I guess this is a serious thing to happen. But he enjoyed reasonably good health. He had his very good days when he was full of energy, and on 15 November he made a speech and had a tremendous row with the Labour peers about it, on a question of a plaque for Tilak, the Indian Nationalist leader. On 16 November he went to the House and made a speech on the situation in Central Africa. I was at the House at a Committee meeting downstairs when the messenger came in at about 4 pm with the message from Lord Amulree.

The following evening, he died.

David Butler: Did he know what was happening?

He had recovered during the first evening and began talking and said, 'If you think you can keep me in hospital you've made a very great mistake.' I sat with him and he held my finger and tried to write with it as if it was a pencil. He was passionately keen to get on with his work, and that was always his character.

Of course, at the moment of his death the only thing on my mind was all the arrangements that had to be made. The moment came, as I had known it always would come, when one had to begin this job at the very moment when one was least inclined to think of anything else at all. But, as it happened, my mother found the battle the thing that really kept her

Arundel Castle

10th December 1960.

The Viscount Stansgate.
12, Holland Park Avenue,
Kensington,
LONDON W.11.

Dear Stansgate.

　　　　You must forgive me if you do not approve of the way I address you, but until such / time as you can effect a change I must be correct.

　　　　I do not think I can be of much help to you, but I must say that there would appear to me to be more difficulties in the way if Peers are to be given the right to renounce their Peerages for Life. After all, there are their children to consider. I suppose there would be fewer difficulties if it is intended to permit Peers to sit and vote in the House of Commons, if elected as M.P's.

　　　　It may be that some of our methods are today out-of-date.

Yours sincerely
Norfolk.

going. The funny thing was I never had a chance to discuss the tactics with him as I'd always imagined I would. I'd always supposed he'd have an illness of a week or two, if not a month or two, and that he and I would have planned every stage together, which he would love to have done. But it didn't work like that.

Looking back on it, I suppose I'm almost ashamed that the thought of the battle came to me so soon. It naturally did because with his last breath I was out of Parliament too. The fact was, his death took two people out of Parliament. I did think then that I might go straight over to the House to take my seat and either not say anything so that I had sat after he died, or else raise a point of privilege and say, 'Mr Speaker I have to tell you that my father has died and I don't intend to be removed from the House', in the way that Lord Selborne had done in 1895. But it would have been a stunt, it would have been a sensational thing to have done, and I don't know that it would have helped very much. The Speaker would have ordered me to withdraw immediately and I don't think it would have contributed anything, so I'm glad I didn't do it.

The letters were already pouring in. I wrote a formal letter to the Speaker. I said: 'I have to tell you that my father's died and that I don't propose to acquiesce in the acceptance of a disqualification. I want to make this clear from the outset. I would like to come and talk to you about it.' I took it over to the House myself on the Friday at about 4 o'clock in the afternoon. The Clerk of the House had gone home – I asked the Clerk in the Table Office to take it to the Speaker that afternoon. Then I went home. The press had, of course, reported Father's death. One or two of them had noted that I had tried in 1955 to get rid of the peerage. But I think they assumed that the battle was completely over and forgotten. It was just another case of an MP being taken out of Parliament against his will.

On the following day, Saturday 19 November, I was with my mother most of the day, and that evening I got out the files that I had kept open over the years. They were dusty and messy; but they were in the right order and they were all categorised.

As soon as Father died the escalator was beginning to move. The gates had clanged in the Commons and I was moved, against my will, up the other end of the building. Of course I was terribly sad and upset, and felt very lonely that the one man who could advise me wasn't there to advise me – Father. At this stage, and regularly throughout the battle, I would plunge into the deepest, blackest depression which really made it impossible to work for sometimes two or three days at a time. I've never been so gloomy about it.

On Sunday 20 November I went along to see Geoffrey Bing at his flat in Portland Street. There he was, larger than life: bushy eyebrows, smoking cheroots at a tremendous rate, pacing about in his braces, all bulging, and like a big American tycoon, but terribly friendly. He and his wife were great admirers of Father's. So I felt a sympathetic atmosphere. His advice was terrific. He suggested all sorts of new lines. He was one who suggested I should draft an Instrument of Renunciation. I ruled this out on the grounds that I'd tried to get it enacted in '55 and had failed. He said, 'Oh, you must try again.' So we drafted a rather clever Instrument of Renunciation which said: 'Inasmuch as I renounced in 1955, I am not now, nor ever have been, nor have any wish to be, a Peer.' This was an extremely useful thing to have done, because it did give me something to hang on to in the days following Father's death when I argued later that I never had been a peer.

I also went to see Gerald Gardiner. He had spoken at a dinner for Father, and I knew him slightly. He is so clearly the brightest brain at the Bar in the Labour Party and I knew that when I went to see Gaitskell, he would say to me, 'Have you seen any lawyers about it?' He wouldn't have had any faith in my legal capacity. So I thought that to put it to Gerald Gardiner would be worth while. I rang him up and he said, come round at once. I went round to his chambers, and it was a very weird interview. He's pasty-faced and impassive and he gave me an icy smile when I went in. I sat down opposite him. I felt in a very uncomfortable position. First of all, I thought I was taking up his time; secondly he showed no signs of interest and thirdly he didn't say anything about Father's death, which I thought was slightly strange. I explained the case that I'd put to Geoffrey. I went through it fairly snappily and at the end I waited. Gardiner didn't say anything at first, and then he said, 'Well, that's very interesting.' So I said, 'Do you think it has a chance of standing up?' And he said, 'I think it's certainly worth trying.' I waited for him to say, 'Why not put it this way or that way,' but instead he said, 'Well, I don't really know anything about this.' So I thanked him and left after about 20 minutes. I was very depressed because I thought: this is just a courtesy. But I gathered afterwards that he is like that; that this is just his manner. Still, it certainly was worth while because I could say I had seen Gerald Gardiner.

On the Monday I made an appointment with the Speaker, and when I went to see him he said, rather facetiously, 'I've made an order, my Lord, that you are to be kept out of the Chamber', which I thought was a bit offensive. Anyway, he was perfectly friendly, but said that he had decided that I was to be kept out.' I asked 'Why?' and he said, 'Because it is now settled, since the Selborne case, that when a man inherits a peerage then he is kept out. Then I asked, 'How do you know that I've inherited?' He said, 'I've got your letter, saying that your father has died, and as far as I'm concerned that is *prima facie* evidence that you've succeeded.'

But the Speaker assumed that this was just a little protest and a struggle before I was carried away. I don't think anybody at that time realised how serious and persistent the campaign was going to be. So that was settled.

I went to see Rab Butler. Butler was very cordial, and I was misled by this. He said, 'Very interesting case.' I told him what I had in mind and he said, 'Well, we'll have to look at that. I'm sure Harold Macmillan would like these little points examined.' I got the idea that he was vaguely on my side, which was clearly quite wrong. He went on: 'By the way, one thing: would your scheme permit Quintin to come back?' So I said, 'Well, no, it wouldn't really.' So he said, 'Ah, well that's all right.' This was an indication, which I've had from time to time, that objection to Quintin's return may be a major factor in the Government's mind; certainly in the mind of all would-be successors to the premiership, of whom Rab was the leading one. Possibly if Quintin came back he might represent a threat to Butler's leadership.

I went from Butler to the office of Sir Edward Fellowes, the Clerk of the House of Commons. I think I should really say a word about Sir Edward Fellowes at this stage, because I saw him regularly right up to the by-election. I haven't seen him once since. My relationship with him, and his feeling about me, is a very important part of this story. He's a man without legal training: big, red-faced, rather like a country squire, in a way. His feeling about me was that of a headmaster to one of his brighter but cheekier pupils. He would like to encourage him, but at the same time, the thing's got to be kept within bounds. I used to go and see him whenever I wanted to, and I am devoted to him as a matter of fact, although I think he could perhaps have done more to help than he did. The conversations would always begin in this way: I would make my main point, he would be very shocked by it, look terribly disapproving and say, 'This is absolutely impossible' and he would indicate that it verged upon the monstrous. Then I would become extremely sweet and he would mellow and in about five minutes he was telling me how to do it. A few minutes earlier he had ruled it out as contrary to the whole spirit of parliamentary life.

We used to have tea together. It was like going to see an old don or a headmaster. His secretary would bring in the tea and a tin of cake would be opened. I would sit at one side of the table, and he would sit at the other, in his black knee-breeches, and offer me cake and we would laugh a great deal.

We went over the drafting of the Petition to the House for a Committee and he went to see Butler regularly; the reference to the Committee of Privileges was partly his achievement.

I was stopped by countless Members with sympathy about Father, which I found very hard to bear. The most difficult thing about a bereavement is people being sympathetic and friendly. It was almost impossible to control oneself. I was conscious of the fact that the affection for Father, which was tremendous – I think he must really have been one of the most popular peers and members of the Labour Party – was working in my favour. A lot of Conservatives came up as well, and I got the feeling at that moment that it was going to be all right.

I worked a great deal with Mrs Small, my secretary, a most wonderful woman. We drafted the Instrument of Renunciation. I had to get my mother and my brother as executors to come with me to the bank to get the brown paper parcel with Father's Letters Patent. I'd never actually seen them before. I took them along with me to the House of Lords because it was my intention that day (Tuesday 22 November) to sign the Instrument, and return the Letters Patent to Buckingham Palace. But before that I went to the Gallery of the Lords to hear the tributes paid to Father, which were very moving. Hailsham made one of the finest speeches I've ever heard. Then Bert Alexander made a speech, and Clem said a word or two, and it was really a lovely occasion.

After that I went to see Gaitskell. That was a very unhappy interview. Of course he was angry with me because of the row over defence. I've a very short memory and my father's death had obliterated from my mind all recollection of the row over the bomb and the Conference and so on. Looking back on it now, I realise that it must have been a much bigger factor in his mind than the peerage case. I had caused him a lot of trouble; he would have thought I'd stabbed him in the back and was now coming along and asking for a favour. So I must give him full credit for his understandable irritation with me.

I sat down in his room at the House and he said three things to me: 'Well, you can't expect the Party to make a fuss over you.' Secondly: 'We do need young peers very badly in the House of Lords, you know; all the peers are so old.' Thirdly he said, 'Meanwhile, in view of the fact that you're no longer a Member of the House of Commons, and you're not yet a Member of the House of Lords, you'd better not come to any more Party meetings.'

I was really knocked back by this because I had expected a rather different attitude. I think I got slightly angry. I said: 'It's all very well, saying you need young peers, but what am I going to live on?' 'Well,' he said, 'I hadn't thought of that. I suppose there is some difficulty in this.'

I'm afraid that, from then on, I never regarded Gaitskell as a particular friend. His attitude throughout the case has been very simple. When it's been in the news and leading articles have been coming out, then he joins in and makes a wonderful speech attacking the primitive tribal customs which hold back a Member, and all that. But as soon as the thing goes out of the headlines and becomes submerged, he forgets it. He thinks the public forgets it and he thinks there's nothing much worth doing about it.

So I thought one thing I ought to do was to go and see the Editor of *The*

Times. I'd never liked William Haley at all. He was the Director-General of the BBC when I was there in 1949 and I'd never thought much of him. His line on all political issues had always annoyed me; nevertheless I felt I must go and see him, because he seemed to be a key figure. But I *was* warmly disposed to him because of the superb and generous obituary he'd written about Father. I went along to *The Times* building and into the Editor's office. Haley settled down in his big wing chair and put me on a couch.

I told him everything; I said, 'I'm going to ask for a Select Committee. This is my argument, which I think has some merit. I've discussed it with certain lawyers, and if they throw me out I shall probably stand again in the Election myself.' I said, 'I would be very grateful if you could keep it quiet.'

He said, 'Oh, the Editor's office in *The Times* has heard many, many secrets. You may rely upon me to be discreet.'

It was like seeing another headmaster, and I thought of all the Foreign Secretaries who'd been there and pleaded with him. It was very pleasant. Then I said, 'What shall I do about the press?' I really needed his advice. He said, 'If I were you I'd be very careful about it, because it might seem that you were using the press to try to get your way against the authorities. I think it might harm you.'

I thanked him and he got up and walked with me out of his office and took me down in the lift with the two clanky gates. He went with me down the steps round the corner to the front door of the *Times* building and took me by the hand. I was really almost overcome with gratitude and emotion, and of course, *The Times* from then on was absolutely a firm and reliable friend.

I went straight back to the Commons from the *Times* building and I saw Jo Grimond in the corridor. That's another good thing about the Commons: you bump into people. Jo was very sympathetic; much more sympathetic than Gaitskell. I told him what I had in mind. He didn't commit himself in any way. But I suppose then I had in the back of my mind the idea that if there was going to be an Election might I be opposed by a Liberal candidate. Grimond's support has been tremendous.

My next job – which I had to complete that same day – was to get the Instrument of Renunciation witnessed. I went back into the Commons Library to sign the Instrument and I looked for a couple of MPs who would witness it. Dick Mitchison was there, a QC, very senior man, and Edwin Gooch, a trade union MP. I thought they would make a good pair. So I signed and they both witnessed it and smiled at me in a slightly tolerant and amused way.

So I now had the Instrument of Renunciation and a letter to the Lord Chamberlain and my Letters Patent wrapped in a brown paper parcel. I took them along to the post office at the House of Commons and I paid sixpence – which is what you pay a messenger per mile – and a boy cycled to Buckingham Palace that night and took the Letters Patent back.

It was a symbolic rejection of the peerage entirely; I didn't want to be a peer or have anything to do with it; it was also a courtesy – the documents that the Crown had given to the family to confer the peerage should be returned to the custody of the Crown. I'm sure that was right. Anyway, that was the end of the day – Tuesday 22 November – and I went home.

On Wednesday morning the avalanche of calls began and one of the nightmares was that the phone rang all day continuously. As soon as one put it down, it rang again. The siege continued throughout that week, and at other stages in the campaign. That night I decided that the best way of dealing with the press was to hold a meeting of press lobby correspondents to give them the points that I was working on. So I called a Lobby meeting and it was absolutely packed out. I did say at that meeting that I wished they wouldn't describe me as 'The Reluctant Peer', which suggested a bored young aristocrat who asked to be excused from public duties, but 'The Persistent Commoner', which suggested a rather aggressive, awkward chap who couldn't be put down. This appeared for a day or two, but the Reluctant Peer was too heavily entrenched in the reporting of the case to be altogether obliterated and it stuck all through.

On the Thursday, Dingle Foot rang up and offered his services. He said he'd be very glad to help in any way he could. This was a tremendous encouragement to me because Dingle Foot is a distinguished constitutional lawyer and I was grateful to him for this. I said that I would be delighted if he would help me. I then went to the House again and saw Fellowes. I was in the Library when a message came that someone was waiting to see me. Outside in the corridor was Mr John Hunt of the Crown Office, with a messenger – and there were my Letters Patent returned to me!

Charlie Pannell – who I used to see a lot of – came up to me that day and we had a talk. His friendship and support throughout this has been absolutely wonderful. He's a very learned man, although quite uneducated in the formal sense. He's a great reader and a great expert on parliamentary procedure; he's a fine Parliamentarian, there's no question about that. I've always regarded him as a great friend, although he's been a critic of mine. He thought I was totally wrong to resign on the defence issue, which was only a little earlier. But he just became my champion – my shop steward, as he used to say. He promised to do all he possibly could to help. I confided in him about my interview with Hugh. He's also a good friend and admirer of Hugh Gaitskell's, he's one of the Leeds members, like Hugh. Later on, he travelled up to Leeds with Hugh and talked to him for the whole of the four-hour journey and as a result of this Hugh made the most wonderful weekend speech. But then, of course, the press had come out and Hugh was rushing to the help of the victor. That's what they used to say about Mussolini.

That day, also, the reshuffle of Shadow Cabinet offices took place and Hugh left me as the Transport Spokesman. That was very decent of him; there's no reason why he should have done it. But I think Charlie put it to him that if I was dropped from there it would indicate that the PLP had given up hope of victory, and Hugh did leave me as Transport Spokesman for about another week.

Butler: Could we get on to the events of Friday 25 November?

On the Friday, the first press comment from Bristol reached me. There'd been a leader saying that this was a scandal and that Bristol was preparing for a by-election. BRISTOL WILL BACK BENN as far as I remember was the headline, with a quotation from Herbert Rogers, the Secretary of the Party and part-time agent. I hadn't at that stage communicated with Bristol, except possibly on the telephone. I had been busy and felt there was nothing much I could say to them, but clearly I did make a mistake not going to them earlier.

Now that day, Martin Redmayne, the Tory Chief Whip, rang me up. He said that the Cabinet had agreed to a Select Committee. He couldn't tell me offhand whether it was going to be a Select Committee or a Privileges Committee, but they had agreed anyway that there would be a Committee to look into my case. I told him I was going to Bristol that day and it would be nice to be able to inform them. A few minutes later I had a further message from Redmayne to say would I be sure not to use my railway warrant. I was extremely angry about this: it was nothing whatsoever to do with the Government Chief Whip whether I used my railway warrant or not. Of course I wasn't going to use it, but it was just the sort of niggling, hostile point that really made my blood boil. That day also, my income tax papers came back from the Fees Office marked 'Viscount Stansgate'. So I got my 'cards', and my pay stopped, on the night of 17 November.

In Bristol on the following morning, Herbert Rogers, who was Cripps' agent for many years, came to collect me and took me to meet the loyal Party officers. His idea at that stage was that there should be a new petition in Bristol which should be signed within the constituency. He said to me: 'It would be much easier, you know, if you could offer some money to the local Party to help to finance this.' He explained 'We haven't got any money. We've got an overdraft of about £2,000.' I said, 'Well look, I'm afraid I can't. My pay has stopped. I'm not in a position to donate an amount, and I think in any case it would be open to the gravest objection if it got out that the local Party was backing me in this fight, and that I had transferred to them £200 or £500 for this purpose.' It would look like sheer bribery.

He never mentioned it again. But, of course, the money problem in the constituency is a continuing one and for this reason it was all the more courageous of them to go ahead with the by-election when there was no guarantee that it wouldn't cost them a great deal. Anyway, this is the key meeting. I went to see Bert Pegler, the Chairman of the Party, and we went to his office. He is a Dock Officer in the Transport and General Workers' Union and he's got an office on the quayside of the docks in Bristol. The press were there. We went into this little room, completely surrounded by cobblestones leading down to the pier, and in the office were Pegler, Emrys Jones, the Assistant Regional Organiser, Les Bridges, the Borough Party Secretary, Herbert Rogers and myself. I noticed, first of all, a slight lack of enthusiasm on all the faces. Pegler had always been dead against this, on the same grounds that George Brown has been, really. Nothing personal, but he doesn't think it has anything to do with the Labour movement.

I outlined the position and told them what the alternatives were and what might happen. Pegler was extremely cautious, laying great stress on the possibility that the constituency might be represented by a Tory and that this would really be a very serious thing. Emrys Jones was non-committal because he was there as an observer for the National Party, and Les Bridges really exploded with irritation and said he hoped it was absolutely clear that what I was doing wasn't in any way an attack on the system of hereditary peerage. I said, 'Of course it does involve this.' He said, 'You can't broaden out into an attack on hereditary peerages', and I didn't pursue that. But from then on I knew that he was very much anti. I realised at this point that I had failed completely in my consultation with Bristol.

On the Monday (28 November) I was really frightened because I was going to Bristol. I didn't know what I would find when they were gathered all together. Sara Barker was sent down from Smith Square on behalf of the Executive, and at 7 o'clock we met in the little office at Unity House. Sara Barker, opening the discussion, said it was a unique situation. The Party had never faced this before and the normal by-election procedure couldn't be followed; the Executive agreed it wouldn't be right to set any procedure in motion in the circumstances; that I was legally disqualified. Therefore, they recommended that no action of any kind should be taken by the local Party. They were prepared to wait on events. They wished me all success in the Select Committee which was going to be set up; if I failed, which she made it pretty clear she thought certain, then the situation would have to be reviewed.

Then there were a number of questions. One chap said, 'What about the possibility of a by-election?' Sara Barker said that it was for the

Labour Whip to decide when he wished to issue a writ, so then the question arose about local political activity. Ted Rees said that they must take certain steps and all that.

I then presented my plan for the Petition and Sara Barker said that the Party would be perfectly prepared to help me in the House of Commons but if a by-election came the whole thing would be quite different. Whatever they did that night, the local Party mustn't prejudge the decision.

As throughout the entire pre-Election campaign, the machine was trying to persuade the local Party to do nothing. This was the key night. We had a meeting first of all at 7 with the officers and the Executives and at 7.45 we met the GMC. This was the night when the support in Bristol crystallised and from then, nothing ever changed.

Butler: I wonder if we could just go back on one or two things during the week following your father's death? I don't think you said anything about the position of Rab.

I regarded Rab subsequently as an enemy. But I must give him credit for three friendly things: first, he did ask about the family and how they were managing, in an extremely friendly way and as if he really realised what a problem this would be. It has been a problem for me financially and so on. The second thing was that I was always able to talk to him very frankly, and I always made a point of telling him everything that I was going to do. He congratulated me on this in a cordial way, which suggests that the tactic of putting all one's cards on the table was an absolutely right one. The third thing about him was a specific point. A few days after Father's death I wrote a letter to the Prime Minister asking him whether, in the interim, he would arrange that Ministers would continue to reply to my constituency correspondence, because I was very worried that my constituents would suffer. I told Rab about this and he said, 'No, no, whatever you do don't send that letter', indicating quite clearly that it was courting a refusal from the Prime Minister which I'm almost certain I would have had. That was the first clear indication I had – there were others later – that the Prime Minister was, really, the principal opponent to the whole business.

In December, Jack Ashley, a producer at the BBC and Labour candidate, wrote to me and said he would be prepared to organise a group of Labour candidates who would refuse to stand for Bristol South-East. That was rather sweet of him, because I didn't know what attitude the Party would take and a letter from a number of them would have been very helpful. As it happened, it wasn't necessary. Dick Taverne also rang me to say he was working flat out on the case.

Butler: Let's talk more generally about your approach to the Privilege Committee.

This is a Committee which has been convened about six times since the war, once or twice on big issues. It's a terribly senior Committee, isn't it?

Yes, the Committee of Privileges is a standing Select Committee. It is set up every session automatically with the Leader of the House in the chair. The Leader of the Opposition, the Attorney-General and other senior Members of Parliament sit on it, and matters of parliamentary privilege are referred to it, as and when required. It's not met more than half a dozen times since the war. But it was felt, in this case, that it was the appropriate body to refer it to because the privilege issue was one of the main ones, and a Select Committee might not have felt powerful enough to deal with that. Dingle Foot had offered to appear for me without fee.

Dingle didn't think anything of my argument on renunciation. He didn't think anything of the House of Commons Disqualification Act. He didn't think anything of privilege. His view was that the only thing – hope – was the argument on the Writ of Summons, ie that I would not be a peer until I had received and responded to a writ and taken my seat. It had never been dealt with by a court of law and, although he helped me with provision of material for my other stuff, he wasn't much impressed by it. When he gave evidence he based himself almost entirely on the Writ of Summons.

The disadvantage of his approach was that he had to concede before the Committee of Privileges that in his opinion I had succeeded to the title. So his evidence and mine were quite out of joint. I was slightly cross with him for having done this because it was cited in the report against me that Mr Dingle Foot had said, 'Wedgwood Benn succeeded'.

The Committee itself was a most unpleasant experience. They met in a committee room upstairs – Number 13 I think – which has a horseshoe table. You come and sit in the middle of the horseshoe, completely surrounded by Members. You're not allowed to have Counsel represent you, although you can petition the House for permission though I didn't know that at the time and I'm not sure I would have wanted it. You're seated the whole time, and so you address the Committee seated. I felt the whole time that they wanted to get it over with very quickly. They were rather impatient. I think I gabbled through my speech.

I asked the Committee whether they would agree to call an expert witness of my choice – Dingle Foot whom I had briefed. But Butler said, 'I'm sorry, we can't allow you to brief a barrister. Nobody can brief a barrister before the Committee. All you can do is to ask us, as a grace and favour, to call Mr Dingle Foot as an independent expert on peerage matters.' So the protocol and rubbish associated with the Bar interfered with the protocol and rubbish associated with the Committee of Privileges.

The Committee of Privileges, by its nature, sets up every obstacle to the people concerned even being able to follow the case during its progress. It's a most unsatisfactory thing. By contrast the Election Court, with the judges sitting there, was a model of courtesy and kindness, respect and tolerance to me. What I discovered was that all the non-lawyers on the Committee were paralysed by the lawyers. You know this awful phrase that keeps recurring: 'I'm not a lawyer but . . .' , as if you were really not entitled to have an opinion unless you are a trained lawyer. And the lawyers there, notably the Attorney-General and Clement Davies, terrorised the other members. They could have reached a different conclusion had they not felt that they were somehow breaking the mystique by doing so.

I felt most uncomfortable. I had my notes close to me, and since I could see they were all very impatient I went through it much too quickly. The whole thing was very unsatisfactory. It is quite unlike the Election Court, where you stand and make the speech in a proper way, dealing with each point in such a way that the judges can make notes on it. I thoroughly disliked it. Then, of course, I was subjected to cross-examination by Members of the Committee.

I then had a very sharp cross-examination from the Attorney-General. Reading the transcript you don't get an impression of the sharpness. But he bullied and hacked at me as if I was a man who had been caught red-handed in the act of rape, and was then pleading mistaken identity. He really behaved in a most unpleasant and hostile way. I discovered from lawyers afterwards that this is his normal manner. But still, after all, I was neither a member of the House of Commons nor a peer, and had done nothing whatsoever wrong. I was arguing a case. Whether it was right or not was inconsequential. I really should have been treated with a little more respect and courtesy by Manningham-Buller and I came to really detest the man. I've always disliked him. I've seen him perform in the House – but that experience is something I shall never forget.

Butler: Did you answer him sharply?

No, I didn't. As a matter of fact I was very respectful, of course. By nature I am, and because I thought it would be very stupid to cross swords with him. But I absolutely refused to be budged and, although he attacked me from fifteen angles, he never found an inner inconsistency in the argument.

Butler: How far do you accept the argument that, in fact, to grant the relief that you sought would have strengthened the House of Lords, and so the Labour Party was right to oppose any assistance being given to you?

Well, in a sense this is true. This absurdity and fierce battle that there's been about it has gravely weakened the House of Lords and so the Labour Party should be grateful to me for having made the Lords look ridiculous. Conversely, if you clear up this anomaly, the Lords goes back to being more respectable again. But this is a marginal thing, of such little importance when contrasted with the right of a constituency to have its own Member, that when you put it in the balance I think there's no doubt that even if this did lead to a slight return to respectability and acceptability by the Lords, it would still be politically worthwhile because it would have broken the front at one point in the hereditary system and would have established the constituency's rights in Parliament to be dominant over the rights of a hereditary system.

Butler: You were, in fact, attacking Monarchy?

In one sense this is true. The extent to which the Crown exercises social influence over our society . . . to that extent the malaise that I later came to articulate is attributable to the way in which the Royal Family now operates in Britain.

Butler: This was one of the embarrassments in your campaign – that you had to pretend that you had no hostile feelings towards the Monarchy?

I never pretended that I hadn't any. But I always took the view that the Monarchy was irrelevant to modern political problems and I didn't challenge it outright. I very much wanted to challenge it outright, and had I received a Writ of Summons from the Crown I would have made an issue of it. But the whole question of one's attitude to republicanism is a complicated one, because it's a matter of timing. I don't think Charles III will ever ascend the throne, myself, because I think something will interfere with it in the meanwhile. I'm a republican in the sense that I would like Britain to be a republic within the Commonwealth. The Queen could still be Head of the Commonwealth and we would then be able to establish a social pattern which was free from this corrupting class system in which all permeates down from the top. But I think to challenge it outright without an occasion would be to stir up a bigger hornet's nest than necessary and might weaken one's appeal on other things.

It is alarming the way we've reverted to our pre-war class patterns in the last ten years. There have been certain structural changes in society which have gone the other way. So I am a republican in the sense that I think that a republic is inevitable, and that, unless you do get a republic, you probably won't be able to alter all this. But the difficulty is emotional.

In general I'm in favour of changing the reality, and leaving the outward form unchanged because an element of stability in society is very useful. That's why even if you completely altered the House of Lords – and I would like to see it altered – I think there's a case for calling it the House of Lords just because that is what people have always called it. Similarly, if the Monarchy were to democratise itself completely and become like royalty in Scandinavia where there's a family of people who lead a more or less normal life and appear on festive occasions to join in the festivity, like the Beefeaters, then I think that wouldn't be a bad thing.

On 30 December I did a television programme on the Honours List with Sir George Bellew, who's the Garter King at Arms. This is such a hilarious story that I think I must put it on the record. He's quite nice – but pretty weak. He told the producer, 'You must address the first question not to me but to the Viscount', because his idea was that the programme would relate to the social order, and that even if he was the natural man to turn to on the Honours List, he said, 'After all, he is a Viscount.' I said to him afterwards when we were having a talk, 'How on earth did you become the Garter?' 'Well,' he said, 'I became a Pursuivant thirty-eight years ago. I'd done a lot of shootin' and huntin', and that's the sort of chap they're looking for.' He was quite open about it. The funny thing about the College of Heralds, as I later learned, and particularly about Sir George Bellew, is that they know nothing whatsoever about peerage law.

After the programme he asked me, 'Would you like me to come over on your side?' So I said, 'Of course. It would be wonderful if you'd come out.' 'How much is it worth to you?' he asked with a laugh. 'You know we live on the fees of the College of Arms and for 150 guineas we get you a coat of arms. Perhaps for 300 we might take it away.'

Well, of course, it was a very funny joke, but it was a joke which tells you something about him and about the way the College of Arms works. It was once said that the College of Arms had so demeaned itself in the interests of lucre that its records were no longer to be taken seriously even in a court of law. That was 300 years ago. Of course, there's something in this. Something else happened in the programme. I had attacked the honour of the GCVO that was awarded to the Duke of Kent on the grounds that he'd got it for greeting someone at the railway station. Afterwards Garter said to me, 'I couldn't comment on that GCVO, it was impossible for me to comment. But of course, it was ridiculous. But there, if you live near the fountain of honour you're bound to get doused.'

I should add that Lady Violet Bonham Carter has been a passionate supporter throughout; really involved, and an intimate friend. I think her influence moved Jo Grimond, and through Jo Grimond, was a very big factor in persuading the Liberals not to oppose me in the Election.

From my point of view, the Privileges Committee was enormously worth having, for two reasons. First of all, it stopped the escalator that was carrying me out of the Commons and throwing me into the Lords. It was a spanner in the works, and it bought me four months when I could think about what to do, mobilise opinion, get Bristol on the right lines, and prepare a campaign. Secondly, it set down in a perfectly clear report the reason why I was being thrown out of the House of Commons. This had never been gathered together so clearly before. It said that Mr Justice Dodderidge in 1626 stated that a Peerage was fixed in blood for all posterity, and this was such patent nonsense that it greatly helped the campaign; indeed, I attacked Mr Justice Dodderidge in my Election address. It is an unusual thing that 320 years later a judge should be attacked. So it was a tremendous help from that point of view.

Do remember this: my only weapon against the Government was to force them to take the law to its own logical absurdity. By refusing to accept a 'No' and going a stage further, I could carry this on as long as I wanted. Indeed, I did carry it on to a point where they had to put a defeated Conservative in the House. So from all these points of view, I've no grumble about the Privileges Committee: they worked for me, and they gave me the time that I needed.

Butler: When you came back from America, what did you do?

Well, I had about a month so I began a tremendous amount of work. I remember I rang Barbara Castle, and asked her whether we should make it an all-Party campaign; should I wait for the Executive and see whether they would give me permission to fight? I wrote down her actual words in my diary. She said: 'Don't be so damned public school and middle class and ask our permission. Thank God *you're* in the fight and the instrument chosen to wage it. Go in and do it.'

Now that was encouraging, because it indicated that the left was interested. I then tested out a lot of other people. Shirley Williams, Secretary of the Fabian Society, had a lot of useful ideas about how we might combine the campaign with an exhibition of architecture. Pat Llewellyn Davies was very enthusiastic, as was her husband. I rang Sidney Jacobson and Gerald Kaufman and various other people to get their ideas as to what the campaign should be about. The *Daily Telegraph* correspondent was extremely enthusiastic, and said it would be the by-election of the century, and all that. So I took a lot of advice during that month and the thing formulated in my mind as a result. Meanwhile, I went to the House of Commons from time to time.

I felt Parliament slipping away from me. It was difficult to persuade them to give me a Hansard in the Vote Office. I just felt a stranger. I began to dislike the House of Commons. It was absolute penance to go there. I also found one other thing, which is rather interesting, happening to me. When you're a Member of Parliament, you're there because your constituency sent you there, and you're not dependent on anybody. But at this time I felt terribly dependent on the Tory Party, because I knew they would be the only people who could save me. I found this gravely affected my political independence. I did an *Any Questions* once, and I remember consciously thinking as a controversial question came up, 'If I answer this in any anti-Government way, is it going to affect Mr Butler's attitude, if he's listening? Is it going to alienate the Tory MPs who are listening?' And I realised something I hadn't realised when I was an MP: what a wonderful and absolutely irreplaceable thing it is to be in Parliament not beholden to anybody.

The magazine *Today*, which is run by Odham's Press, offered to pay the whole cost of the Election if the Labour Party wouldn't pay it, but I couldn't accept it, and I told them so. The whole thing would have been a stunt if a newspaper or magazine had financed the Election. Anyway, I said to them, 'It's very good of you, but I couldn't allow you to finance the campaign, but we are opening a fund and if you would like to contribute, do' – Not a penny came out of them! They wanted to run it as 'Labour lets Wedgwood Benn down – *Today* is the magazine of young people. We are fighting this campaign.' That would have been absolutely disastrous, but it was rather interesting. In the end, we did raise quite a lot of money, although the Election cost something.

Meanwhile, in Bristol itself, there was a lot of interest among the young architects. There's a tremendous controversy going on about the replanning of the centre of Bristol, and all the architects with whom I worked on this – because I tried to help them as best I could – became involved in the by-election. They saw the by-election – I put it to them in the terms I have described – as an opportunity for broadening the range of political controversy. Many of these young architects, who had been apolitical if not unsympathetic, played an enormous part in the Election, hawked their exhibitions around, and joined the Labour Party as a result of it.

But there were some MPs who were not so keen. It turned out that there was a small but vociferous and powerful group of trade union MPs who were dead against this, partly on personal grounds because they disliked me. They thought this had nothing to do with the old-age pensioner and politics and also, of course, it was the inverted class feeling which is strong in the Labour Party.

Monday morning, 6 March 1961, was a key day, because it was the day of the General Council in Bristol. I said to them: 'Now look, by the end of the month you have really two alternatives open. You can either drop me altogether and pick a new candidate, and you'll have a new Member for Bristol. Or you can re-adopt me. Now, if you re-adopt me, first of all you will have to select me. But if the NEC refuse to endorse me I give a pledge that I will never stand against a Labour candidate.'

My Peerage Renunciation Bill was very simple. It simply provided for life commoners. A peer could renounce his peerage and he would be a commoner for life, and on his death his son would inherit the title with, of course, the right to renounce. This seemed to me to be the simplest way of dealing with it. I prepared this Bill to be presented as soon as the Committee of Privileges' report came out because I was very much afraid that people would be so obsessed by the detailed difficulties of dealing with this problem that I would psychologically lose. So this Bill was drafted and presented a few days after the Privileges report was published and it shone a light to show that out of the dark tunnel it was going to be possible to find a legislative way.

I glanced at the conclusions of the report and recommendations, and saw that it was 100 per cent anti on everything. That's the way the Committee treated you. The fact that you have a special interest, or have given evidence, doesn't even give you the courtesy that the press have with Ministerial speeches of receiving them in advance.

Butler: Did you make a statement to the press then?

No I didn't, I dashed home. The phone rang absolutely continuously, but I put them all off. About half an hour later, at 11.30, I did issue a little

✓

JOHN OSBORNE
31, Lower Belgrave St. S.W.1
13.3.61

By all means, you can have my effort, for what it's worth. Frankly, I should think it would deaden your efforts considerably.

Yours,

John Osborne

statement. What I said is, 'This is the beginning of the fight and not the end.' The result was that even by the time the evening papers were published my counter-statement was there and this was a part of the psychological battle of tossing the grenade back.

Butler: You had a lot of friends at this time – people who were interested in the campaign in one way or another. Had you consulted any more regular advisers outside your own family circle?

No, I hadn't. In fact Dingle and Dick Taverne were dropping behind a bit because the legal side was being played down. Remember, one had to put on different hats at different times. When Father died I was a parliamentarian at bay, using the procedure of the House. *Erskine May* was my Bible. When I went to the Committee of Privileges I was the amateur lawyer, presenting the case as best I could.

On 23 March Lynn Ungoed-Thomas introduced the Peerage Renunciation Bill. It was decided at the Party meeting to discuss the matter the following week. Then Charlie Pannell told me again, that afternoon, that George Brown was against it, and that Hugh Gaitskell thought I might lose the Election. Hugh had told Charlie that he was again afraid that if it came to a by-election I would be defeated by my opponent.

On Friday, 24 March there was a special meeting of the General Council in Bristol, an absolutely key meeting from my point of view. The Privileges Committee's report had come out, and it was quite clear that at this meeting a firm decision had to be taken as to whether I would be put forward as a candidate or not. Len Williams had come down from Transport House and he had been told by the Organisation Sub-Committee to take the sense of the meeting to find out what people in Bristol were really thinking, and to report back to them. He had no order to stop anything in Bristol, but he had no orders to encourage anything, so his position was a rather curious one: all the local people wanted to know the attitude of the National Executive, and he couldn't tell them. Again, you see, all these solid trade union chaps came out absolutely firmly in favour of fighting. Fred Newman of the Shopworkers said that every house in Hanham had been canvassed and 2,000 had signed the petition; less than 1 per cent were not prepared to sign. They were fighting for a principle. They were certain of an overwhelming victory. Another chap said, 'Even if they do seat the Conservative this will only be confirmation of the privileges that we're fighting.' It went on and on like this.

Then there was a vote on a resolution pledging support for me in a by-election. The only hope I had was that my constituency wanted me.

from: Earl Russell, O.M.,F.R.S.,

PLAS PENRHYN,
PENRHYNDEUDRAETH,
MERIONETH.
TEL. PENRHYNDEUDRAETH 242.

18 March, 1961.

Dear Mr. Wedgwood Benn,

Thank you for your letter of March 10. I sympathize whole-heartedly with your desire to remain in the Commons rather than be smothered in the Lords, but I do not feel that I can send you a message of support as I am supporting only such candidates as have a policy on nuclear weapons that seems to me desirable. With regrets,

Yours sincerely,

Russell

On March 25th the Speaker wrote to withdraw my remaining rights as an MP. What was interesting about that correspondence, and other correspondence I had with the Speaker, was this. I would go to see Sir Edward Fellowes, and I would say, 'Sir Edward, I think I would like to raise this point with the Speaker.' So he would have tea with me and appraise me how to draft the letter. I would then write the letter and send it to the Speaker. The Speaker would then, no doubt, ring up Sir Edward and say, 'I've had a letter from Wedgwood Benn' – it must have been an awful bore to him – 'What shall I say?' And Sir Edward would say, 'Well, Mr Speaker, I think really the position is this.'

So the Speaker would write me a letter, which I would receive, and I would ring up Sir Edward and say, 'I've had a letter from the Speaker', and I could almost hear him smile. 'He says this. What do you think I can do about it?' He would say, 'Give me an hour or two and then come and have tea again.' I would go and see him and he would say, 'Well, I think the best line really would be to write like this.'

On 29 March a special Parliamentary Party meeting had been called to discuss my case. Hugh put before the meeting the alternatives: either, he said, you could urge that there should be a special bill for Tony Benn himself, and we're not in favour of this – of course, I agreed with that – or, you must stress that whatever bill does come in, it is retrospective so that it includes Tony Benn and then the question of whether the

9 April 1955.

My dear Wedgwood Benn,

As I wrote to you <u>confidentially</u> in September
1953, I certainly feel yours is a very hard case, and I
am personally strongly in favour of sons having the right
to renounce irrevocably the peerages they inherit from
their fathers.   This would not of course prevent them
from accepting another peerage, if they were offered one,
later on.

Yours sincerely,

Winston S. Churchill

renunciation should be for life or for ever is something that you really couldn't decide. It is a matter that would have to be left open. He suggested that they add the addendum which had been agreed. Then he went on to say that, of course, the Party would support the motion that I be allowed to speak from the Bar of the House and, at that time, he said he thought the Government wouldn't oppose this.

I thanked them very much for their support. I agreed with the Party line and said that we should shelve the legal issues. I then went through all the possibilities of how the law might be changed and said that I preferred the extinction of the title. I thought it wasn't a bad thing to make the situation funny. I told them about Hailsham, and Rab saying he hoped Hailsham wouldn't get back (to the Commons).

On 30 March I had a phone call from Lambton. He said that Butler and the Attorney had been extremely effective and that I wouldn't get to the Bar. He said he'd seen Beaverbrook, and Beaverbrook was a strong supporter of my claim to speak. As it happened, the following Sunday an article written by A.J.P. Taylor appeared in the *Sunday Express*. No doubt it had been ordered by Beaverbrook as a result of the conversation. Of course, the *Express* attitude was just anti-snobbery and anti-aristocracy and vaguely anti-Monarchy and that was why they took this up.

Butler: Do you think it was in your favour to have the Express *on your side?*

Well, it's the kiss of death to have the Beaver on your side. But if everybody else is on your side as well, I suppose the Beaver's support is just tolerable. It's better, in some ways, than having him viciously against you. The *Express*, if it's against you, can be really vile. I'm grateful that I didn't have to face that.

I ought, perhaps, to bring you up to date on Churchill's involvement. I had written to him in February, telling him that if I lost in the Committee of Privileges I would like to fight the Election and asked him whether he would give me further support. I had a message back saying, 'Sir Winston Churchill cannot go beyond what he said in 1953 – that is to say, he is prepared to reaffirm it but not go beyond it, as he has withdrawn from controversy.' I took this to be permission for me to use his letter again, without indicating anything else. I did write and tell him I was using his letter again, so as to be absolutely sure that I was on the right side. I let out to the press that, in this message back, he had indicated that he hadn't, in any way, withdrawn. That is to say, his support continued. And it did. He sent me £10 for the Election fund later.

There's no doubt the Churchill letter was a bomb that went off three or four times to great effect. It was most powerful in '55 though it didn't do the trick. It undoubtedly helped in the debate on 13 April 1961 to show that this was not just a left-wing crank attacking the Lords, otherwise Churchill wouldn't support him. And I think the 10,000 Churchill letters during the Election, which were distributed on the eve of the poll in the Conservative areas, made a very substantial contribution to the size of the vote, and threw the Conservative Party into absolute disarray, particularly as St Clair had been Churchill's Private Secretary at one time, which was a thing that made him very embarrassed.

Also on that day – 6 April – I decided to write to the Duke of Windsor. In my letter I said that I had decided to renounce and that I would be grateful for any support that he could give me. I never had a reply of any sort.

On 12 April, the day before I was to address the Bar of the House, Yuri Gagarin rather scooped the headlines. Nabarro had signed the Labour amendment – a terribly bold and cheeky thing to do, to put his name below Gaitskell and George Brown and the others. It just gave that slight air of excitement to the debate. I was working on my speech, which I wanted to make a classic oration, partly because I knew there wasn't much chance of its being delivered. I heard, unofficially, that the National Executive had decided to endorse me. So that when the following day, Thursday 13 April, dawned, I knew that whatever the outcome of the debate, and there was very little doubt about it, I was just about to launch from the parliamentary arena back into the constituency.

That morning *The Times* had a leader saying that the House ought to hear me at the Bar, and the *Telegraph*'s leader said that they shouldn't hear me at the Bar, but that the law should be changed. Gaitskell telephoned me to say, 'Do make your speech very simple, if you're called to the Bar.' I intended to do that. I completed the speech and went to the House of Commons, with Caroline and Stephen, where I delivered my letter to the Speaker, asking to be heard.

The three of us, with various members of the family and friends, sat through the debate until 10.30. That debate has been very fully reported in the press; I don't know if there's much I want to add about it. I had cherished the hope that I might be called and I therefore had my speech with me. I hated the first part, because I wasn't sure, until the vote, whether I would have to go. Gaitskell was extremely unsatisfactory, I thought. He's very bad when he has to argue a case that he doesn't really believe in.

There were 35 Labour Members who were absent. Hugh actually rang me up to apologise about this. I didn't really think much about it. I never have given much thought to the problem of the Labour people who were unsympathetic, because there's nothing I can do about it. But it indicated that the feeling was there, in rather greater numbers than I had realised. The Tory friends were as few as I had expected.

The debate really marked the turning point in the whole story in a way, because as I walked away with Caroline and Stephen at about 11 pm that night, it was the moment of expulsion. It was the moment that I'd been able to delay for five months from November to April, and it was the end of the first stage. Here was the inevitable expulsion, which had been confirmed by the House. I was awfully pleased by this stage to be shot of the House of Commons. I didn't much like being there before the debate, because I was unhappy. But after that, I never felt that I had any place at Westminster at all. I had to counteract the feeling of defeat because, of course, the following day the press was full of it. I think the keynote of what I said then was, 'Well, now, on to Bristol. This is what we've got to look to now.'

It began a wildly exciting period for me. It was certainly the happiest part of the whole battle because, of course, I was shot of the lawyers, I was shot of the Whips, I was shot of the Conservative Party. I was back, really, with my own people in Bristol.

Public opinion, generally, was on my side. Even the sizeable percentage of people who disagreed with it in a way respected me for not wanting to be a peer. That was the least important side of it. But all over the place where I've done meetings before and since, I have sensed this good will. At one meeting, for the Rotarians in Bournemouth where there were about 2,000 present, the other speaker was the Lord Chancellor Kilmuir, so we sat next to him at lunch and went back to London in the same compartment. I thought that Kilmuir was very embarrassed. He was a friend of Father's and he was also very friendly to me. We talked all the way back to London, and Caroline, who's much braver than I am, told him what tremendous support there was from the Tories on this issue, and he looked even more embarrassed and shifty. Anyway, he offered me a lift at Waterloo. He said, 'The House of Lords?' and I said, 'No, I don't think we want to go where you're going.'

That evening I had a letter from the Speaker saying that, in view of the decision of the House, I was to be kept completely out.

I went to Bristol on 17 April and we had two meetings: first the Executive at 7.30. Len Williams, the National Agent, had come down and he was in a very jovial, cordial mood. He said: the Party is going to support Tony, we think an early Election's a good idea. One woman, Mrs Berry, had doubts about whether we should run the risk of the Tories getting the seat. This was a view that was undoubtedly shared by a number of people. I said that quite honestly this is a possibility. If you go into a fight of this kind, you're taking this risk. But I'm taking an enormous risk too of the possibility that when I take my seat I'll find that I'm liable to a penalty of £500 a day. But I'm prepared to take that risk. I've also got the possibility of very high costs in the Election Court. Let's go into this, if we do, knowing – all of us – exactly what risk we're running. The question is: is it worth it, or not?

Anyway, the meeting moved, and seconded, that I be selected and adopted. And it was unanimously agreed. We went into the General Council at about ten to eight. Len Williams opened and traced the history, saying that the NEC officers had been authorised to act; that they had agreed to endorse me and that the by-election finances would be as normal. He said that the constitutional issue would, of course, be the main one, that it did raise the whole question of the hereditary system, and that we should fight it on the policy of the Labour Party.

We appointed Herbert Rogers as the agent. We suspended the Party, as you have to do, under law, during the course of a by-election and we appointed an Election Committee. We ordered the envelopes. That was the moment when the by-election was set up.

At this time, I had a couple of telephone calls: the first was from Tony Greenwood, and the second from Charlie Pannell. This is what they told me, and it was a most remarkable story. On Thursday, 20 April, in the Division Lobby, Dick Crossman, who had heard that I had got Lambton coming to my adoption meeting, went up to Hugh Gaitskell and said to him, 'You must stop the whole Bristol campaign. You must tell Tony Benn that these people are not to come.' George Brown was there and he said, 'The whole of this must be torpedoed immediately, before it does the Party any more damage.' In fact, Dick said to Tony Greenwood, 'You are not to go to speak at the adoption meeting, if Lambton speaks.' Charlie Pannell heard it and they both told me this because they were really worried. The funny thing was that George Brown said to Dick

Crossman, 'Well, Dick, you're the Chairman of the Party. You deal with Wedgwood Benn, if you think he's behaving wrongly. It's your job. It's not our job. It's a National Executive function – by-elections. I do the PLP.'

That evening Caroline, Stephen, my mother, brother and sister-in-law all arrived on the train and we went to the Transport Hall at 7.30 really quavering about what would actually happen. On the same train were Malcolm Muggeridge and Lambton, who had come down. This motley crew went to Transport Hall, which is the new building in Bristol for the Transport and General Workers' Union. It was a jolly good meeting. In fact, even the old militant Party workers, who had been to meetings all their life, said afterwards that they had never enjoyed a meeting so much. Lambton said that he had only been able to come because the Attorney-General had assured the House that every vote for me would be thrown away, and therefore, under no circumstances, could he be held to be speaking against a Conservative in any effective way, which was a moot point.

We got a collection of £92, which at a Labour meeting was really fantastic. The treasurer, a man from USDAW, left the £92 on the table, in the open, all night. It was returned to him in the morning, by the cleaner. We went back to the hotel and talked till midnight and Muggeridge and Lambton were very amusing indeed. It was a lovely relaxed evening. The campaign had begun; it had been a great success. Then we all went to bed.

Malcolm Muggeridge and Lambton went back to London accompanied by Hilary; he had taken a tremendous liking to Muggeridge, who seized his hand and took him over to the sweet shop, where Muggeridge had to dig deep. Hilary then announced that 'Malcolm', as he continuously called him, had invited him to stay with him.

We had a press conference every morning at 11 am. We decided that we would bring out a sheet called the *Bristol Campaigner*. I'd had these printed on a duplicating machine in London, and the idea was that we would furnish the press with all they needed to know about the Election and in this way we would try to keep the initiative. The press sent down an enormous number of people and our headquarters were absolutely flooded with press the whole time. When a new chap arrived he would be brought to see me, I would take him into our long General Council room, furnish him with a complete set of documents – the Election address, the material, the messages – so that he always felt that he had a proper briefing, and then I would say: 'Now, go out and report what you find, but here's what we're trying to do. Do please measure us against our aspiration, and not against some imaginary aspirations.'

The press conferences were really very cordial. I enjoyed them enormously and the press used to bring me news of what was happening at St Clair's headquarters, and of course all the press stayed in the hotel I was staying in. Every night the press were there. To begin with some of them were terribly cynical – the thing was a stunt, a farce, of human interest and nothing else – but gradually, one by one, they were won round to an enthusiasm for the campaign which was really quite impressive, because the press are tough chaps and they don't like to become enthusiastic about anything. But I can honestly say, at the end of the campaign, as individuals, they had mostly been brought round. The *Times* correspondent was Wynford Davies, who looked like Alec Guinness, a very quiet steady chap who asked difficult questions and predicted the result as a 6,000 majority and so on. When he was sent off on a job he wrote a little note, which I kept in my file, saying: of course I was doing a job and I was reporting for *The Times*, but I'm also a human being, and I've been tremendously excited by what you're trying to do. Now that sort of letter from a press man is enormously worth having.

On 25 April the rumours about the Government announcement of a Joint Select Committee to look into the peerage question were getting stronger and stronger and the press view was that this would absolutely spike my guns. It added special point to our treatment of this question. I got to the office at 7.45 am and my first job every morning was to prepare the *Bristol Campaigner*. The main diet of the *Campaigner* was the messages of support that were flooding in from the people we'd asked to send them. I've got a complete set of *Bristol Campaigners* containing messages from

✓   *31, Drummond Place. Edinburgh, 3.*

WAVERLEY 2926.

SIR COMPTON McKENZIE   **14th March 1961.**

Dear Wedgewood Benn,

    Will this do?

    "If the House of Lords can have Life Peers from the Commons, why can't the House of Commons have Life Members from the Lords, subject to the goodwill of the electorate?"

    I hope you will be successful.

    Yours ever,

Compton Mackenzie

Arnold Toynbee, Compton Mackenzie and all the others. There were always two or three well-known people who had sent their support. I had got the *Daily Mirror* to provide me with photographs of my distinguished supporters so that the Committee Rooms had their faces round them. All this gave the impression of a broadly based campaign.

We discussed what to do about the notice that St Clair had put out declaring that all votes cast for me would be wasted. I think it was Jo Grimond who said: 'Look, is it in order for a man to put out a notice saying you are disqualified? Surely this is fraud.' So we worked and drafted a statement saying that it was quite improper, since it could only be decided by the Election Court. This was a very useful point, because it threw some doubt on the validity of St Clair's notice.

The next day we had the *Daily Mail* coming out strongly against me and saying that the whole campaign was too slick, that my image was damaged, and so on. This was the beginning of things turning nasty. But the press coverage was still very good indeed. At a press conference I said that I would issue an answer to St Clair about his notice and it was then that I learned that St Clair, in answer to a question, admitted that *he* was the heir to a peerage. This really reduced the thing to farce. I kicked myself for never having enquired about it. At St Clair's press conference, which was held before ours, so that we could always answer his stuff, Walter Terry had asked, 'Are you, by any chance, connected with the peerage yourself?' St Clair said, 'Yes, as a matter of fact, I am.' So Terry said, 'How closely?' 'My cousin.' So Terry asked, 'Who is your cousin's heir?' St Clair said, 'I am.'

That really settled it. It was the biggest laugh of the campaign. Of course, it gave me my opening in the evening, because I then said that I would be prepared to campaign for St Clair's right to represent the constituency if he could only win it. I offered to speak on his platforms in support of any campaign he might have in mind. This was the type of thing – it was good-humoured but it all bore upon the central point, which was the absurdity of the law, and ridicule that night was very helpful indeed.

The following day we had a legal argument about what we should do about the statement that St Clair had put out. I must admit I was rather rattled and worried about this at the time. This nagging fear that we might be mishandling the legal issue continued through the Election. We also got a great deal tougher with St Clair and I spent the rest of the day going round with John Guinery of the *Bristol Evening Post*, who came with me everywhere. I delivered a letter to St Clair's headquarters asking him to withdraw the notice.

We had James Cameron one night, talking about the freedom of the press, and we had Donald Soper on the ethics of politics, both very good speakers. The seminar went on until about a quarter to one. This time I think there must have been about twenty-five people there. By then, I must admit, I was getting pretty tired: the day was awfully long and I was afraid that I simply wouldn't have the physical strength to carry on at this pace, particularly as the following morning, Friday 28 April, I got up at 5.15. I tried a new technique, which I'd never tried before, of canvassing people at bus stops. It was a brilliant success, because people gather automatically. You go to an empty bus stop and people begin to come up. At the end of ten minutes you've got a crowd of twenty-five. They're all rubbing their hands, they're icy cold and they're bored. So we took the main arterial roads passing through the constituency. We drove from the middle outwards, stopping at bus stops and I suppose, before breakfast, we had talked to and shaken hands with 200 people. I was rather pleased about this. I thought it was an imaginative way of running the campaign and, of course, people have nothing to do on the buses. So as soon as they get on, the word spreads.

We had a message from the Oxford University Conservative Association. I was putting such messages out with great enthusiasm in our *Bristol Campaigners*. One night we had Dick Marsh and Professor Blackett, and Professor Llewelyn-Davies. Michael Zander arrived to advise. Blackett made a really good speech about the development of science and technology in Britain, and what was wrong; how we did the basic work but didn't apply it.

On Sunday morning 30 April, I was up at 6.30 and read all the newspapers. I went to headquarters and we drafted a legal statement for the QCs to sign. We rang Dingle Foot and posted copies of the statement off to him, Frank Soskice, Elwyn Jones and Lynn Ungoed-Thomas. We put out a statement in the *Bristol Campaigner* which we knew would go to every party worker and canvasser, answering St Clair's points and saying that they were untrue. They were misleading; they were illegal; they were trickery, and they were an attempt at dictatorship, because it looked as if St Clair was telling us that whoever we voted for as our MP Mr Macmillan had decided that St Clair was to be the Member.

Harold Wilson arrived that evening and did a meeting for me. He had 100 plus in quite small halls in different parts of the constituency. It was a really excellent response. We had our usual evening seminar which went on until late into the night. By this time the press, who used to avoid the seminar and go and gossip in the usual press way in the bar, began coming in. We had the most interesting exchanges in which students would attack the press and the press would have to defend themselves. They would get drawn in. I'm always reminded about that story of the tremendous Billy Graham type meeting. The Preacher said, 'Stand up those who wish to be saved.' Everyone stood up except one man. The Preacher said, 'What about you?' and he said, 'I'm from the press.'

We released the Churchill letter; it had of course, been released in '55, but somehow, every time someone looks at the facsimile of that letter with the old man's name on it it creates a fresh stir. On 3 May, Eve of Poll, we had a motorcade; it was pouring with rain, blustery and then suddenly sunshiny. We went round the whole constituency standing out in the open in plastic macs, putting them on or off according to whether it was hot or cold. It was a horrible day. But it was showing the flag and we had lots of cars and big banners. This is worth doing. I think it gives the atmosphere of an Election in these rather dull days.

I had got up at about 6.30 on 3 May because I was extremely worried by the knowledge that the Tories were going to put up warning notices on every polling station. It is a characteristic of Elections that although logically a scare by the other side doesn't make any difference, when you actually get up to a scare then you do get worried. We were afraid that the effect of the Tory notices on the polling stations would be to turn away our voters in droves on polling day. On the previous night, 2 May, we had discussed whether we should issue a counter-notice. Michael Zander had been working with me on the telephone from London and he discovered that we were entitled to put up a counter-notice if we wanted to.

So I got up at 6.30 on the day before polling day and I went to the office at 7.30. We had already drafted a counter-notice in which we warned the other party that, by saying that I was disqualified, when this couldn't be known, it was possible that they were guilty of corrupt practice. I went to the printers' and ordered 100 red warning counter-notices, which we intended then to put up at polling stations. I also issued copies to the press – the *Bristol Evening Post* and the *Bristol Evening World*. This was a very difficult decision to take and it led to the most extraordinary consequences. First of all, the *Bristol Evening Post* refused to publish my counter-notice. They said that, in saying that St Clair might be guilty of corrupt practice with the issue of his notice, I might be guilty of libel, so they wouldn't print it. The *Bristol Evening World*, however, did print it.

Anyway, in the end I agreed to cancel the whole lot. I cancelled the counter-notice everywhere, except for the *Bristol Evening World* where it had already appeared. This was interesting, because it was an argument, really, about the level at which you fight the Election at a certain stage.

When you are dealing with the general public, they really are not interested in the Representation of the People Act. They are not concerned with the legal side at all. For them it is a simple vote – do we think this chap's had a raw deal and do we want to keep him as our Member or not? I had made a great mistake of judgement, I think, in issuing this notice. Anyway, we decided to play the whole of their warning notices down and at the press conference that morning I was very confident, and I pooh-poohed the whole thing.

At 9.15 we went into St George's Park, which is the traditional centre for holding meetings in the old Bristol East constituency, and when I arrived there I found a really quite sizeable crowd and a big truck drawn up with a loudspeaker standing on the back. It is a lovely place from which to speak – cars all round, with their headlights lighting it all up. The crowd thickened and thickened and it was the best meeting that I've ever attended in the constituency. It was a wonderful meeting. George Brown got up and delivered a tremendous oration. Ungoed-Thomas, Ian Mikardo, Leslie Plummer . . . they all got up one after the other. I suppose there must have been 200–300 people. I've got photographs of it. Finally, I spoke. It was a rousing end to the campaign and I think it did do some good for George Brown, in a way. I had always felt that he was against it and I was glad that he came down and found the local Party really excited.

Anyway, I went back to the hotel and George said, 'I want to talk to you.' So I took him to my room, and he said, 'I've been sent down by Hugh because you've become a guided missile. From now on, this goes back to the PLP.' I felt my status as a candidate slipping away, and I felt the chains of the PLP upon me, but I was very happy about it, because it was the last stretch home. He said to me that there'd be a Parliamentary Party meeting tomorrow – on polling day – and that I was to come to the House of Commons on Monday. He said I would be stopped by the authorities; I should write to the Speaker. Then he said that there would be two debates again: a debate on whether I should be allowed to speak at the Bar – which, this time, I was pretty optimistic about – and another debate, which Butler would move, on whether to exclude me. Gaitskell would move to seat me. Now this was very good news for me, because if the Leader of the Opposition moves to seat you it is as near a pledge as you can get from Party that, were this to happen again, after a General Election at which the Labour Party won a majority, they would simply say: you take your seat and we'll work this out later. Then George went on to say – and this is very characteristic of him; in some ways I quite like him – that there are 30 to 50 Members of the PLP dead against me on all this. 'I may as well tell you, I'm dead against you myself. I would strongly object to your fighting the seat again. I didn't want to come down here to speak in this by-election, but still, I was asked to do it, and that is my job.'

Polling day was the usual awful business. I do dislike polling day. I was up at 6.30. I was at the office at 8.15 and I went round to all the polling stations and all the committee rooms. It's a killing job. I think in many ways it's a complete waste of time, although it does encourage the Party workers and that's the only case for doing it. There's no point in talking to the returning officers or the clerks. After all, you must look at it from a practical point of view and I suppose you have to get in and out of

New Delhi, India
May 10, 1961

Dear Benn:

Even here in India we note these triumphs of the
common man and I add my voice to the chorus.

Best regards,

Yours faithfully,

John Kenneth Galbraith

Honorable Anthony Wedgewood Benn,
    House of Commons,
        London, England.

a car about a hundred times on polling day and this begins to mount up.
Anyway, the turnout wasn't bad. We were quite encouraged in the earlier
part of the day, although it simply poured first thing in the morning.

At 4 o'clock I went back to the hotel, and was told that Sara Barker
wanted to see me. By then I was tired and a little worried, because you
never know till the end of the day how it will work out. I went to see her
in the lounge of the hotel. She was sitting there with her lips pursed and
she said, 'I've just come down to tell you that in your speech tonight
you're to make no reference whatsoever to the future. I've been asked by
the NEC to come down specially to say this to you. It's going to be
particularly important if the result is better than we expect. The NEC
will not support you, further, in any Election fight.'

I must say I was very resentful of this and the way in which it was
done. First of all, she didn't wish me luck – a candidate on polling day is
like a bride, he wants something said – there was no suggestion of good
will about it. I said, 'You could have sent me a postcard to tell me that.
I've no intention of saying anything about the future.'

But it did send me down to the absolute bottom of depression, the one
thing that was unbearable at any stage was the feeling that my own
people weren't with me and George Brown plus Sara Barker made me, at
this stage, regret the whole business. When I heard that St Clair had

issued a writ for libel, because of my legal notice, it really was the lowest point in the whole struggle. I was frightfully worried about the money. I knew the Election Court might come to that and I really did think that evening that I was an absolute fool. The whole thing had been totally misconceived.

We went out and did our last-minute knocking-up on polling day. It was still pouring with rain. The streets were absolutely empty. There simply was nobody who was going to vote from 8 till 9 – or so it seemed. The street lights shone yellow on the rainy pavement, and our voices echoed back from the loudspeaker. I raised my voice in an almost desperate way to persuade people to come out. I lost my voice completely between 5 and 9 that night; I couldn't speak at all. We came back to the hotel absolutely finished, thinking that possibly we'd get in with a majority of 2,000. We thought it quite possible that we wouldn't win at all, and that was just the end of the whole business as far as we were concerned.

After the polls closed we went and had tea and apples at Temple Meads Station, where I ate most of my meals during the Election, because it was quick and easy. At 11 we went to St George's Grammar School to the count and we forced our way through a crowd of people who were beginning to form outside. The television lights were shining on the school on the main London to Bristol road and there was, of course, as there always is at the count, a great sense of excitement. But we were utterly dejected as we walked in. As soon as we got in people said: 'It's a landslide.' Our people came up and said, 'It's going four to one, it's fantastic.' All of a sudden, the thing changed. From 11 till the result was announced was the most splendid and glorious part of the whole campaign. The clouds had disappeared, our optimism and enthusiasm soared, we walked around. We saw votes pouring out of the ballot boxes; we saw the piles going up. We really thought at one stage that St Clair had lost his deposit.

I think that was the very best part of the Election, just as two hours earlier had been the very worst part of the whole business. I sat on a child's desk in the corner and drew up a little statement of victory, which I hadn't given any thought to at all. All the press were there, and they were so friendly and, of course, the press reflects the current mood. Anyway, it was extremely enjoyable. Then we came to the declaration and the Town Clerk himself came and announced the results: Benn 23,275, St Clair 10,231.

I made a little speech inside, of an uncontroversial kind, and thanked everybody. I think I may have said, I can't remember, that I hoped St Clair wouldn't try to get the seat by the back door because he would then be terribly unhappy. I'd been in Parliament long enough to know that a man who got in this way would be miserable. I also beat the big drum a

bit and said that of course now I had the authority of the constituency
and the House wasn't just dealing with me. They were dealing with the
Bristol people, and they were a very formidable lot. St Clair then got up
inside, and he paid tribute to his wife who, he said, had been 'working
throughout the whole campaign'.

Then we went out on to the steps at the front of the school where
there's a little stone balustrade. There was an enormous crowd. I can't
estimate the number, but it's a broad road, and I suppose there were
2,000 people there. And they were absolutely cheering their heads off. It
was a wonderful moment. The only trouble was, I'd lost my voice so I
had to shout hard to be heard. It sounded rather shrill. I went on from
the uncontroversial bit that I'd said inside, to a highly political bit saying
we'll go on from this till we've removed all privilege in this country. It
received a hysterical welcome, and St Clair was spitting in the
background. Caroline was standing next to him. 'This is absolutely
monstrous,' he said, 'to make a Party political speech at a moment like
this.' Then he came forward, and the crowd shouted at him, and it wasn't
until I held my hand up that they stopped. You must forgive me. Here
was a moment when my buoyancy and enthusiasm really was justified. It
was a fabulous scene.

After the speeches, we came down the steps. We got on top of a jeep
and were driven very slowly from St George's Grammar School right up
the hill along the main road to London, which was utterly blocked by
people, to the headquarters. We went into the Walter Baker Hall and
there were all these people gathered. It was a moment of great drama and
great personal excitement. We were overcome with emotion and
gratitude and I was unable to express it, of course, because I'd lost my
voice. The result was a 13,044 majority with a 13 per cent swing. There
were about 200 supporters in the main hall. This was about 1 o'clock;
how they all got home I just don't know.

The following day we got up at 8.30 and, of course, the press was
terrific. The headlines that day about triumph in Bristol completely
wiped out the memory of the Committee of Privileges, the dull lawyers,
the old nonsense. Here was the response from the people I represented. I
was very arrogant at this stage, extremely arrogant. Here was a clear
answer to all the absurdities and reactionaries – Tories and doubters and
everything else. I admit that at this moment I was getting my own back
in my own feeling against all those who had crabbed or criticised or
opposed, because here was a plain and clear answer. The cartoon I liked
best was one in the *Daily Mail* of me with a trumpet marked 'Bristol
Mandate' and there was Butler and the Government looking out of 'The
Walls of Rab and Co.' One felt that one had come back refreshed and
could really knock them for six.

After my election the *London Gazette* published a statement from the

Crown Office saying: 'Member returned for Bristol South East, Anthony Neil Wedgwood Benn.' I rang the Public Bill Office and arranged to collect the certificate. I phoned the Serjeant-at-Arms to tell him what would happen that afternoon. He said that as far as they were concerned, I was a stranger. I got five Gallery tickets, phoned the Speaker's Office and left at about ten to twelve for the House of Commons. There were four cars full of photographers chasing me there.

At 12.15 I went in to see Gaitskell, Brown, Bowden and Frank Barlow. They were very friendly, and extremely pleased with the result of the Election. Of course, I was full of excitement. They did really feel, then, that it had done the Party some good and this was the new factor: that the Party did recognise that a swing of that kind, and a humiliation for the Government, was a much bigger and better thing than they had previously realised. It did, undoubtedly, push into the background a lot of the doubt and even a lot of the hostility. Anyway, we discussed the tactics to be pursued in the afternoon. It was really that we should try to get me to the Bar and then, again, get me seated. We knew neither would succeed, because no stranger could be admitted to the Bar and the Speaker said I was a stranger.

I went to see the Speaker at 1.25. He had my letter and he said that he had ruled to debar me from the House. He discussed the procedure and said, 'You can't come beyond the door.' So I asked whether he had ordered force to keep me out. He asked why I said that, and I said that I was not prepared to stay out for any purpose other than to avoid a scuffle. He said he would have to think about that. So I said, 'Well, this is quite clear. If I'm ordered to stop I shan't stop. But if you intend to stop me you must give orders that force is to be used to keep me out. That's the only condition under which I'm prepared to bow to your authority.'

He was very upset indeed. He said, 'I had no idea that you were going to put it like that.' So I told him he was responsible for keeping me out of the House. I'd just been elected by a large majority and, 'If you're stopping me, you must take responsibility for it.'

The Speaker was shaken by this. I also raised with him the question of his ruling: his excluding me from the amenities of the House. Peers who have been MPs are allowed to use the House of Commons. He said that because I was not a peer yet, because I hadn't taken my Writ of Summons, I was not allowed to use the privileges of the Commons. Well, he was rather upset, but he said at the end, 'I know this must be difficult for you.'

At 2.15 I went out to St Stephen's entrance and there was Caroline and Mother, and Stephen and one or two others. There were a lot of people and a lot of photographers, and I had the return to the writ proving my election to Bristol South East, which I held up. That was undoubtedly a key point – I was approaching the House armed with the authority of the constituency, and there's a certain dramatic excitement in it. Well, then came the scene at the House.

I knew exactly what was going to happen; I'd even gone up that morning and spoken to Mr Stockley, the doorkeeper, who was a distinguished old Naval Warrant Officer. I said to him, 'It's very important that this shouldn't go wrong, or be in any way undignified,' which he appreciated, because the truth was they were very scared. They were afraid that something would happen. They didn't quite know what. It was, after all, quite a serious thing to keep a man out who had a piece of paper.

It was the first time in history that this had ever happened. The Chief Whip and I walked towards the door of the House. There were lots of Members standing in the Members' Lobby and they formed a sort of 'V' towards the Chamber. I suppose there must have been 50 to 100 there. I came in from the Central Lobby and the journalists were all waiting there too, although they're not allowed to report what happens in the Members' Lobby. I went round and met Bowden and we walked towards the door of the House and the people sort of came in on us.

When we got there Stockley came forward and put his hand up and said, 'You cannot enter, Sir.' I was very, very nervous indeed. It was a moment of high drama, although the press said it was corny because everyone had known what would happen. But I was relieved to get it over, because you couldn't be quite sure *how* it would happen.

Then I went into the Gallery to hear the debate.

It was rather dull, really. It was the same as 13 April, except that there had been the great by-election victory in the middle. They refused to hear me and they refused to seat me. So when I left the House that evening I was, although still a Member of Parliament, really in outer darkness.

When I was outside the Distinguished Strangers' Gallery just by the lift, I lit my pipe and the doorkeeper came out to me and said, 'You can't smoke here.' So I said, 'What do you mean? I always do.' He said, 'You're not a Member.' So I absolutely lost my temper – the only time I did lose my temper in the whole thing – and I really attacked him. I forgot exactly what I said. But here he was, applying the rule. It wasn't his fault. The rule was that Members could smoke there, but non-Members couldn't.

After the debate we went to the Strangers' Cafeteria, the only one we could use, and those dear women who worked there laid out a cloth on two tables so that my mother, Stephen, Caroline and I could have a meal. Now my friends in the House when I go there are the police, the women in the cafeteria, who play a very big part in a Member's life, and some of the badge messengers, the ex-warrant officers who look after the Chamber. The idea that one had been thrown out by the Establishment, yet one was still a friend of the people who work in the Palace, meant a very great deal to me. They were so kind. Whenever I went to the Cafeteria, they always made a point of getting my meal. I didn't have to queue like anyone else. This matters when you feel you've been shut out. Anyway, at 10.30 the votes were over and we went out and went home and that was the end of the Election campaign.

The following morning I had my first visit from Mr Hazledean. Mr Hazledean became quite a figure in this. He was a managing clerk for Lewis and Lewis and Gisborne who were the solicitors for St Clair. This old gentleman, who was about eighty-four, came to my house and presented me with a libel writ, a result of what had happened on the eve of poll. So I offered him a cup of tea and he sat down. I had no solicitors then at all. I asked him what it was all about. He said, 'Well, if you ask me, I don't think anything will come of it.' He said it was a technical thing and that he had to present it. So I asked whether he thought that St Clair would pursue it. 'Oh no, I doubt it.' I then asked, 'What shall I do about it?' He said, 'You'd better give it to a solicitor, because you'll have to enter' something or another 'in response'. Then he said I would just have to wait. I was rather encouraged by this.

Then we got to the Election Petition. He told me that his firm was handling the Election Petition as well. He said, 'Of course, you haven't got a chance in the thing. But I may as well tell you, privately, that I'm on your side.' I asked him what he thought it would all cost. He said that if the case lasted a week, it would cost £5,000 to £6,000. This really threw me. I asked him how on earth he got that. 'Well,' he said, 'Counsel are very expensive and they've got a refresher every day. There'll be a silk, or maybe two.' I said, 'I doubt whether it will last a week, because it's a very simple case.' He said, 'Oh I don't know. By the time all the stuff is read out, it will take a week.'

Mr Hazledean became, in a sense really, my adviser after this as well. I used to ring him up and ask him what was happening. I liked him very much. He was very straight and whenever we met, which we did quite regularly, he always managed to get across something nice about the case. One of the pleasant things was that, with the exception of St Clair whom I didn't see again from the Election until the Court, relations between both sides in the case were extremely cordial. We were always trying to help them and they were always trying to keep us posted about what was happening.

The big question in my mind, at that time, was whether I would fight the case or not. This was a tremendous anxiety, because looking at it from a long-term point of view, I knew that I never could win; at least I thought then that I couldn't win the case. I thought the advantage of this fight was in the political arena, not in the legal arena. No good came out of the Committee of Privileges and why go over that again? So in my mind I was beginning to decide not to fight the case. I also decided, as a

result of what had been said in the press, that perhaps warning everybody what was going to happen had been a mistake. I don't know whether this is right or not. I told the press people exactly what would happen. I'd told the Speaker exactly what would happen. I'd told the doorkeeper what would happen, the Serjeant-at-Arms what would happen, and the press built it up, a little bit, as a farce. As if this had, somehow, been a prearranged minuet in the Establishment. So I decided that the next time this happened, I really would use force to get in or be taken into custody. I don't say I would have fought like a tiger, but I would compel them to take me into custody. Of course, at that time my mind was on another Election. So I've always, at every point in this fight, been thinking ahead and this was what I'd decided.

I had a flood of letters and telegrams. The Italian Socialist Party sent a telegram. The Foreign Minister of the FLN Government in Algeria sent a message. There were many messages from all sorts of people. There was a letter from Galbraith, the American Ambassador in Delhi, saying 'Here we have noticed and applauded the victory of the common man.' This was very pleasant and happy and I greatly enjoyed it.

On 9 May a man drove up from Bristol, to say that they would like to organise a march on the Houses of Parliament from the constituency. I said, 'Look, hold on a minute. Let's wait. After the next Election we can have a march. The machinery is now set for the Election Petition and I don't think it would do any good.' So I managed to discourage him. Then two people arrived, two students from London University, whom I'd never seen before, and I've never seen since. They said, 'We're going down to Bristol to organise a petition in your favour. Can you tell us who we should see while we're there?' So I gave them the address of the agent and they hitch-hiked off to Bristol.

There were visitors all day with things of this kind: people dropping in with money, ideas and ringing up. That was the spirit of that day. I did decide then that I definitely would not fight the Election Court, and I worked till about 2.45 in the morning on a legal statement, explaining why I wasn't going to contest. I said that by its resolution of yesterday, the House of Commons has now taken out of the hands of the Court its power to decide this matter and, therefore, the Court will not be a free agent in deciding. I drafted this very carefully. I then drafted a second statement that I intended to fight the constituency again if I was unseated, and thirdly I wrote to the Speaker asking for the amenities of the House as a man whose Election was being queried by the Court, and I gave many examples to show that when a man is elected and is subject to a Petition he is treated as a Member until the Petition is decided. That was the Tuesday.

On Wednesday, 10 May, I completed all the draft statements and I rang Hugh Gaitskell and said, 'Look Hugh, it seems to me that there's no point in fighting this case. It's going to be very expensive, there's going to be no political advantage in it at all. I think the best thing to do is to make it quite clear, by a statement now, that I do intend to fight again, so that the Tory, if he wins the Election Court, won't resign and precipitate a new Election. The best thing really is for him to stay on at the moment, but we should warn them that this thing is not going to be finished until it's won.'

Hugh was very cross with me. It was a very sharp interview. He said, 'Don't do it. The Party won't have anything to do with it. The NEC were very doubtful about the by-election in any case. We got as much out of this as we possibly could on Monday' – I suppose that was a reference to the political benefit to the Party – 'and I know St Clair intends to apply for the Chiltern Hundreds after winning the seat, so you must say nothing about the future whatsoever.'

So I said, 'Well, you know, Bristol South East will almost certainly re-nominate me, if there is a new by-election.' In the aftermath of the campaign I felt this.

Hugh said, 'You mustn't try to blackmail the Executive. You mustn't do anything at all without consulting the Organisation Sub-Committee.'

I said, 'Of course I will do what you say, but you know it isn't all that easy for me. I've got maybe £6,000 damages against me for the libel action and I've also got to pay the cost of the Election case.'

He then used one of his characteristic phrases; he said, 'I appreciate that.' Then he said, 'Remember this. If there were another Election the result would be likely to be much worse than the last time. It would look very bad for us.' That was a reference to the Party. So that was the phone call with Hugh.

I went into a period of bad depression for the rest of May and about half of June. I couldn't get up in the morning and couldn't bring myself to do any work at all. It was partly the physical reaction after the excitement of the Election and partly the feeling that I had come to the end of the road.

On Tuesday 16 May I went to see Rab Butler at 4 pm. He was very grim and pale, rather different from his urbane and smiling self on my previous interview. I thanked him very much for seeing me, and said I'd come about two things.

'First of all to let you know that I intend to subpoena you at the Election Court and I thought it would be courteous to tell you before you hear officially. Secondly, I've come along to ask what the prospects are for ending this business, which is not very pleasant for me – it'll probably bankrupt me in the end – and it can't be very enjoyable for you.'

Butler was very surprised. 'What do you mean, summon me before the Election Court? The law is very clear. We're the High Court of Parliament. You can't summon me.'

'Oh well, it's not to do with the law, but the question of asking why the Whips were put on is a judicial matter, because it's the first time since 1868 that the House of Commons has intervened between an Election and an Election Petition. Anyway,' I said, 'I'm not arguing the case with you now as to what questions I will put to you in court, but I thought it would just be a courtesy. I don't want to go to the Courts, in any case; the Election Petition is not of my making. But obviously, if it comes to the court, I'm bound to use it as best I can to help to promote the case. That's all I can do.'

'Well now,' he said, 'as to the general position. You'll be very glad to hear that I got you a select committee. This wasn't very easy, I may say. The Attorney-General was very much against doing anything for you at all. There was strong feeling in the Party against you personally.'

Was that true or not? I don't know. My feeling about Butler was that he was sympathetic, but meant to do nothing. I said to him: 'Well, if you wanted to help me, why did you put the Whips on for the vote to exclude me from the House?'

'Oh, there was nothing in that at all.'

So I said, 'I'm an amateur historian and I remember that Bradlaugh had to fight four Elections.' Butler said that it wasn't the same. I replied that I thought it *was* the same, because the principle that a determined constituency can always defeat an entrenched House of Commons seems to me to be the parallel and I couldn't relax now, whatever I wanted to do, because Bristol would put me up again. Butler said, 'Well, what good would that do?'

'It would keep it alive. If I relax for a moment, the steam will go out of it.'

Butler then became more accommodating and said, 'You did very well in the Election and our chaps are politicians, you know. Remember, we're all politicians and we noticed the result and it influenced us. So you've already achieved a great deal.'

'Yes, but if you had a new Labour Member for Bristol South East the matter would be as dead as a dodo. Obviously, I can't contemplate that.'

Butler said, 'Now remember, St Clair is in a difficult position. He's a very decent chap. You must remember that.'

'I know, he's the victim of my case too. I don't mean because he's the heir to a peerage, but he is a victim of the absurdities that are pursuing me. But I am anxious that he should know that, if he wins the Election case and then resigns before the law is altered, I will fight again.'

'He hasn't decided what to do yet,' Butler told me. 'He's going to let me know. If he has as much character as you have it may be his own decision. In any case, he would never fight you again.'

'The best thing for him to do really,' I said, 'would be to stay on in Parliament until the law is changed. That will keep it alive.'

So Butler said, 'I'll make a note of that point and remember it. You'd better come and see me again before he decides.'

'How am I going to know when he decides what to do?' I asked.

'I summon you.'

'Look,' I pointed out, 'it's in St Clair's interest to resign in time to get another constituency before the next Election.'

'Yes, but he will do his duty. I'm sure he'll do his duty.'

I asked about the future and he said, 'Well, after the Election Court is over, we shall go ahead with the joint Select Committee, even if your chaps won't come in and help us. We really do want the Labour Party to come in and we'd even agree to have some of your wild men from the real left on the Committee, if it would encourage your people to come in.' 'If you really wanted them to come in,' I said, 'why didn't you ask them about the terms of reference of the committee, before you announced it?'

'Oh, well, our chaps wouldn't have stood for it. We know the Labour Party difficulties, but honestly, if you're talking to your people, it really would be better for your own case if they did agree.'

'I don't think that they ought to come in on Lords' Reform generally,' I said, 'even if it were better for me – which it may very well be – that they should come in. I'm a politician first and I'm only fighting a personal battle second, and I couldn't possibly ask the Party to make a sacrifice on the whole question of Lords' Reform in my own particular interest.'

'You know, we really do care about Lords' Reform,' Butler said. 'We always have done. After all, Gaitskell is much stronger now that this disarmament thing is settled. After ten years in office it'll be hard to predict the outcome of the next Election. So you see we have an interest in getting Lords' Reform in this Parliament.'

'You mean to have it looking respectable so that it can check the legislation of a possible Labour Government? Because if that's what you mean, that, in a nutshell, is why I don't think the Labour Party ought to have anything to do with it. Why should we help you to leave behind you a little time-bomb to use against us?'

Then he realised what he'd said, and added, 'Oh, you mustn't get the wrong idea. We only want very minor changes in the House of Lords, renunciation and remuneration and other things of this kind; it's all really to help your chaps because they're having a very difficult time in the House of Lords. Anyway,' he said, 'very, very few people would renounce. I'm sure Balniel and Hinchingbroke wouldn't.'

'Of course they wouldn't. I've always known this. If you make the price high enough then you will simply have a natural selection operating. If you say renunciation or extinction, nobody will do it but me. Of course if you make it easy, there'll be more.'

Then Butler said, 'We'll have lot of difficulties with the Lords, especially the independent Unionist peers.'

Later I discovered that this was the thing that was holding up the Select Committee; Macleod had said it at the time. I pooh-poohed it. 'I doubt it,' I said. 'I've been in close correspondence with Jessel and Salisbury, both of whom are very friendly. And can you give me a pledge that you'll act on this before the next Election?'

'I cannot commit the Cabinet but some of our chaps are very well disposed towards you,' said Butler.

'I know that. They ran the risk of displeasing the Whips.'

Butler denied this and said it was ridiculous: 'There was no pressure on the people who voted for you. No pressure at all.'

'Well, I'm very glad to hear that.'

Then out came the characteristic Butler: '*The Times* was quite wrong to say that I fumbled this. It is the only point on which I have run into difficulties as Leader of the House.'

He became very friendly at the end. He said: 'Any time you want to come and have a frank talk with me you can. Of course, on "Club" rules.' Then, 'How's your wonderful family standing up under the strain?'

'Well, they're 100 per cent behind me. But it is a very anxious time for them. This may all look great fun from the outside, but it's a deadly serious business and I've no intention of going into the House of Lords.'

I think that interview was a great success.

I had a message to go and see Gaitskell. I went to see him the following day, 18 May. I wondered what it was about. All he said was that he thought Caroline should run for the constituency and that Dora Gaitskell had suggested it to him – a brilliant idea, he said. So I said, 'Well, there is the difficulty about her nationality and her not wanting to give it up, and all that.'

'Don't reject it too strongly,' he said, 'because I think this might be the best way of doing it.'

One amusing incident occurred later that evening. At a reception at the Tunisian embassy Bourguiba came up to Caroline and said, 'Mrs Benn – or is it Lady Stansgate?' Then he burst out laughing and said, 'I was only teasing.' He told us, 'The whole Tunisian people are behind you in your struggle. Mr Benn, you are the people's choice. You have the confidence of the people.' I said, 'So have you, Mr President.' We passed on.

The ITN took a film unit and interviewed students in the streets of Moscow about the case. The students asked the interviewer about why Wedgwood Been had been kicked out of the House of Commons. All over the place this has been picked up and has been treated as typical, which I think it is, of the illness and malaise that now affects British society – people clutching on to the Queen and Royal Family and the old ways of doing things because they're frightened of a world in which, they suspect, Britain has no future.

On 23 May I decided that I would represent myself at the Election Court. First I wanted to control the case throughout. I was terrified that any lawyer put up – even Gerald Gardiner appearing for nothing – would miss a point or would give away a point of substance. Secondly I felt that I did know this branch of the law as well as anyone else. Perhaps that sounds rather arrogant, but I had been working on it for many years. Some other lawyer would have had to mug it all up and I doubt whether he would have been prepared to give as much time to it. The question of costs was also very much in my mind. And I wanted to fight every stage of the case myself, simply on grounds of public sympathy. Quite honestly, I think the fact that I did represent myself was worthwhile. I thought that the judges would give me at least as good a hearing, as a layman, as they would to anyone else other than a top silk. Michael Zander was a bit doubtful about this. Still, I had reached the decision and I stuck to it. Although Michael Zander continued to worry and tried to persuade me to ask Gerald Gardiner to appear for nothing, by this time my mind was fairly well settled and I never shifted.

I worked for six weeks flat out before the case, and a lot of the basic stuff was parliamentary stuff which I knew a good deal better than a lawyer would have done.

On 26 May I took up the whole problem of where I would do my research. The Speaker said I was to be treated entirely as a stranger, so I was in the position of a Member of Parliament defending his seat before an Election Court, and not allowed to use the House of Commons Library. Charlie Pannell said he would see or write to the Speaker and I wrote too; in the end he gave me the right to use the Library when the House wasn't sitting. I was given a little room up in the *Times* Room, way up under the eaves, where I was allowed to work throughout the whole period. I must say, here, how kind the House of Commons Library were. All the staff, I feel sure, were on my side, and they went out of their way to do everything possible to help me. I suppose they must have brought 300 or 400 books, at different times, up in the lift. I would telephone down and they would bring them up to this little room where I worked opposite a couple of Library clerks. It was very dark, with a small window from which you could just see the river. I lived there really for a month. I took a Thermos and never went down for a meal. I would just stay up there and work. Michael Zander came and worked there too and without the House of Commons Library's co-operation it would have been quite impossible to develop the case as we did.

We worked on a very interesting system. We would simply take general books – anything on the law, or peerages, or the House of Commons proceedings – we would read them through and if we came across anything that had any bearing we would then look it up in the original – in the *Journals* of the House. If we wanted something that was referred to in the original journal, we would ring up the Victoria Tower, where the Chief Archivist was, and he would get us down the original. All the Library staff were rather delighted and pleased, because they felt that here was one man working away on the history of Parliament, not just for academic reasons but because he wanted to be there. I think that influenced them. My sense of gratitude to the Commons, for that, is unbounded, and when they lent me twenty-one books to take to the Court, and I collected them on Sunday without even a signature, it made me feel very grateful. We went on working, I suppose, pretty continuously, every day.

On 31 May I heard from the Speaker that I could use the Library, as a stranger, as I mentioned earlier.

Michael Zander's contribution to the preparation of the case was absolutely phenomenal. My parents had known his parents for some time. His father was a German refugee lawyer who came over here before the war, and is now Head of the Hebrew University in London. Michael just devoted himself whole time to it.

On 9 June I had to go to the Law Courts to fix the time and place of the trial. This was the first time I had appeared in a court, and it was before Mr Justice Gorman and Mr Justice McNair, who were the two senior judges of the three who were on the circuit in which the constituency is. I think this must have been regarded as a little bit more interesting than attempted rape and petty larceny and speeding. So they had allocated themselves to it.

It was certainly worthwhile getting the feeling of a court. Of course, the QCs had their special place, with a desk, where they could stand, but I was just a layman on the solicitors' bench and it was very awkward to speak so low, when the other chap was at an advantage behind you. But the class system operating, in terms of accommodation in a court, is fascinating. You have silks, juniors, managing clerks and the judges. Everybody is graded according to their importance and if you don't have the right grade then you don't have as advantageous a place from which to speak. But it was interesting. Helenus Milmo, QC was appearing for the other side, quite needlessly, since it was an agreed point. He was very cordial, and indeed our relations with the other side were perfectly cordial throughout. There was no point in getting angry about it, though, obviously, it was very irritating to see this gathering of expensive lawyers to get me out of Parliament, with the pretty certain knowledge that I'd be paying their bill at the end.

It was on Saturday 17 June that I got a cheque for £500 from Mr and Mrs Edward Sieff of Marks and Spencer, who were old friends of ours. We were absolutely knocked sideways by this. They said that it was for us personally, to help us over this very difficult period without my salary. We wrote back and said we couldn't possibly accept it for ourselves, but that, if we lost the case, we would have to start a fund and could we put it into that? They wrote back and said they didn't really intend it for that, but if we wanted to, that would be all right.

On that day, which was also our wedding anniversary, Caroline and I went down to a social at the Corn Exchange in Bristol. It was a wonderful evening. All the people who helped in the Election came along and we had a splendid evening, with dancing and cheering and all that.

It was very interesting that the Lords are terribly pleased if you come in to prove a peerage. If I'd come in with string around my trousers and said that I thought I was the Marquis of Granby, they would have treated me with respect, because I would have been trying to get what they had to offer. But there was a feeling of resentment, because I was trying to get rid of it.

Michael Zander and I worked terribly hard. We worked at home or at the House. Once he stayed all night and I went to bed, with my mind in a complete muddle, at about 3 in the morning and I could hear him typing through the night as we sorted out the argument in the right order. This was really the big problem. We had such a mass of material – how were we to present it? I think we could sum it up by saying that we presented the case in a historical way in order to show why these rules had developed. The way to get round the absurdity of the law was to throw light on the history of the matter. This had the merit, of course, of being interesting to the Court; it wasn't dull. We weren't picking on silly little points and making the most of them. We were presenting the whole history of Parliament and its attitude to disqualification, and the relationship of the Crown to the Lords and the Commons, and those to the people, in such a way that it hung together and stood, absolutely, on its own feet. We added the legal points that we thought were helpful. But this, I think, had integrity as a presentation. Although we lost the argument, reading over the transcript again, what was worked on, produced, developed and presented has I think some lasting value. I was very anxious that this should be so – but the difficulty was putting it in the right order. I had to read all the stuff very carefully and Michael had got to try to get a grasp of it. I worked out the most elaborate card index system, under which – by subject, name of case, type of case, reference book – all the page references were there with five or six different-coloured metal tags on the top. So that, literally at my fingertips, I had available the reference to substantiate any of the points we were making. I enjoyed that enormously. But I did find myself rather weak on the pure intellectual side of it, because I found it very difficult to marshal the facts in the right way.

On 29 June we had this talk with Lynn Ungoed-Thomas and Elwyn Jones. I presented in outline, very quickly, in about ten minutes, the whole case that I would present. They sat there with faces absolutely blank. They're great personal friends of mine and they didn't want to discourage me, but they simply said that it wouldn't wash at all. You start with a tremendous jurisdictional argument about whether the Court has power to decide the issue, which was how we were going to start, and then go on to say you are not a peer. You have lost the ear of that Court in half a day. They'll never go on listening. So we came home utterly crushed, feeling that it was completely hopeless. Then, of course, we took the argument and rearranged it in a new form.

On Sunday 9 July we went to the House of Commons and sorted out the books and references. We put a tag in each one. I went through the case, and got completely depressed because I thought the whole thing was hopeless, there wasn't a point that would stand up. That was just anxiety. Anyway, the boys came with me, and we moved eighty books down from the Palace of Westminster to the Law Courts. The press and television were on us all day for photographs and comments and so on, but we were too busy and tired for that. They got the Court unlocked for us, and we went in and set all the books out. I spent an hour in the empty courtroom, looking up at the judges' seats, and preparing the case. It was weird. But I went early to bed because the following day, Monday 10 July, was the day on which the case began.

I felt very much on my own after the early part of May, for about six weeks. Pannell did ring me up from time to time, and one came in contact with individuals when it was necessary, but I never felt that they were taking a continual interest. I had a few friends in the House. Lynn was one and Elwyn was another. There were a lot of people I could ring up if I wanted to or if I needed advice, but very few who took a lot of interest. The House of Commons isn't really like that. If you're sick, you probably get a letter from the Chief Whip and one or two friends may ring up. It's a community, but only in the building. It isn't a community that spreads out and encompasses you if you fall by the wayside. One felt, therefore, a little bit lonely about it. But I was in the House, of course, and I was seeing people.

I tried to keep up with my political work. After all, the whole purpose of this exercise was to be free to get back to politics. It isn't that it had any interest in itself, but it became totally absorbing because one felt one had to put the best possible case forward, in the Court.

Butler: What about the press? Were they relatively quiet about it?

The thing died the death after the Election and the barring in the House, right up until the case, because it would have been contempt of court to have referred to it in any way at all.

On the morning of Monday 10 July we had another of our sieges, by television. I should think there must have been thirty or forty of them in the garden. All the photographs of leaving home and getting into the car and the children waving and all that. We had a few books with us and one or two things we needed. We got into a taxi and went off to the Law Courts in the Strand – and found another reception committee. We arrived about an hour before the case began, to settle in. They had allocated a little room to us, which was a great convenience, because we needed a place where we could keep all our papers and books. My mother was there, and various other members of the family. The jury box was really full of friends, and I saw St Clair arriving and said good morning to him. That was the last time I spoke to him.

We settled in and at 10.30 the case began. It was a moment of great tension and excitement. I knew that I wouldn't be speaking for the first day or two, but I didn't think that Sir Andrew Clark, the QC opposing me, would take very much longer than that. I was amazed when he took three days. The feeling of the Court was quite new to me. I was sitting on the ground floor with a table in front of me and all my books in front, about ninety of them, marked up with tabs. I had my card index right beside me, so that I could find anything I wanted. I had the great big, red Letters Patent and all the piles of documents that would be needed. Sir Andrew Clark sat in the row behind, in the silks' lines, with a reading stand. I was able to borrow one for my speech later on. The biggest bulk was the *Journals* of the House and we didn't use or quote from anything like all of our books. But, if pressed, we could have dealt with any point that arose. Anyway, we had all the stuff ready and we simply sat back.

The judges came in at 10.30 and bowed and sat. I got to know their faces well in the next two weeks. I liked both of them personally. Gorman, who was thin and the senior judge, was, I think, the nicer of the two. McNair had a much better mind, and really asked hostile questions. They both had a sense of humour and I did feel that I got on very well with them. Certainly, they couldn't have been kinder, or more polite to me than they were personally. I did enjoy the case, there's no doubt. I got terribly tired and, on occasions, very depressed, but I did enjoy the atmosphere of that Court. It began by them saying 'I suppose you want to be called Wedgwood Benn?' They did, of course, consistently call me that throughout the case.

Andrew Clark, on the other hand, I took an instant dislike to. He looks like a rodent, with a little moustache, and a very pompous manner. I soon discovered that he really hadn't done his homework. He made a lot of extraordinary slips. He said that a peer of the Realm was a peer who had inherited, and a peer of Parliament was a life peer, and all this sort of stuff. He just hadn't got it right. This gave us a certain satisfaction. We felt that we could trip him up on small things.

Butler: Did you interrupt him at all?

I did a bit. It wasn't awfully popular. I was brought up in the heckling tradition, where, if a man on the other side is making a point that's wrong, you jump up and say so. I was always delighted when he interrupted me, which he very rarely did. It was an added interest to the occasion. But courts don't work like that. You're expected to take your medicine, even if it's the wrong medicine and the chap has the wrong bottle in his hand. You're expected to take it, and not to make any comments.

I was immensely impressed by the fact that the judges would listen to all I had to say. After all, I did talk to them for 22 hours and I gave them 135,000 words. They asked me 537 questions in the course of that, which kept it alive. But there was no sign of impatience with me. I hope I didn't bore them. But, even if I did, they didn't show it. This made a very profound impression on my mind. On the first day of the case, the only thing we could do was to sit and listen attentively, and make notes to see if Clark raised any points we hadn't expected. He didn't.

On the second day, 11 July, we began to get into the routine of going to Court. I got there early, with all the books, notes and materials. Clark went on all day. I ought perhaps, to say a word more about the Court itself. It was crowded out almost all the time. Barristers were coming in and standing by the doors, or sitting. The Gallery was always full. There was a big crowd outside the Court in the morning when we arrived, and quite a number of touching scenes. There was a woman called Mrs Belcher who lives in Shoreham. I had tried, unsuccessfully, to take up a point for her about her eviction from her house a year or two earlier and she came up from Shoreham every day to hear the case. Then there was a chap living in Westminster who was very keen on road safety; I had taken up a point for him and he came to the Court every day. And one realised that there was a floating population of people who, for one reason or another, were interested and were coming in. Various other distinguished people looked in from time to time. It may have been a bit like the Christians and the lions in the local circus. But they were coming in.

Caroline sat beside me making notes of everything, and she was invaluable. Her natural pessimism matched my natural optimism, but she did make most useful points and she latched on to the things that she thought the judges were noticing and that she thought that Clark was pressing particularly strongly, whereas I was much too concerned with the wider thing to be able to follow these carefully.

There were no charges of corruption, as there often are in these Election petitions. I pointed out that St Clair himself was the heir to a Scottish peerage and that the facts were agreed. I was going through the personal points about Father, about my brother and so on when the judges interrupted me and said, 'Mr Benn, you're speaking too quickly.' I couldn't understand this. I thought I was speaking very slowly, but they were finding it impossible to keep up with what I was saying. MacKenzie from Ashurst Morris (Michael Zander's solicitors), who had come in, was extremely worried at the end of three-quarters of an hour; he thought – if this is the sort of case that the chap is going to present, dealing with irrelevant issues like his father's public service, he's going to get nowhere at all.

But, as it happened, I think that my first day was rather successful, because I only had about 45 minutes of this type of preliminary material. I wanted to read it into the record, and it did all appear in *The Times* the following day. *The Times* was doing a brilliant survey of the case, and I wanted to get it out of the way so I could begin the following morning with the legal argument. I made one error. I incorporated some very mild, watery jokes. For example, while tracing the history of it, I said that in the old days, among people who were regarded as inherently unsuitable were the lawyers. I said there were some today who still feel this. There was such a lot of laughter from the Gallery that Gorman banged on the table and said, 'I will not tolerate interruptions in this Court. Any more laughter and I shall clear the Galleries.' I felt that this was directed against me. I tried to disarm him by saying 'My Lord, was that rebuke addressed to me?' He said, 'Not in the slightest' so firmly that I felt I had been exonerated. But, in fact, I deleted a lot of other little jokes after that because I believe that, in Court, only the judges are allowed to make jokes. Nobody else is allowed to do it.

Well, on Thursday 13 July I was speaking all day, and it was very tiring to stand for four and a half hours and go on speaking. It does leave you completely limp at the end because your mind has to be on the job the whole time and, unlike hecklers', judges' questions really go straight to the point. I felt throughout the case that I was never caught by the judges. I don't know whether this is right or not, but they never managed, by their cross-examination, to reveal any inconsistency in the argument. They rejected the whole argument but the thing hung together and they never caught me out once on a reference that I couldn't find, on a request for information, or the meaning of a phrase that I couldn't give them.

I spoke again all day on Friday 14 July, but it seemed to be going wrong. I felt, for the first time, that I was not getting my case over and not making any impression. I didn't know why this was. I still don't know why it was. But the incredulity of the judges that such an argument could be sustained was coming out and they asked so many questions that they were actually robbing my argument of points that I didn't intend to raise until later.

On the Friday, Sir Andrew Clark came up for the first time to me – I don't think I'd done more than nod at him – and enquired anxiously about how long my speech would last. He gave me the impression that he was rather worried about this. He went so far as to suggest that the judges were only tolerating such a long speech because I was a layman, which I think was extremely offensive. He, in fact, had taken just as long as I did. I said, 'Well, I'm awfully sorry, Sir Andrew, I don't want to keep you from another case, but this is life and death to me. Just for the sake of your convenience I can't possibly fall short in my argument.' I didn't put it as rudely as that, but I did make it quite clear that this wasn't just a joke for me, or just another case.

We did feel, as I still feel, that the case had certain merits, which were very hard for the judges to push aside. The thing that really shook me about some of their questions on the following Tuesday was that they had really not appeared to grasp some of the simple factual points. For example, I remember one question put to me by McNair about a Writ of Summons. Every peers gets one on the death of his father. I said, 'Not at all, My Lord, why do you think I haven't had one?' He said, 'Because you've made a fuss about it.' This was an absolutely central point, which I'd been working to get over. He simply hadn't grasped it. I'm not sure whether they did grasp the whole thing. But it was a model argument, and maybe too difficult to absorb at points. It wouldn't have made any difference, even if they had.

I was very near the end of the case then, and I had got everything prepared for the following day. We went out to dinner with the Sieffs. Well, anyway, the following day, Wednesday 19 July, I finished the speech. The concluding passages, which I had polished with such care, really so moved me that I could hardly utter the last sentence because I was almost in tears. The *Times* reporter actually did, I'm told, break down at the end. Anyway, that was the end. Sir Andrew Clark got up, and I thought I had no right of reply, though I subsequently discovered I did have this, and did exercise it. But as far as I was concerned the main strain was over, and I felt very relieved. Clark droned on and on but didn't really take up any of the major points that I had made. He just dismissed them all. He didn't deal with them.

At any rate, it all finished, and when I sat down I think that was the end of the case altogether. The judges said they would reserve judgement, and I was still not sure, of course, what the result would be. But people seemed to think it had gone well, and I was, as I say, pretty certain that St Clair wouldn't be seated. It was really very remarkable that they should have seated St Clair. I'm very glad, from a political point of view, that there wasn't a new Election. But I obviously had to try to stop them seating St Clair. If there had been a new Election, it would have created considerable problems for me, but it would have been something of a triumph, of course, to have disposed of St Clair after all he had said about the votes being thrown away. It was the first time, since 1868, that an English court had ever seated a defeated candidate in an Election case. This was another reason why I didn't think they would do it.

On Tuesday 25 July, I had a phone call from Len Williams. He said two things – he said, 'You can't stand again, if there's another Election.' I said that the matter hadn't arisen yet. But then he said, 'By the way, your nomination for the NEC and your status as a delegate to Conference will both be ruled out if the Election Court goes against you,' on the grounds that I would then be neither a candidate (endorsed) nor a Member of Parliament. So I said that I had idly thought of this at one time or another, but had anybody raised it? He said that nobody had, but that he was going to, with the NEC, if the matter came up. He said, 'Of course, when you lose the case . . .' This was before the judgement and there was no hint in his voice that I might win, or that something might happen to alter it. 'Of course, if you become a peer and represent the PLP in the House of Lords, then you'll be able to go to Conference.' So I said, 'My dear Len, do you think I've been fighting this battle for a year just in order, at the end, to get a seat at Conference by capitulating completely?' That thought had never really occurred to him.

I went to see Gaitskell, and coming out of his room I passed Butler in the corridor. He saw me and stopped for a moment and frowned at me. I said to him, 'Are you all ready to receive me back on Monday? When the result of the Court is presented to the Speaker?' He looked very worried. I heard from a number of people afterwards, particularly from David Wood of *The Times*, that during the case there had been great anxiety amongst Butler, and others, that we might have won. But, of course, that was a bit of bravado, because the following day the judgment went against me.

We went off early in the morning – it was another of the siege days – and sat in this packed Court. It was fuller than it had been on any other day, and we heard the judgment, which was read by the judges alternately. I suppose the judgment took about two hours to read. I should think that for the first 45 minutes it was just a recapitulation of the facts. There some phrases like, 'we cannot allow our feelings or the feelings of the respondent to enter into our consideration.' Then one realised that it was lost. Then it all poured out in a most extraordinary form: that while the hereditary system is retained, it cannot in any way be modified. The phrase is there, and is the phrase which is quoted in the Soviet reports of the trial. The idea that the hereditary system was necessary took precedence over the democratic element in our constitution. This is a view of our constitution that simply doesn't fit in with the facts, because of course in no respect, except in this, does the hereditary system have anything but a very minor role to play in the Government of this country. Any rate, that was the end of it and we kept our end up. It was a grim moment. It was the clanging of the gate. It was obviously the end of the first stage of the struggle, some eight or nine months after it had begun. But we were very cheerful and gave interviews.

Butler: What about costs?

Ah yes. The costing came up. I realised that I was faced with the absolutely crippling bill, and so simply made one submission to them. I said that I had tried to keep the case as short as I could. I'd represented it myself. I hadn't engaged expensive Counsel. I had not contested any of the evidence. I had dropped several of the points that Clark had thought I might raise, and warned him in good time that I was going to. Anyway I said that this was a very important constitutional principle that is being decided: whether the rights of a constituency or the hereditary system should take precedence. I had no alternative but to defend my seat in this case, and really it was most unfair that costs should fall upon me. I therefore asked that there should be no award as to costs. I wish I had said that the judges should report to the House that the costs should be borne by public funds. It would have been a precedent, but a perfectly fair one. Then Clark jumped up and said, 'This is monstrous. Here are two men fighting, absolutely by themselves, one against the other, and the loser must simply pay.' All the costs were duly awarded against me. If no award had been made to costs, Tory Central Office would have paid his, and I would have paid mine.

I had an interview with the BBC and ITN outside in the street. Then I went to Broadcasting House and did an interview at 10 pm. I came up against the first little struggle as to whether I was to be Mr Benn or Lord Stansgate. The BBC 10 pm programme tried to introduce me as Lord Stansgate. I said that I wouldn't go on if they called me that. I was rather depressed by the whole thing and the end of the day felt as if it was the end of the road.

The bill, when it came in from the other side, was £7,500 and our own was £1,000. We realised that a public fund was urgently needed, and we had various talks with people. Michael Zander carried on and we got a list of sponsors, including some fairly distinguished people who agreed to give their names. Attlee, Lady Violet Bonham Carter, Bronowski, Fenner Brockway, Jo Grimond, Augustus John, Elwyn Jones, Sir Compton Mackenzie, Christopher Mayhew, Gerald Nabarro, Harold Nicolson, Charles Pannell, C.P. Snow and the Bishop of Southwark all agreed to be sponsors of the Bristol Fund. We set up a committee of Ungoed-Thomas, Robin Day and Michael Zander, who would be empowered to sign the cheques. Michael worked on this. It was difficult for me because I didn't want this presented as a hard-luck story; clearly that would have been wrong.

Out of the £5,500 raised only £2,000 came from big contributions. There were some hundreds, some £50s and £25s. But the vast majority of contributions came from local Labour Parties, in shillings and guineas.

FROM HAROLD NICOLSON. C.1. THE ALBANY. PICCADILLY. W.1

TELEPHONE: REGENT 2470

14th March 1961.

Dear Wedgwood Benn,

Of course I will send you a message of support. Not since the days of Wilkes has a Member of Parliament been exposed to such injustice as you are.

Yours sincerely,

p.s. I thought I had better send you a draft statement herein.

The truth was that I panicked at that stage: £8,500 to have paid myself would have been an absolute hammerblow. It seemed essential to get the Fund going. It was a horrible moment. I had my worst period of depression from 29 July to the end of August. It was certainly the worst period of the whole case, because it was over.

There was a definite attempt to try to prevent St Clair from taking his seat. Some Tory MPs rang me up and said, 'Can we do anything to stop St Clair from taking his seat?' I said, 'I don't think you can. It's binding on the House of Commons.' But I did go, on Monday 31 July, to the House of Commons and I sat under the Gallery, with the intention of seeing St Clair take his seat. But on that day Macmillan made his statement saying that we were going into the Common Market, and there was a row, and I had to go to Bristol, so I wasn't there after all when he did take his seat.

I went along to the House simply because I wanted to show that I wasn't altogether beaten. And in Bristol that evening the General Council passed a resolution of support. This resolution said that they would continue to work with me as if I was the Member, and called on the Parliamentary Party and the National Executive to continue so to regard me. It was a very skilfully worded resolution that didn't re-adopt me as a candidate, which they couldn't do. But, at the same time, it established my status in the constituency, and I had hoped that the PLP might conceivably have allowed me to attend Party meetings.

On Wednesday 2 August the Labour Party telephoned to tell me that the nomination for the Executive would not be in order and would not be accepted and that I would not be allowed to attend Conference *ex officio*.

John Stonehouse wanted to raise this on the floor of Conference, and one or two other people suggested that I might try to get this thing reversed on the floor of Conference. I think it could have been done, if it had been worked on. If I'd gone to see Frank Cousins and told him the story, I'd have got the TGWU vote. I've no doubt that one could have mobilised a considerable – even a decisive – amount of support. The reason I didn't do it was that I thought it could only do harm. If there'd been a debate, pro and anti Benn at the Conference, whatever the outcome – and I might not have won – it would have been very damaging.

To be excluded from Conference, and that Bristol who had fought all year to put its man into Parliament should be denied for hereditary reasons the right to have its own man at Conference, was an absolute disgrace. You can't really justify it at all. The Executive certainly had the power to allow me to speak. There was a debate on the Lords: they could have invited me to speak at that. They could have found some way, as they did after the 1959 Conference.

Butler: Just after Conference, Dick Crossman made a statement to me saying, 'At

Conference, for the first time, I really did something dirty to Anthony Benn. I really damaged him.' Do you know what he did?'

I don't actually know what Dick Crossman did at the Executive, but, of course, he had the power as Chairman of the Party to have helped me to a very great extent. He could have said that this clearly came within the terms of the power of waiving the rules, and he could have exercised that. He could also have postponed the whole thing until Conference, so that the full Executive could consider it, which would then have made it impossible for them, I think, to strike me out. Dick was afraid that I was going to make an issue of this at Conference, and I did consider whether I should and came to the conclusion, as I said earlier, that it would be absolutely fatal to do it.

I did write to Hugh about the Wednesday debate at Conference on Reform of the Lords and asked him if he would give a pledge. He did make reference to my case in his speech, but it was reference to the absurdity, which he was very fond of stressing. It wasn't a clear, categorical statement that a Labour Government would deal with it. But I think that that will be forthcoming at a suitable moment and undoubtedly a Labour Government, if it has the time, will do something. What I'm afraid of, of course, is that if there is a Labour Government, they'll be too busy to do anything and anyway, when Gaitskell is forming his Government he will be looking for peers to go into various offices. I must confess, I think I have a better chance, in many ways, under the Tory Government, than I would under a Labour Government.

I hadn't spoken to St Clair, except to say good morning to him at the Election Court, since the declaration in May, and then only very briefly. But I had a letter from him dated 12 August, saying that he would be prepared to resign, but 'before I do resign I must have your assurance that you would not assent to nomination at any by-election or Election in this constituency.' This was the result of a compromise. He wanted to resign because he was very unhappy and the Government didn't want him to, so I've no doubt Butler said to him: make this offer. Benn will refuse it – because he knew I would – and then you'll be able to sit with a clear conscience. So that was the way it came.

I got that letter on the morning of the 14th and I then telephoned through a statement to the press at 1.45 on the same day, in which I said that I could well understand St Clair's embarrassment, that it had now been explained to him that an MP ought to be elected by a majority vote, which was the very point on which the Bristol Election was fought. Then I went on:

'He now asks me to solve his problems for him, by abandoning the whole campaign, so that he can withdraw from the difficulties into which the Government have led him. But it is not for Mr St Clair, or the

Conservative Party, to decide who the Labour candidate at the next Election shall, or shall not, be. To ask for that right is to add a fresh absurdity to the present law. If Mr St Clair's resignation makes a fresh Election necessary, the Labour candidate will be chosen by the Bristol South East constituency, together with the National Executive Committee of the Labour Party, in the usual way, and by no one else. I can, therefore, give him no assurance whatsoever. Mr St Clair's duty is perfectly clear. He should seek an immediate public pledge from the Government that the law will be changed when Parliament meets in October, and when it has been changed, he should resign immediately. This is the only honourable course open to him.'

That was a really defiant reply. St Clair made a statement saying he was disappointed.

After Father's death a number of papers referred to me as Lord Stansgate. Then they went back to Wedgwood Benn. After the Committee of Privilege's report they said, Lord Stansgate it is, and I became Lord Stansgate for a bit. Gradually I fought my way back again. The Election in Bristol was very largely reported as Wedgwood Benn. And at the Election Court some people thought that the judges had said I must be called Lord Stansgate. Of course, this was nonsense. A man can be called what he likes. When I saw the *Guardian* and *The Times* calling me Lord Stansgate I wrote to the editors, Alastair Hetherington and Haley William very informal letters, saying: 'I notice your papers have slipped into this habit. Could I, at least, have my name back?' Hetherington of the *Guardian* wrote back and said, 'Of course. I'll give an order, but I can't guarantee that it won't happen from time to time.' But Haley wrote and said 'I'll consider it.' Then he wrote back and said, 'I have considered it and it would be a legal fiction to do this.'

I wrote to the *Telegraph* to Colin Coote, and he wrote me an awfully nice letter back saying, 'I've always defended your right to call yourself what you like and to be what you like.' So I sent this to Haley. I had a very unpleasant reply. In the previous correspondence he had written 'Dear Anthony Wedgwood Benn', but in this letter he wrote 'Dear Lord Stansgate', which was offensive to a degree, repeating that this was perpetuating a legal fiction. I did not reply to him: I simply put a little bit in the Personal column of *The Times* saying 'Caroline and Anthony Wedgwood Benn are continuing to use these names and would like to be known as such.' I shall win this in the end, of course, because when I'm active again, which at the moment I'm not, then it'll be Wedgwood Benn, and the Stansgate thing will go into brackets, and then, I think, ultimately disappear. After all, Haley is himself Sir William Haley and when you go on too far to try to get rid of a title, you begin to make people with titles feel slightly worried. I'm sure that in Haley's own mind, perhaps not consciously, is the idea that this represents an attack upon the Establishment which he is not prepared to tolerate. That's my feeling about it.

Butler: Would you like to describe what happened when you went to see Iain Macleod the new Leader of the house to lobby him?

I went to the Commons, and I was a little early, so I had to sit in the Central Lobby for an hour with my old overcoat and parachute bag of documents, with nowhere to go. I felt very, very miserable. I went down to Macleod, and waited outside his room. I was taken in to see him. I've never spoken to him before, though I've often seen him. I respect him. He's a very competent chap, obviously the most likely successor to Macmillan. I've always thought this.

He smiled so I said, 'Thank you very much for seeing me. I'm sure that after your experience of constitutional change, this is easy for you.' He smiled at that. Then he said, 'Now I take it that our discussion is on Lobby terms.' So I said, 'Of course, and the recording that I'm now making is on Lobby terms.' Then he said, 'Well, the position is really this: Rab had a scheme last summer for a general Committee to investigate the composition of the Lords. But your people weren't in favour of it. And the peers weren't in favour of it.'

This was very interesting to me because I'd always known that the real reason why the Government have never been able to reform the House of Lords is not because the Labour Party wouldn't agree, but because the Conservative peers would never agree to anything that involves thinning out the backwoodsmen. On this one issue, the backwoodsmen are not pro-Tory. So he had had to negotiate it, and he thought he had now found something which was acceptable to Gaitskell, to Grimond and to the Conservative peers. The peers said they would only come to the Committee if the Labour Party came in, so it looks as if the thing is going to work.

It will discuss Scottish peers, peeresses in their own right and the whole question of renunciation and hereditary disqualification. I was very highly pleased about this. I said I was sure that the Labour Party would come in. And I was sure this was the right way to go about it – if you tacked it on to anything else it would fail. Then he said, 'As you know, I've very sympathetic with you, I want to see you back here, because I regard the House of Commons as your home.'

I thought that was very cordial. I thought, 'My goodness, this is going extremely well.' I raised the question about what St Clair would do in the interval: 'May I raise just one other point with you, about St Clair. I know that he wanted to resign after the Election, but Rab persuaded him to stay. If we are now so near a solution of the problem I, naturally, very much hope he doesn't resign.'

Macleod said, 'I had no idea that you still had any idea of keeping up with Bristol South East. We've never regarded Bristol South East as having had anything to do with this Committee whatsoever. I never heard anything so arrogant in my life – that you should be sitting there thinking that you can hold the constituency and the Government to ransom. Change the law so that you can go back? You càn get a seat some other time, somewhere else. You wouldn't have any difficulty with your Party. I haven't seen St Clair, but I know he wants to resign. He's been offered some other constituencies, and he may go in the recess. It's quite possible we could hold him till the spring.'

I was terribly upset. I didn't get excited but I felt that this was such an unjust accusation that I admit my eyes filled with tears. I said, 'I'm very sorry that you should think it arrogant, but what do you mean? What could I do? I'm out of Parliament, I may be out for life. I was only expressing to you my hopes as to how the thing might end. I can't force you to do anything about it at all.'

'What about the pledge St Clair asked you to give?' he said.

So I told him, 'I can't possibly give the pledge. If I give it now, why not before the last Election?'

He said, 'We don't want any more by-election farces.'

By this time I was a bit frightened that if I said anything about I'll fight, and fight, and fight again, which I'd said to Rab, that he would say, 'Well, if that's your attitude, the whole thing will go down.' Instead I said, 'Well, I haven't said I wouldn't fight; I have said I will fight. But I must admit that my model here has always been Bradlaugh. Bradlaugh's constituency stuck by him.'

He said, 'There's no parallel there, because Bradlaugh wasn't disqualified as a candidate.'

I pointed out that this was a technicality: in fact he was as effectively disqualified as I was – he was thrown out four times in six weeks. So then I said, 'Over the last year my relations with my constituency have been the only thing that has really mattered. You've been a Member of Parliament for many years, you know how intimate the relationship is in any case. But this year, beginning with the bereavement, and losing my job and being thrown out of Parliament, then having a huge bill to pay, these chaps have stuck absolutely firmly by me. I'm not prepared to give up. I'm not prepared to desert them.' I think Macleod said 'I'm sorry I said you were arrogant. Arrogant wasn't the word I should have used', or something of the kind. But, he said, you should give the pledge. I said, 'I'm very sorry but it isn't really for me to do anything, it's entirely for St Clair to act on his own, and if it's your view that this had nothing to do with Butler, why did Rab suggest to me that my wife should stand last summer? He suggested that Caroline should stand and, of course, if it were just in an interim period while the Bill was going through, that would be reasonable. But she's a young woman with four children and to ask her to sit there for many, many years is just impossible.'

He couldn't really answer that one. He didn't know what Rab had said. I went on, 'You know, this isn't a Party thing. I've got an awful lot of Conservative support. I've had hundreds of pounds from Conservative organisations for the Fund, and from Churchill and a lot of young people as well.'

He said, 'I can only tell you that I'm in a better position to know than you are what the attitude of the Conservative Party is, and feeling against you has very much hardened' – or something like that.

'Maybe,' I said, 'but this is not a Party matter as I've ever understood it to be.' By this time I was utterly dejected. I thought the whole thing was completely lost, and Macleod – I may be wrong – struck me as the sort of chap who might go round to everybody and say 'Oh, old Wedgwood Benn thinks that now we're going to run round and let him get back in the House of Commons. Let's postpone the whole Committee.' I couldn't be sure now precisely what would happen. Clearly, I may have made a grave tactical error.

This is David Butler interviewing Anthony Wedgwood Benn at his home on 12 July 1962. We are going to take up where we left off six months ago and try to pick up the thread of what has happened in the peerage case since then.

The main development has been the setting up of a Joint Select Committee of Lords and Commons to investigate the issues raised by your case and some wider issues.

There were talks going on all last autumn, after Parliament met, and these talks took the following form. The Labour Party said: we won't touch the composition of the Lords, we just want renunciation, and Macleod put forward a plan – he was the new Leader of the House – that there would be talks about renunciation and the pay of peers. The terms of reference were narrowed to the position of UK peers for Parliament, the position of Scottish peers, Irish peers and women.

I was abroad from 4 January for about seven weeks lecturing, but the rumours of an agreement between the two Parties began to appear; and at this point it got all confused with the question of whether Lord Home or Lord Hailsham should be the next Prime Minister. I am not at all sure whether this issue is a helpful one to me. But all the press comment was along those lines because Macmillan was at the nadir of his popularity; this therefore was an interesting news line. The New York papers had a report on it and it was very encouraging when I was in America to get news direct as well as from Caroline.

On 31 January the Parliamentary Labour Party had a meeting to consider whether to go in under the new terms and I only heard very indirectly what happened. They did decide, but Anthony Howard in the

THE RED HOUSE, ALDEBURGH, SUFFOLK.

27th March, 1961.

My dear Mr. Wedgwood Benn,

Please forgive the delay in answering your card, only I have been terribly busy.

Of course if the matter comes to a by-election I would happily let you use my name as one of your supporters. It would be a tragedy if a person of your sterling abilities and strong fighting qualities would be lost to the House of Commons.

With all good wishes.

Yours sincerely,

[signature]

New Statesman, who usually gets his information right, says that Charlie Pannell attacked Hugh Gaitskell for his flippancy in approaching this subject and Howard went on to say that the whole thing got round to whether Hailsham and Salisbury and Home should be allowed back, which was just a cheap political issue and nothing to do with the main issue. On 8 February the terms of reference were tabled and on 19 February the Tory MP Captain Kerby made a speech in which he indicated that he was very keen on this reform scheme because if Hailsham could come back as Prime Minister, this would settle the question of the leadership for ever.

On 10 April 1962 the Lords debated the Committee. I read the reports of this with great care. I didn't go to either debate, deliberately, but it was a typical Lords debate, full of self-congratulation and the role of the House of Lords. The general use of the word 'democracy' to indicate the role of the Lords just makes me want to throw up.

On 17 May, when it had been announced that the Committee would ask for evidence to be submitted to them, I released a statement which in fact only the *Guardian* published, saying that I was not going to give evidence because the case was very well known. The *Guardian* ran it as a little story 'Benn in the Wings', and one or two people thought it surprising. It was part of the continued policy of keeping out of it. I thought it would only annoy them. And I didn't even put a memorandum in to the Committee.

Charlie Pannell rang me up, after the second meeting of the Committee, and told me that he himself had read the reports of all the last hundred years of Joint Select Committees in order to understand it, which is typical of Pannell. He said that Lord Morton of Henryton was a very important member of the Committee. He carried a great deal of weight and had successfully persuaded the Committee that they ought to get straight on to the main point, which was renunciation, and leave the Scottish peers who wanted to give evidence and the women and everything secondary; he had said: 'Get this straight and everything else will be all right.'

So it was agreed at the meeting on 16 May that Kilmuir would issue a draft list of questions to members and the Committee would meet two weeks later to discuss what their answers to these questions would be. Kilmuir said at the Committee that whatever the recommendations were, they would certainly apply to existing peers, that is to say those who hadn't taken the Writ of Summons.

I had lunch with Pannell on 23 May and he gave me a photostatic copy of the papers from the Committee – the highest breach of privilege you could possibly imagine – but he says he always takes the broad view of these things. He says: I'm only interested in this because of you, and therefore I give it to you. I went through it with tremendous care and was intensely impressed by the thoroughness of the Committee. They considered every sort of consequence of the consequences: what would happen to the precedence of a widowed aunt of a peer who renounced, for example. They had gone into it in enormous detail. I went through this list of questions, and annotated it and said, 'Look, this must have a yes.' 'It doesn't matter what you do to this one.' 'This one must have a no.' There were only two critical points where a complete no or yes – I forget which way it was – was required. I wrote a memorandum and sent it to Pannell and he circulated it to all the Labour members of the Committee under his own name, saying, 'If you want to help Wedgwood Benn, this is what you must do.'

What the Committee is now going to recommend – I gather this was unanimous, which is highly significant – is that if a man renounces he will be a statutory commoner for life; not a life commoner, but a statutory commoner. The peerage will be dormant. He will lose absolutely everything. He will lose the peerage, his wife will lose the title, his children will lose the 'Honourable', he will be ineligible to receive the hereditary peerage to the end of his days – although he could get a life peerage. But the title cannot be recreated for him except in one case, and here is a rather amusing story.

Charlie said as this was being discussed he thought Salisbury was looking rather anxious so he said, 'I chipped in and said, "My Lord Chairman I think there may be one anxiety in Lord Salisbury's mind. Is he wondering whether if a man wanted to be Lord Chancellor, he couldn't have his real title restored to him?" and Salisbury said, "I am grateful to Mr Pannell, it is just what I was thinking about."' So they have agreed that if you are to be made Lord Chancellor your actual peerage can be recreated in you. But my mother will be left alone because she derives it from my father, and so will my brother.

The Committee have gone into it in enormous detail. What happens if the man is a lunatic when he inherits? The Committee unanimously agreed that he remained a peer, which I think is rather splendid. They obviously hadn't quite thought it out.

Charlie tells me he has never been on a Committee which is so anxious to be shot of the whole business. He says they have really broken the back of it, and they are perfectly happy with their solution, they don't want to hear evidence. They just want to leave the Lord Chancellor enough material to write his draft report in the recess.

That is the end of the Committee's story. As I say, I feel the turning point has now been reached and I am almost preparing for an Election return before the end of this Parliament, for this reason: I think that the Government will put a mention in the Queen's Speech that they intend to deal with this even if the report isn't out. They will then prepare the Bill. They will send the Bill to the Lords first and the Lords will not be busy because the Lords never have anything to do at the beginning of a session. The Lords will examine it very carefully, but with Kilmuir and the Government Whips on, and the fear of a Labour threat to extinguish behind them, they will pass it. The Bill will then come to the Commons, having been fully examined and amended by the Lords. It will come with the support of Macleod and the support of Gaitskell. There will be a minor revolt on it from Jennie Lee on the left and from a few nuts on the right. But it will go through the Commons, probably very quickly – it will be a shortish Bill. If it comes into operation at once – which I think it is almost bound to do – then I suggest St Clair will resign immediately. The whole story will have come to a conclusion in the summer of 1963. That is the most optimistic. But the least optimistic – or the next least optimistic – is that I fight the next Election as a qualified candidate and otherwise possibly that I fight it as an unqualified candidate.

There is a bit of gossip which arose out of the case. Edward Boyle had dined with Sir Michael Adeane who had said, or indicated, that the Queen had intimated something like this: 'However dear the Monarchy is to the British people, I can't think that the conscription of unwilling peers is a necessary prop to the popularity of the Crown.' And he seemed annoyed at the whole business. But what I an not clear is whether the Queen said it or whether Sir Michael Adeane said it.

One other amusing thing is that on 2 July my mother went to Mansfield College, Oxford, where she is on the Board of Governors. She is the only peeress, I think, on it and normally when she goes there she is considered a great nob and is introduced to everybody. But that day the Queen Mother came down to open a a new wing or dedicate something and the Principal introduced the Queen Mother to almost everybody there except my mother, and she feels that this was because there was disapproval at the name of Stansgate. Again it is only a hint, but that I think is likely to be the view.

On 4 May we went to the Royal Academy private view (our doctor has another patient, an artist called Ruskin Spear, and we were invited along). When we got there it was half empty and as we walked through the halls I saw a vaguely familiar figure. I didn't recognise him, but when I got closer I realised it was the Speaker, and I had a word with him. Caroline was there too. He said, 'I hear that the wheels are grinding slowly' in a rather facetious way.

During the summer Lord Kilmuir undertook to write the Committee's draft report, and it was circulated to the Committee just before Parliament met. Lord Hailsham had an idea of what was happening, and he wrote a very powerful memorandum, which is published in full in the Committee's report, urging the necessity of extending the right of renunciation to hereditary peers who had done their duty by going to the Lords earlier on when there was no prospect of staying in the Commons. This memorandum produced the one close vote in the Committee. The Labour members, with the exception, I think, of Leslie Hale, voted with some Conservatives to defeat the official view that Lord Hailsham, and people in his position, should not be allowed back.

I saw Jennie Lee at the Durham Women's Miners' Gala in July and I saw Barbara Castle at the Miners' Gala later. I also saw Michael Foot at the Labour Conference and I made a particular point of seeing Dick Clements of *Tribune*, and I put to all of them exactly what the Select Committee would recommend. I pointed out that it was only the removal of anomalies and that in fact it would leave the House of Lords weaker than before because there will be some new hereditary deadbeats in the place. The peeresses and the Scots and the guys with guts will leave and, I said, it will be just as easy to attack in the future. This is what the left mainly worries about, but frankly it is my only hope of getting out and I'm afraid I am in favour of it. It doesn't prevent the Labour Party dealing with it later, if I thought it would, which I am afraid I think it won't, and this I must say has produced results. I see that *Tribune* today says exactly this: that the case for the report is that it is a reward for the campaign that I have been fighting, and *Tribune* still urges abolition.

The Labour side is, I think, pretty well all right. The Shadow Cabinet met on 19 December, and their attitude was really this – the Labour Party doesn't want to have to deal with this problem; the Labour Government will be much too busy with other things and so the best thing is for this Government to deal with it. Although, I think, the Labour Party is not prepared to push this very hard they are prepared to offer facilities to the Government to get the bill through, provided the Government sticks to the Select Committee report *in toto* and doesn't try monkeying about with it. Macleod and Butler were both distinctly unenthusiastic about it. I am afraid, frankly, that for reasons of crude self-interest neither of them wants Home or Hailsham to come back. This is the only real explanation, because on grounds of principle you would imagine that both of them would side with the younger element in the Government who want a new and modern image, and here is a way to be popular without spending any money.

Butler: The other day I met Rab at a party, and he said, 'I don't think Macmillan is ever going to go. You know what he said to me last weekend? "I don't see why I should make room for you, old cock."'

I think that while Macmillan remains there, he might well think it unattractive to have Home back. Home would be a godsend to the Labour Party. His qualities are completely overrated by his own Party and are preserved for the public mind by the fact that he is not subjected to cross-examination. So I would be very much in favour of him, but incidentally the Labour Party's attitude now is slightly altered by the fact that we might appear to be helping the Government to find a more effective Leader, and quite a number of people have said to me, including Dick Crossman, 'Of course the price we pay for you is having Hailsham as the Leader of the Conservative Party.'

I had lunch with the editors of the two Bristol papers and I told them the contents of the report a week before it was published. They ran exactly the sorts of leader I wanted – that this was a victory for Bristol – because civic pride in Bristol is playing a very much bigger part in it than anywhere else. Now everyone in Bristol thinks it's all over and I have to persuade them that it isn't, yet not take away from the terrific sense of victory they have. They want a campaign and that is going to be arranged, with a public meeting and literature, but now it's patience and toughness. However, I am pretty sure that after this report, unless the Government turns it down absolutely flat, there will be no question of them wanting a new candidate. That was my big fear – that they would feel so discouraged that I would lose my main source of strength. I think that now Bristol knows that they will win in the end, I mean literally within two or three years, they might want to hang on to me. The question is – what sort of interim candidate? Caroline's name has been suggested, and although I would be very much against this, it might be right. The other thing would be to take a man like Alderman Hennessy who is about eighty, a very distinguished man in the constituency, and say that Bristol is going to put its own man in just to keep a watch and then to resign at the end. That would give you your by-election, beat the Government over the head for inactivity, give you a Labour MP for Bristol South East and at the same time keep the seat warm pending the change in the law.

Funnily enough, when I was in America on my lecture tour, as you would expect, lots of local papers got the story wrong. The best of all was one college magazine which said, 'Mr Wedgwood Benn, better known as the Earl of Snowdon, is coming to address us.' They were very much embarrassed by this and I said at the beginning that Princess Margaret was very sorry not to be able to be with me. I did send this magazine to Snowdon with a little note saying, 'My dear Snowdon, I thought you might be amused by this, they were very disappointed to find that I wasn't, Yours sincerely, Anthony Wedgwood Benn', and I got a note in his own handwriting saying, 'Dear Mr Wedgwood Benn, Thank you for sending me the paper. The press never says anything as nice about me as that, and I hope they keep it on their files, Yours sincerely, Snowdon.'

Epilogue

The end of the peerage campaign came quite quickly; the Joint Select Committee reported in 1963 in favour of a change in the law to allow renunciations, which enabled me to renounce my own title, which I did in July 1963. I was the first person ever to do so and the following month, in a by-election which the other main parties did not contest, I was re-elected for Bristol South East.

All this is described in *Out of the Wilderness*, my political diaries 1963–7.

The whole campaign, which took ten years to win, through many setbacks and disappointments, taught me many lessons which greatly influenced my thinking about the whole political process, about the shallowness of democracy in out parliamentary system, about the nature of our society and about how political campaigns have to be organized if they are to be successful.

From birth to death the British people are taught to be subservient, deferring to those 'above them', and this is how feudalism over succeeding generations has been adapted to serve the interests of a new ruling class so as to protect their power and privileges.

It therefore follows that polite appeals for justice directed to those in political power or positions of responsibility will almost always fall on deaf ears; the only way to win, as I discovered in Bristol South East, is to make the argument a popular one, and gain the people's support. When it is strong and powerful enough popular opinion will force the establishment to change.

When it is clear that opinion has shifted – then, concessions are made and I learned how to apply this principle to other campaigns since then; for those at the top will always retreat under pressure, and thus avoid the greater threat of losing their power altogether.

Every effort is always made to defuse those movements that seem to be most threatening – and that includes co-opting progressive leaders by the subtle use of patronage, honours and peerages too.

Anyone who doubts the power of this patronage has only to go to the House of Lords and see the Labour and trade union leaders of yesteryear, including some ex-communists, sitting alongside the old aristocrats, industrialists, bankers, press lords, former MPs and other life peers in the cozy atmosphere of a club where all controversy has been submerged into gentle exchanges between friends.

This whole system is thoroughly corrupting partly because of the patronage it gives Prime Ministers and partly because of the credibility it gives to the House of Lords, which still has real political power.

This is why a growing number of people would like to see Britain become a democratic Commonwealth controlled by its own people in their own interests.

Principal Persons

Family

BENN, William Wedgwood (Lord Stansgate 1941) (1877-1960) Elected to Parliament 1906. Labour MP for Gorton. Secretary of State for India 1929-31 and Secretary of State for Air 1945-6. President of the Inter-Parliamentary Union 1950-60.

BENN, Margaret Wedgwood (nee Holmes) (later Lady Stansgate) (1897-1991) First President of the Congregational Federation and Honorary Fellow of the Hebrew University, Jerusalem.

BENN, Michael Wedgwood (brother) (1921-44) RAF pilot. Won the DFC.

BENN, David Wedgwood (brother) b 1928, lawyer, author and broadcaster. Former head of the BBC Yugoslav service. Married in 1959 June Barraclough, teacher and writer. Two children.

DeCAMP, Caroline b. 1926. Married Tony Benn 1949. Educated at Vassar, University of Cincinnati, University of London. Lecturer, researcher, author.

BENN, Stephen Michael (son) b. 1951

BENN, Hilary James (son) b. 1953

BENN, Melissa Anne (daughter) b. 1957

BENN, Joshua William (son) b. 1958

Political and Personal

ACLAND, Sir Richard. Founder of Common Wealth Party 1942. Liberal MP (Barnstaple) 1933-45, Labour MP (Gravesend) 1951-55.

ATTLEE, Clement. Leader of Labour Party 1935-55. Prime Minister 1945-51.

BARKER, Sara. Labour Party official from 1935. National Agent of the Labour Party, 1962-9

BEVAN, Aneurin (Nye). Labour MP for Ebbw Vale. Minister of Health 1945-51, Minister of Labour and National Service 1951. Married to Jennie Lee.

BEVIN, Ernest (Ernie). General-Secretary, TGWU 1921-40. Labour MP for Central Wandsworth, subsequently for Woolwich East. Minister of Labour and Woolwich East. Minister of Labour and National Service 1940-45. Foreign Secretary, 1945-51.

BEVERIDGE, Sir William. Long-time civil servant, working with Liberal Governments before the First World War. Director of LSE, 1919-37. Author of The Beveridge Report (Report on Social Insurance and Allied Services 1942).

BING, Geoffrey. Labour MP for Hornchurch.

BONHAM-CARTER, Lady Violet. President of the Liberal party 1945-7. Daughter of Liberal Prime Minister Herbert Asquith.

BOOTHBY, Robert (Bob). Conservative MP for Aberdeenshire East. Broadcaster.

BOYLE, Sir Edward. Friend from University days. MP for Birmingham Handsworth. Resigned from Treasury over the Suez War.

BRADDOCK, Bessie. Labour MP for Liverpool Exchange.

BROCKWAY, Fenner. Labour MP for East Leyton (1929–31), subsequently for Eton and Slough. General Secretary of ILP and founder of the Movement for Colonial Freedom.

BROWN, George. Labour MP for Belper. Deputy Leader of Labour Party 1960–70.

BUTLER, David. Friend from university. Author and inventor of psephologist; Fellow of Nuffield College.

CALLAGHAN, James. Labour MP for Cardiff South, later Prime Minister (1976–9).

CASTLE, Barbara. Labour MP for Blackburn. Chair of Labour Party 1958/9.

CHESHIRE, Group Captain Leonard. Much decorated wartime bomber pilot, British Cabinet observer at the Nagasaki atomic bombing.

COUSINS, Francis (Frank). General Secretary of the Transport and General Workers Union 1956–69.

CRIPPS, Stafford. Labour MP for Bristol East. Chancellor of the Exchequer 1947–50.

CROSLAND, Anthony. Friend from Oxford University. Labour MP for South Gloucestershire. Author of *The Future of Socialism*.

CROSSMAN, Richard. Labour MP for Coventry East.

DALTON, Hugh. Labour MP for Bishop Auckland. Chancellor of the Exchequer 1945-7. Forced to resign over inadvertent budget leak in 1947.

DAVIES, Clement. Leader of the Liberal Party 1945–56. Liberal MP for Montgomeryshire.

DE FREITAS, Geoffrey. Labour MP for Central Nottingham and later Lincoln.

DRIBERG, Tom. Labour MP for Maldon and later Barking. Chairman of the Labour Party 1957/8.

EDE, (James) Chuter. Labour MP for South Shields. Home Secretary 1945–51.

EDEN, Sir Anthony. Conservative MP for Warwick and Leamington. Prime Minister 1955–57.

EISENHOWER, Dwight. War-time Supreme Commander Allied Forces in Europe. President of the United States 1953–60.

FREEMAN, John. Labour MP for Watford. Later British High Commissioner in India and Ambassador in Washington.

GAITSKELL, Hugh. Labour MP for South Leeds. Chancellor of the Exchequer 1950–1. Leader of Labour Party 1955–63.

GRIFFITHS, James (Jim). Labour MP for Llanelli. Deputy leader of the Labour Party 1955–59.

HALL, Glenvil. Labour MP for Colne Valley. Financial Secretary to the Treasury 1945–50. Chairman of the Parliamentary Labour Party 1950/1.

HARRIS, Kenneth. Friend from University. Journalist. Biographer of Attlee.

JAY, Douglas. Labour MP for Battersea North. Financial Secretary to the Treasury, 1950–51.

JENKINS, Roy. Labour MP for Southwark and later Stechford.

KAUFMAN, Gerald. Political Correspondent, Daily Mirror Labour.

KHAMA, Seretse. Barrister educated at Oxford. At the age of 4 became Chief of the Bamangwato tribe of Bechuanaland (Botswana). He was removed from the British Protectorate by the Labour Government in 1950 over objections to his marriage to Ruth Williams, a white British woman, in 1948. Close friends, Seretse Khama was godfather to Melissa Benn and Tony Benn was godfather to Anthony. Later President of Botswana.

LEE, Jennie. Labour MP for Cannock, married to Nye Bevan.

LLOYD, Selwyn. Conservative MP for Wirral. Foreign Secretary 1955–60. Chancellor of the Exchequer 1960–62.

MacARTHUR, General Douglas. Commander in Chief, US Forces, Far-East until 1951.

MACLEOD, Iain. Conservative MP for Enfield West. Minister of Labour and National Service 1955–9.

MACMILLAN, Harold. Conservative MP for Bromley. Prime Minister 1957–64.

MAYHEW, Christopher. Labour MP for South Norfolk then Woolwich East.

MIKARDO, Ian. Labour MP for Reading, subsequently for Poplar.

MONCKTON, Sir Walter. Conservative MP for Bristol West. Minister of Labour, Minister of Defence and Paymaster General consecutively 1950–57.

MORRISON, Herbert. Labour MP for South Hackney, subsequently for Lewisham. Deputy Prime Minister 1945–51. Deputy Leader of Labour Party 1951–55.

NEHRU, Jawaharlal. Prime Minister of India 1947–64.

NKRUMAH, Kwame. Prime Minister and President of Ghana 1953–67.

PANNELL, Charles. Labour MP for West Leeds.

PEAY, Ken. Broadcasting officer, Labour Party headquarters.

POWELL, Enoch. Conservative MP for Wolverhampton South West. Financial Secretary to Treasury, 1957–8.

ROBINSON, Kenneth. Labour MP for St Pancras North.

ROOSEVELT, Franklin D. President USA 1933–45.

SHAWCROSS, Sir Hartley. Labour MP for St Helens. Attorney General 1945–51. President of Board of Trade 1951.

STRACHEY, John. Labour MP for Aston subsequently for Dundee. Minister of Food 1946–50. Secretary of State for War 1950–51.

THORNEYCROFT, Peter. Conservative MP for Stafford, subsequently for Monmouth. Chancellor of the Exchequer 1957–8.

WILSON, Harold. Labour MP for Ormskirk, subsequently for Huyton. President of the Board of Trade 1947–51, later Prime Minister.

WYATT, Woodrow. Journalist and Labour MP for Aston, subsequently for Bosworth.

YOUNGER, Kenneth. Labour MP for Grimsby. Resigned to become Director General of the Royal Institute of International Affairs.

ZANDER, Michael. Lawyer and academic. Gave legal assistance to Tony Benn during Peerage Campaign.

Benn Family Tree

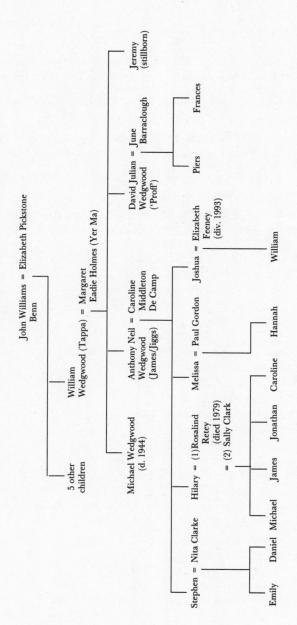

John Williams = Elizabeth Pickstone
Benn

5 other children

William
Wedgwood (Tappa) = Margaret
Eadie Holmes (Yer Ma)

Michael Wedgwood
(d. 1944)

Anthony Neil = Caroline
Wedgwood   Middleton
(James/Jiggs) De Camp

David Julian = June
Wedgwood   Barraclough
('Proff')

Jeremy
(stillborn)

Piers   Frances

Hilary = (1)Rosalind
         Retey
         (died 1979)
       = (2) Sally Clark

Stephen = Nita Clarke

Melissa = Paul Gordon

Joshua = Elizabeth
         Feeney
         (div. 1993)

Emily   Daniel   Michael

James   Jonathan   Caroline

Hannah

William

Abbreviations

AC	Aircraftsman
ADA	Americans for Democratic Action
ADC	Aide-de-camp
AEU	Amalgamated Engineering Union
AFV	Armoured Fighting Vehicle
AG	Air Gunner
ATC	Air Training Corps
ATV	Associated Television Ltd
BAC	British Aircraft Corporation
BBC	British Broadcasting Corporation
BEF	British Expeditionary Force
BGA	British Guiana Association
BTC	British Transport Commission
CCK	Christian Council in Kenya
CFI	Chief Flying Instructor
CGI	Chief Ground Instructor
CI	Chief Instructor
CLP	Constituency Labour Party
CO	Commanding Officer
CP	Communist Party
DG	Director General
EC	Executive Committee
EDC	European Defence Community
FBU	Fire Brigades Union
FLN	Front Libération Nationale (of Algeria)
F/Lt	Flight Lieutenant
FO	Flying Officer/Foreign Office
GMC	General Management Committee
GMT	Greenwich Mean Time
GPO	General Post Office
HQ	Headquarters
ILP	Independent Labour Party
IPC	International Petroleum Company
IPU	Inter-Parliamentary Union
ITA	Independent Television Authority

ITN	Independent Television News
ITW	Initial Training Wing (RAF)
LAC	Leading Aircraftsman
LCC	London County Council
LEA	Local Education Authority
MCF	Movement for Colonial Freedom
MEF	Middle Eastern Forces
NATO	North Atlantic Treaty Organisation
NCO	Non-Commissioned Officer
NEC	National Executive Committee of the Labour Party
NUS	National Union of Students
OC	Officer Commanding
OTU	Operational Training Unit
PLP	Parliamentary Labour Party
PM	Prime Minister
PMG	Postmaster General
PO	Pilot Officer
PPP	Progressive People's Party (of British Guiana)
PPS	Parliamentary Private Secretary
PRO	Public Relations Officer
PS	Private Secretary
RAF	Royal Air Force
SHAPE	Supreme Headquarters, Allied Powers, Europe
S/L	Squadron Leader
SPD	Social Democratic Party (Sozialdemokratische Partei Deutschlands)
SS	Schutzstaffel (Nazi Police and Military Organisation)
TGWU	Transport and General Workers' Union
TUC	Trades Union Congress
ULR	*Universities and Left Review*
UN	United Nations
UNA	United Nations Association
USDAW	Union of Shop, Distributive and Allied Workers
VERA	Visual Electronic Recording Apparatus
WAASIE	Women's Auxiliary Air Service (member thereof)
WEA	Workers' Educational Association
WingCo	Wing Commander
WO	Warrant Officer
YWCA	Young Women's Christian Association

Index

NB Names and titles etc. are contemporaneous with the diaries